Multisensory Living in Ancient Rome

Also available from Bloomsbury

A Cultural History of the Senses in Antiquity, edited by Jerry Toner
The Hellenistic Home: Interior Design and Domestic Decor, Craig I. Hardiman
The Boundaries of Art and Social Space in Rome, Frederick Jones
Roman Architecture, Martin Thorpe
Houses and Their Furnishings in Bronze Age Palestine Domestic Activity Areas and Artifact Distribution in the Middle and Late Bronze Ages, P.M. Michèle Daviau

Multisensory Living in Ancient Rome

Power and Space in Roman Houses

Hannah Platts

BLOOMSBURY ACADEMIC
LONDON • NEW YORK • OXFORD • NEW DELHI • SYDNEY

BLOOMSBURY ACADEMIC
Bloomsbury Publishing Plc
50 Bedford Square, London, WC1B 3DP, UK
1385 Broadway, New York, NY 10018, USA
29 Earlsfort Terrace, Dublin 2, Ireland

BLOOMSBURY, BLOOMSBURY ACADEMIC and the Diana logo
are trademarks of Bloomsbury Publishing Plc

First published in Great Britain 2020
Paperback edition first published 2021

Copyright © Hannah Platts, 2020

Hannah Platts has asserted her right under the Copyright,
Designs and Patents Act, 1988, to be identified as Author of this work.

For legal purposes the Acknowledgements on pp. xv–xvi constitute
an extension of this copyright page.

Cover design: Terry Woodley
Cover image © Lawrence Alma-Tadema, The Vintage Festival. Archivart/Alamy Stock Photo

All rights reserved. No part of this publication may be reproduced or
transmitted in any form or by any means, electronic or mechanical,
including photocopying, recording, or any information storage or retrieval
system, without prior permission in writing from the publishers.

Bloomsbury Publishing Plc does not have any control over, or responsibility for,
any third-party websites referred to or in this book. All internet addresses given
in this book were correct at the time of going to press. The author and publisher
regret any inconvenience caused if addresses have changed or sites have
ceased to exist, but can accept no responsibility for any such changes.

A catalogue record for this book is available from the British Library.

Library of Congress Cataloging-in-Publication Data
Names: Platts, Hannah, author.
Title: Multisensory living in ancient Rome: power and space in Roman houses / Hannah Platts.
Description: New York: Continuum International Publishing Group Inc., 2019. |
Includes bibliographical references and index. | Summary: "Classicists have long wondered what
everyday life was like in ancient Greece and Rome. How, for example, did the slaves,
visitors, inhabitants or owners experience the same home differently? And how did
owners manipulate the spaces of their homes to demonstrate control or social
hierarchy? To answer these questions, Hannah Platts draws on a diverse range of
evidence and an innovative amalgamation of methodological approaches to explore
multisensory experience - auditory, olfactory, tactile, gustatory and visual - in domestic
environments in Rome, Pompeii and Herculaneum for the first time, from the first
century BC to the second century AD. Moving between social registers and locations,
from non-elite urban dwellings to lavish country villas, each chapter takes the reader
through a different type of room and offers insights into the reasons, emotions and
cultural factors behind perception, recording and control of bodily senses in the home,
as well as their sociological implications. Multisensory Living in Ancient Rome will
appeal to all students and researchers interested in Roman daily life and domestic
architecture"– Provided by publisher.
Identifiers: LCCN 2019021056 (print) | LCCN 2019981615 (ebook) |
ISBN 9781788312998 (hardback) | ISBN 9781350114326 (epub) | ISBN 9781350114319 (pdf)
Subjects: LCSH: Architecture, Domestic—Rome. | Senses and sensation. |
Rome—Social conditions.
Classification: LCC NA324.P59 2019 (print) | LCC NA324 (ebook) | DDC 728.0937–dc23
LC record available at https://lccn.loc.gov/2019021056
LC ebook record available at https://lccn.loc.gov/2019981615

ISBN: HB: 978-1-7883-1299-8
PB: 978-1-3501-9449-6
ePDF: 978-1-3501-1431-9
eBook: 978-1-3501-1432-6

Typeset by RefineCatch Limited, Bungay, Suffolk

To find out more about our authors and books visit www.bloomsbury.com
and sign up for our newsletters.

For my parents,
Anne and Nigel
and my dearest Jez
Thank you

Contents

List of Figures	viii
List of Tables	xiv
Acknowledgements	xv
List of Abbreviations	xvii

1	Smelling, Touching, Hearing, Tasting and Seeing the Roman Home	1
2	Sensing Status? Multisensory Awareness and Power Display in the Roman Domestic Realm	23
3	The Impact of Streetscapes on the Domestic Realm	31
4	Initial Perceptions: Controlling Access and Multisensory Experience in the *Atrium-Tablinum*	77
5	'Public' and 'Private': Multisensory Perception and the Roman *Cubiculum*	131
6	Beyond Taste: The Multisensory Experience of Roman Dining in the Domestic Sphere	157
7	Housing the Foul: Kitchens and Toilets in the Roman Home	193
8	Conclusion: Sensing Status – Approaching a Lived Experience of the Roman House	231

Notes	237
Bibliography	291
Index	329

Figures

3.1 Fragment 11e of the *Forma Urbis Romae* showing the close proximity of domestic and commercial properties opening directly onto the Vicus Patricus, Rome. Roma, Sovrintendenza Capitolina ai Beni Culturali.   33

3.2 Map of Pompeii showing the location of different types of commercial, religious and other productive premises. Bloomsbury Academic with base map courtesy of E. Poehler, Pompeii Bibliography and Mapping Project, 2019, and further information from R. Laurence *Roman Pompeii: Space and Society*, 2007.   35

3.3 Floor plan of the house and connected *thermopolium* of Vetutius Placidus (Reg I.8.8), Pompeii. See no. 41, fig. 3.5 for location. © Bloomsbury Academic.   36

3.4 View of façade of house of the Ceii opening on to the Vicolo del Menandro (Reg I.6.15), Pompeii. See no. 24, fig. 3.5 for location. Note the benches outside. Photo: Hannah Platts.   36

3.5 Map of Pompeii showing houses and commercial properties opening directly on to pavements. © Bloomsbury Academic.   40

3.6 Map of Herculaneum showing houses and commercial properties opening directly on to pavements. © Bloomsbury Academic.   41

3.7 Deep cart ruts gouged in to the Via Stabiana, Pompeii. See E, fig. 3.5 for Via Stabiana location. Photo: Hannah Platts.   44

3.8 *Cave Canem* mosaic at the entrance to the *fauces* of the house of the Tragic Poet (Reg VI.8.3), Pompeii. See no. 38, fig. 3.5 for location. Photo: Hannah Platts.   50

3.9 Close up of map of Pompeii showing streets and properties located near the amphitheatre (Reg II.6) and palaestra (Reg II.7), Pompeii. © Bloomsbury Academic.   55

3.10 Floor plan of the house of Octavius Quartio (Reg II.2.2), Pompeii. See no. 13, fig. 3.5 for location. © Bloomsbury Academic.   56

3.11 Floor plan of the house of the Marine Venus (Reg II.3.3), Pompeii. See no. 34, fig. 3.5 for location. © Bloomsbury Academic.   57

3.12 Floor plan of the house of the Garden of Hercules (Reg II.8.6), Pompeii. See no. 29, fig. 3.5 for location. © Bloomsbury Academic.   58

Figures ix

3.13 Fresco depicting the riot between the Nucerians and the Pompeians (from Pompeii). Naples, Museo Archeologico Nazionale inv.112222. © DEA PICTURE LIBRARY/ Getty Images. 60
3.14 Floor plan of the house of the Vettii (Reg VI.15.1), Pompeii. See no. 39, fig. 3.5 for location. © Bloomsbury Academic. 62
3.15 Floor plan of the house of the *Fullonica* of Stephanus (Reg I.6.7), Pompeii. See no. 42, fig. 3.5 for location. © Bloomsbury Academic. 64
3.16 Close up of map of Pompeii showing properties near the *Fullonica* of Stephanus (Reg I.6.7), Pompeii. Cf. nos. 14, 24, 27, 33, 42, fig. 3.5 for location in Pompeii. © Bloomsbury Academic. 64
3.17 Floor plan of the house of the Chaste Lovers (Reg IX.12.6), Pompeii. See no. 26, fig. 3.5 for location. © Bloomsbury Academic. 66
3.18 Floor plan of the house of the Ceii (Reg I.6.15), Pompeii. See no. 24, fig. 3.5 for location. Note that rooms (i) and (j) back onto the Fullonica of Stephanus. © Bloomsbury Academic. 69
3.19 Close up of map of Pompeii showing the buildings and tombs outside the Herculaneum Gate, on the Via Consolare. Pompeii. Cf. nos. 2, 3, 4, fig. 3.5 for location in Pompeii. © Bloomsbury Academic. 70
3.20 Floor plan of the villa of Diomedes situated on the Via Ercolanense, Pompeii. See no. 2, fig. 3.5 for location. © Bloomsbury Academic. 70
3.21 Cart ruts on the Via Ercolanense, outside villa of Diomedes, Pompeii. Photo: Hannah Platts. 72
3.22 View into the small peristyle garden from the entrance of the villa of Diomedes, Pompeii. Photo: Hannah Platts. 73
3.23 View from the Via Ercolanense looking up to the entrance of the villa of Diomedes, Pompeii. Photo: Hannah Platts. 74
4.1 Floor plan of the house of Pansa (Reg VI.6.1), Pompeii. See no. 15, fig. 3.5 for location. This residence's structure is often seen to reflect the 'canonical' layout of Pompeian houses where the *fauces* leads to the *atrium*, which in turn leads into the *tablinum* and peristyle. © Bloomsbury Academic. 79
4.2 Entrance door casts from the house of the Ceii (Reg I.6.15), Pompeii. See no. 24, fig. 3.5 for location. Photo: Hannah Platts. 83
4.3 Secondary entrance door remains in the middle and at the top of the *fauces* of the house of the Anchor (Reg VI.10.7), Pompeii. Photo: Hannah Platts. 84
4.4 *Posticum* from the house of Tragic Poet (Reg VI.8.3), Pompeii. See no. 38, fig. 3.5 for location. Note the post hole in the *fauces* for

	securing the door, and cardine and vertical bar cuts in the threshold. Photo: Hannah Platts.	93
4.5	Bottom righthand side of picture is entrance #20 in the Vicolo Proculus Paquius (Reg. I.7.20), Pompeii. Note the peristyle at (n) (in fig. 4.7) from the house of Proculus Paquius in the top left of this picture. Photo: Hannah Platts.	93
4.6	View across the peristyle (n) and garden (j) (fig. 4.7) towards wall remains of room (m) of the house of Paquius Proculus (Reg I.7.1), Pompeii. Rooms (k), (l) and (m) are located directly above the storeroom at #20 on the Vicolo di Paquius Proculus (Reg. I.7.20). Photo: Hannah Platts.	94
4.7	Floor plan of the house of Paquius Proculus (Reg I.7.1), Pompeii. See no. 16, fig. 3.5 for location. © Bloomsbury Academic.	95
4.8	Floor plan showing the peristyle at the rear of the house of Caesius Blandus (Reg VII.1.40), Pompeii. See no. 6, fig. 3.5 for location. Entrance to storerooms at #43 on the Vicolo del Lupanare (Reg. VII.1.43) are located under this peristyle. © Bloomsbury Academic.	95
4.9	Entrance #43 on Vicolo del Lupanare (Reg VII.1.43), Pompeii. Note that this storeroom is located under the peristyle of the house of Caesius Blandus (Reg VII.1.40), the columns of which are also pictured in this photo. Photo: Hannah Platts.	96
4.10	View through shop of M. Noni Campani (Reg VII.1.41) showing thresholds leading into *cubiculum* (c) and *atrium* (b) of the house of Caesius Blandus (Reg VII.1.40), Pompeii. Photo: Hannah Platts.	97
4.11	Floor plan of the house of Caecilius Iucundus (Reg. V.I.26), Pompeii. See no. 10, fig. 3.5 for location. Note the possible access between this residence and its neighbouring residence (Reg. V.1.23) situated to the left of the room (k) in the house of Caecilius Iucundus. © Bloomsbury Academic.	98
4.12	View of threshold from shop (d) (Reg VI.6.22) leading into *cubiculum* (c) of house of Pansa (Reg VI.6.1), Pompeii. See no. 15, fig. 3.5 for location. Note also the remains of door architecture between *cubiculum* (c) and *atrium* (b) in the house of Pansa. Photo: Hannah Platts.	99
4.13	*Posticum* and steps down on to Vicolo della Fullonica from house of Pansa (Reg VI.6.8), Pompeii. Photo: Hannah Platts.	100
4.14	Threshold at #13 opening onto the Vicolo di Modesto, Pompeii. Photo: Hannah Platts.	100

Figures

4.15 Doorway and step down between the kitchen at (l) and the paved area at (m) of the house of Pansa (Reg VI.6.1), Pompeii. Photo: Hannah Platts. 101

4.16 Floor plan of the house of the Ara Maxima (Reg VI.16.15), Pompeii. See no. 21, fig. 3.5 for location. © Bloomsbury Academic. 101

4.17 Floor plan of the house of Marcus Holconius Rufus (Reg VIII.4.4), Pompeii. See no. 8, fig. 3.5 for location. © Bloomsbury Academic. 102

4.18 Threshold at (n) (Reg VIII.4.49) connected to house of Marcus Holconius Rufus (Reg VIII.4.4), Pompeii. Photo: Hannah Platts. 103

4.19 Threshold between kitchen at (d) and *atrium* at (b) in the house of the Ceii (Reg I.6.15), Pompeii. See no. 24, fig. 3.5 for location. Note the evidence of door architecture remains. Photo: Hannah Platts. 111

5.1 View from the end of the *fauces* (a) across the *atrium* (b) and towards the *tablinum* (e) in the house of the Wooden Partition, (Ins III, 11), Herculaneum. See no. 11, fig. 3.6 for location. Note the wooden partition used to separate the *atrium* and the *tablinum*. Photo: Hannah Platts. 137

5.2 Tri-fold doors from the villa of the Mysteries, Pompeii. See no. 1, fig. 3.5 for location. Photo: Hannah Platts. 140

5.3 Fresco of bi-fold doors from the *tablinum* frescoes at (e) in the house of M. Lucretius Fronto (Reg IX.13.3), Pompeii. See no. 11, fig. 3.5 for location. Cf. fig. 5.8 for floor plan. Photo: Hannah Platts. 141

5.4 Floor plan of the house of Trebius Valens (Reg III.2.1), Pompeii. See no. 40, fig. 3.5 for location. © Bloomsbury Academic. 144

5.5 Floor plan of the house of the Prince of Naples (Reg VI.15.8), Pompeii. See no. 36, fig. 3.5 for location. © Bloomsbury Academic. 145

5.6 Fresco of cupids making and selling perfume from *oecus* at (h) in the house of the Vettii (Reg VI.15.1). See no. 39, fig. 3.5 for location. © De Agostini/Archivio J. Lange/Getty Images. 146

5.7 Floor plan of the house of the Menander (Reg I.10.4), Pompeii. See no. 12, fig. 3.5 for location. © Bloomsbury Academic. 147

5.8 Floor plan of the house of M. Lucretius Fronto (Reg IX.13.3), Pompeii. See no. 11, fig. 3.5 for location. © Bloomsbury Academic. 147

5.9 Floor plan of house VI.16.26, Pompeii. See no. 5, fig. 3.5 for location. © Bloomsbury Academic. 148

6.1 Fresco of an outdoor banquet from the *triclinium* (f) of the house of the Chaste Lovers (Reg IX.12.6), Pompeii. See no. 26, fig. 3.5 for

	location. Naples, Museo Nazionale 9015. © DEA/A. DAGLI ORTI/ Contributor/Getty Images.	173
6.2	Fresco of an indoor banquet from the house of the *Triclinium* (Reg V. 2.4.), Pompeii. Naples, Museo Nazionale 120029. © DEA/A. DAGLI ORTI/Getty Images.	173
6.3	Fresco of a banquet between a young man and *hetaera* from Herculaneum. Naples, Museo Nazionale inv. 9024. © AGB Photo Library/Alamy Stock Photo.	174
6.4	Floor plan of the house of the Cabinet Maker (Reg I.10.7), Pompeii. See no. 23, fig. 3.5 for location. © Bloomsbury Academic.	176
6.5	Food warmer from the house of the Four Styles (Reg I.8.17), Pompeii. Naples, Museo Nazionale 6798. © DEA/L. PEDICINI/Contributor/ Getty Images.	177
6.6	Floor plan of the house of the Mosaic *Atrium* (Ins IV, 1–2), Herculaneum. See no. 13, fig. 3.6 for location. © Bloomsbury Academic.	179
6.7	Enclosed peristyle colonnade in the house of the Mosaic *Atrium* (Ins IV, 1–2), Herculaneum. Photo: Hannah Platts.	180
6.8	Floor plan of the house of the Golden Bracelet (Reg VI.17.42), Pompeii. See no. 30, fig. 3.5 for location. © Bloomsbury Academic.	181
6.9	View of summer dining area (n) and fountain (m) (fig. 3.20) in the large peristyle of the villa of Diomedes, Pompeii. See no. 2, fig. 3.5 for location. Photo: Hannah Platts.	185
7.1	Window above masonry hearth in kitchen at (i) (fig. 7.7) in the house of the Tragic Poet (Reg VI.8.3), Pompeii. See no. 38, fig. 3.5 for location. Photo: Hannah Platts.	196
7.2	Floor plan of the house of the Neptune Mosaic (Ins V, 6-7), Herculaneum. See no. 5, fig. 3.6 for location. © Bloomsbury Academic.	213
7.3	Floor plan of the house of the Priest of Amandus (Reg I.7.7), Pompeii. See no. 35, fig. 3.5 for location. © Bloomsbury Academic.	213
7.4	Floor plan of the house of the Golden Cupids (Reg VI.16.7), Pompeii. See no. 31, fig. 3.5 for location. © Bloomsbury Academic.	214
7.5	Floor plan of the house of the Centennial (Reg IX.8.6), Pompeii. See no. 25, fig. 3.5 for location. © Bloomsbury Academic.	215
7.6	Floor plan of the house of the Corinthian *Atrium* (Ins V, 30), Herculaneum. See no. 6, fig. 3.6 for location. © Bloomsbury Academic.	216
7.7	Floor plan of the house of the Tragic Poet (Reg VI.8.3), Pompeii. See no. 38, fig. 3.5 for location. © Bloomsbury Academic.	217

7.8	Floor plan of the house of Gavius Rufus (Reg VII.2.16), Pompeii. See no. 7, fig. 3.5 for location. © Bloomsbury Academic.	218
7.9	Floor plan of the house of Siricus (Reg VII.1.47), Pompeii. See no. 20, fig. 3.5 for location. © Bloomsbury Academic.	220
7.10	Room (k) of the house of Siricus (Reg VII.1.47) showing uneven floor layers and location of possible partition wall dividing room in two. Pompeii. Photo: Hannah Platts.	221
7.11	Floor plan of the house of the Bronze Bull (Reg V.1.7), Pompeii. See no. 22, fig. 3.5 for location. © Bloomsbury Academic.	222
7.12	Steps from kitchen at (k) up to corridor (j) in the house of the Bronze Bull (Reg V.1.7), Pompeii. Photo: Hannah Platts.	223
7.13	Floor plan of the house of the Deer (Ins IV, 21), Herculaneum. See no. 14, fig. 3.6 for location. © Bloomsbury Academic.	224
7.14	Floor plan of the house of Queen Margherita (Reg V.2.1), Pompeii. See no. 17, fig. 3.6 for location. © Bloomsbury Academic.	227
7.15	Kitchen at (k) in the house of the Cabinet Maker (Reg I.10.7), Pompeii. See no. 23, fig. 3.5 for location. Note the partition wall used to separate this space off from the rest of the ambulatory at (i) (fig. 6.4). Photo: Hannah Platts.	228

Tables

1	Presence of doors in *cubicula* leading off *atria and peristylia*	138
2	Pompeii: kitchen location and proximity to road outside and internal *atrium*	200–2
3	Pompeii: kitchen location in residence and proximity to *atrium* and road, expressed as percentages	202
4	Herculaneum: kitchen location and proximity to road outside and internal *atrium*	203
5	Herculaneum: kitchen location in residence and proximity to *atrium* and road, expressed as percentages	203
6	Pompeii: door architecture in dining room and kitchen thresholds	208–9
7	Pompeii: door architecture in dining room and kitchen thresholds expressed as percentages	209
8	Herculaneum: door architecture in dining room and kitchen thresholds	210
9	Herculaneum: door architecture in dining room and kitchen thresholds expressed as percentages	210

Acknowledgements

Ideas in this book stemmed from an AHRC grant on the 'Lived Environment', 2016–2017, where colleagues and I collaborated to develop a multisensory recreation of a Roman dwelling. Whilst not technically connected with this manuscript, the theories developed from this project have proved invaluable in refining my thinking in this area.

This book would not have been possible without the support, help and interest from a large number of people. I am deeply indebted to the Isobel Thornley Fund for their generous grant to fund the publication of this work. I must also thank the RHUL Santander Grant for the financial support they gave for field trips that allowed me to understand and record these dwellings in detail.

I would especially like to thank Stefania Peterlini at the British School at Rome who secured permissions enabling me to access and photograph the residences discussed in this volume. A huge debt of gratitude must also go to the Soprintendenza and custodians of Pompeii and Herculaneum who provided this access. Special mention is made to the Italian archaeology students at these sites, particularly Gervasio Illiano, who spent much time discussing the houses he was looking after, as well as his own research into Pompeian dwellings – good luck with your work, I look forward to reading it in the future. I must also say a big thank you to Eleanor Dickey who helped me get to grips with the *Colloquia of the Hermeneumata Pseudodositheana* by giving me tremendous insight into an amazing source. Likewise, the excellent work of Ray Laurence, particularly his *Roman Pompeii: Space and Society*, which provided much of the evidence for my map of land use at Pompeii, should also be noted. This really helped me consider both the relationship between properties and the way in which the world outside might impinge on how they are experienced. Thanks must also go to the fabulous editors at Bloomsbury, particularly Alice Wright and Lily MacMahon who have worked so tirelessly with me on this text, and to the two anonymous reviewers who gave me such fantastic advice on the original manuscript of the book. All errors in the text that follows, of course, remain my own.

Words cannot express how grateful I am for the unfailing help, guidance and enthusiasm offered to me by my colleagues. Particular thanks must go to John Pearce at KCL, whose generous help over the years in providing career and academic advice, has been invaluable. I am grateful also for the vibrant and friendly research atmosphere in Royal Holloway's School of Arts and Humanities. Being able to work alongside colleagues in Classics, Modern Languages, and English has introduced me to wonderful friends and colleagues including Hannah Thompson, Liz Gloyn and Richard Alston, all of whom have offered help, a chat and a cup of tea when very much needed. Polly Dalton and David Howard have proved a wonderful source of cross-departmental multidisciplinary inspiration and collaboration. In particular Polly has given so much time and encouragement that I am not sure I will ever be able to repay the kindness.

Within the History Department at Royal Holloway, I would like to say a big thank you to Jane Hamlett and Sandra Cavallo, my co-directors of The Centre for the Study of the Body and Material Culture, and to Kate Cooper, for her support since her arrival as Head of Department. Huge thanks must also go to Niki and Jonathan Phillips, and Andrew Jotischky who have been the most wonderful friends and supporters – whether that is reading my work and helping me to improve it, or listening to me chatter on and on over dinners, lunches and train rides to and from work. Hannes Kleineke, too, has spent valuable time reading this text and pulling out errors! Above all I must thank David Gwynn. Ever since I started in the History Department, he has been an amazing friend and colleague, giving time, energy and enthusiasm to supporting my work and reading this text. For this, I am truly grateful.

Finally, I owe my biggest thanks of all to my family. Their assistance and encouragement has been, and continues to be, immeasurable. Their unquestioning belief in me is what has made this book possible. To Pippa, thank you for laughing at me and supporting me all at the same time – I really love you for that! That I have managed to raid and re-use your collection of archaeology books and see your name in them makes me smile. To Mum and Dad, I give my thanks for your unwavering support over the years, and in the writing of this book. To Jez, I give my unending thanks for your love, for listening to me talk about Rome, houses and multisensory experience, and for trekking around Pompeii and Herculaneum in the boiling sun. Words really are not enough.

Abbreviations

AA	Archäologischer Anzeiger
ADAJ	Annual of the Department of Antiquities of Jordan
AE	L'Année épigraphique: Revue des publications épigraphiques relatives a l'antiquité romaine (Paris 1888–)
AJA	American Journal of Archaeology
AJP	American Journal of Philology
AJAH	American Journal of Ancient History
AnalRom	Analecta Romana Instituti Danici
AntK	Antike Kunst
Antiquity	Antiquity: A Quarterly Review of Archaeology
ArchNews	Archaeology News
AZ	Archäologische Zeitung
BABesch	Bulletin antieke beschaving: Annual Papers on Classical Archaeology
BAR-IS	British Archaeological Reports, International Series
BdI	Bullettino dell'Istituto di corrispondenza archeologica
BullCom	Bullettino della Commissione archeologica Comunale di Roma
CAH	Cambridge Ancient History
CAJ	Cambridge Archaeological Journal
CÉFR	Collection de l'École française de Rome
CIL	Königlich Preussische Akademie der Wissenschaften zu Berlin, *Corpus inscriptionum latinarum* (Berlin 1893–)
ClAnt	Classical Antiquity
ClMed	Classica et mediaevalia: Revue danoise de philologie et d'histoire
CP	Classical Philology
CQ	Classical Quarterly
CR	Classical Review
CronErcol	Cronache ercolanensi
CronPomp	Cronache pompeiane
CW	Classical World
EchCl	Echos du monde classique: Classical Views

EJA	European Journal of Archaeology
G&R	Greece and Rome
HistriaAntiq	Histria Antiqua
Fiorelli, *Descr.*	Fiorelli, *Descrizione di Pompeii*
Fiorelli, Scavi	Fiorelli, *Gli Scavi di Pompeii dal 1861 al 1872*
GdSc	*Giornali degli Scavi di Pompei*, n.s. vol. III, 1874–1877
ILS	H. Dessau, ed., *Inscriptiones latinae selectae* (Berlin 1892–1916)
JAR	Journal of Archaeological Research
JGH	Journal of Garden History
JRA	Journal of Roman Archaeology
JRS	Journal of Roman Studies
Klio	Klio: Beiträge zur alten Geschichte
LTUR	E.M. Steinby, ed., *Lexicon topographicum urbis romae* (Rome 1993)
MAAR	Memoirs of the American Academy in Rome
MANN	Museo Archeologico Nazionale di Napoli
Meded	Mededelingen van het Nederlands Historisch Instituut te Rome
MH	Museum Helveticum: revue suisse pour l'étude de l'Antiquité classique
NSc	Notizie degli Scavi di Antichità
Ocnus	Quaderni della Scuola di Specializzazione in Beni Archeologici
OpArch	Opuscula archaeologica
OJA	Oxford Journal of Archaeology
PastPres	Past and Present
PBSR	Papers of the British School at Rome
Prilozi	Prilozi Instituta za arheologiju u Zagrebu
RANarb	Revue archéologique de Narbonnaise
RendPontAcc	Atti della Pontificia Accademia romana di archeologia: Rendiconti
RhM NF	Rheinisches Museum für Philologie (Neue Folge)
RM	Mitteilungen des Deutschen Archäologischen Instituts, Römische Abteilung
RM-EH	Mitteilungen des Deutschen Archäologischen Instituts, Römische Abteilung: Ergänzungsheft
RivIstArch	Rivista dell'Istituto nazionale d'archeologia e storia dell'arte
RStPomp	Rivista di studi pompeiani
SAP	Catalogue of the Soprintendenza Archeologica di Pompei
TAPA	Transactions of the American Philological Association

TLL	R. Estienne and J. Hollins, *Thesaurus linguae latinae* (London 1734–1735)
WorldArch	World Archaeology
VAMZ	Vjesnik Arheološkog muzeja u Zagrebu, Zagreb

1

Smelling, Touching, Hearing, Tasting and Seeing the Roman Home

Introduction

Once on a time – such is the tale – a country mouse welcomed a city mouse in his poor hole, host and guest old friends both. Roughly he fared, frugal of his store, yet could open his thrifty soul in acts of hospitality ... At last the city mouse cries to him: 'What pleasure can you have, my friend, in living so hard a life on the ridge of a steep wood? Wouldn't you put people and the city above these wild woods? Take my advice: set out with me ... while you may, live happy amid joys; live mindful ever of how brief your time is!' These words struck home with the rustic, who lightly leaped forth from his house ... And now night was holding the mid space of heaven, when the two set foot in a wealthy palace, where covers dyed in scarlet glittered on ivory couches, and many courses remained over from a great dinner of the evening before, in baskets piled up hard by. So when the town mouse has the rustic stretched out on purple covers, he himself bustles about in waiter-style, serving course after course, and doing all the duties of the home-bred slave, first tasting everything he serves. The other, lying at ease, enjoys his changed lot, and amid the good cheer is playing the happy guest, when of a sudden a terrible banging of the doors tumbled them both from their couches. In panic they run the length of the hall, and still more terror-stricken were they, as the lofty palace rang with the barking of Molossian hounds. Then says the rustic: 'No use have I for such a life, and so farewell: my wood and hole, secure from alarms, will solace me with homely vetch.'[1]

The story of the town and country mouse, as rewritten by Horace, presents a colourful account of the pleasures and trials of urban and rural living. Focusing on the differences between life in the two spheres, Horace emphasizes the frugal way of rustic life and the opulence of the urban realm. Thus whilst the country mouse survives on and entertains with meagre rations in his humble home, in contrast we read of the sumptuous and plentiful fare, in decadent surroundings, of ivory couches and scarlet coverlets that the town mouse provides for his guest.

For the purposes of this book, the story above is more than a delightful tale that has been retold through the centuries.[2] Rather it opens the door onto the world of the Roman home, the sensory experiences to be had within it as well as the chances of disapproval or praise to which house owners exposed themselves when they welcomed guests into their residences. Just as the country mouse risked criticisms of plain and simple food in the bacon and oats he himself serves (*aridum et ore ferens acinum semesaque lardi frusta*) in his unattractive home, which is described as a 'poor' hole (*paupere cavo*) situated in a seemingly uncomfortable location perched on the ridge of a steep wood (*praerupti nemoris*), so too the urban mouse opens himself up to similar critique when he invites his friend to dine with him. For although the setting and foods are opulent and plentiful, the interruption of the dinner by Molossian hounds and the fear that ensues likewise leaves the country mouse with an unpleasant experience.

Key to both stories are the attempts by the house owners to control the multisensory experiences of their guests and it is this notion which is to be examined throughout the following chapters. By reconnecting the literary accounts with the archaeological remains of life in the home, this book explores the embodied Roman home, reconnecting it with the vivid sounds and smells, the vibrant tastes, textures and sights experienced by those within. Such an approach in turn seeks to develop further our understanding of the complexities behind the organization and manipulation of space and surroundings as a means for displaying power and status to others.

The embodied experience of the home

The experience of home is structured by distinct activities – cooking, eating, socializing, reading, storing, sleeping, intimate acts – not by visual elements. A building is encountered; it is approached, confronted, related to one's body, moved through, utilized as a condition for other things. Architecture initiates, directs and organizes behaviour and movement. A building is not an end in itself; it frames, articulates, structures, gives significance, relates, separates and unites, facilitates and prohibits. Consequently, basic architectural experiences have a verb form rather than being nouns. Authentic architectural experiences consist then, for instance, of approaching or confronting a building, rather than the formal apprehension of a façade; of the act of entering, and not simply the visual design of the door; of looking in or out through a window, rather than the window itself as a material object; or of occupying the sphere of warmth, rather than the fireplace as an object of visual design. Architectural space is lived space rather than physical space, and lived space always transcends geometry and measurability.[3]

In his book on architectural theory, *The Eyes of the Skin: Architecture and the Senses*, the Finnish architect Juhani Pallasmaa explores in depth the role of multiple bodily senses in the experience of the built environment. As the passage above highlights, for Pallasmaa full corporeal immersion within a building is critical. Engagement with the home is not just about 'visual elements' but, as importantly, is embedded in bodily experience of the lived space and the physical responses that this realm, and the activities within it, engenders. For him, the fireplace is not merely something to be seen, but is to be physically felt as its heat warms the skin; the door is not only to be looked at, but is something to be moved through, changing a person's surroundings and physical sensations as he or she enters a different environment.

It might appear odd to begin a book about Roman housing with references to contemporary architecture. But this insight into the multisensory aspects that make up the meanings and values of the built environment of the home was as pertinent then as it is today. From the architectural treatise of Vitruvius, which ascribes an idealized blueprint to the layout of Roman residences according to social standing, to the remains of dwellings destroyed by the eruption of Vesuvius in AD 79, the wealth of extant evidence on the Roman domestic sphere is substantial. Examination of Roman literature and the archaeological remnants of houses emphasizes the extent to which the home played a crucial role in displaying a person's standing to contemporaries. Beyond the views, vistas and ways of movement within the home, however, there has been little consideration of its full, embodied experience and the way in which this could be manipulated as a further means for displaying personal power and wherewithal. It is, then, this concept of the 'lived experience of the home', that sits at the heart of this monograph on Roman domestic space. This book examines the sensorially charged environment of the Roman home by focusing on textual and material evidence of housing from the Bay of Naples and Rome. It explores the diverse corporeal responses (including smell, touch, sound, taste and sight) to be had within the Roman house, and investigates how owners, inhabitants and visitors of various social levels physically experienced the Roman *domus*. To what extent and in what ways did the sounds, smells and textures of Roman domesticity affect perception of a home and how far and for what reasons were multisensory experiences open to manipulation by house owners?

Approaches to the past: The problems of the pre-eminence of sight in the western sensorium

Evidence from ancient Rome is diverse and requires varied approaches in its interpretation.[4] Engagement with literary materials differs significantly from examining tangible artefacts and scholars need to balance carefully discrepancies between types of evidence.

When trying to understand the remains of antiquity from a sensory perspective, one of the biggest issues is the dominant role that vision has played when approaching evidence. Sight has been accepted as the most important sense of the traditionally recognized five senses in the Western sensorium since the fourth century BC, when Aristotle ordered the bodily senses in terms of importance.[5] Sight, hearing and smell he labelled as the 'human' senses, whilst taste and touch were 'animal' senses.[6] Although some medieval scholars, such as Aquinas, equated the importance of sight to that of touch, thereby confusing the traditionally accepted hierarchy of the Western sensory realm, the primacy of vision above other sensory experiences has remained.[7] As Day points out, the development of visual instruments such as cameras, telescopes and microscopes, which enabled knowledge of, and access to, sights and locales that were otherwise too small or far away to see, ensured that 'sight became the gateway to new worlds', thus increasing the 'intellectualization of vision'.[8] The voyages of discovery that brought Europeans into contact with other civilizations emphasized further the dominance of the sense of sight in the West, since those with whom they made contact were seen as 'primitive' peoples whose connections with the world were perceived to revolve around the 'lesser' senses of taste, touch and smell.[9] The culmination of this was the combination of sensory and racial hierarchies determined by the natural historian Lorenz Oken who categorized races according to the senses they were understood to prefer. At the top of the cultural ladder Europeans favoured the sense of vision whilst at the lowest level were Africans for whom touch was perceived to be most vital.[10]

The continued dominance of vision becomes more obvious when we consider attempts to re-engage with the full array of human senses through which the world is perceived since these have struggled to dislodge the perceived preeminence of sight. Key to this was the work of the mid-twentieth-century French philosopher Merleau-Ponty.[11] At the heart of his attempts to interpret the physical, visual, literary and dramatic experiences of human life was an emphasis placed upon the ability to 'read' all types of evidence. For him the study of music, dance, religious ritual or the visual and dramatic arts required a relatively standardized approach similar to that used to study the written word.[12] The problem with this methodology was that 'reading' evidence inherently emphasized vision, whilst other sensory responses – touch, sound, smell and taste – faded into insignificance. This logocentric bias resulted in scholars questioning whether such examination of human action based on linguistic study of human experience should be considered reductive. Can we really 'read' all examples of human endeavour like a text? As Serres, one of Merleau-Ponty's severest critics explains,

> I laughed a lot at Merleau-Ponty's *Phenomenology of Perception*. He opens with the words: 'At the outset of the study of perception, we find in language the notion of sensation.' Isn't this an exemplary introduction? A collection of examples in the same vein, so austere and meagre, inspire the descriptions that follow... What you can decipher in this book is a nice ethnology of city dwellers, who are hypertechnicalised, intellectualised, chained to their library chairs, and tragically stripped of any tangible experience. Lots of phenomenology and no sensation – everything via language.[13]

For Serres, Merleau-Ponty's insistence on considering all human experience as verbal expression and language reduced human engagement with the world to an inflexible, one-dimensional interpretation that left its audience's comprehension incomplete.[14] Serres' alternative approach sought to rehabilitate the human body's full sensory perceptions at the core of understanding the world and human interaction with, and within, it.[15] Thus, although Merleau-Ponty attempted to rehabilitate the full human sensorium, it was only the ensuing criticism and developments in exploring the wide range of corporeal experience from scholars such as Serres that caused considerations of the olfactory (smell), auditory (sound), tactile (touch), gustatory (taste) as well as the ocular (visual) to feature within numerous academic disciplines.[16]

Seeing and 'reading' houses

The last forty years have seen growing interest in research into domesticity across the Roman Empire. Sites from as far afield as Dura-Europos, Egypt, Africa, Ephesus and Britain have been explored, as have examples of different housing styles within mainland Italy.[17] In addition to investigating disparate housing locations, typologies and temporalities there has been developing study of the Roman domestic realm across the social spectrum. Thus, whilst housing of the upper echelons remains a focus of many investigations, the dwellings of Rome's lower classes have increasingly proved a fruitful area of research.[18]

A number of recent studies of Roman domesticity have focused in particular on the examination of sightlines within and outside Roman houses in addition to studies of movement and access in houses for both owners and slaves.[19] By using Hillier and Hanson's justified access-maps, numerous studies have also concentrated upon analysis of spatial configuration.[20] These maps, which render visually the accessibility of spaces, have become and remain popular within the field of archaeology, particularly as a means of representing space.[21] Through this method of mapping building location or room distribution, networks of movement and the sense of sight are emphasized, since these access-maps present a way of showing space and its subdivisions in a two-dimensional form rather like a floor or archaeological plan.[22] One particular way of employing Hillier and Hanson's space syntax theories has been developed by Mark Grahame in his investigation of how space within residences of *Regio* VI of Pompeii was organized and the effect of this on social encounters, surveillance and levels of privacy and visibility within residences. For Grahame it was not just the footprint of buildings, but the built space encompassed by the walls and boundaries of houses that was a vital aspect of reading and understanding buildings of the past.[23]

Whilst space syntax analysis raises important points regarding the domestic sphere, it is not without problems. Just as the issue of sight dominating the Western sensorium was highlighted above with reference to Merleau-Ponty's assumption that all aspects of human experience could be read, this materializes again when we consider the justified access-maps of Hillier and Hanson and their application to Grahame's study of the Roman domestic realm. Such approaches to space privilege only one sensory experience in the home, namely that of sight, whilst undermining the sensorial richness that is so clearly portrayed in our ancient literary sources such as Pliny, Seneca and Statius.

Let us consider Grahame's use of space syntax analysis for the study of Roman houses in greater detail. According to Grahame, 'if we want to learn about a society from its architectural remains, we will need to "read" those remains.'[24] He goes on to suggest that 'architecture can be thought of as having textual properties' including syntaxes (or rules) that order space in a manner not dissimilar to the syntaxes that dictate word order to make sentences comprehensible and accordingly raises the question of how we might go about '"reading" this text'.[25]

His assumptions raise two key issues. In his discussions of how we can 'read' space, he draws parallels between how text tries to fix speech and the way architecture tries to 'fix' the 'contextuality' of space, in other words the social encounters within it.[26] Grahame rightly asserts that text fails to 'fix' speech, because 'Texts are consequently open to numerous readings because what is inscribed into them is not the actuality of speech, but rather an interpretation of it. Likewise, architecture tries to "fix" social interaction, but also fails.'[27] In his further discussion of 'fixing' speech, however, difficulties arise.

> Built space, as Bourdieu reminds us, is analogous to a 'book' that is read through 'displacements' of 'the body' (1977: 89–90). However, just like a written text, once the 'text' of space has been read, the knowledge inscribed in that text becomes available to the 'reader', making continuous readings unnecessary. Only when changes are made to the built environment does it become necessary to read it again.[28]

Grahame appears to set aside his previous important point that texts are open to various readings by implying that once read there is no need to revisit a text. For Grahame then, it is only when structural changes to buildings or word changes to texts occur that 're-reading' the text or building becomes necessary. Herein lies a problem. Whilst written words might be unchanging, their interpretation can constantly change depending on the context in which they are read.[29] In this way we might also reconsider his comment about changes to the built environment. Certainly, when built structures are altered, the manner in which they are understood will also change and, as Grahame suggests, it becomes necessary to re-read the built environment.[30] As with understanding texts and the changing contexts of reading, however, we also need to consider that interpretation of the built environment can be altered without modification to the structure, but by changes in the sensory landscape. Changes to a building's lighting, temperature, smells, sounds, or the time of day or season, can significantly affect the manner in which a building is perceived, and thus an individual response to it.[31] Additionally, like texts, buildings are open to multiple simultaneous interpretations, which can be affected by numerous factors, including viewer/visitor status or background, time of day/season/weather.

Imperative within attempts to understand texts and buildings, then, is the context in which the printed word or building is approached. It is not just when visible changes are made to a written word or to the structure of a building that we need to consider how interpretation and/or use might change – though these will probably alter perception. Rather, when approaching any written text or any building's space and structure, we should ask how non-visual sensations might affect its audience. If prose or a poem is read aloud, will the listener's response be the same as if they had read it themselves? Similarly, if a person stands in a room, will their response to the space be the same as when viewing it on an architectural plan? Indeed, two individuals can experience a room (or a text) contemporaneously but in entirely different ways. To read a building as a text, is to respond to it in a one-dimensional fashion which relies on vision over other senses and fails to allow an understanding of the changes to a space when other corporeal responses are also taken into account. The focus on movement and vision in Grahame's justified access-maps, for instance, encourages a gap in understanding the complete bodily responses to a space since other sensory experiences of the environs, such as sounds and smells, are not represented on these plans.[32]

In an attempt to build upon space syntax analysis as a means of understanding dwellings, Hanson has argued that the way in which houses are organized presents a method of communicating social and cultural information about inhabitants to each other and to guests. She has termed this method of communicating to others via house structure and décor as 'domestic space-codes', emphasizing that '[t]he manifest variety of ordinary people's lifestyles seemed to point away from behavioural universals and basic human needs and towards a view that, if space had a purpose, this was to encode and transmit cultural information.'[33] For Hanson, understanding housing revolves around the examination of access networks between rooms, as well as considerations of architecture and décor and the relationship of the residence's interior to its exterior, in order to allow identification of the various social relations experienced within the house.[34]

Domestic 'space-codes' developed to articulate the spatial layout and hierarchies of a residence to inhabitants and visitors are not restricted to studies from modern history but have been applied to ancient Roman housing. Wallace-Hadrill's investigations of Pompeii and Herculaneum have presented a detailed insight into Roman housing, spatial organization and its role in the articulation of social identity.[35] Here, Wallace-Hadrill explored the development of space codes and the role they played in the formulation of the Roman domestic realm. Once again architectural form, decoration and artefacts play an important role in the interpretation of these spatial codes as they help to 'refin(e) the hierarchical contrasts between the different social spaces of the house'.[36]

Yet, just as Hillier and Hanson's initial process of spatial mapping and its later application to the Roman domestic realm encouraged an emphasis on vision and movement, investigations into 'decoding' domestic space equally rely on sight and movement-through-space and the role these play in 'reading' different facets of the domestic realm and its layout. For Wallace-Hadrill and Hanson, approaches to interpreting the domestic realm continue to highlight the importance of vision and the permeability of spaces within dwellings. As Hanson explains, 'In moving around in buildings, people orientate themselves by reference to what they can see and where they can go.'[37] Similarly for Wallace-Hadrill emphasis is placed upon the ability of individuals to see into the heart of the house from the street as well as the plotting of visual axes throughout residences.[38]

Once again, then, sight dominates scholarly approaches to interpreting spaces from the past or present. Herein lies a methodological problem: emphasis on sight defining how we understand the domestic realm is unsurprising, given the nature of the two-dimensional plans used to map the size, shape and surroundings of houses. Investigations into spatial conditions, street networks, houses and their environments do not preclude smaller-scale sensory analysis of the relation of buildings to the street, to next-door properties and even within individual buildings. However whilst floor plans and axial views through buildings emphasize their size and shape in archaeological reports, they give little consideration to the impact of smells, sounds, texture and light and an individuals' response to surroundings even though, as outlined below, literary descriptions of dwellings are often fully immersed in the range of the body's complete sensory experience. A broader multisensory view can affect the way in which individuals perceive and experience the spaces they inhabit, and may render as simplistic current visually dominated approaches to understanding space and spatial organization.

Developing a multisensory approach to archaeology: Problems

Within the field of archaeology, recent attempts to take advantage of increasing interest in sensory approaches across numerous scholarly disciplines have encouraged the development of new questions and frameworks for examining tangible remains of ancient societies. For studies of antiquity, understanding the relationship between the images portrayed in texts and what emerges from archaeology can be complex. Texts verbally and visually guide the reader as to how the author wishes words to be understood, and of course this book is no exception to this reliance on the visual medium of words. Archaeological remains, however, although likewise visually perceived and interpreted, also offer individuals the immediacy of physically 'experiencing', rather than merely 'viewing' them. Different building materials present various physical sensations, which in turn are affected by many factors, including footwear and clothing, meteorological conditions, seasons and time of day. Striding across marble in dry weather wearing hard-soled sandals, for example, will give certain auditory sensations for the walker and those in near proximity. Change the weather to rain, however, and the experiences will likewise vary, as clothing becomes damp and heavier, the rain splashes noisily on the marble and the ground surface becomes slippery and possibly unsafe for walking. The tactile qualities of artefacts are similarly significant and variable. That obtaining any information from physical remains requires unearthing, and consequently touching, objects or buildings emphasizes the tactile nature of excavation and thus the importance of multisensory engagement with archaeological remains. Compare, for example, the rough warm texture of sandstone or limestone to the smooth and cool touch of marble. Likewise, we might contrast the relatively neutral olfactory experience of spacious household *atria* such as the house of the Faun with the damp, cool and musty smell of the remnants of Nero's *Domus Aurea* or the tombs and columbaria dotted along the roads leading into and out of Rome.

It is, then, vital to be aware of the differing sensory ways in which audiences can interact with the historical past from archaeological remains. When considering possible experiences of past spaces and objects, however, it should not be assumed that a person's modern-day sensory experience of a site or item will be the same as that of people from antiquity. Not only do physical changes from weathering and decay affect the structures of items and buildings over time, causing variations across the spectrum of sensory experiences, but also it cannot be assumed that cultural perceptions of embodied engagement with places or objects were similar in the past. Where many today are accustomed to the sounds of cars, planes, helicopters, burglar alarms and mobile phones, such noises would have been completely inconceivable to those living in the ancient world. Likewise, given that even today acceptable smells and tastes vary globally, both between and within countries, it is difficult to assume similarity between ancient and modern-day experiences of and responses towards olfactory, gustatory or even visual stimuli.

In addition to the evident difficulties faced trying to compare sensory landscapes, experiences and responses of the ancient past with those of the present day, it is equally important to realize that sensory experiences can also be substantially affected by questions of class, gender and age. Age and gender, for example, impact upon the ability to smell, with the young and women perhaps having a more perceptive sense of smell than men.[39] Likewise, age can affect hearing and sight, with both often declining with advancing years. Many physical senses can also be affected by excessive exposure: extreme contact with loud noises or strong smells in the work place, for example, can negatively affect hearing or sense of smell (and a reduction in the latter can impinge on the sense of taste).[40]

Let us explore these concerns of 'corporeal bias' and individual sensory experiences a little further in relation to the possible inhabitants of the Roman home. We must bear in mind that the Roman house was occupied not just by the owner but was experienced by others including slaves, guests, children and women. Their status, background, gender, age, and physical ability would all influence and elicit varying responses to the multisensory environment of the dwelling. Whether slave or free, visitor, inhabitant or owner, differences would affect a person's immersion in, and response to, a dwelling. Moreover, when trying to comprehend these disparities, there are considerable issues since many sections of Roman society remain relatively 'silent' in literary sources. This makes reconstructing and understanding their potential multisensory responses to the domestic realm difficult. As such, it is important we are aware that sensory experiences of buildings or artefacts are likely to vary between individuals, thus again raising queries regarding the complexities and potential biases that the analysis of the ancient sensory world by a modern 'western' individual might pose.

The very prospect of attaining multisensory insight into the past has until recently been regarded as posing considerable problems for historians. As Hamilakis points out, the fleeting and intangible nature of the senses means that, 'the archaeology of the senses appears a contradiction in terms'.[41] Furthermore, the highly individual nature of sensory responses together with the fragmentary remains of most buildings from antiquity ensures the virtual impossibility of reconstructing the corporeal experiences of bygone eras. How can we hope to understand the sounds of the Roman gladiatorial arena, for example, or the smells of the Roman baths without any sort of solid physical evidence? Such impalpable experiences cannot, after all, be packaged and stored for future study and yet the very activity of archaeological study to interpret the past relies on secure material evidence.

Current research into sensory experience

Irrespective of the perceived problems posed by the ephemeral and individual nature of the sensory realm, in the last two decades there has been an emerging interest in the study of the senses and multisensorial response to the world around us. Rapid advances in technology have enhanced visual, auditory and tactile experiences. Commercial and home cinema systems, for example, assure heightened sensory engagement with movies and television, whilst the development of Virtual Reality headsets has enabled the creation of corporeally immersive video games. In parallel to these attempts to intensify multisensory engagement with the world, deeper understanding has also developed of the individual ways in which people, for example those with autism or sensory impairment, experience the different senses.[42]

Significantly, the agenda of entertainment and commercial enterprises for creating embodied experiences has increasingly been echoed within academic research. Disciplines as diverse as healthcare, construction, philosophy, architecture, and archaeology have begun to study multisensory environments from various empirical and theoretical standpoints. Modern-day concerns with mapping and understanding the sociological role of the senses within contemporary cultures, for example, have begun to be adopted in scholarly examinations of the past and, whilst initial investigations focused upon sight and how this helped the understanding and potential reconstruction of past and present environments, more recently there has been increasing examination of multiple senses. This is well demonstrated by the work of David Howes and Constance Classen, both of whom have explored combined sensory experiences of past and present cultures.[43] Building from their ground-breaking research into multiple sensory experiences of the world, scholarship in various disciplines has started to consider not just sight, but also sound, smell, touch and taste, and how these senses play a crucial role in human response to the world. For example, recent work exploring historical, cultural, aesthetic and sociological interpretations of the individual senses across a range of academic disciplines can be found in the *Sensory Formation Series* where individual edited volumes focus on a particular sense.[44]

Perhaps surprisingly, given the concerns raised above regarding both the potential issues of interpreting ancient 'sensoryscapes' today and the problems of understanding individual experiences of buildings, places and objects, explorations of multisensory engagement with past societies is becoming an increasingly important tool for archaeological research. Indeed, according to

Hamilakis it is the very material nature of archaeology, which enables us to explore the sensory realm of the past.

> Archaeology relates to materiality and time. It explores the material presence and the concrete and specific formal qualities of beings and things (including space), and their social and cultural lives and meanings in diverse temporalities. These formal and physical qualities of the world are the properties that our sensorial engagements rely upon: the smoothness or roughness of surfaces, the sound-amplifying qualities of houses and other spaces, the odorous effects of plants and other substances. The archaeology of the senses is therefore feasible in very tangible terms.[45]

Whilst some examples of sensory archaeology remain dominated by the sense of sight and attempts to restore the whole human sensory realm to studies of ancient cultures remain incomplete, in recent years there have been increasing attempts to modify this ocularcentric approach.[46] Efforts have been made, therefore, to combine visual aspects of archaeology with other sensory experiences in order to highlight the complex linking of the senses.[47] Thus investigations have been made into relationships between visual aspects of rock art and human auditory and tactile senses.[48] There have also been wide-ranging studies into non-visual aspects of archaeology and archaeological sites that have encouraged scholars to think beyond a sight-based approach to past cultures.[49] Here important work has helped provide foundations for future studies in archaeoacoustics, and although the archaeology of smell is not common, Insoll presents a discussion of a possible methodology for understanding scents of the past.[50] Also crucial in developing further an understanding of smell in ancient cultures is the article of Hamilton and Whitehouse on measuring olfactory senses in Neolithic villages of Italy and Bradley's edited volume on smell in antiquity, which examines olfaction in various different environments in the ancient world. Both of these works pose questions on the cultural role and societal responses to smell in antiquity.[51] Taste is closely connected with smell and, like smell, has received relatively little attention, although there have been some attempts to bridge this gap by Rudolph's edited collection on taste in antiquity and by Hamilakis, Fox and Hopwood who have started to explore, amongst other topics, multisensory responses to the feast in the Aegean Bronze Age.[52] Moreover there have been recent examinations of archaeological sites that have investigated a combination of senses in an attempt to develop understanding of possible multiple sensory interactions within ancient cityscapes and the way in which these might have impacted social interaction.[53] Ancient Rome presents an excellent site for this type of examination.

In addition to exploring imagined journeys through the city that take into consideration constantly changing views of the surroundings, analysis of interconnecting street networks and their urban surrounds has enabled consideration of how vision and movement during these journeys might combine with other sensory experiences of sound, smell and taste to affect an individual's interpretation of location.[54]

Key to this brief overview of studies in the field of multiple bodily senses and sensory engagement with past and present societies is the relative newness of this area of enquiry. As recent studies from Betts, Hamilakis, Bradley, Rudolph, Squire, Purves, Butler and Nooter's and Butler and Purves' edited volumes as well as selected papers in Day demonstrate, Greece and Rome have proved fruitful areas for exploration into the role of multiple senses in the past.[55] Multisensory environments are an emerging area of interest but there are still areas that lag behind and one is the Roman domestic sphere. As suggested above, study into sensory responses to ancient domestic space has largely been restricted to examining vision, sightlines inside and outside the house and movement within it.[56] By not considering other bodily experiences within a dwelling, we create an unrealistic one-dimensional understanding of life in the Roman home, without revealing all its messy complexities.

Key terms, structure and methodological approach

This book develops further our understanding of the ancient Roman domestic sphere by exploring how and why individuals were able to, and interested in, affecting and modifying the sensory realm of their dwellings. The types of residence under consideration here are the *domus* and villa dwellings of Rome's elite and, since the Bay of Naples provides substantial and measurable archaeological evidence, as well as detailed excavation reports, it is this region, in particular the city of Pompeii, that provides the majority of evidence. As the largest part of our evidence on housing dates from late Republic and early Empire, the time period is from the second century BC to the second century AD.

Defining the Roman villa and *domus* has proved contentious.[57] For present purposes, the villa is identified as an extra-mural residence, whilst the *domus* is an urban dwelling that housed a single-family unit, including both family and slaves. Whilst these definitions appear relatively clear cut, it is important to note in particular that both the terms villa and *domus* can be used to describe dwellings from the unpretentious to the extravagant and rich mansions of Rome's aristocracy and Imperial family. Size of dwellings can vary substantially from those with ten rooms or fewer to those boasting in excess of fifty, yet both are still perceived as *domus* or villa residences that would hold a single family unit and corresponding slaves. Likewise, levels of decoration can differ and it should not be assumed that only the larger houses boast opulent décor.[58] Indeed as Mayer demonstrates in his examination of the house of the Ara Maxima that measured about 180 square metres, sumptuous wall paintings were often employed in small dwellings.[59] The present book looks at dwellings that range from the relatively modest to those of Rome's elite. It will not, however, consider dwellings of Rome's emperors. 'Elite' is a multivalent term encompassing those from numerous levels of social status and different backgrounds within Rome's social hierarchies. Such individuals might possess significant social prestige through wealth, ancestry, political or religious status. Elite, then, might refer to members of a variety of groups in society including senators, equestrians, local civic administrators such as *decurions*, cult priests or freedmen. Since we are unsure of the owners of many houses from Pompeii and Herculaneum, we are often unable to comment with any certainty on their position in society.[60]

By considering residences ranging from the non-elite urban *domus* and villa to elite upper-class country retreats and urban abodes, this monograph explores how Romans of varying levels of social prominence could employ their domestic realms to engender specific multisensory responses. When comparing different dwellings, for example, can we identify approaches, capacities and desires to influence the physical experiences to be had within them? In what ways might house location, size and architectural layout, environmental surroundings and topography shape an individual's corporeal engagement with a particular domestic sphere? Such investigations encourage insight into the complex and diverse methods used by Roman homeowners to parade and manipulate the image they presented to others and enable enquiries into the reasons, emotions and cultural pragmatics behind the perception, recording and control of the bodily senses in the home.

In recent years studies of the Roman home have shown interest in examining the visible and 'public' nature of the house, particularly its impact on construction and display of elite status.[61] Understanding the terms 'public' and 'private' is complicated, and whilst the applicability of these concepts to particular rooms in the Roman house will be considered in the relevant chapters below, it is important to outline in general principles the issues faced when attempting to grasp a comprehensive interpretation of these terms in antiquity. As Riggsby highlights, 'English "public" and "private" are … structured rather differently than their

Roman counterparts.' He goes on to highlight that 'private' today revolves mainly around an individual's family and friends whilst,

> the Roman system is reversed; it is anchored not by a core ... that always counts as private, but by an outer layer that is always public. Persons ... (say gladiators or *negotiatores*) are in ordinary circumstances *privati*, despite coming into contact with many individual members of the populace, because they have no particular connection to the people as a whole.[62]

As an example, somewhat disconcerting in today's terms, public multi-seater toilets such as those found at Pompeii and Herculaneum, help us understand how concepts of 'public' and 'private' differ today from Roman times. These ancient toilets could house numerous users, defecating and urinating and perhaps only 30 cm apart, wiping themselves on sea-sponges tied to sticks that sat in shallow trenches situated before them.[63] Whilst such images might 'jolt our modern sensitivities', we cannot judge Romans from personal or indeed contemporary cultural perspectives.[64] Rather if '*privatus*' can be translated as 'apart from the state' or 'of or belonging to an individual' whilst '*publicus*' translates as 'of or belonging to the people, state or community', then defecating in front of twenty other people was surely not perceived to be a 'public' act, or an act in 'public' since it had no sense of belonging to the people or the community.[65] It was, rather, an act that belonged to the individual in question and thus 'private', irrespective of whether it was carried out alone or in company and where it occurred.[66]

Applying the terms 'public' and 'private' to the domestic sphere highlights further their complexities. According to Vitruvius,

> Into those [rooms] which are private (*privatis*) no one enters, except invited; such are bedchambers, *triclinia*, baths, and others of a similar nature. The common rooms (*communia*), on the contrary, are those entered by anyone, even unasked. Such are the vestibule, the *cavædium*, the *peristylia*, and those which are for similar uses.[67]

This passage has generally been interpreted as presenting an unobstructed and accessible home, with permanently open entrance doors that enabled pedestrians outside to wander into the house as they traversed the city's streets. The house has thus been seen as being divided into 'public' spaces for unquestioned access to all and more protected 'private' areas restricted to an 'invited' few.[68] The ambiguity behind Vitruvius' use of '*privatus*' and '*communia*', however, requires thought.[69] He explains that the house should be laid out according to the status of the owner. People from the lower echelons do not require grand vestibules and reception areas since they do not have people visiting them, rather they visit others. For those of higher status, such as advocates or those with public office who hold the highest social position, houses should reflect the nature of their standing. Of those from the highest echelons, Vitruvius stipulates,

> for nobles, who in bearing honours, and discharging the duties of the magistracy, must have much intercourse with the citizens, princely vestibules must be provided, lofty *atria*, and spacious *peristylia*, groves, and extensive walks, finished in a magnificent style. In addition to these, libraries, *pinacothecæ*, and *basilicæ*, of similar form to those which are made for public use, are to be provided; for in the houses of the noble, the affairs of the public, and the decision and judgment of private causes are often determined.[70]

According to Wallace-Hadrill, we are dealing here with 'a spectrum that ranges from the completely public to the completely private, and with an architectural and decorative language that seeks to establish such relativities'.[71] He goes on to outline the 'subtle grades in relative privacy' and explains,

> The *triclinium* will be private relative to the main circulation and open reception areas; yet the *cubiculum* is private relative to the *triclinium*, and this is a place not only for rest ("bedroom") but for the reception of intimate friends and the conducting of confidential business – and even for emperors conducting their notorious trials *intra cubiculum*.[72]

Thus, for Wallace-Hadrill, 'An area may be public and grand (the magistrate's *atrium*) or private and grand (his *triclinium* or *cubiculum*). It may be private and humble (the slave's bedroom, the farmer's storeroom)'.[73] The notion of gradations of public and private is important, but needs further thought. That a 'public/private antithesis in terms of a black/white polarity' does not exist when we consider the Roman house is clear.[74] However, there need not be as fixed a hierarchy of rooms on a spectrum of 'public' or 'private' as Wallace-Hadrill indicates. If we apply the meaning 'of or belonging to the people, state or community' to the term '*publicus*', and the meaning of '*privata*' as being 'apart from the state' or 'of or belonging to the individual', concepts of 'public' and 'private' in the Roman house become more complicated than mere concern with the situation of one space relative to another in terms of physical circulation and its relationship to the main reception areas of the house. Questions of the nature of activity within a room, the timing of its occurrence and the presence of doors, curtains or other barriers to physical or sensory access might also influence the extent to which a room in a house is perceived as 'public' or 'private'.

Vitruvius highlights that the nature of business undertaken within the houses of the elite might be 'public' affairs or 'private' concerns (*publica consilia et privata iudicia*). In the case of the *cubiculum*, for example, whilst reception of friends and intimates occurs here as well as rest and sex, we also find examples of trials and business being conducted in these spaces.[75] Although it is a space that is 'private' relative to other parts of the house in terms of location and circulation, 'public' business pertaining to the state or community might also occur thus complicating the usual interpretation of the space as purely 'private'. Likewise, as we will see, partitions at the thresholds of *cubicula*, the presence or absence of lighting and visual access, might also complicate how the terms 'public' or 'private' should be interpreted. Throughout this book, then, a more complex and flexible approach to the conception of 'public' and 'private' spaces in the Roman house is suggested, which takes into consideration not merely room location relative to circulation and décor, but also activities undertaken and their timing, as well as the presence and impact of partitions and lighting on the physical experience of space and its interpretation as 'public' or 'private'.

Corporeal engagement with the home is affected not just by the edifice itself, but also by the surrounding environs in which it is situated. To understand the ways in which the sensory experiences of the world beyond the home might enter a dwelling and how life in the home might merge with the street outside, it is necessary to understand the residence structure, including thresholds and room location and detailed information on street layout and networks, traffic flow, and the location of amenities such as fountains, taverns and shops. To gain an understanding of the sensory realm of the Roman home, the sites under consideration need to have been excavated extensively: this has a major influence on the choice of locations examined in this monograph. The Bay of Naples provides considerable knowledge about the built environment of the Roman city and its surrounding landscape. The region's destruction in AD 79 preserved vital information that has enabled historians to develop a macroscopic overview and a microscopic insight into the Roman built environment. Sizeable remains, including whole street networks and dwellings, together with smaller and more specific vestiges such as guttering, thresholds – including, in places, door and window architecture – enable exploration of the sensory experience of dwelling in the towns of Pompeii and Herculaneum. Moreover, two and a half centuries of excavation serve to provide an incomparable wealth of evidence for understanding the domestic realm.

Evidence from Rome is more problematic. Given its continued occupation and constant rebuilding over time, detailed exploration of the relationship between roads and houses is more complicated. Thus, whilst we have substantial information about journeys through Rome and insight from texts and material culture into typical buildings, locating such buildings on the actual remains of Rome's ancient streets is often impossible.[76] Towns on the Bay of Naples and even Ostia, albeit to a lesser extent, exhibit traces of daily life and travel in their streets such as cart ruts, street shrines and fountains, but these have been built over in Rome as the city has developed. Remains of Rome's ancient residences are scarce: most have been replaced or used for building material in later centuries. Thus whilst the fourth century AD Regionary Catalogues of Rome suggest there were in excess of 46,000 multi-storey dwellings or *insulae* in Rome and 1,790 single family occupancy residences, or *domus* dwellings, today only a handful of these houses stand, often in such fragmentary state that understanding even the residence itself, let alone its relationship to its environs, is virtually impossible.[77]

Texts from Roman authors, however, provide significant insights into Roman housing. References to houses in letters, satires, histories, architectural treatises, plays and poems serve to develop a picture of life within many types of homes. The bulk of literary evidence is focused on dwellings in the city of Rome, and literature about daily life and houses outside Rome is scarce. Those that remain refer principally to residences belonging to Rome's elite, generally male, which is an important consideration when looking at corporeal experience in the Roman home. Over the centuries of its excavation, Pompeii has been seen as similar to Rome, thereby ensuring its primary significance in studies of Roman history. In reality, however, we must be aware that it was a relatively small town in Campania, how many Romans ever went there or how many Pompeians visited Rome, we cannot say. As Hales comments

> We must remind ourselves that she [Pompeii] was, in the larger scheme of things, fairly insignificant, a prosperous market town in Campania, famous only to the people of Rome for her amphitheatre riot and, of course, the eruption of Vesuvius, which destroyed her along with Pliny the Elder on 24 August 79 AD.[78]

Yet there were social and cultural similarities to Rome in Pompeii and Herculaneum. That Pompeii was a Roman *colonia* and Herculaneum was a *municipium* by the early first century BC highlights at least a basic comparability between life in these towns and Rome.[79]

Having summarized the developing scholarly interest in multisensory perception and the issues posed by the range of evidence concerning the ancient Roman domestic realm, this chapter concludes by outlining the methodological approaches and structure of the book.

Drawing on archaeological factors including size, layout and finds such as lamps, mosaics and graffiti, evidence of drainage and the presence or absence of partitions from Pompeii (and to a lesser extent Herculaneum); and comparing these with literary accounts of the domestic realm, the monograph examines in detail how, and why, owners sought to control and manipulate corporeal engagement in their domestic sphere and the extent to which this is evidenced in the literature and archaeology. Whilst the owner's role is the focus here, we will also explore, where possible, alternative potential embodied experiences of the home, for example those of slaves, to highlight the variety of interactions to be had with the sensory realm of the house.

In terms of the book's structure, Chapter 2 moves on to explore the key relationship between an owner's ability to organize and control the multisensory domestic realm and the role this plays as a means of personal status display. Using as a starting point an initial examination of the highly complicated term 'power' and the varying ways in which it can be presented and perceived in the built environment, the chapter presents a theoretical model of a multisensory reading of the Roman home. Focusing on two well-known villa letters of Pliny the Younger, we consider how and why owners used other bodily senses to shape the image they presented to others in order to help us understand more clearly the various strategies Romans exploited to parade their wherewithal and status to contemporaries.

Following this, the remaining chapters have been structured to resemble an imagined walk through the Roman *domus* or villa, exploring numerous corporeal experiences stimulated for individuals by different spaces and rooms and their internal and external environmental factors. Each chapter presents a particular room associated with the Roman domestic realm and considers the daily or regular multisensory experiences to be had and the possible factors such as time of day, season or weather that might affect the house and an individual's response.

Chapter 3 considers the relationship of the house to the street, examining the visual and other sensory relationships between the residence, the street outside and surrounding environs. Moving into the house, Chapter 4, the first chapter on the interior realm of the Roman home, considers the question of access to the dwelling and the multifaceted role of the *atrium-tablinum*, which hosted familial and social rituals and also the more mundane chores of daily life. As spaces with numerous functions, often open to the outside world, corporeal engagement with *atria-tablina* was variable. This chapter considers potential multisensory experiences to be had in this space and how far and why we see evidence of attempts to organize or control them.

Located around the *atrium* and peristyle were rooms traditionally called *cubicula*. As spaces leading off areas deemed by Vitruvius to be accessible to anyone invited, Chapter 5 examines these rooms and focuses on the nature of the relationship between public and private with reference to these spaces and considers how the senses of sight, sound and smell might be manipulated in order to alter the levels of public access or privacy within *cubicula*.[80] In Chapter 6, our imagined journey through the dwelling takes us further into the house to explore the possible multisensory responses to be had in *triclinia*, both those located in the house, and in house gardens. Chapter 7 considers the role and location of rooms and spaces from which either powerful or foul sensory experiences might be expected to emanate, such as toilets, kitchens, workshops or stables. The practice of locating kitchen-toilet-bathing suites together at some distance from reception areas of the dwelling perhaps confirms the desire to control or manipulate potential unpleasant smells (and sounds and sights) coming from these rooms. Yet it raises the question of how the sensorially foul were housed in smaller dwellings where employing distance as a means of sensory control might not have been an option. To what extent, then, can we see attempts, and indeed the ability, to control and manipulate the multisensory experiences that kitchen, toilet and/or bathing areas might encourage? What do studies of these rooms of ancient Roman houses tell us about ancient perceptions of 'unpleasant' sensory experiences particularly those arising from bodily functions and do these vary according to social standing?

Conclusion

Using evidence from residences of Rome, Pompeii and Herculaneum, this monograph offers a new interpretation of the multifaceted nature of the Roman domestic realm. Traditionally the sense of sight has dominated much of our understanding and engagement with the world around us. Similarly, this is the case with much of our current interpretation of the Roman home, which relies on vision and the plotting of sightlines to discover what can be seen from one part of a residence into other areas and the environs. More recently, however, emphasis on singular sensory interpretations have been recognized as one-dimensional, and there has been increasing awareness of the plurality of human sensory experience. It is this developing understanding of the range of corporeal responses to environs that I bring in here to interpretations of the ancient Roman domestic realm. Such insight is crucial for helping develop a deeper comprehension of these complicated locales, since over reliance on the sense of sight in engaging with the Roman domestic realm may lead to problems of interpreting accurately the role of the home in Roman culture and society. I am aware of the irony that to communicate multisensory experience within the Roman home in this book, I am forced to do so via the particularly visual medium of the written word. Through the following chapters, however, this monograph brings together literary accounts of ancient Roman dwellings together with their archaeological remains in order to help develop our comprehension of how important the full body experience of a dwelling was perceived to be, in terms of sights, sounds, smells, tastes and textures. Through exploration of the potential and varying multisensory experiences to be had within the home, we can explore Roman perceptions of the sensory realm. We can also examine the roles of the multiple senses, beyond that of sight, in the organization of the domestic sphere and investigate how far attempts to 'condition' sensory experiences of the lived environment may be perceived and what this tells us about modes of display of individual power, status and belonging in the Roman world.

2

Sensing Status? Multisensory Awareness and Power Display in the Roman Domestic Realm

Introduction

> Almost opposite to the middle of the portico is a suite of rooms set back a little, with a small open space in the middle shaded by four plane-trees. In the centre is a marble fountain, from which the water plays upon and lightly sprinkles the roots of the plane-trees and the ground beneath them. In this suite of rooms is a bedroom which excludes all light, noise and sound, and next to it is a dining-room where I entertain my friends, which faces on to the small court and the other portico, and commands the view enjoyed by the portico. There is another bedroom, which is leafy and shaded by the nearest plane-tree and built of marble up to the balcony; above is an equally beautiful fresco of a tree with birds perched in the branches. Here is a small fountain with a basin surrounded by little jets, which make a charming murmuring sound. In the corner of the portico is a spacious bedroom facing the dining-room, some of its windows look out on to the terrace, others on to the meadow, while the windows in front face a fish-pond which lies just below them, and is pleasant to see and hear as the water falls from a height and foams white as it hits the marble basin. This bedroom is warm even in winter because it is bathed with sunshine.[1]

In his letter to Domitius Apollinaris, Pliny the Younger gives a description of the wonders of his Tuscan villa. An earlier letter, addressed to Gallus, similarly presents an idyllic account of his Laurentine dwelling.[2] Pliny paints extraordinary mental impressions of these houses, which generations of scholars have sought to identify in archaeological sites and portray in paper–recreations of the intricate descriptions.[3] Yet the enduring legacy of these accounts is not merely the visual image that they convey to the reader. Rather, just as Pallasmaa demonstrates the importance of full sensory engagement with today's domestic sphere, as seen in Chapter 1, so Pliny's *Letters* on his villas highlight the existence of similar concerns with full bodily experience. Within his written words lie rich tapestries of the multisensory experiences at his houses. From his description of babbling fountains, auditory peace and shelter from excessive heat, cold and light in his Tuscan villa to the sea's murmur and the tranquillity and seclusion at Laurentium, these letters tantalize and encourage sensory responses, evoking the reader's full corporeal engagement with the houses and surroundings described.[4] Not only do these letters demonstrate authorial awareness of the potential for residences to effect a range of sensorial responses in visitors and inhabitants, as we will see they also highlight the importance of manipulating bodily experience in the home as a means of controlling displays of power and standing in the Roman world.

Power and the Roman home

In Chapter One we considered the complexities of defining the terms 'public' and 'private' with reference to the Roman home. Implicitly embedded within notions of the 'public' nature of Roman dwellings is the way houses were seen as a means of visually displaying an owner's social standing to contemporaries. Thus, the connections between houses and personal status, particularly with reference to décor and architecture, are clear in the Roman world.[5]

When examining his *Letters*, Pliny's high social standing is a key factor that impacts upon our understanding of his villa descriptions. For members of Rome's elite, the capacity to parade power and influence over others was of fundamental importance. Pliny's writings on his villas demonstrate how he employed his letters to emphasize not just the bodily immersion that was possible, but also that he could organize those feelings. Physical experiences whilst in Pliny's domain were under the control of Pliny himself and served to highlight his influence. Such displays over another person's bodily experience presented an important way of demonstrating personal status and power.

Connections between power and the built environment might initially seem obvious; a cursory glance at the Parthenon or the *Forum Romanum* shows clear visual messages of both democratic and Imperial power, or oligarchic and military power respectively. The means by which individuals could parade power and their capability to control environments, however, deserves deeper attention. Recent investigations into the notion of power emphasize the significant problems in reaching a clear understanding of the term.

> The very term [power] makes many of us uncomfortable. It is certainly one of the most loaded and polymorphous words in our repertoire. The Romance, Germanic, and Slavic languages, at least, conflate a multitude of meanings in speaking about *pouvoir* or *potere*, *Macht*, or *mogushchestvo*. Such words allow us to speak about power as if it meant the same thing to all of us.[6]

For anthropologist Wolf, it is the nebulous yet multi-layered qualities of power that make it so difficult to define completely. Of the four methods that Wolf outlines for interpreting displays of power, the third and the fourth modes are the most useful for our discussions.[7] Wolf describes his third approach to the term power as 'tactical or organizational power' or how people 'circumscribe the actions of others within determinate settings'. The fourth mode of power he sees as one that 'not only operates within settings or domains but that also organizes and orchestrates the settings themselves'.[8] Here he draws closely upon Michel Foucault's theory of power as being the ability 'to structure the possible field of action of others'.[9] For him, 'structural power' is not a purely economic relation, but a political one as well: 'it takes clout to set up, clout to maintain, and clout to defend; and wielding that clout becomes a target for competition or alliance building resistance or accommodation.'[10]

What is particularly relevant to this book in Wolf's third and fourth interpretations of power is the recognition of power displayed through the control and management of the environs of others and their actions, or movement. This is achieved not just by the erection of buildings and the construction of views and vistas but equally importantly, I would argue, with control of an individual's full sensory and kinetic engagement with a site. Whilst the organization and control of sightlines into and movement throughout the house were important, other sensory experiences could be manipulated in the Roman house: this needs consideration in order to help us develop deeper understanding.[11] After all, as Lefebvre has shown, it is the physicality of spaces, where smells, sounds and textures can be bodily experienced, that makes space something more than the written word and which highlights the need for us to consider other corporeal feelings in the Roman home.[12]

Wolf's exploration of power's overriding complexity helps demonstrate its nuanced relationship with architecture in society. Thus, although not specifically focused on the role of power in antiquity, his work provides important theoretical underpinnings for this book's examination of the relationship between power and display in the Roman domestic realm. That various modes of power display were an important part of understanding the Roman domestic realm is well attested. Pliny the Elder, for example, describes the display of *spolia* at the homes of triumphing generals.

> Outside the houses and round the doorways there were other presentations of those mighty spirits, with spoils taken from the enemy fastened to them, which even one who bought the house was not permitted to unfasten, and the mansions eternally celebrated a triumph even though they changed their masters.[13]

For those military commanders who achieved the ultimate accolade in military prowess of the triumph, the entrance of the house presented the ideal location for exhibiting the evidence of their successes for all to see. That such proof of their achievements could not be removed even once the dwelling had passed into new ownership further emphasizes the extent to which the house played a vital role in parading the supremacy of individuals over their contemporaries. Another way in which power was demonstrated within the domestic realm was the manner in which the dominion of the *paterfamilias* extended over all members of the *familia*, giving him control over all aspects of the property, inheritance, marriage and divorce, and even the life or death of family members.[14] Although rather different types of power display within the home, both examples emphasize the important role of the domestic realm as a vehicle through which owners could display personal clout and wherewithal to the *familia* and the community as a whole.[15] Importantly, Wolf's multi-stranded interpretation of the modes of power develops such concepts further, not just by highlighting the power of individuals *per se*, but also by allowing us to consider **how** a person's power can be expressed. We are encouraged not only to understand power as the interaction and physical or emotional domination of another's actions or capabilities but also to examine how power can be used to affect the surroundings of an individual or an event. It is this notion of power over people and the environment that is fundamental to developing further our understanding of the role of the domestic sphere in Roman society.

Bringing the home to life: The *Letters* of Pliny the Younger

A person's being is intimately intertwined with their home. Within the decoration, architecture and organization of the domestic sphere, as the architectural theorist and philosopher Pallasmaa has suggested, is found the very essence of an individual's self; not just the body but their 'memory and identity' also.[16] Thus, embedded within a dwelling are the aspects that make up an individual – both the recollection of past experiences and their current physical engagement with the world around them. People and their residences are consequently, for Pallasmaa, physically inseparable and one's corporeal experience of home epitomizes this. In the following pages, the developing modes of multisensory research that Pallasmaa advocates are applied as a theoretical model through which to open up and develop further ways of interpreting the organization and experience of the ancient Roman domestic sphere. Two villa letters of Pliny are used to explore literary accounts of multisensory interactions with the domestic environment and to examine evidence for manipulation of the corporeal experience of the home as a means of controlling displays of power and standing in the Roman world.

In Pliny's Laurentine villa, the vistas and views across the sea, over neighbouring villas and within his own domain are clearly crucial. Sight is fundamental to his perception of the villa and how he wants others to understand its displays of wealth and personal power. We read about how the house can be visualized within the landscape: 'The shore is beautified by a most pleasing variety of villas, some of which are close together while others are far apart. They look like a number of cities.'[17] Likewise, we can visualize how the rooms of the villa relate to one another and the views to be had from within the dwelling. When describing the hall of his Laurentine villa, Pliny writes,

> It [the hall] has folding doors or windows as large as the doors all around, so that at the front it seems to look out onto three seas, and the back has a view through the inner hall, the courtyard with the two colonnades, then the entrance-hall to the woods and mountains in the distance.[18]

There is a similarly visual account of his Tuscan villa in his letter to Domitius Apollinaris. 'Picture to yourself a vast amphitheatre, such as could only be a work of nature.'[19] He goes on to emphasize the importance of visual reaction to the setting.

> You would be delighted if you could obtain a view of the countryside from the mountain, for you would think you were looking not so much at a real landscape but rather at a landscape picture of unusual beauty. Such is the variety, such the arrangement of the scene, that the eye is refreshed wherever it turns.[20]

The sight of his house in the landscape and the panoramas it commands across the mountains are key for Pliny: 'My house is on the lower slopes of a hill but commands as good a view as if it were higher up, for the ground rises so gradually that the slope is imperceptible, and you find yourself at the top without noticing the climb.'[21] So too are the vistas to be had from within the residence, for he comments: 'From the end of the colonnade projects a dining room: through its folding doors it looks on to the end of the terrace, the adjacent meadow, and the stretch of open country beyond, while from its windows on one side can be seen part of the terrace and the projecting wing of the house, on the other the tree tops'.[22]

Closer examination of both letters, however, emphasizes the importance to Pliny of other senses within his villa depictions.[23] The manipulation of the aural senses, for example, is emphasized in his discussion of the effect of the closing or opening of shutters when he writes of his Laurentine residence: 'this is the winter-quarters and gymnasium of my household for no winds can be heard there except those which bring the rain clouds.'[24] Likewise here Pliny refers to the 'deep seclusion and remoteness' of his detached garden building because of 'a dividing passage which separates the wall of the chamber from that of the garden, and so all sound is lost in the empty space between'.[25] Similar auditory sensations and attempts to reduce excessive noises are drawn upon at his Tuscan villa when he observes that 'in this suite is a bedroom which no daylight, voice, nor sound can penetrate',[26] and when he discusses the fountain in a room near a plane-tree, with its 'lovely murmuring sound' or the 'ornamental pool, [which is] a pleasure to see and hear'.[27]

Moreover, it is not just sight and sound that are emphasized in Pliny's letters. Olfactory and haptic (or tactile) references proliferate, from the 'terrace scented with violets' and the 'western breezes' which ensure 'the atmosphere is never heavy with stale air' at his Laurentine dwelling[28] to the implied aromas of the 'roses', the 'meadows bright with flowers' and the 'cypresses' dotted around his Tuscan house and its surroundings.[29] Suggestions emerge of heady arrays of pleasurable scents at both dwellings and the feeling of breezes on the skin. Likewise, references to the 'full warmth of the setting sun' on the ball court and the organization of suites in both houses in order to take advantage of seasonal climate, demonstrate a desire to take advantage of, and indeed manipulate, different types of physical experiences for both owner and visitor when at these villas.[30] We find even gustatory references in Pliny's description of his dwellings. From his Laurentine villa, he describes the fishing from the sea nearby, whilst from his Tuscan villa the references to the 'abundant and varied hunting to be had' and the crops on the descending slopes of the mountain likewise serve to inform the reader of the sumptuous culinary delights to be sampled whilst staying with Pliny.[31]

Pliny's accounts of his villas are not just about bringing to the fore a multitude of pleasurable sensory experiences for his readers. Throughout his letters, Pliny is equally keen to parade the power that he wields over even the extremes of

Nature. There is a clear desire where and when necessary to block or avoid unwanted corporeal experiences from parts of his villas. Thus at his Tuscan villa Pliny writes about the various rooms which can be used in either summer or winter, as well as the numerous references to protection from unpleasant weather, 'joining the cold bath is one of a medium degree of heat, which enjoys the kindly warmth of the sun, but not so intensely as the hot bath. This last consists of three several compartments, each of different degrees of heat; the two former lie open to the full sun, the latter, though not much exposed to its heat, receives an equal share of its light.'[32] At his Laurentine residence he writes about parts of the villa that can be opened up in fine weather, but also closed and offering protection in storms, thus highlighting the ability and desire to manipulate sensory experience in the dwelling. 'Here begins a covered arcade. It has windows on both sides. These all stand open on a fine and windless day, and in stormy weather can safely be opened on one side or the other away from the wind.'[33] Moreover, it is not just cutaneous, or feelings on the skin of warmth and wind or rain, to be had in the residence that Pliny demonstrates a desire to control. At his Tuscan home, Pliny describes a *triclinium* and attached bedroom and, explaining its architectural layout, highlights both the dark sanctity of the bedroom protected from the daylight and also the quiet and solitude to be had here.[34]

These examples from Pliny's villa letters demonstrate extensive comprehension of, and concern for, the multisensory experiences to be had within his homes. Whilst the visual aspects of his homes are clearly emphasized, Pliny's letters include descriptions of corporeal experiences in what appear to be almost ekphrastic portrayals of his dwellings.[35] In the same way that Pallasmaa promotes fully embodied encounters as a means of completely comprehending the domestic realm, Pliny's *Letters* display an intriguingly similar approach that physically brings his villas to life for readers delighting in the pleasurable haptic, olfactory, ocular, auditory, kinetic and even gustatory experiences to be had within his houses, which he had the power to arrange. Indeed, he emphasizes his role in the organization of both his Laurentine and Tuscan villas and outlines the structures, arrangements and location of his houses according to the multisensory experiences to be enjoyed there, explaining how they are manipulated in order to ensure the best possible experience.[36] As we will see throughout the remaining chapters of this book, that the Romans were acutely aware of the importance of complete bodily experience in the domestic sphere is visible in the texts of many other authors and within the archaeological remains. Not only do these different types of evidence identify visual experiences to be had within residences and their environs, they also highlight the crucial role of the careful control of other sensory experiences.

3

The Impact of Streetscapes on the Domestic Realm

Introduction

Imagine what a variety of noises reverberates about my ears! I have lodgings right over a bathing establishment. So, picture to yourself the assortment of sounds, which are strong enough to make me hate my very powers of hearing! When your strenuous gentleman, for example, is exercising himself by flourishing leaden weights; when he is working hard, or else pretends to be working hard, I can hear him grunt; and whenever he releases his imprisoned breath, I can hear him panting in wheezy and high-pitched tones. Or perhaps I notice some lazy fellow, content with a cheap rubdown, and hear the crack of the pummelling hand on his shoulder, varying in sound according as the hand is laid on flat or hollow ... Add to this the arresting of an occasional roisterer or pickpocket, the racket of the man who always likes to hear his own voice in the bathroom, or the enthusiast who plunges into the swimming-tank with unconscionable noise and splashing. Besides all those whose voices, if nothing else, are good, imagine the hair-plucker with his penetrating, shrill voice, – for purposes of advertisement – continually giving it vent and never holding his tongue except when he is plucking the armpits and making his victim yell instead. Then the cakeseller with his varied cries, the sausageman, the confectioner, and all the vendors of food hawking their wares, each with his own distinctive intonation.[1]

In his letter to Lucilius *On Quiet and Study*, Seneca the Younger enumerates the range of disturbing noises he experienced as he tried to study in accommodation above a baths. We must be wary of his comments, for he is making a rhetorical point about the importance of personal and emotional tranquillity to the peaceful life. Yet his presentation of the hubbub of city life highlights the multisensory relationship between the home and its environs and the impact the corporeal experience of urban living in ancient Rome could have upon individuals. Visual links between house and street have been examined in depth in terms of framed views into and out of dwellings.² This chapter seeks to develop understanding of the relationship between house and street by exploring other sensory connections between these two spheres thereby giving further insight into the embodied experience of the Roman home and life for owners, inhabitants and visitors.

The fluidity of the boundary between the civic and domestic realms is emphasized by the ways in which sensory experiences of the street and neighbouring properties had the potential to penetrate a dwelling.³ As such, we must start by looking at the 'sensoryscapes' of the street and environs of a dwelling and the extent to which these might impinge upon the domestic realm. Where Chapter 2 explored a theoretical multisensory reading of the Roman home, which focused solely on the letters of Pliny, this chapter seeks to take this further using both archaeological remains and literary evidence to develop a practical methodology that can be applied to understanding the sensory impact of the street on the Roman home.

Beginning with how a city's basic organization, in terms of the location of its shops, workshops and taverns, might affect the lived experience of a city's residences, we will then focus our investigations more closely upon the potential impact of the street outside, both in terms of pedestrian and cart traffic, upon life within the home. Since daily life in the home is not static but constantly changing, crucial to investigating the embodied realm of the home is a consideration of how such experiences change across time of day and seasons, and between different neighbouring settlements. After exploring a methodology for investigating corporeal connections and experiences that mingled between the world of the *via* and the domain of the house, this chapter concludes with a series of case studies exploring the possible ways in which house owners in particular parts of Pompeii might seek to control the impact of multisensory experience from external environs within their domestic sphere.

Sensory streetscapes in Rome and Pompeii

The impact of neighbouring buildings and surroundings on the domestic realm

> Do you ask why I often visit my bit of land near dry Nomentum and my villa's dingy hearth? Sparsus, there's no place in Rome for a poor man to think or rest. Schoolmasters deny you life in the morning, bakers at night, the hammers of the coppersmiths all day. On one hand the idle moneychanger rattles his grubby counter with Nero's metal, on the other the pounder of Spanish gold dust beats his

well-worn stone with shining mallet; neither does Bellona's frenzied throng give up, nor the garrulous sailor with his swaddled trunk ... Who can count up the various interruptions to sleep at Rome? ... within your own premises there's a retired drive for your carriage, in your deep recesses sleep and quiet are unbroken by the noise of tongues, and no daylight penetrates unless purposely admitted. As for me, I am woken by the laughter of the passing crowd; and all Rome is at my bed-side.[4]

Of significant importance when considering the relationship of houses to streets in the ancient Roman world is that residential, industrial and commercial sectors were distributed across cities, rather than being grouped together. In many examples, we see residences and commercial enterprises combined within the same building.[5] This lack of land use 'zoning' was first identified in Pompeii by Eschebach and later in Herculaneum by Guadagno.[6] Similarly, using literary sources, together with the *Forma Urbis Romae*, we can see the mingling of domestic and commercial properties (Fig. 3.1). Just as Seneca complains of the disturbances from the nearby baths, Martial tells us of the clamour from people

Figure 3.1 Fragment 11e of the *Forma Urbis Romae* showing the close proximity of domestic and commercial properties opening directly onto the Vicus Patricus, Rome. In the top right hand side of this fragment, the Vicus Patricus is flanked by a series of buildings with shops in front of them, by corridor apartments and by another large building with shops in front. The bottom half of this fragment depicts 3 *atrium*-style houses opening out directly on to the Vicus Patricus. © Roma, Sovrintendenza Capitolina ai Beni Culturali.

from various occupations, including schoolmasters, the corn grinders and metal workers, money-lenders, cult worshippers and sailors all disrupting the peace of those in nearby dwellings. Both men show the irritation that the lack of zoning could cause for a city's inhabitants, particularly from multisensory experience: people lived amongst pervading smells from cookshops and bakeries or the racket of metalworking and hawkers selling their wares to passers-by.

The situation was similar elsewhere. According to Wallace-Hadrill at Pompeii there was 'no real attempt at segregation or concentration beyond the tendency of shops to line the main roads and horticulture to cluster on the margins'.[7] As can be seen from Pompeii, within city walls shops, taverns, inns, fulleries, workshops, fountains, bakeries, street shrines, brothels and houses mingle together whilst outside the city's boundaries workshops, cookshops, taverns, villas and tombs were similarly interspersed (Fig. 3.2).[8]

In Pompeii's *Regio* VII *Insula* II, for example, the *pistrinum* of Popidius Priscus was next to the house of Vettius and the house of Popidius Priscus. In this bakery was a substantial oven and numerous mills for grinding flour, which were turned either by slaves or donkeys.[9] This emphasizes the possible smells and noise associated with bread production and working animals that might have emanated during working hours. Further evidence of the proximity of businesses and residences is highlighted by the example of the *thermopolium* of Vetutius Placidus, *Regio* I, *Insula* 8, 8–9, which was connected to the house of Vetutius Placidus (Fig. 3.3). Here, a bar and tavern area opened directly onto the Via dell'Abbondanza. *Dolia* which held food were fitted into a marble counter top, and a stove for heating food was also located here. This shop frontage and two connected rooms could be separated by doors from the residence located behind, and an alternative entrance to the residence, away from the shop front, was also possible via the *fauces*, which opened onto a different and narrow unnamed street at 1.8.9 on Fig. 3.4. That shop and dwelling could be partitioned off from each other suggests a desire to reduce, at least to some extent, the sensorial impact of the cooking of foods and the sight and noise of customers from household inhabitants and *vice versa*.

The lack of zoning within Pompeii is further emphasized by the remains of 100 masonry benches dotted around the city and located outside a variety of properties ranging from the domestic to the commercial and civic (Fig. 3.4.).[10] As Hartnett points out, it is likely that at times wooden furniture would also have lined the streets, although no examples survive.[11] The sheer number of these benches would have meant there would have been numerous instances of benches placed outside bars and taverns in close proximity to residences. In *Regio* I *Insula* 15, benches have been found outside properties of either a domestic

Figure 3.2 Map of Pompeii showing the location of different types of commercial, religious and other productive premises. Bloomsbury Academic with base map courtesy of E. Poehler, Pompeii Bibliography and Mapping Project, 2019, and further information from R. Laurence *Roman Pompeii: Space and Society*, 2007.

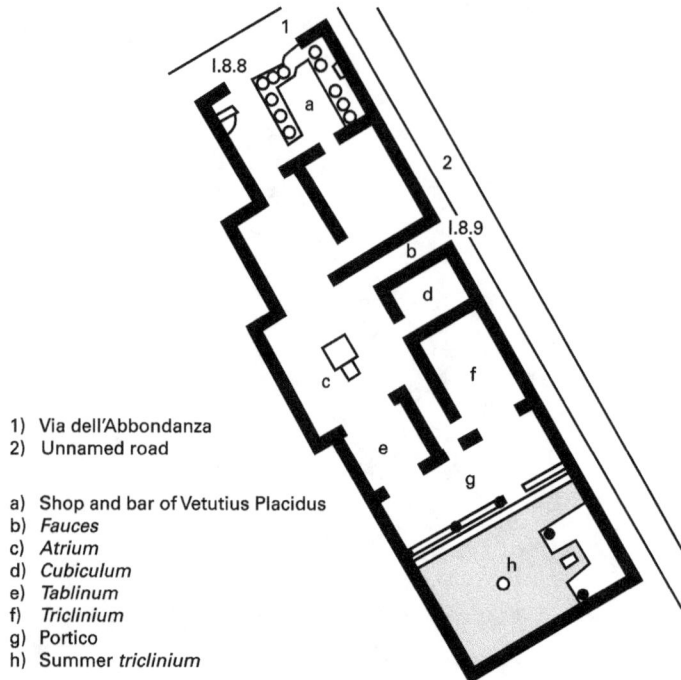

1) Via dell'Abbondanza
2) Unnamed road

a) Shop and bar of Vetutius Placidus
b) *Fauces*
c) *Atrium*
d) *Cubiculum*
e) *Tablinum*
f) *Triclinium*
g) Portico
h) Summer *triclinium*

Figure 3.3 Floor plan of the house and connected *thermopolium* of Vetutius Placidus (Reg I.8.8), Pompeii. © Bloomsbury Academic.

Figure 3.4 View of façade of house of the Ceii opening on to the Vicolo del Menandro (Reg I.6.15), Pompeii. Note the benches located outside. Photo: Hannah Platts.

or a less clearly defined role. On the opposite side of the street, another bench was located outside a property identified as having a commercial or industrial role.[12] Similarly, along the Via dell'Abbondanza in *Regio* III, many benches have been found outside properties that had a variety of purposes. Assuming that these were used by customers, pedestrians, residence owners and their *clientes*, either for relaxing and chatting, for sitting outside taverns and drinking or eating, or for queuing and awaiting admission into residences, this street furniture provided a focal point for people to mingle. The noise from the resultant groups could be substantial and once again, we can imagine it filtering into nearby homes and disturbing any quiet.

In the same way that there would have been substantial auditory disturbances filtering into and out of dwellings due to this lack of zoning, we must also consider other potential sensory experiences, including smell. The measuring of smell from a source is complex. When a smell source emits an odour, the odour molecules are transmitted into the surrounding air via diffusion from an area of higher to lower concentration until they are equally spread out within the surroundings.[13] Without the influencing factor of wind, these odour particles will linger in the area around the source. The introduction of wind, however, will serve to transmit the smell further from the source as the odoriferous molecules are carried by the wind in the direction in which the wind is blowing.[14] This changeable, yet vital, environmental factor in smell dispersal helps to make 'smell-mapping' (the plotting of smell transmission from source into surroundings) so complicated.

Irrespective of how difficult it is to measure and map the diffusion of smells within an area, it is crucial for us to be aware of the presence of odours and to consider their impact upon the physical experience of an environment. Consider, for example, the smells coming from workshops, cookshops and the urinals in the street used by fullers to collect the urine that they used for cleaning clothing.[15] Houses too would have provided substantial olfactory nuisances in the areas in which they were located, given that chamber pots were regularly emptied of out windows onto the heads of unsuspecting passers-by.[16]

Just as importantly, however, in addition to the stink from the living inhabitants of the ancient city, we must also consider the reeking dead. Like all other Roman towns, the city of Pompeii buried their dead outside the city walls. Whilst remains are limited outside the Nolan, Stabian and Vesuvian gates, excavations outside the Stabian Gate have uncovered 119 cremations that date to the Roman period.[17] There is more evidence for Pompeian burials outside the Herculaneum and Noceran gates, both of which have been published in some detail and which give some good insight into monumental burial styles and commemoration of the dead.[18] Cremations took place either in public areas of a necropolis designated for the purpose called *ustrina*,[19] or sometimes in a private tomb enclosure and would, when burning, have emitted a strong stench.[20] Depending on the direction of the wind, the smell would have impacted not only those living and working around the Herculaneum gate, but also those within relatively close proximity.[21] Whilst relatively simple burials and cremations suggest at least some level of burial provision for the poorer members of Pompeian society, we must also note that many living in Roman cities, including some in Pompeii, had no financial wherewithal for dealing with death: for these people disposing of corpses was difficult. The discovery of a decree from Puteoli which fined those caught abandoning bodies, and inscriptions from the city of Rome which prevented people from disposing of rubbish and bodies suggest that for at least some of the poorest adequate disposal of human remains was not possible.[22]

When we compare such evidence to Rome, we observe close similarities as to the problems of disposing of the dead. Literary sources, for example, suggest the possibility that human remains might be found in the streets of Rome. Suetonius tells of a dog that dropped a human hand beneath Vespasian's table and the rearing of Nero's horse at the smell of a dead body left in the road.[23] In AD 276, wolves dragged a half-eaten body into the Forum, whilst about a century earlier Martial describes the fears of a destitute and dying poet who envies those who can afford a proper funeral pyre and who fears 'the wrangling of dogs for his body and flaps his rags to drive off birds of prey'.[24] In addition to the likelihood of abandoned bodies and body parts being left to rot in the street, according to Varro, corpses were thrown into pits called '*puticuli*' that were possibly located outside Rome's Esquiline gate.[25] Using comparative evidence from mass graves employed for burying the poor in France and England from the sixteenth to the eighteenth centuries, Bodel has suggested that the 75 mass-burial pits uncovered outside the Esquiline Gate might have housed between 550 to 800 bodies each, which would have meant that they remained open for several weeks possibly even months before being filled and closed.[26] Having the pits open for such periods of time would have been long enough to allow the 'putrefaction of their deposits … to set in and the unpleasant symptoms of decay (stench and putrid air) would have emanated into the environs.'[27]

The impact of roads, street networks, traffic flow, pedestrians and animals on Pompeian homes

Beyond the lack of zoning of commercial enterprises and domestic spaces an additional factor which intensified the impact of sensory disturbances between street and home was the relative proximity of the two. In today's towns, certainly across the United Kingdom, the front doors of many modern residences do not open directly onto the pavement or road. It is regularly the case that house doors open onto private front gardens or driveways, thus giving at least some distance from the roads and pavements that are open to public use. The situation was different in many ancient cities. The plan of Pompeii, for instance, demonstrates that most houses opened directly onto the city's bustling streets (Fig. 3.5). It would appear that such closeness between house entrances and streets was typical of other cities, including Herculaneum and Rome. Housing remains from Herculaneum demonstrate that, as in Pompeii, houses opened straight onto pavements (Fig. 3.6), whilst fragments of the Severan Marble plan from Rome likewise depict *atrium*-style houses opening out onto Rome's Vicus Patricus (Fig. 3.1). Likewise Plutarch's biography of Publicola provides evidence of a literary nature of houses opening immediately onto pavements in Rome. In honour of his military achievements, the entrance doors to Publicola's home were allowed to open outwards onto the street so that he would constantly be honoured as passers-by would have to move out of his way.[28]

We should also note the inherently close relationship not just between houses and pedestrians on the pavement, but also between residences and the cart and animal traffic on roads outside, particularly in view of the potential multisensory impacts they might have had upon inhabitants. The typical lack of a space, such as a front garden, situated between house entrance and pavement ensured there was less of a separation zone to reduce penetration of sensory experiences such as sounds, smells and sights from road into house and vice versa. Given this lack of sensory 'buffer' spaces, not only would pedestrians affect and be influenced by life in houses, but, as we will explore below, cart flow and movement on roads would equally impinge upon the corporeal experience of life in the Roman home.

That proximity to road and pedestrian traffic affected the lived experience of domestic spheres can be observed in literary evidence. Not only does the frustration of Martial and Seneca emphasize how daily activities in the urban realm impacted upon life in the home but Juvenal's famous *Satire* III gives considerable detail of the numerous unpleasant aspects of living in the city of Rome, from poverty and violence to crumbling houses and dirt. In particular he emphasizes sensory disturbances caused by cart, animal and pedestrian traffic, 'Which lodgings allow you to rest, after all? You have to be very rich to get sleep in Rome. That's the source of the sickness. The continual traffic of carriages in the narrow twisting streets and the swearing of the drover when his herd has come to a halt would deprive a Drusus … of sleep'.[29]

Figure 3.5 Map of Pompeii showing houses and commercial properties opening directly on to pavements. © Bloomsbury Academic.

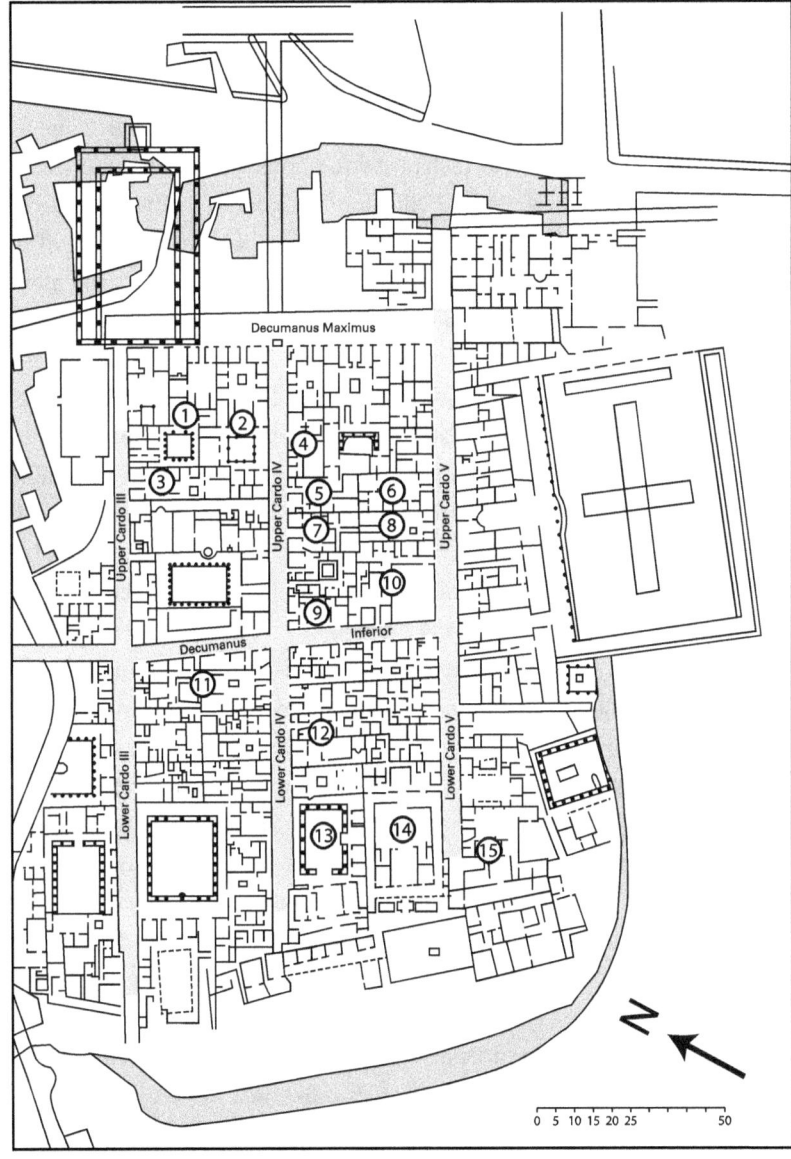

1 – House of the Tuscan Colonnade	9 – Samnite House
2 – House of the Black Hall	10 – House of the Great Portal
3 – House of Double *Atrium*	11 – House of the Wooden Partition
4 – House of the Beautiful Courtyard	12 – House of the Alcove
5 – House of the Neptune Mosaic	13 – House of the Mosaic *Atrium*
6 – House of the Corinthian *Atrium*	14 – House of the Deer
7 – House of the Carbonised Furniture	15 – House of the Gem
8 – House of the Wooden *Sacellum*	

Figure 3.6 Map of Herculaneum showing houses and commercial properties opening directly on to pavements. © Bloomsbury Academic.

As with our reservations above regarding Seneca's *Epistle*, we must note concerns about the possible accuracy of both Martial's and Juvenal's satirical attempts to depict life in Rome. Whilst we know little about their lives, we know they were both writing about the same time and that they probably came from relatively wealthy backgrounds, which raises questions about their understanding of the difficulties and privations of life for the poorer members of Roman society.[30] Connected to this question of reliability is the satirical nature of their work and the issues this poses for us in terms of their credibility.[31] To entertain successfully, satirical texts require a balance between exaggeration for comedic effect and a level of accuracy to engage audiences.[32] Applying this to Juvenal and Martial, we must understand that whilst there will be substantial elements of hyperbole in the scenes they create, it is unlikely that all aspects of their descriptions are without substance. Thus, we see that Juvenal's presentations of life in a noisy and sleepless Rome are supported by both Seneca's description of life in a Roman home, and by Martial's account of life in the metropolis in his *Epigram* addressed to Juvenal, 'While you perhaps, Juvenal, wander restlessly in noisy Subura'.[33]

It is not just the satirical nature of their works that raise issues regarding Juvenal's and Martial's presentations of life in Rome. We must also explore the problems faced when trying to apply their words on life in Rome to living elsewhere in the Roman Empire, for example in Pompeii. As outlined in Chapter One, ancient cities such as Rome and Pompeii varied considerably from one another, hence lifestyles and experiences within them were unlikely to be identical. Yet, whilst not directly analogous, we saw above similarity between numerous Roman cities, including Pompeii, Herculaneum and Rome, in the way dwellings open directly onto the pavement. This comparability between the house entrances and their relationship to the streets is important when trying to understand corporeal experiences of the bustling city and the lived home, and the impact these might have had upon each other. Just as Juvenal, Seneca and Martial complain about the disagreeable sensory distractions of life in Rome and the problems posed by closeness, it is plausible to assume, given equivalent proximity of houses, pavements and roads, and thus house residents, pedestrians and carts, that similar multisensory experiences would arise in Pompeii and elsewhere.

In recent years there has been increasing interest in exploring the ways in which people might have travelled around cities of the ancient Roman world. Using an initial theoretical framework for understanding how people today 'read' and traverse cities, developed by the urban geographer Lynch, scholars including

Corlàita, MacDonald, Zanker, Favro and Malmberg and Bjur have proposed descriptions of journeys through ancient Rome and Roman cities and the landmarks visitors would have encountered.[34] Yet it is not merely what people possibly saw on their travels that help an understanding of how individuals travelled around cities. Given its destruction by Vesuvius shrouding the city in lava and ash, which therefore protected much of its footprint, Pompeii in particular presents an excellent example of a settlement where road systems offer the potential for in-depth investigation into how people navigated it.[35] Remnants of journeys past have been etched into Pompeii's streets in the form of cart ruts and grooves on stepping and kerbstones.[36] Both cart rut depth and evidence for two-way and one-way streets have been mapped by scholars.[37] Debate continues as to which roads were blocked to vehicular access, but by examining remains we can identify the more heavily and less used patches of road and, when combined with investigations into traffic control and calming measures, these develop our understanding of types of travel utilized in Pompeii.[38] These studies have advanced understanding of streets in the civic sphere, however it is through combined investigations into Pompeian roads and buildings, as initiated by Laurence, that scholars are able to comprehend further the potential experiences of urban spaces by inhabitants and visitors.[39]

One particular area for consideration is how far traffic systems and road networks impact upon multisensory life in the city and home. Observing cart rut and traffic impediment remains from Pompeian streets in order to explore how past journeys through the city might have sensorially impacted its inhabitants is difficult, but possible (Fig. 3.7). Establishing the street networks of the city of Rome and the exact relationships between roads and buildings is more complicated, given its continued occupation and constant rebuilding over time: this has meant that complete archaeological comprehension of the relationship between street and dwelling is virtually impossible. In addition, it must be remembered that Rome itself is atypical in history, structure, function, size and population. Crucially, however, similar examinations of cart ruts and traffic control to that of Pompeii have been carried out in other cities of the Roman Empire, including Ostia, Silchester and Empúries. The data from these cities allows us both to understand further the nature of street networks and traffic systems within other Roman cities and provides us with a better idea as to just how comparable Pompeii's data is with that of settlements from across the Empire.[40] Moreover, the expansion of Rome's Empire throughout mainland Italy, and specifically the foundation as a *colonia* of Pompeii (in 80 BC) and Herculaneum as a *municipium* (in 89 BC) allows us to assume some form of

Figure 3.7 Deep cart ruts gouged in to the Via Stabiana, Pompeii. Photo: Hannah Platts.

'Roman' culture common to these settlements and the metropolis itself. This permits us to consider in greater depth the complexities of the relationship between street and home and the implications of this on multisensory experience of the Roman house, and to envisage similarities to Rome itself.

Houses vary, and the embodied experience of homes will likewise differ; so, too, streets themselves are not identical and their impact upon life in the home will also not be uniform. How far the bustle of daily life on the street affected life in a house, or indeed whether household activities would impinge upon those of the street, would vary depending on the road on which a particular house was located. Individual streets of cities varied in length, width, and even presence of pavements.[41] Indeed as Hartnett points out, consistency even within individual streets cannot be assured, as is demonstrated by the Via dell'Abbondanza in Pompeii, which measured 14 metres at its widest outside the Stabian baths, and only 8 metres in the east towards the Sarnus Gate. The average width of Pompeii's streets from façade to façade measured between 5 and 6 metres, which was only slightly less than the average width of Rome's streets, and most of Herculaneum's streets measured between 5 and 7 metres.[42] Thus, although there were streets of exceptional width, such as Pompeii's Via dell'Abbondanza, or Herculaneum's

Decumanus Maximus, there is some level of comparability in terms of average street width in the cities of Pompeii, Herculaneum and Rome.

It seems fairly obvious to state that the wider the street, the more traffic and social activity it experienced. Accordingly, then, one might argue that the broader roads of Pompeii, probably were amongst the most vibrant in sensory terms. Those that carried larger amounts of cart, animal and pedestrian traffic and which housed the most shops, taverns and workshops would probably be the smelliest, noisiest and most colourful areas, with the greatest incidence of bodily contact between individuals. In recent years, there has been much research into recording the incidence of graffiti and the presence of doorways on Pompeii streets in order to explore just how busy were the streets of Pompeii.[43] According to Laurence, by counting the number of doorways located on roads, indications of social activity on particular streets can be obtained.

> The placement of doorways and the use of street frontages would seem to reflect how the urban environment was used. For example, in a main street, there would have been a tendency for the maximisation of street frontages. In contrast, in a side street, the use of the street frontage would reflect the lower incidence of activity. Therefore, the number of doorways opening into a street directly reflects the level of social activity and interaction that occurred in the street.[44]

Laurence also suggests that understanding of levels of social interaction can be gained by recording the number of graffiti either on each house façade or metre of the street. Roads with higher levels of graffiti or those with more doorways indicated higher levels of social activity.[45] Results, from Pompeii's wider main arteries, such as the Via dell'Abbondanza and the Via Stabiana, showed evidence of more graffiti and doorways, thereby supporting the notion that the broader the street, the more social activity it experienced. There were, however, also some unexpected results. In particular, one part of the Vicolo di Tesimo, one of the narrowest streets in Pompeii, shows significant evidence of social activity with large amounts of graffiti and a higher incidence of doorways. As Hartnett explains this is 'perhaps because it offered an attractive alternative to the Via Stabiana, which ran parallel just to the west and hosted much more vehicular traffic.'[46] Vicolo di Tesimo highlights the need to refine Laurence's theories. We need to consider more carefully a street's individual characteristics and how these might affect the level and type of social activity within it and in turn the potential impact on the sensory experience of the street for those dwelling and travelling along it.

Laurence's notion that levels of street activity can be measured by numbers of doorways and amount of graffiti has been further complicated when comparing evidence of both within individual streets of Pompeii. He suggests that roads with more doorways often have fewer examples of graffiti because numerous doorways reduced the amount of space available for writing messages.[47] Looking at many of the main thoroughfares through Pompeii, including the Via dell'Abbondanza, Via del Vesuvio and Via Stabiana, revealed both a high incidence of doorways **and** graffiti, thereby suggesting that at least on some of the main streets of Pompeii, the number of doorways had little impact on the levels of graffiti daubed or carved into walls. These main roads that often led directly to the city's gates experienced high levels of traffic and social activity from both incomers and inhabitants, and with the bustle of carts and residents, there were more individuals milling around to write graffiti and more people to read the scrawled messages. A high incidence of doorways situated on these particular streets did little to detract from this.

That the main routes through Pompeii display evidence of substantial social activity reflected by high levels of graffiti and doorways is unsurprising. What is more remarkable, however, are instances where relatively minor roads, for example the Vicolo del Lupanare, the Vicolo del Centenario and the Vicolo di Lucrezio Frontone, show high levels of graffiti, with messages appearing at less than every 4 metres along the streets.[48] This is where factors particular to specific roads, such as proximity to public buildings and main thoroughfares in addition to the amount of doorways present, perhaps influence the levels of social activity experienced as indicated by graffiti.

The number of doorways on the narrow Vicolo del Lupanare is high, with entrances appearing approximately less than 5 metres along the street, the amount of graffiti here is also substantial, with messages occurring at least every 4 metres if not more frequently. The street permitted one-way traffic and therefore restricted the levels of cart traffic along it, but it housed a brothel, numerous shops, and entrances to the Stabian Baths.[49] This road would have seen substantial, particularly pedestrian, activity and so, just as with the main streets of Pompeii, levels of graffiti were high irrespective of the number of doorways.

The examples of the Vicolo del Centenario and the Vicolo di Lucrezio Frontone are rather different. These narrow roads both display graffiti messages occurring at least every 4 metres and often more frequently. They have comparatively lower incidence of doorways (occurring every 6–10 metres and every 11–15 metres respectively) and both lead off the important through route of the Via di Nola.⁵⁰ The proximity of both roads to the Via di Nola perhaps meant that they both saw fairly substantial social activity, but both roads also show evidence of traffic calming measures, such as the introduction of one-way traffic routes which, as with the Vicolo del Lupanare above, would restrict to some extent the road traffic travelling along them.⁵¹ It is perhaps these specific factors of street location, building set-up and traffic that meant these roads were popular access routes from the Via di Nola for pedestrians who then took the opportunity to daub messages on the walls unhampered by doorways, hence there was a high incidence of graffiti. Indeed, we might also add to this that some narrower streets perhaps **encouraged** numerous examples of graffiti specifically because they had reduced traffic and fewer doorways, which meant less people entering and exiting from buildings into the street and *vice versa*. Whilst busy roads with much traffic might encourage graffiti due to increased amounts of social activity, it is equally possible that some roads with less traffic attracted high levels of graffiti of an illicit or anonymous nature because there was less chance of perpetrators being caught in the act.⁵²

It is into this more nuanced approach towards the social activity that Pompeii's roads experienced, which considers specific factors of topography, road size, landmarks and buildings as well as the incidence of graffiti and doorways to understand possible levels of street activity, that we might place Hartnett's particular example of the narrow Vicolo di Tesimo. Although this alleyway had more doors, which made writing graffiti more difficult, and was narrower with less vehicular traffic than other nearby streets, it perhaps saw more footfall from pedestrians avoiding the nearby noisier, smellier and cart filled Via Stabiana. As they wandered down the street, many pedestrians in the Vicolo di Tesimo took the opportunity to scrawl their messages on the street's façade.

Graffiti and doorways hint at the levels of social interaction on ancient roads but they provide us with only part of the means by which to understand the streets of the ancient city. Careful comparison of the amount of graffiti and doorways together with consideration of nearby roads, public buildings, road width and traffic calming measures enables us to think in more detail about the nature and type of the social activities occurring in specific streets. This in turn offers us the ability to explore the potential varied sensory experiences of travelling around and living along the different roads of Pompeii.

In general, the widest roads of Pompeii acted as the city's key arteries that connected to the city's gates. The remnants of deep cart ruts gouged in parts of these routes of the Via Stabiana, the Via del Vesuvio, the Via di Nola and the Via dell'Abbondanza, for example, show that these two-way routes must have experienced significant levels of cart traffic (Fig. 3.7).[53] Furthermore, in addition to road size affecting the corporeal experiences of traffic as it travelled through the city, the materials used for road construction would have an impact, particularly on the soundscape of the street. Road surfaces in Pompeii, for example, included beaten ash, cobbled, lava stone and debris surfaces, and by the time of Vesuvius' eruption, 61 per cent of the city was paved, 31 per cent was unpaved and 8 per cent unknown.[54] The various surfaces would produce different sounds, as metal-covered cart wheels and horses hooves travelled along them, cobbles or paved surfaces producing the most noise, and beaten ash the least.[55]

The above evidence allows us to consider in greater detail the main routes people took to travel by foot or cart around Pompeii, and to consider the possible sounds from such journeys. These would have included cart wheels and animal hooves clattering along uneven roads and the shouts of drivers as they cajoled whinnying horses and braying mules, and warned pedestrians of their presence and swore at them along the way. Additionally, traffic impediments and calming measures such as the implementation of one-way routes are likely to have reduced the sounds of traffic flow through the city. At least some of these noises would have affected those living in the houses and shops that lined the streets, particularly along the main streets of Pompeii that carried large amounts of traffic.

When we think about the transmission of sound from the street into a dwelling, it is worth considering the nature of sound, the way in which it reduces the further it travels from the source of the noise, and the additional factors that affect that attenuation. Sound is a movement of energy that travels in waves through various media, including air. As these waves travel from a sound point-source and hit surfaces, some of the energy of the sound wave will be absorbed by the materials they encounter, whilst some of it will be reflected. The levels of absorption and reflection vary according to the material of the surface in question. When noise such as a shout is made in the street outside a house, for example, not only will the sound decibel level decrease by 6 decibels as the distance from the sound point-source doubles, but the size of the space in which the sound was made and the material of the surfaces the waves hit as they travel will also affect sound levels, since materials both absorb sound and reflect it back into the space. These factors can therefore affect acoustic properties of a space.[56] The levels at which various materials absorb or reflect sound is called the absorption coefficient and can be measured accordingly. The frequency of a sound, whether low frequency like hammering or higher pitched like children squealing, affects the levels of its absorption by the surface materials it hits. Thus depending on the pitch (whether low or high) as well as its level at source (in decibels) and the materials through which the sound must travel, a noise will be experienced differently in neighbouring spaces.[57] The absorption coefficient of solid wooden panel doors, for example, demonstrates that they absorb more energy from sound waves of lower frequency noises than higher frequency ones, whilst the absorption coefficient of painted plaster marginally increases with higher frequency sounds. The consequence of this is that noise levels travelling from the street through a closed wooden door into an *atrium* will be diminished as some of the sound's energy is absorbed or reflected on hitting the wooden door surface.[58]

The other important measurement that affects sound levels passing through materials and being heard on the other side is transmission loss (a measurement of the number of decibels that are stopped as a sound passes through a material). It is calculated according to the mass of the material through which the sound must travel: the greater the mass, the greater the transmission loss of the sound.[59] Wood has a low transmission loss rating (between 17 and 34 decibels), whilst concrete has a much higher one (45–71 decibels).[60] The frequency of a sound will also affect the ease with which a sound passes through a material. Low frequency noise pass through materials more easily than high frequency ones. So, in summary, how far a sound made in the street outside is heard within a dwelling will depend on the decibel level of the original sound, its pitch and the materials with which the sound waves make contact as they travel.

Of course, it was not just traffic that caused multisensory experiences for the inhabitants of Pompeii. We must also consider the daily hustle and bustle of the street and the impact this would have had upon domestic life in the city. The excavations of Pompeii have unearthed some wonderful, yet poignant, remains which give a tremendous insight into the city's sensory landscape. The nineteenth-century cast of a dog found in the house of Orpheus together with the discoveries of floor mosaics saying '*cave canem*' remind us of ancient Pompeii's canine population who, like dogs of today, would have defecated, howled and barked around the streets and homes of the city (Fig. 3.8). Whilst dog excrement on the streets of the city would not impact significantly upon individuals in the home (unless brought in on the sandal of an unsuspecting individual!), dog barks can register around 100 decibels, making it likely that hounds barking in the street would have been heard to some extent in the home, and vice versa.[61] Birds, too, are capable of producing considerable noise. Not only have nightingale song levels in excess of 90 decibels been

Figure 3.8 *Cave Canem* mosaic at the entrance to the *fauces* of the house of the Tragic Poet (Reg VI.8.3), Pompeii. Photo: Hannah Platts.

recorded, but recent studies into bird song characteristics have shown that urban songbirds, including the nightingale, amplify their voices when background noise is raised. When living in noisy urban areas, nightingale songs have been recorded at 14 decibels higher than those produced by nightingales in quieter areas.[62] Not only was the remarkable singing ability of nightingales recorded by Pliny the Elder, but from the remnants of wall paintings preserved by Vesuvius we know that nightingales, amongst other birds, existed on the Bay of Naples.[63] As such we can start to add to the clatter and the din of traffic in the streets the potential avian soundscape of Pompeii, for whilst the city's urban soundscape would have been quite different from today, it would have been noisy. Thus, it is probable that birds, such as nightingales, would have needed to sing or call loudly in order to be heard by mates over the sounds of the city and would have been heard within Pompeii's dwellings.

It is not just birds who raise vocal levels against loud background noise. Humans and mammals likewise amplify the volume of their voices, and thus we must consider the auditory impact of people conversing in the street and home.[64] We have already seen from Martial that sounds from the street would have filtered into the home.⁶⁵ As Bruce Smith highlights in his discussion of historic soundscapes, 'in the absence of ambient sounds of more than 70 decibels (barking dogs excepted), the sound of outdoor conversations would become a major factor in the sonic environment'. He goes on to explain that where cities have been pedestrianized, for example in Bologna, the streets act like 'highly reflective corridors' and increase the audibility of conversations occurring at a distance of over 100 feet away.⁶⁶

Here, then, we have archaeological support for the sensory life of Pompeii. The smells of cooking and fulling mingled with both the odour of excrement from animals and people dumped in the streets and stench of corpses buried outside the city walls.⁶⁷ Added to this was the combination of animal sounds such as birdsong, dogs and horses with people shouting and chatting and carts clattering must have resulted in Pompeii's streets being rowdy and pungent. Just as our literary evidence from authors such as Seneca, Juvenal and Martial suggest that such sounds and smells of life filtered into dwellings in Rome, the din and odours from workshops and taverns, from clients waiting outside residences, and from cart and pedestrian traffic made through Pompeii would likewise have impacted upon inhabitants. The likelihood that urban sensory disturbances impinged upon the life in the domestic realm is then, as our sources suggest, increasingly plausible.

A changing multisensory streetscape

Every town or city has its own 'multisensory streetscape'. Even though located relatively close to one another, Herculaneum's 'multisensory streetscape' would have differed from that of Pompeii. Herculaneum was closer to the sea and had an underground drainage system, which Pompeii lacked; both of these factors would affect many aspects of sensory feeling, including olfactory, visual and haptic experience.⁶⁸ Similar comparisons might be drawn regarding multisensory streetscapes of Rome and Ostia, although they were also in close proximity. The evidence of fewer cart ruts and the lack of stepping stones across streets in Ostia and Herculaneum, for example, highlights the different possible sensory experiences between these settlements and Pompeii.⁶⁹ Ostia's port, with its emphasis on a seasonal work force and its concentration of high-rise apartments, would equally impact upon the sensory experience of the city.⁷⁰

A city's 'multisensory streetscape' is affected by numerous factors including location, size, population density, weather and seasonal changes. Likewise settlements vary considerably in their 'multisensory streetscape' according to time of the day or night. The arrival of autumn and winter, for example, brings about visual, haptic, and olfactory changes, as fires, braziers, candles and lamps are lit, and partitions or windows are shut, closing off sections of houses to block out inclement weather. Days shorten and in settlements lacking permanent street-lighting much activity is likely to find its way indoors out of the cold and dark. Streets are likely to experience an auditory change, too, as people stay inside, rather than venturing out. For many places, seasonal change brings changing meteorological patterns including increased wind and precipitation in autumn and winter. This further alters the multisensory landscape as the sound of raindrops, whistling of wind through trees and the feeling of both on the skin impact auditory and haptic experience. Increased rain, wind and cold change the olfactory backdrop of a site. Frosty and dewy mornings strengthen smells and cold can help to deaden them, rainfall can cleanse the olfactory landscape, but can also increase certain smells, such as 'elder flower, hemlock and dog roses'.[71]

Pompeii's coastal location is a key factor in understanding its multisensory impact. Although now located a few kilometres from the shore, prior to the eruption of Vesuvius, it was situated only a few hundred metres away. Proximity to the sea will have impacted upon seasonal weather conditions, since cool sea breezes give relief in hot summers, whilst the warming effect of the sea provides milder conditions in winter. That ancient Romans appreciated the climatic conditions experienced on the Bay of Naples is demonstrated by its continued popularity as a summer retreat destination, where Rome's elite sought escape from Rome's oppressive heat.[72] Another influence are Pompeii's prevailing winds, which change direction between summer and autumn.[73] Wind direction and speed will have played a significant role particularly in the cutaneous, olfactory and auditory experience of the city. Thus, the breezier days of winter would have helped dissipate strong odours more quickly, whilst in warmer months not only would organic materials and food stuffs rot more quickly and produce stronger odours, but the typically reduced air flow of the summer would encourage smells to linger. Haptically and visually, windier winter months provoke different bodily experiences from those of summer, as wind is felt on the skin impacting temperature and encouraging general feelings of being hot or cold whilst rustling leaves and flowers can be seen. Similarly, in terms of an auditory experience, stronger winds not only increase noise levels (wind through trees, waves breaking) but wind direction also impacts upon sound levels. Thus, the changing direction of Pompeii's prevailing winds would alter the acoustic profile of the city. With prevailing winds blowing towards the west in the summer, a sound's dominant direction would be generally skewed towards the west, whilst in the winter it would be regularly skewed either towards the north-east or the south-east, thus making different regions of the city noisier at varying times of the year.[74]

It was not just changes to wind between the seasons that would have affected the corporeal experience of the city. Autumn and winter in Pompeii typically had increased levels of rain and decreased sunshine with November generally seeing the most rainfall and the least sunshine. Whilst we should not assume the weather in Pompeii approximately 2,000 years ago would be the same as that experienced today, general similarities in weather patterns, at least in terms of hot, dry summers and mild, wetter winters are likely.[75] Warmth and humidity do not just affect haptic or tactile experience, but also levels of sound. Dry weather makes sounds louder and clearer, whilst increased humidity and wet weather serves to muffle.[76] Temperature increases would serve to decrease the levels of sound heard in the city with the result that the fewer noises of the cooler night air would sound louder. Whilst individual sounds might be heard more loudly or clearly at night because of the temperature of Pompeian evenings, the greater levels of activity in the street during the day would produce overall a noisier soundscape in the city during the day.[77] Varying climatic conditions would have little impact upon sound levels over short distances, for example noises in the street immediately outside residences, but have the potential for substantial impact upon sound perception over long distances.

Embedded within the question of the changing multisensory experience of different settlements is the fact that within individual settlements there will be a variety of multisensory backdrops. Essentially, we can divide settlements into both macro and micro-multisensory streetscapes. In addition to road width, traffic calming and pedestrian accessibility measures impacting the sensory experiences of different sections of a town or city, as explored above, so too will types of buildings or the presence of public amenities, such as latrines and fountains. Likewise, given the seasonal changes to the prevailing wind direction and the impact of this on the dissipation of odour, certain parts of town or other sites may be more or less smelly. It might also alter haptic experiences of parts of the city, making some areas cooler and others warmer at different times of the year. The direction of precipitation; more built up and sheltered or open and exposed areas are; the varying seasonal arc of the sun, are all factors which will affect multisensory experiences of the city outside, and in turn may influence significantly the bodily experience of the home.

Controlling domestic sensory experiences around Pompeii

The examination above of factors affecting Pompeii's various and changing 'multisensory streetscapes' provides an example of how we might consider bodily experience within a settlement. It is not an attempt to reconstruct the manner in which inhabitants of Pompeii experienced the city's streets. The reconstruction of perceptions of people from antiquity is challenging because engagement with surroundings is both individual and affected by cultural background.[78] Rather, developing further Derrick's recent 'olfactory geography' of Vindolanda, which sought to 'illustrate a new way of engaging with the archaeological record of [Vindolanda] in order that we might consider, if not better understand, the 'sense of place felt at this Roman military site', I have outlined a possible 'multisensory geography' of Pompeii specifically to explore its potential impact upon inhabitants in the streets and homes of the city.[79]

In the final section of this chapter, the focus is on applying the above enquiry into Pompeii's multisensory streetscapes to specific dwellings throughout the city. Here we will explore both how multisensory experience within these residences might be affected by their particular location within the city, and examine how inhabitants sought to control possible corporeal disturbances upon life in their homes.

Case study one: Controlling the impact of the amphitheatre on Pompeii's residences

The potential impact of various factors on multisensory experience in the city of Pompeii is significant, particularly if we consider the location of residences in the city and the ways in which corporeal experience in and around them might be affected. Take, for example, the amphitheatre in the furthest eastern reaches of the city and its potential multisensory impact upon houses in the vicinity. As can be seen from Fig. 3.9, numerous dwellings were located on the roads leading to the amphitheatre in *regiones* I and II, particularly on the main route from the Forum, the Via dell'Abbondanza. This raises the question as to how residents in

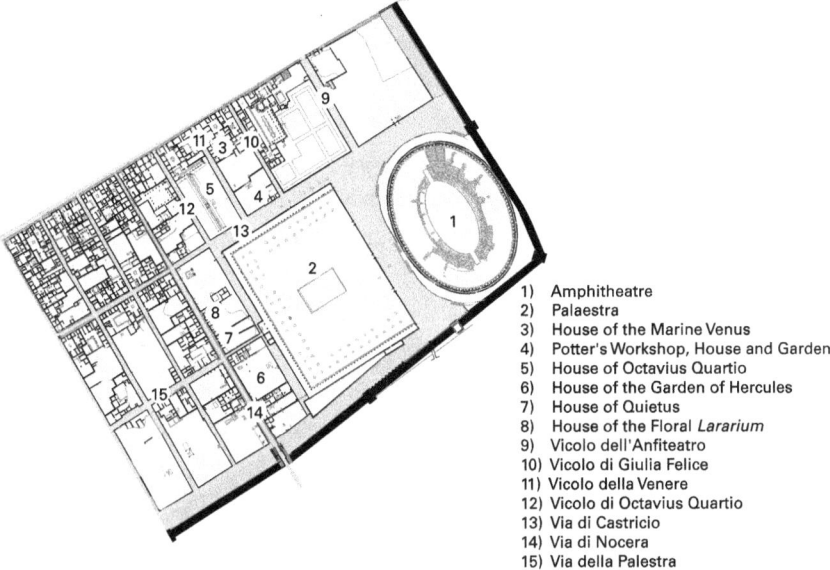

Figure 3.9 Close up of map of Pompeii showing streets and properties located near the amphitheatre (Reg II.6) and palaestra (Reg II.7), Pompeii. © Bloomsbury Academic.

the locality might have attempted to diminish, or at least control, the sensory impacts that this entertainment venue might have upon their domestic sphere.

As a general introduction to understanding the environs of the amphitheatre and its possible sensory impact on residents in nearby houses, it is important to observe that painted notifications give us insight into some of the displays put on at Pompeii's arena. They also indicate that the amphitheatre would not have been in constant use for gladiatorial display.[80] When in use, the amphitheatre could house 20,000 spectators. The sound level of such a crowd might reach around 100 decibels, perhaps more at times of particular excitement.[81] Most theatrical and gladiatorial events would be put on in the daytime, though accounts of Caligula's reign show that some displays were in the evening. Day or night timing of these events would affect significantly the experience within the city. As Suetonius highlights, '[h]e [Caligula] exhibited stage-plays continually, of various kinds and in many different places, sometimes even by night, lighting up the whole city.'[82] Although this comment refers to Rome, not Pompeii, epigraphic evidence confirms the construction of stone seating in Pompeii's amphitheatre thanks to a benefactor who chose this gift for the city, rather than the provision of lighting or sponsorship of the games themselves. This implies that lighting was available to enable gladiatorial games to take place at night and that its provision was a recognized mode of benefaction in Pompeii.[83] Similarly, whilst the painted notices show a number of games in Pompeii were staged during spring and early summer (March to June), there were also events occurring in November (11 days of games) January (2 days) and February (2 days). Given the cooler and darker time of these months, the sensory experience of these games would be quite different from games put on in warmer summer months and would probably have a substantial impact on residences in the vicinity of the arena.

On approaching the amphitheatre, the sound of the crowd cheering, although dampened by the structure of the amphitheatre, its seating and the people within it as well as nearby buildings, would have been loud and would have filtered into surrounding streets. As distances increased between the amphitheatre and residences, sound would have been absorbed by surrounding architecture,

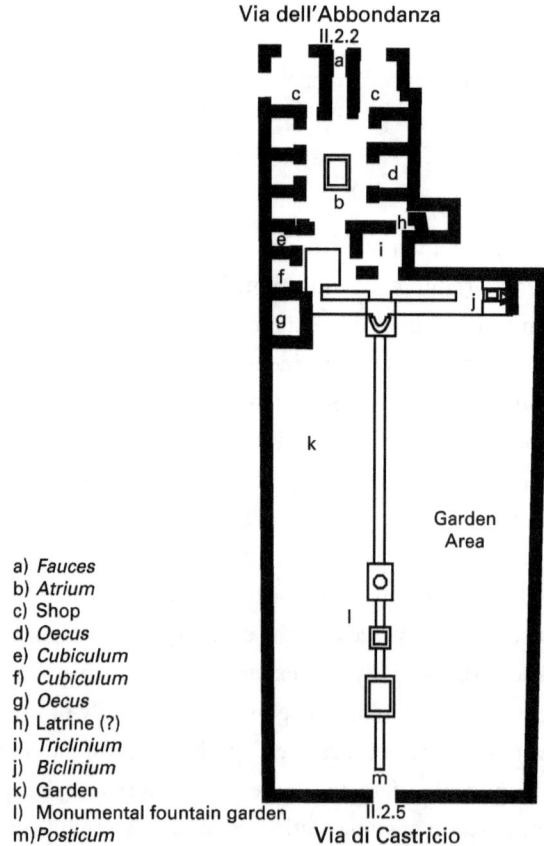

Figure 3.10 Floor plan of the house of Octavius Quartio (Reg II.2.2), Pompeii. © Bloomsbury Academic.

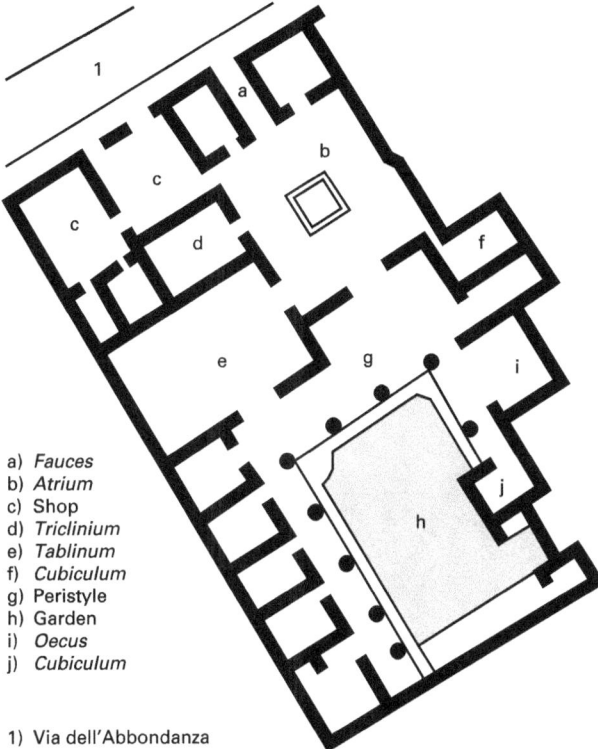

Figure 3.11 Floor plan of the house of the Marine Venus (Reg II.3.3), Pompeii. © Bloomsbury Academic.

thereby reducing the levels of noise impacting on houses. From the floor-plans of many of the houses in the immediate vicinity of the amphitheatre/palaestra complex, such as the house of Octavius Quartio (Fig. 3.10), the house of the Marine Venus (Fig. 3.11), the house of the Garden of Hercules (Fig. 3.12), the house of Quietus and the house of the Floral *Lararium* (Fig. 3.9), we can see attempts to distance these residences from the arena. None of these residences have their front entrances opening onto the amphitheatre/palaestra complex. Rather, the houses of Octavius Quartio, Quietus, the Floral *Lararium* and of the Garden of Hercules all have gardens which immediately back on to the amphitheatre/palaestra complex, whilst the house of the Marine Venus' substantial garden does not back onto the amphitheatre/palaestra complex at all, but onto an area identified as a potter's workshop, house and garden.[84] Furthermore, only the potter's house and garden (II.3.8–9) and the house of Octavius Quartio have doors that lead onto roads near the amphitheatre/palaestra complex. These

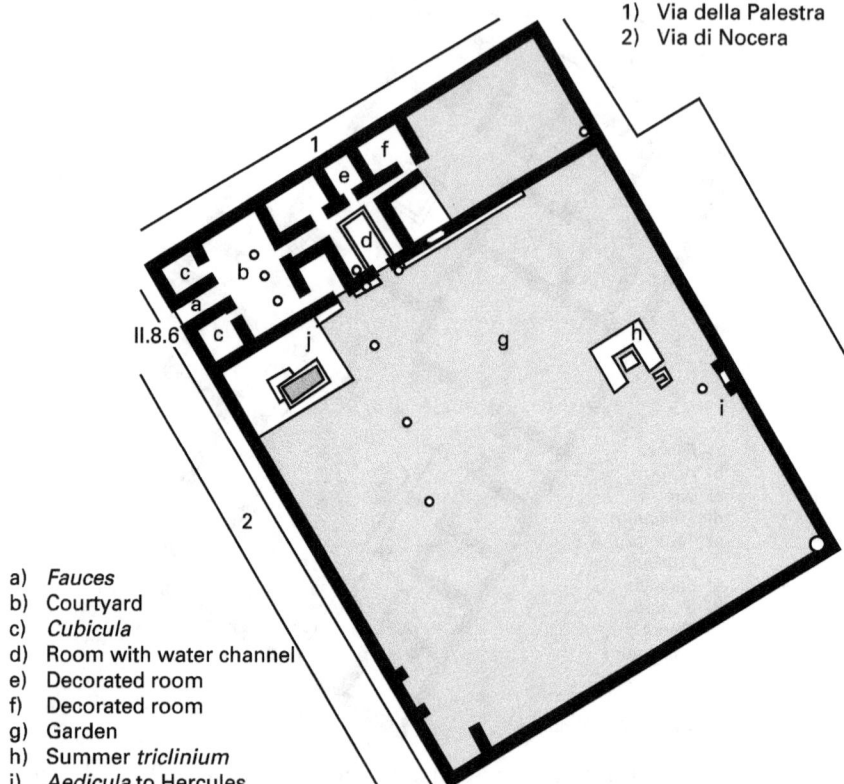

Figure 3.12 Floor plan of the house of the Garden of Hercules (Reg II.8.6), Pompeii. © Bloomsbury Academic.

entrances, a secondary one in the case of the house of Octavius Quartio, open onto the wide Via di Castricio, which is situated next to the palaestra. The gardens sitting between the houses and the amphitheatre/palaestra complex increase the distance between the cheering crowds of the games and the domestic sphere, thereby serving as 'sensory buffer zones' that diminish the levels, particularly of auditory disturbances, leaking from the arena into residences.

For winter shows in the cooler months of February, such as those of Lucius Valerius Primus in February or the November games of Gnaeus Alleius Nigidius Maius, however, it is likely that the sounds of the cheering crowd would spread further through the cold air ensuring that increased numbers of inhabitants sensorially experienced the generosity of the games giver. Light from candles, braziers and torches that provided artificial lighting after sunshine hours would have been visible from some distance, especially since the amphitheatre lay at the lowest point of the city. As people made their way, sometimes in procession, towards the games, lights flickering in the gloom would locate the gladiatorial contests.[85] Whilst we do not know the routes to the amphitheatre, it is likely, if starting from the Forum, that processions would move along the main road of the Via dell'Abbondanza, passing numerous houses along the way, including those of Casca Longus and Paquius Proculus, the house of the Priest of Amandus, the houses of Julius Polybius and Trebius Valens and the house of the Orchard (Fig. 3.5). If the entrance doors and shutters were open at these residences, noises, flickering lights from torches and perhaps even the passing scent of burning were likely to have filtered into the houses along the route, catching the attention of those within the dwellings, if they were not already taking part in the procession.

When thinking about the possible routes to the arena, and the multisensory impact that crowds travelling to the amphitheatre/palaestra complex might have had upon residences, it is important to note that many of the roads in the immediate vicinity of the arena were blocked to cart traffic.[86] Hence the Via di Castricio, the Vicolo di Octavius Quartio, della Venere, di Guilio Felice, dell'Anfiteatro and the Piazzale Anfiteatro would only have experienced pedestrian noise. So whilst the front entrances to many houses in this area, such as the houses of Octavius Quartio, the Marine Venus, Quietus, the Floral *Lararium* and of the Garden of Hercules would have experienced two-way traffic from the roads outside their front entrances, the other roads around them would have been considerably quieter, particularly when the amphitheatre/palaestra complex was not in use. Furthermore, the Via di Castricio, the Vicolo di Octavius Quartio, della Venere, di Guilio Felice, dell'Anfiteatro and the Piazzale Anfiteatro demonstrate doorways less than every 15 metres, and graffiti messages likewise are relatively sparse, occurring less often than every 12 metres. Only in the Vicolo di Guilio Felice does graffiti appear more frequently at every 4–8 metres.[87] As such, if we follow Laurence's theory that graffiti and doorways present evidence of substantial street activity, it can be argued that most of the alleyways around the palaestra/amphitheatre complex probably only saw heavy footfall when the arena was in use. In terms of multisensory experience for the residents of many houses in this area the environs around them were probably relatively quiet for much of the year, but they experienced substantial auditory disturbance on games days, hence the layout of the dwellings and gardens sought to block out where possible excessive noise. The corollary of heighted sensory experiences in the vicinity of the amphitheatre/palaestra complex on games days is the simultaneous reduction in traffic, noise and activities elsewhere in the city as the town's inhabitants are concentrated in the arena and are thus largely absent from the rest of Pompeii.

Figure 3.13 Fresco depicting the riot between the Nucerians and the Pompeians (from Pompeii). Note the depiction of street hawkers selling food and drink outside the amphitheatre. Naples, Museo Archeologico Nazionale inv.112222. © DEA PICTURE LIBRARY/ Getty Images.

Archaeological evidence highlights the activity of street vendors around the amphitheatre/palaestra complex at times of gladiatorial shows. In particular, the famous fresco of the riot of AD 59 between the Pompeians and the Nucerians shows street hawkers selling their wares of food, drink and possibly trinkets to spectators (Fig. 3.13).[88] The cries of vendors, who probably filled much of the open space of the Large Palaestra next to the arena, the smell of cooking snacks and alcohol from numerous nearby *popinae* and temporary stalls, as well as the stink of body odour and urine, would likewise drift into the neighbouring *Regio II* and into houses situated there.[89] Given that the Via di Castricio measures about 13 metres wide from the wall of the palaestra to the back garden wall of the house of Octavius Quartio, and drawing on Whitehouse and Hamilton's research that the maximum distance smells of cooking meat can travel in an enclosed outdoor setting is 122 metres, this suggests that the odour of snacks being cooked by street vendors outside the palaestra would filter into the gardens, and possibly the residences, of the nearby houses such as the house of Octavius Quartio and the house of the Marine Venus.[90]

Compare this potential 'multisensory streetscape' to how such an event might be experienced in dwellings elsewhere in the city. For residences on the other side of Pompeii in *Regio* VI near the Herculaneum gate, for example the houses of Sallust, Pansa, the Small Fountain, the Labyrinth, the Vetti and that of the Golden Cupids, it was likely they would be affected rather differently by disturbances associated with gladiatorial contests (Fig. 3.5). Unlike those living close by the amphitheatre/palaestra complex, houses at a distance would not be affected by the smells of the street vendors nor would they see the crowds of people milling about the arena, the palaestra and the neighbouring roads and in the nearby taverns. It is possible that on cool winter nights, some of the louder cheering from the arena might drift towards houses on the western reaches of the city, but the noise disturbance experienced here would be greatly reduced in comparison to that experienced by houses in the neighbourhood of the arena itself, especially given the prevailing winds mostly blow in a north-easterly direction in winter, which would limit the distance that sound would travel.[91]

In terms of the visual impact of the arena on the inhabitants of *Regio* VI, they might catch glimpses of the glow of torches in processions to the amphitheatre, particularly since *Regio* VI is topographically higher up than *Regio* II situated around the amphitheatre, and of course, were processions to pass these dwellings, inhabitants would probably see, hear and smell them. Residents of some houses or apartments in the area might have views across the city towards the amphitheatre, probably from upper floors. Whilst reconstructing the upper floors of Pompeian residences is complicated, given the nature of the settlement's destruction, excavations of the house of the Vettii, for example, have shown the remains of a stairway leading to an upper floor which stretched across the southeast part of the dwelling (Fig. 3.14). This would have pointed in the direction of the amphitheatre/palaestra complex, thus making it more plausible that residents on this upper floor might have been able to see the processions towards the arena.

This case study sets out the possible ways in which the sensory experience of residences in two different *regiones* might have been affected by the Pompeii's amphitheatre/palaestra complex and the activities associated with it, across both different times of the day and year. Other sectors of the city would experience games days differently. Change the time of year or day, the activity, the year, the

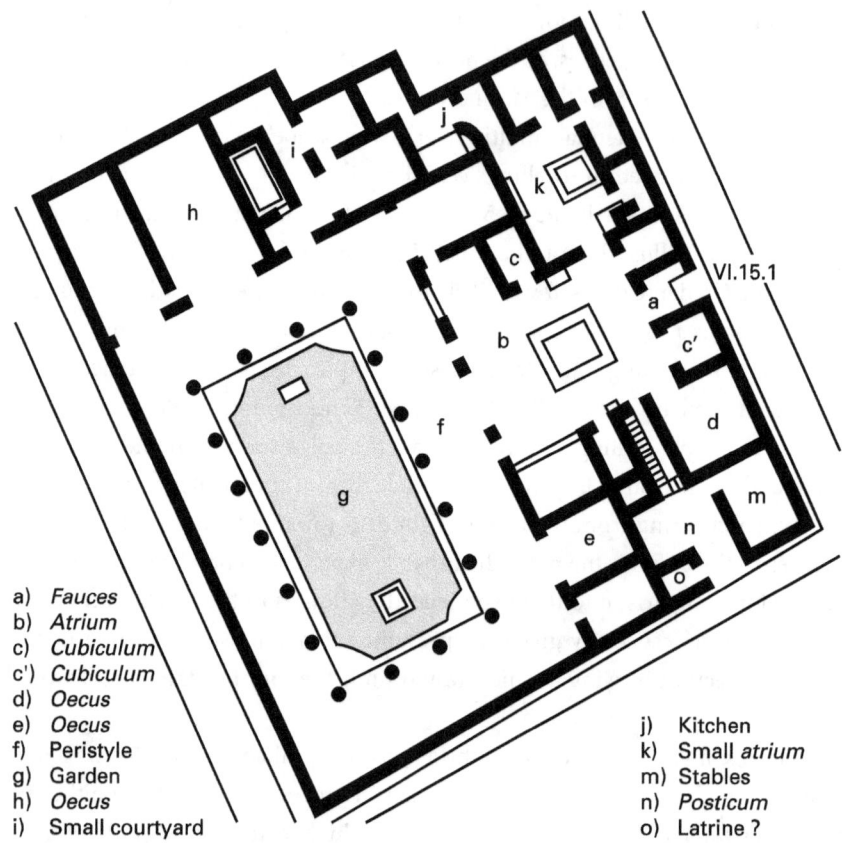

Figure 3.14 Plan of the house of the Vettii (Reg VI.15.1), Pompeii. © Bloomsbury Academic.

a) Fauces
b) Atrium
c) Cubiculum
c') Cubiculum
d) Oecus
e) Oecus
f) Peristyle
g) Garden
h) Oecus
i) Small courtyard
j) Kitchen
k) Small *atrium*
m) Stables
n) Posticum
o) Latrine ?

city, the inhabitants in terms of their ages, gender, ethnicity, abilities or disabilities and social status, and the sensoryscape of the amphitheatre/palaestra and its impact upon the lived experience of homes across the city will also alter. As such, it is important to be aware that each person's experience of the home, whether they are visitor or inhabitant, will vary. There is no single multisensory experience of the gladiatorial arena, either on or off games days, to be had within the Roman home.

Case study two: Controlling the sensory experience of fulleries, workshops and cookshops

Pompeii's lack of residential zoning according to status, commercial enterprise or domestic inhabitation raises interesting questions regarding the extent to which the multisensory experiences, particularly sounds and smells from cookshops, taverns and different workshops, might have impacted upon neighbouring residences and the surrounding environs (Fig. 3.2). Workshops excavated at Pompeii have been identified as bakeries, tanneries, fulleries, dye houses (*officiae tinctoriae*) and *officiae lanifricariae*. It is unclear exactly what manufacturing operations occurred in the last category of workshops.[92] Recently, however, Flohr has argued persuasively that the practices undertaken in *officiae lanifricariae* possibly revolved around some aspect of meat production for eating or bone rendering after the bones had been stripped.[93] The fifteen *officiae lanifricariae* are focused in two areas of the city, in *Regio* VI to the east of the forum and near the theatre, in *Regiones* I and VIII. The six *officiae tinctoriae* were more evenly spread around the city.[94] The twelve fulleries excavated at Pompeii follow a slightly different pattern and are fairly evenly located around the city (albeit with lesser density in the western corner of the city and near the forum). We might also add to this the four felt-making operations and thirty-nine bakeries dotted around the city, of which many of the latter had mills.[95] These mills, in turn, suggest the use of slaves or possibly mules to help grind the flour.[96]

In recent years there have been important debates as to how these manufacturing operations might have impacted upon their surroundings. Scholars have investigated the extent to which they might have posed a sensory nuisance, especially an olfactory disturbance, to city inhabitants. Thus Potter, Bradley and Koloski-Ostrow emphasize the smell that such workshops would have caused.[97] In particular, fulleries have been understood as having been particularly malodorous.[98] In contrast to these depictions of the stink from fulleries and the overall stench of the Roman city, there have also been attempts to reconsider just how unpleasant these smells from manufacturing and daily life really were. Thus whilst Morley has considered the impact of habituation on an individual's experience of the Roman city's olfactory scene, Flohr has argued that fulleries, in particular larger ones, were often organized in order to reduce the multisensory nuisance they posed for others and that the smells from other processes had the potential to be far worse than that emanating from fulling.[99]

Let us take, for example, the well-known *fullonica* of Stephanus, (*Regio* I. 6. 7) and consider the steps taken within it to mitigate against the possible seepage of

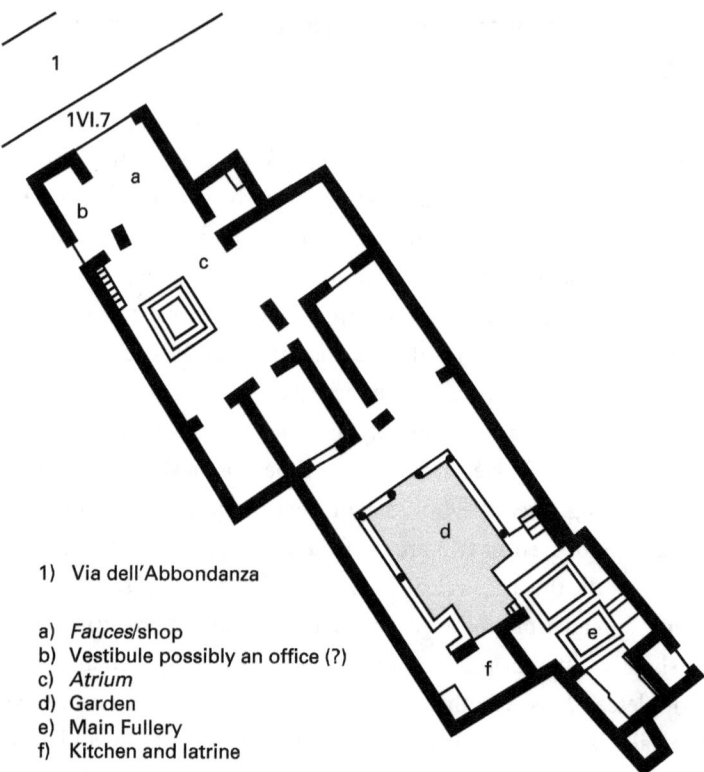

Figure 3.15 Plan of the house of the *Fullonica* of Stephanus (Reg I.6.7), Pompeii. © Bloomsbury Academic.

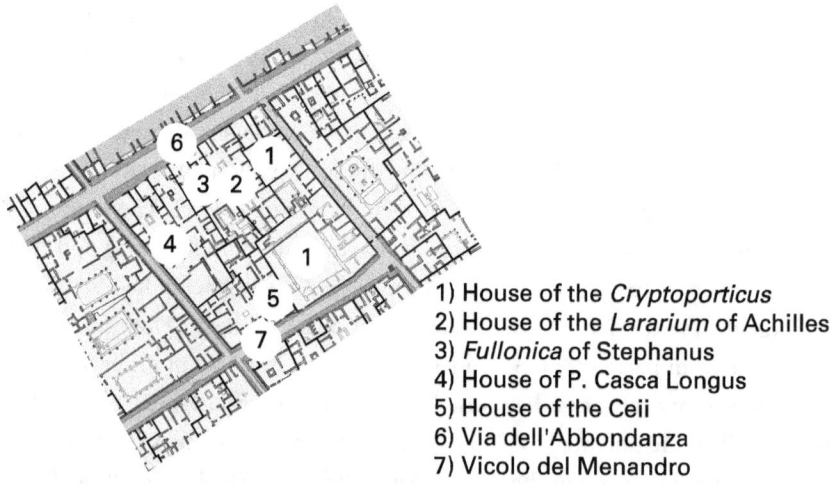

Figure 3.16 Close up of map of Pompeii showing properties near the *Fullonica* of Stephanus (Reg I.6.7), Pompeii. © Bloomsbury Academic.

sensory nuisances into the surrounding environs (Fig. 3.15). In addition, let us also explore its potential sensory impact upon the neighbouring residences of the house of the *Lararium* of Achilles, the house of the Ceii, the house of the *Cryptoporticus* and the house of P. Casca Longus and the extent to which these residences attempted to control any corporeal disturbances from this commercial enterprise (Fig. 3.16).[100]

Traditionally scholars have perceived the premises of Stephanus' *fullonica* as having been 'converted' into a fullery after losing its original residential function following the earthquake of AD 62.[101] Such interpretations have tended to be influenced by the work of Maiuri and Spinazzola.[102] Dating the building history of this dwelling is complicated because of walls being covered by plaster. It would appear, however, that the development of the *fullonica* section was part of a larger building project throughout the dwelling as a whole which, due to the building techniques and fourth-style decoration used, probably occurred during the third quarter of the first century AD, although obviously before the eruption of Vesuvius in AD 79.[103] It is, then, plausible that the commercial aspect of this residence saw substantial development after the earthquake of AD 62; however, as Flohr persuasively argues 'what emerges [is] ... the care taken in ensuring that the house remained a good place to live'. He goes on to point out the presence of doors between the shop at (a), the narrow adjacent room at (b) and the *atrium* at (c) which could be closed when required, and highlights the fact that these boundaries could be both spatial and temporal, allowing the space to be used as work space during the day, and domestic space at night.[104] These doors, together with finds of artefacts of domestic and personal functions and the sumptuous fourth-style decoration of the *atrium*, surrounding rooms and *impluvium*, highlight that rather than the domestic character of the property being subsumed into the *fullonica*, it retained an important domestic role even with the development of a substantial fulling enterprise.[105] It would seem, therefore, that for the inhabitants of this domestic *fullonica* there were attempts to ensure the presence of a visually pleasant sphere, which could be closed off from the smells and sounds of the fulling process when required.

Of the four dwellings abutting or in close proximity to the fullery, the houses of the *Lararium* of Achilles, the *Cryptoporticus* and of P. Casca Longus all open out onto the Via dell'Abbondanza, the road on which Stephanus' fullery entrance is situated (Fig. 3.16). In contrast, the house of the Ceii opens onto the parallel street, the Vicolo del Menandro, whilst its rear section backs onto the *fullonica*. Both the house of the *Cryptoporticus*, and the house of P. Casca Longus are well set back from the Via dell'Abbondanza behind lengthy *fauces*.[106] As well as affecting views into and out of these houses, the length of these *fauces* would have reduced sounds and smells from the street outside and its environs entering into the residences, in particular the noise of customers in the fullery's shop front, and smells produced by the fullery, such as those of the urine used in cloth cleaning and the sounds of carts delivering key constituents of the cleaning process. This is because the longer a *fauces*, the more sounds travelling along it decreased and, although smell works differently from sound, again the greater the distance smell travels the weaker it becomes as it diffuses via osmosis.[107] Thus the presence and length of a *fauces* at the entrance of these dwellings served to provide both visual distance from passers-by for residents and a layer of control over multisensory experience between house and street.

Few of the fully excavated residences from Pompeii lack *fauces* at their entrances. Of those that do, the house of the Chaste Lovers (IX. 12. 6–8) located relatively near the *fullonica* of Stephanus is believed to have been a dwelling of mixed use.[108] This house had a vestibule at its entrance that opened onto the

Figure 3.17 Plan of the house of the Chaste Lovers (Reg IX.12.6), Pompeii. Stables gave access onto a side street. © Bloomsbury Academic.

building's bakery, which comprised an oven, four millstones worked by mules (skeletons of which were found in the residence's stables) and a room for preparing dough (Fig. 3.17). Attached to this workshop were residential quarters, which included a *triclinium* decorated in the third style and various *cubicula* decorated in the fourth style. The lack of *fauces* here is perhaps explained by building use and the desire to engage more closely with the outside and encourage business with passers-by.

Long *fauces* were not the only way to distance the domestic realm from the sensory nuisances connected with a neighbouring fullery; we should also consider how else the front entrances of Roman houses might serve to diminish the effect of living next to smelly or noisy commercial enterprises, such as a fullery. The house of the *Lararium* of Achilles presents us with an interesting example. In contrast to the opulent interiors of many Roman houses, Roman house exteriors were relatively plain, save for graffiti and electioneering posters carved or daubed into the plaster. Many Roman houses had small windows set high up in their front walls, often well above head height. Due to the way in which the house of the *Lararium* of Achilles has been damaged, it cannot be absolutely confirmed that the frontage had such windows in its front wall, however it is certainly possible, given that they are present in the front walls of other residences in the vicinity, such the house of the Ceii (Fig. 3.4).[109]

In her book on the Roman *domus*, Hales highlights the comparison between these 'small windows set high out of reach' in the outer walls of dwellings to the wider window opening of shops and taverns. For Hales, the traditional explanation for these small, high up windows of 'shelter from the weather... are rather disproved by the proliferations of wide openings inside the house, particularly the *triclinia* and *tablina*, which face onto the open peristyle'. She concludes, 'the houses themselves are deliberatively secretive – whether for security against crime or against the forces of vituperative rhetoric'.[110] This explanation, however, needs further thought, particularly if we bear in mind the surrounding environs of many residences and their proximity to commercial establishments whose activities were likely to produce multisensory disturbances for neighbouring residents.

Returning to our example of the house of the *Lararium* of Achilles and assuming that like nearby properties it **did** have high windows in its front wall, we should explore further the possible reasons for the specific positioning of these windows. Control over views or access into the house from the busy Via dell'Abbondanza, for reasons of privacy or security, would have played an important role in terms of the organization of its façade. The use of doorkeepers, as highlighted in literary and archaeological evidence, certainly suggests an interest in monitoring who was, or was not, permitted admittance into the household.[111]

Whilst security and/or privacy must have been a consideration, however, we should also note other possible reasons for their location and size. The presence of wide doorways particularly, for example, those of the *tablinum* opening onto the peristyle and/or *atrium* and those of the *triclinium* that often opened similarly, does not necessarily undermine the suggestion that small windows were employed principally to provide protection from bad weather whilst allowing air to circulate in the house.[112] In other houses from Pompeii and Herculaneum, the evidence of wooden partitions and possible evidence of curtains being used to separate spaces such as the *tablinum* from the rest of the house, as well as evidence from curtain architecture such as rods, bosses and hooks, suggest a strong desire to control the physical sensations from the weather in dwellings.[113] We might easily view small high up windows similarly. Whilst allowing privacy and control over what was visible to passers-by, such windows enabled controlled airflow and light into the residence. In addition to this, whilst the *fullonica* of Stephanus, like other commercial premises, had wide doorways opening onto the street which gave passers-by multisensory experiences of, and insight into, the small-scale manufacturing processes going on inside, the small and irregular street-facing windows of houses like the possible ones of the house of the *Lararium* of Achilles served to reduce substantially the leakage of sounds and smells from the neighbouring fullery into the residence's interior.[114] The size and position of house front windows thus served multiple purposes. As well as reducing visual accessibility of the house from outside, they also allowed an element of control over sensory 'nuisances' filtering into the dwelling. These might include both inclement weather or the dissipation of unpleasant sounds and smells from neighbouring commercial establishments.

One final means by which neighbouring dwellings sought to diminish the sensory impact of commercial enterprises upon them was by locating storage areas and open areas of garden next to the business premises which, just as we saw with the gardens of houses near the amphitheatre/palaestra complex, would serve as 'sensory buffering zones'. The house of the Ceii provides a particularly good example of this. Its two rear rooms (j) and (i) overlooked the residence's garden and thus also backed onto the *fullonica* of Stephanus. By AD 79, these were probably used for storage (Fig. 3.18).[115] At any rate there is little evidence for any décor within these two rooms, thus supporting the assumption that they were not used for entertainment purposes. This area of the house of the Ceii was

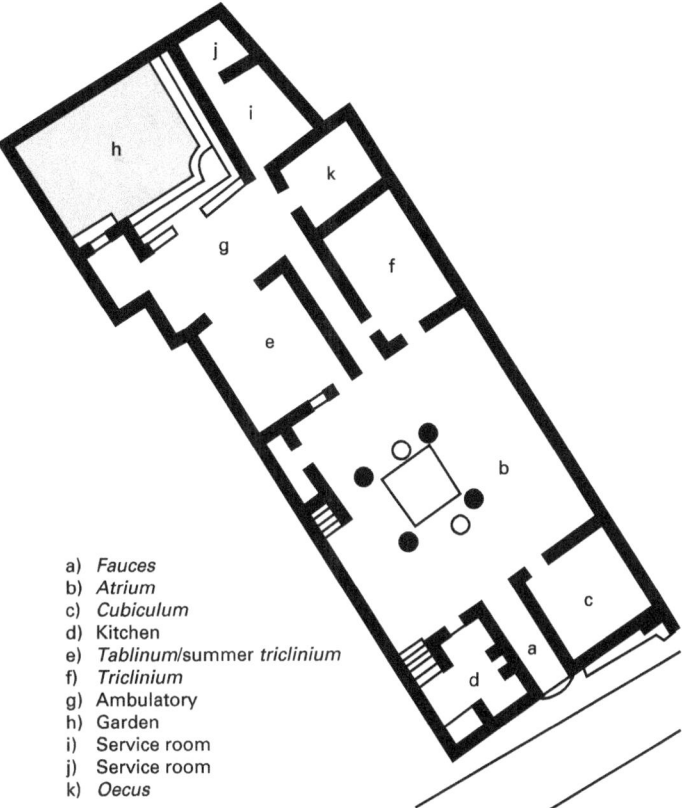

Figure 3.18 Plan of the house of the Ceii (Reg I.6.15), Pompeii. Note that rooms (i) and (j) back onto the *Fullonica* of Stephanus (Reg I.6. 7). © Bloomsbury Academic.

a) *Fauces*
b) *Atrium*
c) *Cubiculum*
d) Kitchen
e) *Tablinum*/summer *triclinium*
f) *Triclinium*
g) Ambulatory
h) Garden
i) Service room
j) Service room
k) *Oecus*

adjacent to the workshop at (e) of Stephanus' fullery where the initial and most problematic stages of fulling, in terms of 'sensory nuisance', would have occurred. These parts of the process in particular would have certainly been noisy and probably smelly to some extent, given the products used in fulling.[116] It is, therefore, plausible that this part of the house of the Ceii was organized specifically to reduce the impact of unwanted sounds and smells wafting from the fullery into the entertainment or public areas of the house. If, as has been suggested, Stephanus' property underwent substantial redevelopment in order to include, or expand, its commercial character during the third quarter of the first century AD, it is possible that the house of the Ceii, which backed onto it was also redeveloped in response to the growth of the fullery and the possible sensory disturbances that ensued. By moving the kitchen to the front of the dwelling (d) and storage rooms (j) and (i) to the back by the garden (h), the owner of the

70 Multisensory Living in Ancient Rome

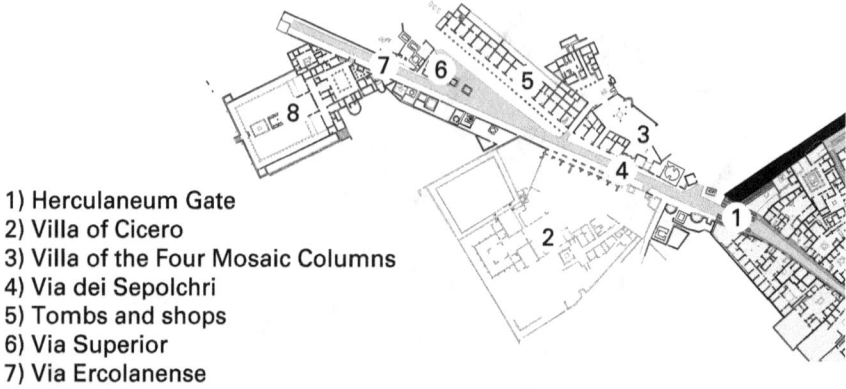

1) Herculaneum Gate
2) Villa of Cicero
3) Villa of the Four Mosaic Columns
4) Via dei Sepolchri
5) Tombs and shops
6) Via Superior
7) Via Ercolanense
8) Villa of Diomedes

Figure 3.19 Close up of map of Pompeii showing the buildings and tombs outside the Herculaneum Gate, on the Via Consolare. © Bloomsbury Academic.

a) Entrance
b) Small Peristyle
c) Triangular peristyle/*frigidarium*
d) Kitchen and latrine
e) *Triclinium*
f) *Tablinum*
g) Stairwell to lower floor including service area
h) Cart area
i) Possible kitchen/hearth area
j) Court with hearth
k) Peristyle
l) Garden
m) Fountain
n) Summer *triclinium*
o) *Dieta*

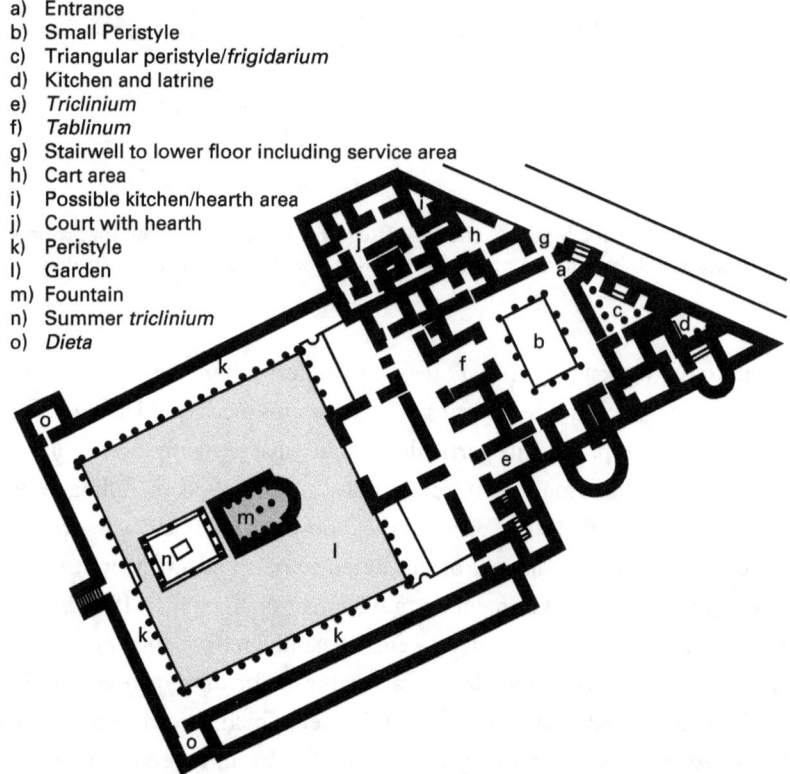

Figure 3.20 Plan of the Villa of Diomedes situated on the Via Ercolanense, Pompeii. © Bloomsbury Academic.

house of the Ceii was perhaps seeking to reduce exposure of the main rooms of the residence to the sounds and smells from the extended *fullonica*.

Case study three: Controlling multisensory experience in extramural dwellings

A further example from Pompeii for examination of multisensory control in the domestic sphere concerns residences outside the Herculaneum gate on the western edges of the city (Fig. 3.19). Interspersed between shops and tombs, four villas have been excavated on the roads leading into and out of the city. Two of these, the villas of Cicero and the Four Mosaic Columns, were situated on the Via dei Sepolchri. A third, the villa of Diomedes (Fig. 3.20), was located past the last group of tombs on the Via Ercolanense, whilst a fourth, the villa of Mysteries, was on the Via Superior. Of these four villas, the latter two remain in the best condition. The villa of the Four Mosaic Columns, although excavated in the eighteenth century, is now in a partially ruined state, whilst the villa of Cicero was reinterred following the completion of its initial excavation in 1763.[117] Unfortunately this early excavation date led to rather disorganized recording of the site and its finds, which has consequently meant that we have an imprecise understanding of the villa's layout and architecture.[118]

This area of Pompeii topographically slopes, which is reflected in some of the villa architecture. The villa of Diomedes, for example, has been built on numerous levels to take account of the sharply sloping land. Hence, while the entrance to the residence is about 1 metre above street level, the rear section of the dwelling is considerably lower. Likewise, the layout of the villa of the Four Mosaic Columns is also affected by the area's underlying sloping topography which inclines from the west to the east of the Via dei Sepolchri and from the south to the north. The greater height of the land to the north side of the residence has left a drop of more than 4 metres from the upper floors and terrace of dwelling to the lower entrance section of the residence.[119] The plot used for the villa of Mysteries similarly sloped, so the residence was laid out on a square platform with a *cryptoporticus* underneath. By making use of the sloping terrain, all three took advantage of vistas over the Bay of Naples. To do this, the geographical layout meant that terraces were constructed at the furthest distance from the street. Not only did this ensure beautiful panoramas over the coast, it also increased the distance from the villa entrance on the street to their belvederes at the dwellings' rear. Consequently, this would reduce the dispersal of sounds and smells from passing traffic, people and neighbouring shops in the villas in question.

Figure 3.21 Cart ruts on the Via Ercolanense, outside villa of Diomedes, Pompeii. Photo: Hannah Platts.

Lack of excavation of the environs of the villa of Mysteries means that we cannot be sure what type of sounds and smells from the vicinity might have been experienced within the residence; the road on which its original entrance stands remains unexplored, meaning we have an absence of information on cart tracks, neighbouring shops or tombs. We can, however, consider the possible multisensory impact of street traffic, shops and carts on the villas of Diomedes and the Four Mosaic Columns and, to a lesser extent, the villa of Cicero.[120]

As one of the main routes leading into and out of Pompeii, the Via Ercolanense and the Via dei Sepolchri would have seen substantial cart traffic, as is evidenced by the remains of cart ruts gouged into the road (Fig. 3.21). The numerous tombs and shops located on this stretch of road meant pedestrian activity would similarly have been substantial (Fig. 3.19). In addition to the associated noise and sights emanating from these tombs and shops, we should recall the sensory nuisance produced by the stench from numerous tombs and cremations situated outside the Herculaneum Gate.[121] Given the number of tombs in this area, it is likely that regular commemorative feasts and cremations would have taken place in the vicinity. Evidence from wills and epitaphs from across the Roman Empire suggest both the celebration of the birthdays of many of the deceased and the provision of roses, each to be provided in perpetuity.[122] These feasts celebrating the *dies natalis* together with others such as the *silicernium* (on the day of the funeral) and the *cena novendialis*, which marked the ninth day post burial, occurred near the tomb and were celebrated by surviving relatives.[123] Such evidence, together with the three masonry dining benches situated outside the tomb of Gnaeus Vibrius Saturninus outside the Herculaneum Gate suggests that necropoleis such as that on the Via dei Sepolchri could be fairly lively with regular banquets to celebrate the city's deceased.[124]

Both the villa of Cicero and that of the Four Mosaic Columns are set back at some distance from the Via dei Sepolchri. Whilst obtaining an accurate measurement of the length of the *fauces* for the villa of Cicero is difficult, sketchy plans of this residence made when initially excavated suggest a long *fauces* led

Figure 3.22 View into the small peristyle garden from the entrance of the villa of Diomedes, Pompeii. Photo: Hannah Platts.

Figure 3.23 View from the Via Ercolanense looking up to the entrance of the villa of Diomedes, Pompeii. Photo: Hannah Platts.

into the entrance of this dwelling.[125] The length of the *fauces* from the main entrance of the villa of the Four Mosaic Columns is 9 metres. Whilst surrounded by tombs and shops at the front of these dwellings, which would have been both noisy and smelly, sounds and odours from these environs would be required to travel some distance in order to be experienced within the dwellings.[126] Not only that, but the narrow, covered *fauces* in the villa of the Four Mosaic Columns would further serve to reduce the amount of sound and smell that might pervade into the dwelling.

In contrast, the villa of Diomedes has a rather different architectural layout as it lacks a *fauces*. Instead, the entrance (a) leads straight into a small peristyle garden at (b) (Fig. 3.22). Being so close to the street, it is likely that sounds from carts and passers-by coming into and leaving the city would probably filter into the front section of the dwelling. The loudest sound experienced at this time would have been thunder (120 decibels) and few sounds above 75 decibels – equivalent to a human shout at a distance of 1 metre – would have regularly been heard.[127] The proximity, then, of the villa's small peristyle courtyard to the road outside meant that conversations, shouts and clatter of carts would probably be heard within the front section of the villa, even though the villa's substantial walls and relatively small entrance would have helped to reduce some of the noise of the bustling street.[128] The height of the villa's front section from the street, being 1 metre higher than the road outside, is likely to have deflected some of the noise from the street as would front entrance doors (Fig. 3.23). Whilst we cannot be sure whether doors to this residence would have been shut or remained open, it is likely that this would alter according to the time of day and perhaps season. When closed, doors would have helped to diminish the dissipation of sounds from the street into the dwelling, although the lack of a roof over the courtyard at (b) would have allowed more noise to filter in than if the entire area had been covered.

In terms of its location on the Via Ercolanense, this villa also had a rather different environment to that of the villas of the Four Mosaic Columns and Cicero. It was situated beyond the last excavated group of tombs and there were no shops immediately surrounding it (Fig. 3.19). The consequence of this is that the sounds and smells associated with the business and activities of the tombs and shops elsewhere on this road leading into Pompeii would have further to travel in order to be perceived inside the Villa of Diomedes. It is plausible, then, that any smells and sounds emanating from shops and tombs would not filter into the Villa of Diomedes to any large extent.[129]

Conclusion

Walking through the streets of Pompeii or Herculaneum today, amongst the jostling, laughing and chatting tourists as the heat of the summer sun bears down, one is encouraged to reflect on the experience of living within these cities for the original residents. Of course, the numerous visitors to Pompeii and Herculaneum only help 'populate' the sites to a certain extent. Cart and animal traffic, sewage, obstacles, and the sounds and smells of productivity in workshops no longer dominate sensory experiences. To understand fully the possible embodied domestic realm, however, one must consider the relationships between a dwelling and the environs in which it is situated including the potential impact of nearby streets, workshops and taverns on life. What this chapter has explored, then, is the multisensory relationship of the home and its environs, exploring how a residence's specific location might impact upon how it was physically experienced – on a seasonal, daily or even hourly calendar. Looking beyond a general overview of how street life might impact upon the embodied life of houses, this chapter has also explored a series of examples of possible multisensory streetscapes, their impacts upon specific residences within Pompeii and the possible ways of controlling corporeal interaction between the street, the environs and the home.

This is not an attempt to outline all possible corporeal experiences and relationships between house and street, but it questions how far life in city streets impacted upon life within residences and vice versa, and the extent to which we might be able to ascertain attempts to control potential bodily experiences within domestic architecture. Change the house and surrounding environs, remove or add fulleries, tanneries, and *lanifricariae,* vary the direction of the traffic, unblock or block the street in question and the multisensory relationship between house and street will likewise change. If we ask the same questions in different weather or a different season, or in a different city entirely, the multisensory landscape will again alter as will its impact upon the residences in question. It is not enough to consider the visual relationship of the Roman street to the house. As Seneca shows there were other sensory factors to be borne in mind and, for those with the status or financial wherewithal to control corporeal experience of their residence, this served as an important means of establishing and reinforcing social standing and hierarchy.

4

Initial Perceptions: Controlling Access and Multisensory Experience in the *Atrium-Tablinum*

Introduction

[W]e must go on to consider the situation of the private rooms for the master of the house and those which are for the guests. For into the private rooms no one enters, unless invited [*nisi invitatis*], such as the bedrooms, dining-rooms, baths and other apartments which have similar purposes. The common rooms, on the contrary, are those entered by anyone, even unasked [*quibus etiam invocati suo iure de populo possunt venire*] such as vestibules, courtyards, peristyles and other apartments of similar uses. Hence magnificent vestibules and *tablina* and *atria* are not necessary to persons of a middling condition in life, because they pay their respects by visiting others, and are not visited by others.

... [T]he houses of bankers and receivers of the revenue should be more spacious and commodius and safe from burglars. Advocates and professors of rhetoric should be housed with distinction, and in sufficient space to accommodate their audiences. For persons of high rank who hold office and magistracies, and whose duty it is to serve the state, we must provide princely vestibules, lofty halls and very spacious peristyles, plantations and broad avenues finished in a majestic style. In addition to these, libraries and basilicas arranged in a similar fashion with the magnificence of public structures, because, in such palaces, public deliberations and private trials and judgments are often transacted.[1]

It is, perhaps, unsurprising that to look in the first chapter on the multisensory experience of the interior of the Roman house, we start with Vitruvius. Written in the reign of Augustus, the first emperor, Vitruvius' *De Architectura* provides us with the only surviving Roman architectural treatise.[2] For numerous aspects of Roman architectural practices, from city design and location to advice on temple building and acoustics in theatres, Vitruvius provides a key insight into structural and functional principles of the Roman domestic realm.³ When taken together with archaeological remains, particularly those from Pompeii and Herculaneum, we have the principal sources for information on Roman houses. In many houses excavated in Pompeii and Herculaneum, the ground plan follows a layout deemed 'canonical', where the *atrium* is the first main room reached on entering the residence from the street outside and then other parts of the dwelling's front section are connected to the *atrium* including the *fauces, alae, tablinum* and peristyle.⁴ Thus the *tablinum* (f) was often located behind the *atrium* (b) and in front of the peristyle (h), whilst the *fauces* (a) led into the *atrium* (b) from the entrance (Fig. 4.1). This style of *atrium* house is closely allied with the descriptions provided by Vitruvius.

In addition to outlining spatial structures and relationships between the rooms of the Roman house, the text of Vitruvius has been mined for details of room function. Accordingly, the *atrium* has been generally understood as an area used for receiving visitors, where the owner paraded self and family wealth, achievements and ancestry: much scholarship on this part of the dwelling has been focused on its 'public-facing' role.⁵ The attached *tablinum* has been recognized as the owner's study where family archives were stored and business transactions occurred. Other rooms perceived to follow this rigid labelling of space and household activity include *cubicula* (bedrooms) and *triclinia* (dining rooms).⁶ In recent years, however, there has been a move away from narrowly defined spatial classifications and their associated functions, as scholars have sought to examine multifunctional roles for rooms in Roman houses.⁷

The multi-functionality of rooms and their respective positions within houses is an important consideration in understanding the role, and possible multisensory experiences, of the Roman home. Indeed, the varied purposes of the *atrium* and connected *tablinum*, together with their location in the *domus* present a key focus for this chapter, since they are the initial space(s) that visitors encountered. The role of the *atria-tablina* in rituals and ceremonies including the *salutatio*, funerals and weddings, has been explored by other scholars.⁸ Yet, whilst Graham, Hope and Hersch have considered multisensory aspects of the funeral and wedding respectively, most studies of the rites in these spaces consider them solely in terms of their visual impact on those involved. The rituals of the *salutatio*, wedding and funeral will be discussed in detail later in the chapter. It is, however, worth first exploring the relationship of the *atrium-tablinum* to the house as a whole and the world outside through the multisensory experience to be had there. The wide-ranging functions that occurred within the *atrium* would impact variously and significantly upon possible physical

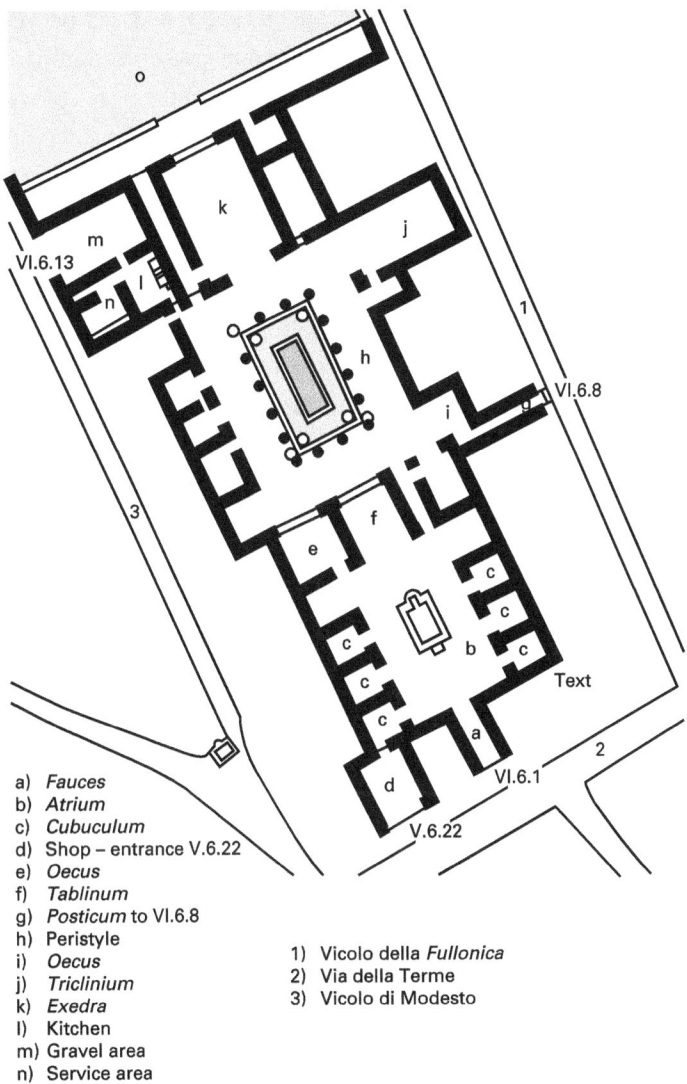

Figure 4.1 Floor plan of the house of Pansa (Reg VI.6.1), Pompeii. This residence's structure is often seen to reflect the 'canonical' layout of Pompeian houses where the *fauces* leads into the *atrium*, which in turn leads into the *tablinum* and peristyle. © Bloomsbury Academic.

experiences of the space. By exploring the corporeal experiences of the *fauces-atrium-tablinum* space we can start to consider how far the civic world outside might be involved with this part of the domestic realm of the house and thus develop understanding of these rooms and the role they performed in the display of personal wealth and status to the community beyond.

In the previous chapter, we examined the blurred boundaries between street and home, exploring how they interacted and impinged on each other through multisensory experiences filtering into the house from the street. Moving on to focus on the entrance and *atrium-tablinum* section of the Roman home, we will explore further how 'public' and 'private' intervened and interacted in the front rooms of dwellings, investigating how multiple bodily senses might serve to differentiate between 'public' and 'private' in the liminal area of the *atrium-tablinum* during certain times of the day or activity. Up to now, sight has been perceived by scholars as key to understanding the rooms at the front of the Roman home and their relationship to the street outside, both in terms of the axial layout of spaces, sightlines into and between the *fauces-atrium-tablinum*, and of the ancient texts describing houses, entrances and front rooms. This chapter argues that when we explore the possible corporeal experiences of the area(s) both during and outside the rituals and activities that occurred here, we realize in just how precarious, perhaps even dangerous, a position the *atrium-tablinum* placed the owner of the Roman *domus*, given it was a space often open to prying eyes **and** an array of physical experiences. We shall consider how far the *atrium-tablinum* complex was organized and structured in order to control the sensory experiences to be had in these spaces.

Ideal vs Reality? The 'openness' of the *atrium-tablinum*

According to Wallace-Hadrill, 'a public figure went home not so much to shield himself from the public gaze as to present himself to it in the best possible light'.[9] For many scholars, perceptions of the elite Roman home's public role have revolved around the dwelling's visibility. Insight into this stems from anecdotes recorded in ancient texts: thus Livius Drusus wished his home be arranged by the architect 'so that whatever I do should be visible to everybody' and Cicero commented, 'My house stands in view of virtually the whole city'.[10] From such passages the importance of a house's visual prominence for those who held public positions in society can be observed.

Comments such as these have, understandably, encouraged scholars to regard the houses of Rome's elite as being consistently open and accessible to all, thereby playing an important role in the construction of an individual's display of power and social standing as owners used them to parade their wealth and successes to others. There have been two key factors behind this perception of the openness and accessibility of the Roman home. First has been the suggestion that there were certain parts of the house, in particular the *atrium-tablinum*, into which anyone could enter, even those who were uninvited and merely wandering in from the street outside. Second has been the assumption that entrance doors to elite houses were constantly open, which in turn would make admittance into a residence that much more possible. Establishing the accuracy of these arguments is central to understanding in greater depth the roles played by the *atrium-tablinum* in status display. If the entrance to a house was constantly open and the *atrium-tablinum* accessible to all, how would this impact the multisensory experiences to be had here for guests and inhabitants? Conversely, if admittance was regulated at certain times of the Roman day or household calendar, this raises significant questions as to when and why this might occur and presents us with a picture of residence owners attempting to have rather more control over what was visible and accessible to outsiders and thus the image they were presenting.

According to Wallace-Hadrill, 'except when closed as a symbol of mourning, the doors of noble houses stood open to all, a feature that allowed the entrance of ransacking Gauls in 390 BC, and of Livius' own assassin in 91 BC'.[11] This notion that residential entrance doors were perpetually open, except when in mourning, has been understood to emphasize just how open to the street the Roman house was most of the time.[12] Indeed, the assertion that the only time when elite Roman houses closed their doors was following bereavement highlights just how extraordinary an occurrence this was. Funerals, after all, would have been rare, rather than regular, activities.

Unsurprisingly, however, examination of ancient texts actually shows numerous references to closed doors at the entrance to houses at different times of the day. Many instances centre around the morning *salutatio*, with clients arriving and knocking on doors to be admitted. In his *Satires*, Horace talks of the client at Maecenas' house who 'towards cockcrow ... comes knocking on his door (*ostia pulsat*)'.[13] Similar references to closed doors in the early morning at the start of the *salutatio* are found in Seneca's *Letters* where we read references to individuals having to 'knock at the haughty doors of the influential (*pulsare superbas potentiorum fores*)'.[14] We can similarly observe discussions of closed entrance doors occurring at other times of the day that show particular connections to Rome's system of patronage. In his advice regarding the best moment to deliver his book of *Epigrams* to Pliny, Martial instructs on the inopportune moments for disturbing Pliny: 'But mind you don't knock tipsily on the eloquent door at the wrong time (*pulses ianuam*)'.[15]

In addition to these accounts, are numerous other literary references to barred or closed, locked doors in various different situations. For Seneca, the importance of seclusion and closing the door (*fores clusi*) against distractions is key to his ability to undertake philosophical musings, whilst in a later letter to Lucilius he rejoices in the games which allow him to revel in his freedom from disturbances. 'My door has not been continually creaking on its hinges nor will my curtain be pulled aside (*Non crepuit subinde ostium, non adlevabitur velum*)'.[16] Elsewhere, from Horace, we read of doors being closed at night against the pleas of lovers (*prima nocte domum claude*) and the problems of old age meaning the chance of fewer assignations with lovers: 'rattl[ing] your closed/ shutters, with volleys of pebbles, depriving you of rest;/ and the door that of old would, most obligingly, move/ its hinges hugs the threshold' (*Parcius iunctas quatiunt fenestras/ iactibus crebris iuvenes proterui/ nec tibi somnos adimunt amatque ianua limen*).[17]

These allusions to knocking on closed doors or barred doors are not important primarily for the **reality** of the precise situations being described for, after all, we should bear in mind the inherent issues of reliability behind the authors cited. Horace, for example, wrote poetry which sought to recount personal experience and social, cultural and occasionally broad political commentary for a relatively wide audience, whilst the problems of accuracy in Juvenal's, Martial's and Seneca's works have been outlined in the previous chapter.[18] Rather, these references to knocking on doors, shut doors or the disturbances that open doors cause, demonstrate a social and cultural perception of the need, at least at some points of day or night, for respite from the world outside. As Martial demonstrates, it is Lesbia's unguarded promiscuity and wanton behaviour in view of all, which is not shielded behind either door or curtain, that leads to his acerbic critique. Whilst we should note that Martial's censure here is directed towards a woman of standing, rather than a man, it is not her sexual appetite which earns reproach but rather her actions of openly parading her sexual desires for all to see that is perceived to be socially repugnant. Martial's conclusion of his diatribe serves to emphasize further the socially perceived need for removal from public view of certain people at particular times.

> A prostitute, on the other hand, drives witnesses away with curtain and bolt and rarely does a chink gape in a suburban brothel. Learn modesty from Chione or Ias, if from nobody else. Even dirty whores take cover in tombs. Does my censure seem too harsh? I do not exhort you to be chaste, Lesbia, but not to be caught.[19]

In order to engage their readership such descriptions of *clientes* banging on front doors at the start of the *salutatio*, of Rome's elite closing the door against regular interruptions, of lovers being locked out at night, or of women needing to conceal, not cease, their sexual assignations speaks to some level of social expectation or ideal regarding necessary occasions of removing oneself from public view, via the closing of doors and front entrances.

This notion of need for household entrance doors to be closed, and thus not perpetually 'open', is supported by material evidence in the form of door remains at and near house entrances. When studying thresholds for the remnants of door architecture we are mainly reliant on Pompeii and Herculaneum. The eruption of Vesuvius preserved organic materials (e.g. wood) from doors at Herculaneum, whilst from Pompeii there are numerous examples of casts of front doors, for example from the houses of Octavius Quartio, the Ephebus, the Orchard and the house of the Ceii (Fig. 4.2). These door, or cast, remains show that houses could be closed off or opened up to the street as required. In addition to these, discoveries of methods for securing doors including postholes, further undermine the notion of consistently open entrances to houses.[20] More interesting, however, is not just the presence of entrance doors and bolts, but the evidence of secondary internal doors situated within or at the exit of the *fauces* into the *atrium* (Fig. 4.3). The existence of extra doors within the *fauces* raises implications for a residence's

Figure 4.2 Entrance door casts from the house of the Ceii (Reg I.6.15), Pompeii. Photo: Hannah Platts.

Figure 4.3 Secondary entrance door remains in the middle and at the top of the *fauces* of the house of the Anchor (Reg VI.10.7), Pompeii. Photo: Hannah Platts.

'openness' and relationship to the street, even when the dwelling's main entrance doors were themselves open.

For many scholars the traditional view of the *fauces* has been one of a narrow, open space that led uninterrupted into the *atrium*.[21] According to Taylor Lauritsen in his study of doorways in houses from Pompeii and Herculaneum 'the doorway between the *fauces* and the *atrium* ... is rarely obstructed in any house'.[22] Examination of archaeological remains from house entrances of Pompeii and Herculaneum, however, undermines this assertion. Indeed, as early as the nineteenth century, some scholars put forward alternative ideas on the presence of secondary doors between front doors and *atria* in Pompeii.[23] Thus Mazois and Gell highlighted the remains of secondary doors at the end of the *fauces* in reconstructions and excavation reports, albeit without providing supporting evidence for their suggestions.[24] More recently, Proudfoot's study on the presence of numerous different types of secondary doors situated between front doors and *atria* from Pompeian residences has provided necessary detailed evidence. Proudfoot's non-exhaustive list of fifty examples highlights the regular use of doors at the *atrium* end of the *fauces*.[25]

Connecting archaeological evidence of secondary doors with the above reinterpretation of literary evidence concerning the 'openness' of dwellings serves to emphasize further that even with open entrance doors, we cannot be certain that contact with the rest of the house behind was likewise unimpeded. Firstly, it is eminently possible that curtains or portable wooden partitions could be drawn across the entrance to the *atrium* from the *fauces*, which would serve to 'close' off the rest of the house from the street outside. Moveable items of this nature would be less likely to leave any form of archaeological evidence although there are remains of partitions (some of which were fixed and others moveable) found in the *atria* of houses on the Bay of Naples.[26] The presence of more permanent doors in this part of the house likewise serve to diminish the 'open' nature of a dwelling in relation to the street outside.[27] Such partitions provided the house owner with greater capacity to influence the amount of contact between the interior of the house and the world outside. This in turn permitted further control over what was otherwise a potentially problematic boundary zone sandwiched between the civic and domestic spheres, which would encounter within it activities of both a public and private nature.

The significance of this flexibility should not be underestimated. As will be discussed below, *atria* were multifunctional and depended on factors such as owner, time of day and ritual in progress. The presence of, and thus potential to close, interior secondary doors/curtains would enable activities of the *atrium* to be carried out in private to a greater or lesser extent from the rest of the community, without the need to close grand entrance doors.

Bearing this analysis in mind, let us return to the suggestion that elite household entrance doors were, apart from times of mourning, uniformly left open. Citing supporting evidence, Laurence points out, 'It would appear that in Rome it was normal to keep the main doors of houses open during the day, with a porter to control access to the house'. He goes on to comment, 'However, it is uncertain whether this was universal', and suggests that such practices were probably only followed by Rome's elite, since they were likely to be the only ones able to afford to do so.[28] Such questions, this time regarding the status and universality of houses with **open** doors, require further examination, again not so much for the exact **reality** of the anecdotes our sources present, but rather in terms of what such claims of 'open' houses within the ancient literature might reveal about social ideals or expectations in terms of Roman elite behaviour and its reflection in the domestic realm. That these open entrances to Roman homes sit at the boundary zone between the domestic realm and the civic sphere is significant. Their location and openness symbolize Roman elite life as one of perpetual duty and being constantly 'on-call', as reflected in sources such as Vitruvius and Cicero. Whether or not this reflected reality, open entrance doors served to signify elite ability to control their domain, the liminal threshold between their dwelling and the civic realm and the experience of others within both spheres.

Firstly, let us consider the question of status and open house entrances. An owner's status was critical to whether doors were kept open: as Laurence points out, few of Rome's poor could have afforded guards for their doors and yet we know from literary evidence that porters were regularly used.[29] In many textual references to open entrance doors, status is a key factor, yet what we might consider here is how and why emphasis upon open elite residence entrances is made within our texts. An often-cited passage from Livy's account of the sack of Rome by the Gauls, given as evidence of open entrance doors, emphasizes the high status of house owners with open entrance doors.

> After all the arrangements that circumstances permitted had been made for the defence of the Capitol, the old men returned to their homes to await the coming of their enemies [the Gauls] with hearts that were steeled to die ... They put on the stately robes which are worn by those who conduct the chariots of the gods or celebrate a triumph, and, thus habited, seated themselves on ivory chairs in front of their houses ... the dwellings of the plebeians were barricaded (*plebis aedificiis obseratis*), but the halls (*atriis*) of the patricians stood open; and they [the Gauls] hesitated almost more to enter the open houses than the shut. They gazed with feelings of religious awe upon the men who were seated in the vestibules of their mansions.[30]

This passage requires thought. Livy emphasizes the patrician status of these men who sat in front of their houses in their finery and with their doors open, in contrast to the plebeians who barricaded themselves in their homes. What must be remembered here, however, is the nature of Livy's text. Written in the reign of Augustus, this text should be viewed with an eye to the troubles Rome had experienced during the later Republic that had led to its collapse. Interpreting Livy's history requires an understanding of Augustus' influence within the text. In his preface Livy acknowledges the declining morality of Roman society, echoed in Augustus' own *Res Gestae*.[31] Once in power, Augustus implemented a variety of social, religious and moral reforms, with the professed intention of returning Rome to the golden age of the early Republic. Embedded within these actions were clear attempts to reinforce social hierarchies and values perceived as becoming lax in the latter stages of the Republic. Thus, Augustus reduced senatorial numbers back to pre-Caesarian levels, sought to implement new laws on festival expenditure and dress codes, banned certain inter-status marriages and the appearance of senatorial members on the stage, as well as reinforcing neglected legislation on theatre seating arrangements.[32]

Given that Augustan legislation sought to clarify and display hierarchies and expected social values, we should bear in mind that this is perhaps what Livy is trying to draw upon in his presentation of the elite with open doors and the plebs barricading themselves away. In Livy's passage the patricians are visually distinctive as they sit outside their open houses in their finery. Nothing is hidden, all is open to the Gallic raiders. Livy draws on important and recognized markers of Roman status display including dress, wealth and residence to highlight standing. Irrespective of the reality behind such anecdotes, such accounts emphasize important social ideals or expectations regarding the behaviour of Rome's elite: namely, that Rome's upper echelons consistently parade the acknowledged markers of their Roman identity and social status even in the face of adversity. This behaviour, including the open nature of their homes, denotes elite standing. Irrespective of the accuracy of Livy's presentation, we should note that in his moralizing history of Rome's past, begun in the declining and troubled years of Rome's Republic, he seeks to speak to and reiterate traditionally perceived values and actions of Rome's upper echelons.[33]

The notion of open house doors reflecting Roman social values is further visible when we consider the question of universally open residence entrances, again raised by Laurence. Of the two passages from Livy that Laurence cites, it is the second which is particularly useful.[34] Here Livy recounts Rome's early conflict with neighbouring Veii; a plague-ridden summer led to the consultation of the Sibylline books as well as public and private propitiation of the gods. Livy comments

> All through the City, they say, doors stood wide open, all kinds of things were set out for general use, all comers were welcomed, whether known or not. Men who had been enemies exchanged kind and courteous words with each other; there was a truce to quarrelling and litigation; even chains were removed from prisoners for those days, and afterwards it seemed an act of impiety thenceforth to imprison men again whom the gods had thus befriended.[35]

What is depicted here is an ideal of civic behaviour and social activities: making items available for general use, (*rerum omnium in propatulo posito*); sharing between strangers and friends; friendly relations between enemies; ceasing of litigation and the unshackling and freeing of prisoners at a time when Romans again find themselves facing adversity. Open dwellings are, once more, indicative of idealized values and expected behaviour within Roman society.

It is not just the representation of the open house entrance that is a sign of socially idealized values. We have already seen that our literary sources present numerous examples of closed entrance doors, and these further support the notion that social and cultural ideals are heavily embedded within literary representations of household entrances, particularly of aristocratic residences. I argue that when considering literary references to elite houses with open or closed entrance doors, we should be aware of the idealistic nature of such portrayals and the extent to which they seek to present a level of social expectation or reality behind a door being either open or shut. Those accounts depicting open house entrances, such as Livy, suggest an owner's openness to, and preparedness for, the world beyond as well as a power and ability to control the experiences of inhabitants and guests of the dwelling in that prominent and precarious liminal space where domestic and civic spheres met. Conversely, anecdotes emphasizing closed doors demonstrate a recognized need for times to close oneself off from society, either by individuals themselves, as was the case with Seneca, or by others, as illustrated by Martial's invective against Lesbia. To avoid public criticism and judgement about upsetting public *mores*, the sexual indiscretions of elite women in particular were expected to occur behind closed doors. The requirement to close the house following a bereavement similarly highlights this concern for traditional customs and values as it was a time when a household entered an alternative state, becoming a *familia funesta*, which marked them out as different. Ritual enactments of grief deemed socially 'appropriate' and expected which included closing a residence's doors, were required in order to reintegrate a mourning family back into society.[36]

We should, then, think more critically about the threshold to the Roman dwelling and its literary presentation, since the discussion of textual references to Roman house entrances above shows how challenging it is to see fixed rules regarding this area of the home in relation to the street outside. In order to start understanding multisensory experience within the Roman home, not only do we need to examine the street on which a residence is located but we also need to explore how and where these two contrasting zones come into contact and to consider the behaviours and possible corporeal experiences to be had within this threshold area. A dwelling's entrance sat in the liminal realm between the civic and domestic spheres. As such its location made it a precarious space where activities or behaviours typical of both realms could be assumed to occur. There are, undoubtedly, numerous examples of doors being left open onto the street, and likewise there are plenty of anecdotes which highlight the closure of entrance doors as well as the need for individuals to retreat behind closed doors. Within such a mixture of accounts are instances of reality, that doors were shut at night and early callers for the start of the morning *salutatio* might indeed be faced with a need to rouse the household by banging on the door. So, too, are examples that served a deeper purpose of speaking to society's traditionally upheld expectations and reiterating idealized behaviour: whether that is closing the house at a time of mourning, removing sexual indiscretion from the public eye or parading unflinchingly one's standing, accessibility and the traditional markers of Roman identity particularly during periods of hardship or difficulty.

'Leaky' houses?: Reconsidering 'public' access into the *atrium*

Wielding control over the domestic and private, yet at times also public and civic, boundary zones of the *fauces-atrium-tablinum* in the Roman house did not merely revolve around the ability to 'open up' or 'close off' parts of a dwelling to the world outside. Rather, the presence of open or closed doors in the vicinity of the entrance and *fauces-atrium-tablinum* complex, and the questions these raise surrounding 'openness' to the street lead us to a connected issue regarding 'public' accessibility to houses and the level to which this was also (un)controlled. In particular, entrance doors are key to the 'open' or 'closed' nature of the relationship between street and front of house, particularly because they actively impact upon the physical accessibility of the front part of the dwelling from the street and vice versa, and thus the publicly accessible nature of this space.

In exploring this further let us consider Vitruvius and return to two matters raised by him in the passage cited at the start of this chapter. First, Vitruvius emphasizes the importance of delineating social position through house organization, decoration and size. Embedded within the passage above, and his chapter VI as a whole, is the articulation of residential space according to an owner's standing. For the upper ranks of society, housing should demonstrate status, whilst for those of the lower orders dwellings should equally reflect their social position, with no opulent and sizeable reception halls. Second, and connected to this, is the 'public' nature of this space since, according to Vitruvius, it was a place where deliberations occurred and favours were granted to those of lower standing.[37]

> For into the private rooms no one enters, unless invited, such as the bedrooms, dining-rooms, baths and other apartments which have similar purposes. The common rooms, on the contrary, are those entered by anyone, even unasked such as vestibules, courtyards, peristyles and other apartments of similar uses.[38]

This passage from Vitruvius has often been understood to define parts of the house as accessible only to those **invited** [*nisi invitatis*] whilst other areas of the dwelling were open to all – even **without invitation** [*communia autem sunt in quibus etiam invocati suo iure de populo possunt venire*]. Wallace-Hadrill, in particular, has employed it in depth to suggest the accessible nature of the Roman house to all, whether invited or not.[39] If we examine Vitruvius' description together with other texts, however, a more complex situation becomes apparent.

Numerous ancient authors suggest admittance into the *salutatio* and thus into the house, was not guaranteed. Rather they suggest the existence of a hierarchy between individuals **before** being permitted into the house, together with continued social demarcation once inside. Seneca, for example, demonstrates the existence of a hierarchy between visitors awaiting entry into a residence when he comments on the categorization into groups of those admitted to houses. From the time of Gaius Gracchus and Livius Drusus in the last two centuries of the Republic, only some were permitted a private audience when visiting residences. Others were forced to remain in the *atrium*, whilst the least fortunate might not even make it past the threshold.[40] There is extensive literature to support suggestions of exclusion from houses during the *salutatio*. Returning to Horace's *Satires* we see him document a man's futile attempts to see Maecenas.[41] Likewise, from various authors we hear not only of further examples of exclusion from the *salutatio* but also read of the concerns of individuals that they might be prevented entry.[42] Such evidence suggests that accessibility to the house was not necessarily improved during the ritual of the *salutatio*, and also that at all times accessibility and admittance into and around the Roman *domus* was carefully monitored: Vitruvius himself makes this clear.[43]

According to Speksnijder, Vitruvius 'disregards the fact that many uninvited visitors could and would be excluded from the house in the first place'.[44] Such neglect to explain the typical practice of excluding some callers from a residence during the *salutatio* resulted, perhaps, from an awareness that the process of 'ordering' visitors who mingled at a threshold prior to entry was a common occurrence that he perceived did not require clarification. Given the liminal domestic/civic zone of this space on the boundary of contact between the house and the street everyone, even passers-by, would be aware of the judgements of status imposed by the owner on those gathered outside his home: those who were worthy of entry and those who were not. Once inside however, the 'grading' of visitors continued, although the hierarchies themselves potentially became less obvious since, at the very least, those inside were now no longer milling around in the public street awaiting entry or exclusion. Vitruvius had identified the proper parts of houses in the preceding chapter (VI.4.1–2). Now at the start of Book VI Chapter 5 he emphasizes the importance of continued categorizing of visitors to the home after admittance.

> When we have arranged our plan with a view to aspect, [w]e must go on to consider the situation of the private rooms for the master of the house and those which are for the outsiders.
>
> *Cum ad regiones caeli ita ea fuerint disposita, tunc etiam animadvertendum est quibus rationibus privatis aedificiis propria loca patribus familiarum et quemadmodum communia cum extraneis aedificari debeant.*[45]

This means of ranking others ultimately served to continue controlling access around and within the home as well as acting as a means to display personal power.

Key to interpreting Vitruvius, then, is that there **were** levels of accessibility to the Roman house and that uncontrolled access into the house in the first place, for anyone and everyone, should not be assumed. Scholars have misinterpreted the 'public' extent of the *domus*, seeing parts of Roman houses such as *atria*, *vestibula* and *peristylia* as open to all, even passers-by wandering in from the street. What Vitruvius was referring to, however, when talking about 'invited' and 'uninvited' visitor access into parts of the home, related to those who had already passed the threshold into the dwelling proper. When an individual was accepted into a residence, access to the 'inner confines' of the home – the baths, bedrooms and dining areas – might be available to those with express invitation from the owner. For the remaining parts of the house such as vestibule, reception hall and peristyle(s), access required no specific permission from the owner **after** the guest had been accepted across the threshold. These parts of the house were open to all guests assuming they were allowed into the dwelling in the first place.[46]

Archaeological remains strengthen this reading of Vitruvius and suggest the need for a more nuanced interpretation of the accessible nature of Roman houses. The fact that dwellings were 'blocked in reality', particularly by architecture according to Hales, warrants detailed consideration in terms of the obstacles to **physical** access to the interior of a residence.[47] Yet, although Wallace-Hadrill's suggestion that Roman residences were accessible to all, even those uninvited, has been subject to criticism, it remains popular.[48] In particular David

Balch, Professor in New Testament, has attempted to employ the physical remains of Roman houses to support Wallace-Hadrill's suggestion that houses were accessible to all. He refers to this as the 'leaky' nature of Roman dwellings.[49] Central to Balch's argument is that as well as numerous household front entrances having mosaics and frescoes which visually welcomed visitors in, many homes had at least one secondary entrance (*posticum*). These *postica* made managing those admitted in from the street outside difficult because it meant residences often had at least two access points that needed monitoring.[50] According to Balch, the fact that Roman houses often had multiple entrances made them 'leaky' and, when combined with Vitruvius VI.5.1, meant house architecture welcomed 'uninvited guests into their *caupona*, domestic *atria* and peristyle'.[51] For Balch, then, these 'uninvited visitors' would be members of the public walking in from the street outside.[52]

Given the liminal position of the *atrium* on the boundary between the street and the heart of the dwelling, and the fact it served numerous functions with the capacity to engender many corporeal responses, however, how welcoming and accessible the *atrium* was to members of the public outside requires more examination. If we combine evidence already set out in Chapter Three regarding *fauces*' length and décor and evidence of doorkeepers, with finds of doors at entrances, secondary doors within *fauces*, at *postica* and in doorways between shops and taverns connected to residences, we can observe that Balch's assumption of 'leaky' houses with uncontrolled and unobstructed entrances or exits that anyone from the street could use at any time becomes questionable.[53] Instead, we should perhaps consider ways in which Roman house owners sought to control the 'leaky' and accessible nature of their dwellings with regards to the world beyond.

The examples Balch cites to support his argument are problematic. His citation of the *posticum* into the peristyle of the house of the Tragic Poet ignores that this entrance shows substantial remains of door architecture, which presumes an ability to control when this door is used. In the centre of the slope leading from the *posticum* into the peristyle are remains of a post hole which would have held a pole for securing the door when closed (Fig. 4.4).[54] Further problems exist in Balch's citation of the house of Paquius Proculus, the house of Caesius Blandus and the house of L. Caecilius Iucundus. Balch's reference to a shop at #20 of the Vicolo Proculus Paquius, which he argues is a back door leading onto the peristyle of the house of Paquius Proculus, is incorrect. The door at #20 does not belong to a shop, but rather to an underground service and storage area beneath the house of Paquius Proculus (Fig. 4.5). Walking through

Figure 4.4 *Posticum* from the house of Tragic Poet (Reg VI.8.3), Pompeii. Note the post hole in the *fauces* for securing the door, and cardine and vertical bar cuts in the threshold. Photo: Hannah Platts.

Figure 4.5 Bottom right hand side of picture entrance #20 on the Vicolo Proculus Paquius (Reg I.7.20), Pompeii. Note the peristyle at (n) from the house of Proculus Paquius in the top left of this picture. Photo: Hannah Platts.

Figure 4.6 View across the peristyle (n) and garden (j) towards wall remains of room (m) of the house of Paquius Proculus (Reg I.7.1), Pompeii. Rooms (k), (l) and (m) are located directly above the store room at #20 on the Vicolo di Paquius Proculus (Reg I.7.20). Photo: Hannah Platts.

the door of this storage area does not lead directly into the peristyle of the house of Paquius Proculus at (n) (Fig. 4.6), but underneath the three rooms at (k), (l), (m) on the south side of the peristyle and to a ramp that connects the dwelling's storage and service area to the peristyle at (n) (Fig. 4.7). Similar issues arise with Balch's use of door #43 on the Vicolo del Lupanare, which he suggests leads straight into the *atrium* (b) of the house of Caesius Blandus (Fig. 4.8).[55] Not only has Balch misidentified the peristyle (h) of this house as being the *atrium*, but there is a misunderstanding of the different levels typical of many Pompeian houses. Looking at a 2D floor plan of this dwelling suggests indeed that door #43 leads directly into the peristyle at area (i). When this floor plan is read, however, with an understanding of the topographical layout of Pompeii and its particular impact on this house, it can be seen that entrance #43 on the Vicolo del Lupanare actually leads into an underground storeroom located below the back section of the peristyle (Fig. 4.9).[56]

Further issues arise regarding Balch's reference to the shop connected to the house of Caesius Blandus. As Balch points out, situated on the corner of two

Initial Perceptions

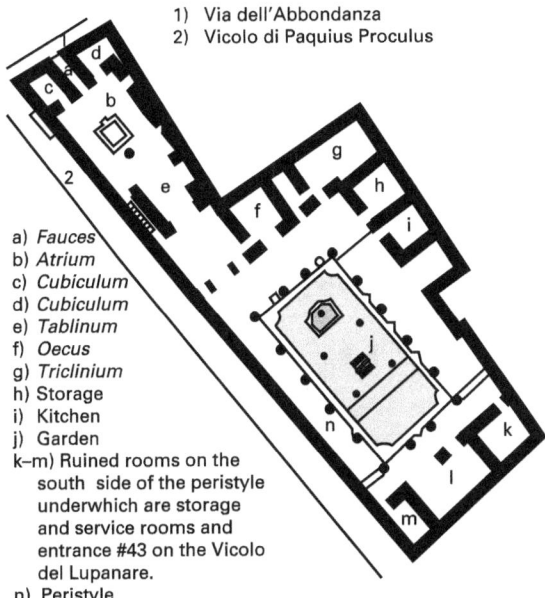

Figure 4.7 Floor plan of the house of Paquius Proculus (Reg I.7.1), Pompeii. © Bloomsbury Academic.

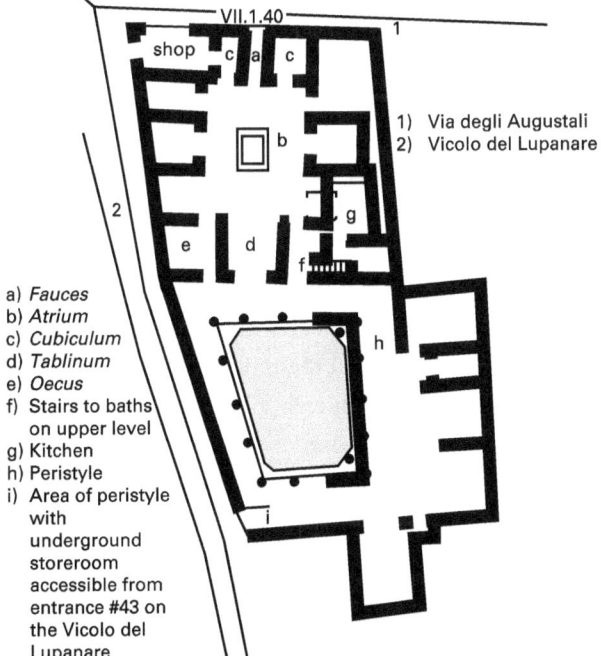

Figure 4.8 Floor plan showing the peristyle at the rear of the house of Caesius Blandus (Reg VII.1.40), Pompeii. Entrance to storerooms at #43 on the Vicolo del Lupanare (Reg VII.1.43) are located under this peristyle. © Bloomsbury Academic.

Figure 4.9 Entrance #43 on Vicolo del Lupanare (Reg VII.1.43), Pompeii. Note that this storeroom is located under the peristyle of the house of Caesius Blandus (Reg VII.1.40), the columns of which are also pictured in this photo. Photo: Hannah Platts.

roads, the wide shop frontages face the two streets (Fig. 4.8). These are the Via degli Augustali and the Vicolo del Lupanare. As is typical with many shop frontages from Pompeii and Herculaneum, the entrances to these shops show evidence of wide sliding doors that would open up or close off the shop to the street. At the back of this shop was a door, which led into a small room (c) in the house of Caesius Blandus. This small room likewise had a door into the *atrium* (b) of the residence (Fig. 4.10). Although evidence of door architecture in the doorway leading from the back of shop into room (c) in the house of Caesius Blandus cannot be fully ascertained due to damage, the threshold demarcation suggests the possibility of a curtain separating the shop from the house room at the very least, thereby providing a visible barrier. Between the small room (c) and the *atrium* (b) there is a further door that does show evidence of door architecture, thus highlighting the ability to close off this room from the rest of the house. Moreover, that there are two thresholds to pass through before one reaches the atrium itself further highlights the increased ability to control unwanted access to the house from the shop and the street beyond.

Initial Perceptions

Figure 4.10 View through shop of M. Noni Campani (Reg VII.1.41) showing thresholds leading into *cubiculum* (c) and *atrium* (b) of the house of Caesius Blandus (Reg VII.1.40), Pompeii. Photo: Hannah Platts.

The final example of Balch's 'leaky' houses, that of L. Caecilius Iucundus (V.I.26), is complex and requires considerably more detailed examination than he affords (Fig. 4.11). In the first instance, it must be noted that this residence was only combined with its neighbouring dwelling (V.I.23), through doorways at (h) and (i) in the early Imperial period.[57] Hence the various points of access between the two dwellings were only developed relatively late in the life of the dwelling, which should be acknowledged in any analysis.[58] Whilst Balch points out numerous points of access to the house from the street outside, for example from the shop at entrance #24 on Via del Vesuvio and the *posticum* at entrance #10 on Vicolo di Cicilio Giocondo, it should also be explained that both of these routes access the neighbouring residence at V.I.23, which had been merged into the house of L. Caecilius Iucundus, and not the house of L. Caecilius Iucundus itself. Only the shops (c) at entrances #25 and #27 lead directly via back doors into the house of Caecilius Iucundus (Fig. 4.11). Moreover, and essential to understanding the extent to which

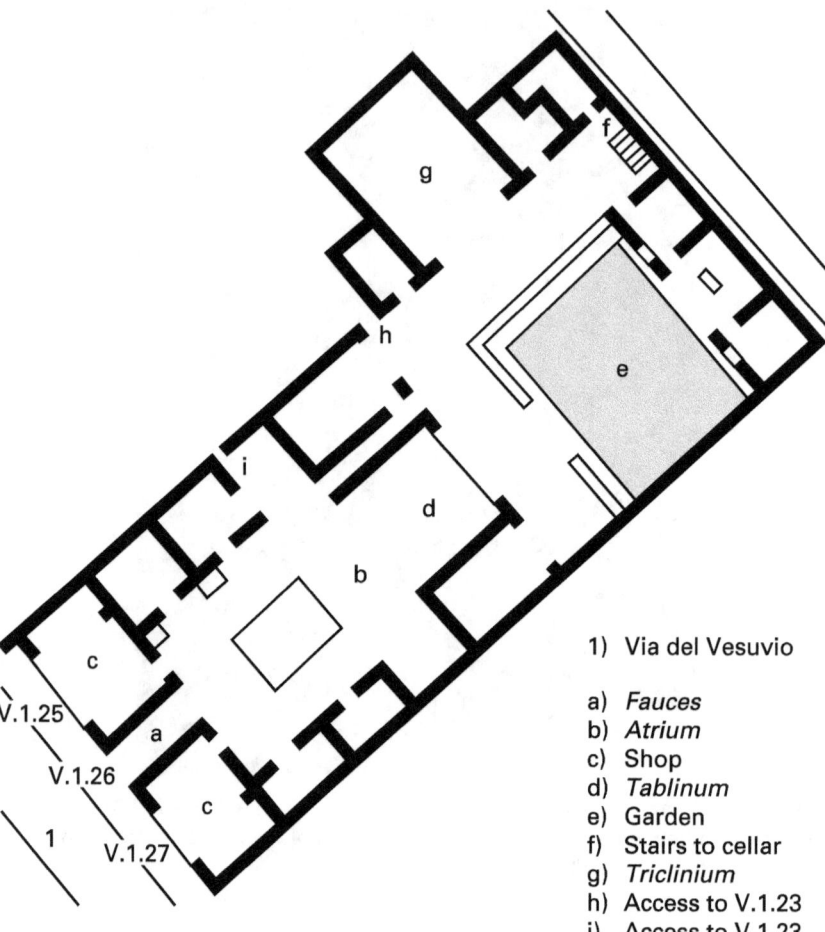

Figure 4.11 Floor plan of the house of Caecilius Iucundus (Reg V.I.26), Pompeii. Note the possible access between this residence and its neighbouring residence (Reg V.I.23) situated to the left of room (k) in the house of Caecilius Iucundus. © Bloomsbury Academic.

these routes enabled possible access to the rest of the residence at V.I.26, both these points of entry to the house itself show evidence of door architecture, which would have served to prohibit, or at least control, access if and when required.[59]

There are numerous other examples, which complicate further Balch's concept of 'leaky' houses, three of which benefit from consideration. One house that presents an excellent example of the problem of assuming that the existence of *postica* and/or attached shops necessarily results in a 'leaky' dwelling with numerous uncontrolled entrances and exits, is the house of Pansa in Pompeii. The main entrance to this residence was from the Via della Terme (Fig. 4.1). The house had one shop (d) connected by a doorway and step to a *cubiculum* (c), which itself has a single entrance with evidence of door architecture that suggests the room could be closed off from the *atrium* (Fig. 4.12). This residence also had a *posticum* at (g) with a door and four steps leading down onto the Vicolo della Fullonica and evidence of door architecture and a doorway 1.1 metres wide which suggest control over access from the street to this part of the house (Fig. 4.13). Similarly, the paved area at (m), which led onto the Vicolo di Modesto, could be closed off by a door from the street, and the presence of a doorway and step between the kitchen at (l) and the paved area at (m) is equally suggestive of partitioning architecture that could be employed to hinder access of the uninvited from the street to the rest of the dwelling (Figs 4.14 and 4.15).

Two other examples where careful control over additional access to the street via doors can be found are the house of Holconius Rufus and the house of the Ara Maxima. Both residences have shops with separate entrances to the street (Figs. 4.16 and 4.17). The shop frontages to the streets of both houses show evidence of the sliding door architecture regularly used in Pompeian shops. In the house of the Ara Maxima, the storeroom at (i) and the shop at (g) and latrine

Figure 4.12 View of threshold from shop (d) (Reg VI.6.22) leading into *cubiculum* (c) of house of Pansa (Reg VI.6.1), Pompeii. Note also the remains of door architecture between *cubiculum* (c) and *atrium* (b) in the house of Pansa. Photo: Hannah Platts.

Figure 4.13 *Posticum* and steps down on to Vicolo della Fullonica from house of Pansa (Reg VI.6.8), Pompeii. This entrance show evidence of door remains in the form of symmetrical cardine cuts on either side of the threshold on the top step. Photo: Hannah Platts.

Figure 4.14 Threshold at #13 opening onto the Vicolo di Modesto, Pompeii. Note view of doorway at back of this area into kitchen at (k) of the house of Pansa (VI.6.1). Photo: Hannah Platts.

Initial Perceptions 101

Figure 4.15 Doorway and step down between the kitchen at (l) and the paved area at (m) of the house of Pansa (Reg VI.6.1), Pompeii. Photo: Hannah Platts.

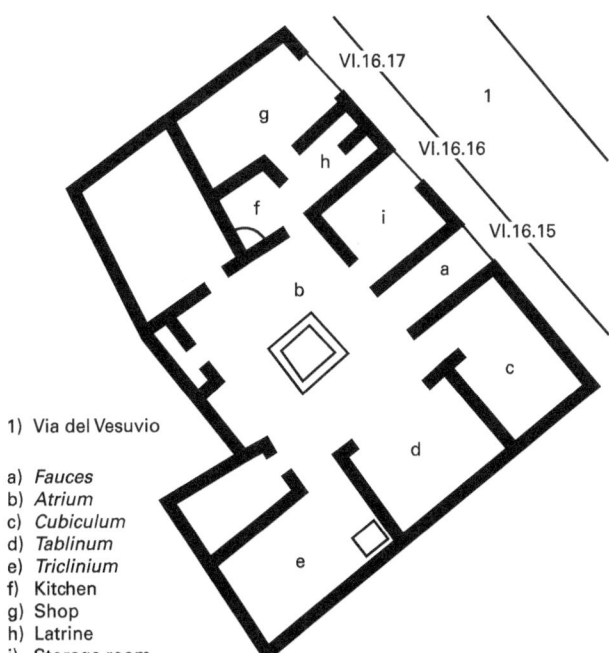

Figure 4.16 Floor plan of the house of the Ara Maxima (Reg VI.16.15), Pompeii. © Bloomsbury Academic.

Figure 4.17 Floor plan of the house of Marcus Holconius Rufus (Reg VIII.4.4), Pompeii. © Bloomsbury Academic.

area at (h) were blocked off from the *atrium* by doors for which architecture remains in situ, thereby highlighting the opportunity to control access from the street into the dwelling via entrances that were alternative to the main entrance via the *fauces* at (a).

The house of Holconius Rufus likewise displays door architecture and steps between the shops at the house front (c) and the *atrium* (b) and *cubicula* (d) and (d') with which these shops were connected (Fig. 4.17). In room (d), remains of bronze hinges were found in situ for the room's two doors, together with locks and three nails, which also show how shops could be physically separated from connected houses.⁶⁰ The narrower door into room (n) from the Via della Teatri at VI.4.49 has a threshold and step showing evidence of scratches in the middle from doors being closed and secured (Fig. 4.18), whilst the side entrance into (n) from the neighbouring workshop similarly has a connecting doorway and threshold, which also suggests an ability to control movement into and out of the space at (n). A modern gate blocks the doorway leading from the peristyle garden at (g) into (n), making it difficult to scrutinize remains of possible door architecture. What must be remembered here is that these examples outline the presence of durable door architecture, rather than curtains or other temporary, more flimsy partitions, remains of which are less likely to have survived, making it more difficult to ascertain their positioning in the house. Where it is not clear from archaeological evidence that there were doors, we cannot be sure that other, less durable means of partitioning were not employed.⁶¹

These examples show in particular the issues posed by relying on two-dimensional plans of houses which do not show either how topography influenced architectural structure or the presence of door architecture and its

Figure 4.18 Threshold at (n) (Reg VIII.4.49) connected to house of Marcus Holconius Rufus (Reg VIII.4.4), Pompeii. Note scratches on the door plate from where the doors have been closed and the cuts for cardines on either side of the plate. Photo: Hannah Platts.

possible impact on obstructing movement within the dwelling. Numerous entrances and exits to dwellings might initially imply a residence had many points of unfettered access and could be seen initially as 'leaky' as Balch has suggested, in other words allowing anyone in. Linking a residence's floor plan to the site's topographical layout and populating it with doors and steps for which there is firm evidence, as well as the potential use of curtains and other modes of partition which no longer survive, however, changes perceptions of the ease of accessibility. These alternative entrances to the residences in question do not emphasize Balch's notion of the 'leaky' nature of houses but instead demonstrate, either through clear door architecture or their situation on lower levels, the ability to control possible entry points into the dwelling. Given their numerous entrances, houses had the potential to be 'leaky', but to perceive dwellings as open to uncontrolled public access from outside either during the *salutatio* or indeed at any point throughout the day or night, is simplistic. When these archaeological remains are combined with a more nuanced reading of Vitruvius' discussion on access to the Roman home, it becomes clearer that the ability to regulate who came in to a dwelling, who went where within it and who left it provided yet another means by which an owner could parade power to others, both outside and inside his domain.

'Public' and 'Private' activities in and around the *Atrium*

It is not just physical access and openness to the street outside that has encouraged a perception of the constantly 'public' nature of the *atrium-tablinum* complex in the Roman home. The assumed function or usage of the space has also played a vital part. As the front hall of the Roman *domus*, the *atrium* played host to numerous important social and family rituals and customs, all of which engendered numerous significant corporeal responses on the part of those involved, as we will shortly see. It was here that ancestor masks, family trees and military trophies were displayed to visitors. This space experienced the daily morning ritual of the *salutatio*, as well as the start and finish of the wedding procession, the beginning and completion of funerary rites, and the coming of age ceremony, when boys of the family assumed the *toga virilis*.[62] Bearing these rituals in mind, the *atrium*'s function as a reception hall from the late Republic into the early Empire is undeniably important and presents a key component in interpretation of the role of the *atrium-tablinum* complex. The short-lived nature of these activities together with the often contradictory accounts of them in texts highlight the problems faced when trying to identify the specific 'facts' of these ceremonies.[63] Yet numerous references to them in Rome's written and material culture emphasize the crucial role they played in society as a means of displaying values of group belonging and standing within Rome's social hierarchy.

The incidence of key family and social rituals in the *atrium-tablinum* complex, together with its proximity to the residence's entrance and the street beyond, and the fact that numerous rooms led off from this space into the rest of the house has, then, played a vital role in interpreting its 'public' nature. Indeed for Wallace-Hadrill, public and private space in the Roman home was situated on a spectrum 'that ranges from the completely public to the completely private'.[64] Although he makes the important point about the *atrium* as ungendered space at the centre of household activity for its inhabitants including the *paterfamilias*, the *materfamilias*, the housekeeper and occasionally for children, embedded in his discussion is a focus on the continual 'public' role of the *atrium*, where the 'promiscuous crowd of the traditional *atrium* house was not a novel or transitional phenomenon, but rather its natural condition'.[65] Consequently the *atrium* has often been considered as being located on the 'completely public' end of the spectrum of 'public-private space' in the Roman domestic realm.

Just as scholars have started to explore the question of unfettered 'public' access into the *atrium* from the street, however, so too have they started to question the notion of a uniform 'public' function for the *atrium-tablinum* for those inside the *domus*. Citing its location as a space between Rome's public and private worlds, Dickmann persuasively argues that '[the *atrium*] marked a borderline between the public life of the town and the privacy of the family'.[66] Being neither public like the civic realm, nor tucked away and inaccessible like other parts of the Roman house,[67] the *atrium*'s position between the street and the deeper confines of the house is significant when trying to understand its role in personal display and construction of the social identity of owner and family. Its liminal nature was not merely due to its physical location, however. Equally important, as Dickmann highlights, the social function of a room (including the *atrium*) varies according to individuals within it and time of day. Thus, the *atrium* might play the role of grand reception hall in the morning, whilst in the afternoon it might be where the master of the residence met his *amici*. Goldbeck has further complicated the traditionally held image of the *atrium-tablinum* as the grand reception hall of the *domus* by proposing a reduced focus on the *salutatio* in many Roman houses, suggesting that far fewer residences held this ritual and that it only happened in senators' houses.[68] In between the *salutatio* and the meeting of *amici*, other members of the *domus* might have used this space, for example playing children and women weaving.[69] Dickmann's statements that 'the *atrium* cannot simply be called a public hall' and his suggestion that 'we need to investigate when and how it was used for other purposes' are particularly pertinent.[70]

A multisensory experience approach to daily routine in the *atrium*

The transitional status of the *atrium* as performing both 'public' and 'private' functions posed potential problems for the owner. As a boundary between Rome's 'public' and 'private' realms, it was fundamentally connected with, and echoed the ways in which individuals corporeally experienced, physically navigated, and used the space. Embedded within the ceremonies and customs of the *salutatio*, wedding and funeral, as we will shortly see, were a multitude of smells and sounds, tastes and textures, from the scent of burning incense or candles and the smell and taste of food at the wedding banquet to the sounds of *clientes* as they jostled their way up the *fauces* to see their *patronus*. Away from these rituals, however, the corporeal experiences of the *atrium* would vary and would certainly be different from those of the *atrium* during these traditional social and familial customs. When thinking about multisensory experiences in the *atrium* with regard to daily routine, we need to understand the sort of activities that typically occurred there and consider them in terms of the multiple sensory responses that they might have encouraged.

Let us start by returning to textual references to weaving and children playing in the *atrium* discussed above. Substantial archaeological finds support the suggestion of weaving occurring in the *atrium*. In *Pompeian Households*, Allison suggests 'weaving seems to be an activity associated with these front halls' and cites evidence, mainly in the form of loom weights, found in the *atria* of eight surveyed residences.[71] The auditory experience of weaving, perhaps the quiet clacking of the weights and the low chatter of voices, would have been considerably different from the bustle of the *salutatio*, particularly if front or secondary entrance doors were closed during times outside the regular *salutatio*. The likelihood of locating weaving in the front hall is supported by the well-lit nature of this room during daylight hours as light came from the *compluvium* in the roof. If so, then, we might also infer both temporal and seasonal differences to the corporeal experience of the *atrium*.[72]

Irrespective of season, the Roman clock had 12 hours of daylight and 12 of darkness. Levels of sunshine today vary between summer and winter with summer receiving considerably more daylight hours, perhaps 15 hours of sunlight, in comparison with possibly 8 or 9 in the winter.[73] Given the comparable amount of daylight in ancient Roman times to today, then it is likely that more weaving occurred in the *atrium* during the summer months, whilst in the winter, weaving might be reduced by the shorter daylight hours.[74] Moreover, with October, November and December receiving the most rain and cooler temperatures, the sound of rain and the haptic experience whilst weaving would vary across the year. During the winter, regular rainfall splashing into the *impluvium* might compete with noises of weaving, whilst colder temperatures might require the use of portable braziers to warm people as they wove. Portable braziers have been found, for example, in the peristyle garden areas of the house of the Menander and the house of the Lovers.[75] If we look to ancient literature, we find evidence of these being employed to ward off winter chill. Whilst Varro emphasizes the need for doors and windows to be adjusted according to the seasonal uses of rooms and Seneca discusses curtains and windowpanes in winter *triclinia* as protection from the cold, both Seneca and Suetonius also refer to the use of moveable braziers for the same purpose.[76] It is reasonable to suggest that braziers might be moved from elsewhere in the house and used in the *atrium* when required in winter months.

Archaeological evidence for children in the *domus* is harder to ascertain. There is, for example, no evidence for the spatial segregation of children.[77] In terms of identifying children's material culture from Pompeii or Herculaneum, it can rarely be securely distinguished from material belonging to adults.[78] According to Huntley there is a propensity to connect small items, games and dolls with the existence of children.[79] There is, however, the problem of securely differentiating between dolls and votive figurines, or miniature pots or tools, which might have been votive objects.[80] Dice and gaming counters from Pompeii and Herculaneum could equally be used by children and adults and thus finds of gaming counters in the *tablina* of the house of the Ephebe, the house of the *Lararium* of Achilles, house VI.16.26 and perhaps house VIII.2.29–30, cannot be specifically connected with the presence of children in this space.[81] Indeed, the only clear discovery of a child's item is that of a child's bed from Herculaneum.[82] We should not assume from this, however, that children were not present in either Pompeii or Herculaneum. Rather, as Allison points out, our lack of ability to identify children in the archaeological record is perhaps because of either 'a lack of specific material culture pertaining to children or perhaps more pertinent, our lack of study and therefore knowledge of what constituted that material culture'.[83]

Huntley's recent work into identifying children's graffiti, which are frequently found in the houses of Pompeii and Herculaneum, presents a development from previous issues of identifying children in the archaeological record.[84] What is interesting about Huntley's finds is the lack of children's graffiti in any of the *atria* or *tablina* of residences examined.[85] This links well with Huntley's supposition that this reflects 'children's comprehension of the social expectations for behaviors within these spaces. Rooms associated with ceremonial functions certainly would have had more stringent rules for children's behavior', ensuring that 'children were conforming to the examples set by elders and peers'.[86] Furthermore, her suggestion of the continued monitoring of activity in these spaces is also key. The lack of children's graffiti in the *atrium* or kitchen might reflect that these spaces presented a safety concern because of their looms and cooking apparatus, thus necessitating supervision and caution.[87] Closer examination of references from both Vergil and Lucretius, however, suggest children playing in a carefree fashion including running and chasing spinning tops in the *atrium*,[88] or spinning themselves round so that they lose their ability to stand and walk in a straight line, so 'they can hardly now believe all the building is not threatening to fall in upon them.'[89] According to Huntley 'When young children were allowed in these spaces, it must have been under supervision'.[90] Such spaces in the house were a constant centre of activity with slaves working, women weaving and other domestic activities occurring. The *atrium-tablinum* was rarely left unattended, even if only being monitored by the *cella ostiarius*.[91] Thus children would constantly be overseen here, even if not explicitly watched by supervisors or slaves assigned to the role.

The primary multisensory experience of children playing in the *atrium* is clearly one of noise. If Lucretius' and Vergil's reflections of childhood activity in the *atrium* are accurate, then one might imagine the slapping of bare feet or sandals on the ground, squeals and laughter, shrieks and maybe tears as children toppled over on hard floors when running. When thunderstorms broke the heat of the summer months, would children in the *atrium* cry and need comfort, especially given the open nature of the roof and the loudness of the sound? At the very least, from Lucretius and Vergil we see the suggestion that children's games in the *atrium* were likely to be fairly boisterous.

Populating the *atrium-tablinum* with children as well as those weaving would clearly impact upon the corporeal engagement with the space. That is not to say these activities necessarily occurred separately but what we need to consider are the various ways in which inhabitants might experience the space during different activities. In addition to literary evidence of weaving and children playing in the *atrium*, recent archaeological finds have suggested this space to have been employed for numerous other, sometimes mundane, daily activities including household worship at the *lararia* (altars to the household gods), and provision of space for storage of goods including tools for domestic activity such as building, fishing and agriculture and ornate strong boxes (*arca*) for displaying family wealth.[92] Whilst some of these uses might not impact substantially upon multisensory experience in the *atrium-tablinum*, except perhaps for the noise of inhabitants regularly fetching and replacing items in cupboards, discoveries that suggest sleeping, eating and washing also occurred here show that the *atrium-tablinum* was multifunctional and a hub of mundane as well as ceremonial activities. All of these would impact in varying fashions upon the multisensory experience of the space for individuals.

As we will see in greater detail below, the *atrium-tablinum* complex was the location for extraordinary family events and rituals including funerals and weddings. The finds in some dwellings of *lararia* in *atria* suggests that this space was also employed for the practice of regular, probably daily, worship. In the house of the Menander, for example, a substantial and decorated *lararium* was situated on the wall nearest the street. On certain feast or festival days, the *lararium* would probably be an important focal point for the household.[93] It was also the focus for the start of rituals celebrating a boy's transition to manhood and a girl's coming of age at the time of her wedding.[94]

Daily rituals around the *lararium*, would likewise engender particular sensory experiences in the vicinity of the altar. These might include placement of food, wine or even blood offerings on the altar, which would evoke both olfactory and visual sensations for those undertaking worship.[95] Likewise burning of incense would have a strong olfactory impact upon those nearby. Vocal incantations celebrating and praying to the household gods would equally provide an auditory experience for those in the *atrium-tablinum* and nearby surroundings, including perhaps the street if the house's entrance doors were open and the *lararium* situated in close proximity to the street, as is the situation at the house of the Menander.

In terms of the mundane activities of daily life, dishes for cooking have been discovered in the houses of the Cabinet Maker, the Menander, houses I.10.1 and I.10.2–3.[96] Allison rightly highlights the surprising location of these items, given that they were not near any form of cooking apparatus such as hearths or braziers and suggests finding pots used for cooking might be evidence of the practice of 'keeping the necessities of daily life in the *atrium* area'.[97] Braziers were discovered in the garden areas of both the houses of the Menander and of the Cabinet Maker, as well as the house of the Ephebe and house VIII.5.9. Their portability raises the possibility that the braziers might be moved and used anywhere in the residence, including the *atrium*, perhaps to keep dishes warm, boil water or even for some simple cooking.[98] If so, this would potentially have a significant impact upon the physical experience of the *atrium*, since not only would braziers warm their immediate surroundings, but together the hot embers and the heating of food would have an olfactory impact. Added to this, if inhabitants ate in the *atrium-tablinum*, then the noise of people in the space as they gathered together and ate would intensify and the smell of the food being consumed would linger.

Whether braziers were employed in the *atrium* for food preparation and consumption cannot be ascertained. Given the absence of cooking facilities in most *atria*, the finds of cooking hearths in the houses of Stallius Eros and house I.6.8–9, complicates the question, since they suggest that for some dwellings, at least, cooking facilities were present in the *atrium*, at least at the time of the eruption.[99] However, these hearths require consideration, as there remains significant debate over the occupancy and use of these residences. The lack of décor and poor find state of the house of Stallius Eros was taken by Mauiri as evidence of this residence's change of use and possible abandonment post AD 65, whilst house I.6.8–9 may have been used to store building materials.[100] If correct, such change in function together with the apparently 'rustic' nature of the semi-circular hearth in the house of Stallius Eros and the clear downgrading of these spaces in both houses suggests that it was perhaps only once these residences' functions had altered and their residential function declined, that large-scale cooking on fixed hearths was allowed to occur within the *atrium*.[101] If so, it is possible that the *atrium* was rarely used for substantial cooking activities. Perhaps it was limited to the boiling of water or keeping food warm specifically to protect against dispersion of unwanted smells that might linger in these parts of the house that retained a substantial 'public' role at certain times of the day.[102]

In addition to considering cooking in the *atrium*, we should also examine cooking in rooms immediately situated to the front or rear of the *atrium*, as this is equally likely to impinge upon sensory experiences of the space.[103] I undertook a survey of sixty house plans from Pompeii and sixteen from Herculaneum the results of which suggest it was relatively rare to locate the kitchen immediately off the *atrium*.[104] From the residence samples of Pompeii and Herculaneum there are only five houses in each settlement that have kitchens next to the *atrium*. In Pompeii all five of these dwellings are small (having under fifteen different rooms/spaces). For Herculaneum the picture is similar, four of the houses that had kitchens leading off *atria* again having fewer than fifteen rooms in their individual footprints. Only one house, the house of the Mosaic *Atrium*, is larger, with about twenty different rooms/spaces. That so few kitchens are located off *atria* suggests that there was a desire to shield this room from the smells, sounds and possibly excessive temperatures from the kitchen. The smaller the dwelling, the more difficult it would have been to locate kitchens at a distance from the *atrium*. Where the kitchen led off the *atrium*, there is often evidence of door architecture between the rooms, suggesting that an attempt was made to reduce the sensory impact that the kitchen might have (e.g. Fig 4.19).[105]

The smell from house kitchens was judged unpleasant and unwanted. Accordingly, Seneca in his quest for health and peace of mind comments: 'As soon as I escaped from the oppressive atmosphere of the city, and from that awful odour of reeking kitchens which, when in use, pour forth a ruinous mess of steam and soot, I perceived at once that my health was mending.'[106] For many Roman authors, unpleasant smells were associated with poorer members of Roman society. Thus Petronius suggests that cooks smelt bad, whilst for Martial, in his *Epigram to Mamurianus*, society's poor were forced to exist on the smells from kitchens because they had nothing else.[107] If to be associated with food

Figure 4.19 Threshold between kitchen at (d) and *atrium* at (b) in the house of the Ceii (Reg I.6.15), Pompeii. Note the evidence of door architecture remains. Photo: Hannah Platts.

smells was perceived as a sign of low social standing, this would perhaps explain the architectural pattern of kitchen location in the houses of Pompeii and Herculaneum.[108] Where possible, owners sought to situate the kitchen at some remove from the *atrium* and, where this was not possible, other architectural structures such as doors could be employed to provide a barrier to unwanted sounds, smells and heat.[109] By ensuring some distance between kitchen and *atrium* to stop or reduce unpleasant sensory influences seeping into the *atrium*, kitchen slaves were able to continue cooking unhindered by the owner's concerns of how cooking might adversely affect the *atrium* during its 'public' functions. Even in smaller, less opulent residences, which Vitruvius suggested had a less 'public' function, there would still be a desire to maintain standing by being seen to have control over transmission of smells, sounds and heat from the kitchen, hence the use of doors or other partitions between the kitchen and the *atrium*. Slaves had no choice but to toil in smelly, noisy and hot kitchens, their bodies smelled of the foodstuffs they handled, and their hands and arms bore the scars of injuries from cuts and burns received whilst working there.[110] For the house owner distancing the *atrium* from the kitchen, or at least partitioning it off, presented a means of status differentiation that was clear to all, inhabitants and visitors alike. Separating the kitchen from the *atrium-tablinum* diminished the extent to which the sensory nuisances from food production dispersed throughout the house and impacted upon guests.[111]

Evidence for eating in the *atrium-tablinum* complex includes finds of serving and tableware as well as chairs, benches, tables and couches. With tableware and serving items, it is difficult to ascertain whether they were located in the *atrium* because they were stored rather than used there. Storage is certainly a possible reason for the substantial finds from the *atrium* of the house of the Cabinet Maker.[112] The two couches found in the *tablinum* of the house of the Menander, however, were probably used there for reclining either for eating or sleeping.[113] We should remember the effect that dining in the area of the *atrium-tablinum* had on the multisensory experience of the space itself, with noises of chatting, laughing, perhaps arguing, the clattering of dishes and in some cases silverware, intermingling with the scent and tastes of the food and drink being consumed. With entrance and secondary entrance doors to the house open, passers-by would experience sights, sounds and perhaps smells of any gatherings. Shut the doors, however, and the dissipation of these sensory experiences into the world of the street outside would be significantly reduced, perhaps even stopped altogether. Thus, if dining in the *atrium*, here again the *atrium-tablinum* complex demonstrates its ability to transition between 'public' and 'private' space, thereby further reaffirming its liminal status. An owner's choice to dine in the *atrium-tablinum*, with household entrance doors open or closed, might be interpreted in terms of the 'public' or 'private' image the owner wished to present to neighbours and passers-by.

Multisensory experience of 'public' activities in the Roman home: The dangers of the *salutatio*, marriage and funeral rituals in the *atrium*

The above discussion of the multisensory experience of 'private' daily domestic tasks that occurred in and around the *atrium-tablinum*, many of which were not for 'public' consumption, presents only one side of the complex's function. Formal rituals occurred in this space, including the *salutatio*, weddings and funerals. These were key events for Rome's elite as a means of parading themselves and their status to others. As a consequence of these rituals in the *atria* of Rome's elite, scholars have deemed the elite Roman house, and particularly the *atrium*, as 'a stage deliberately designed for the performance of social rituals.'[114] Rituals that occurred in the *atrium-tablinum* not only occupied the realms of personal display and political business, but often contained a strong religious dimension that further demonstrates the varying uses of this space. Given its multifunctional role, the *atrium* had an important threshold or liminal status, sitting between the 'public' and civic worlds of society and the seemingly more 'private' and domestic domain of the home, and was thereby able to fulfil duties required of both spheres.

Just as we have seen the *atrium* as a transitional zone, so too we should consider the Roman elite family itself as existing in both the public **and** private realms. In families from Rome's upper echelons, successes and celebrations brought the family into the limelight of the public arena and served to locate and cement a family's *gloria* into Rome's history. In addition to displays of military and political achievements that helped to secure renown, ceremonies relating to births, marriages and deaths equally found their way into the public realm through processions in the city streets.[115] The daily domestic chores of family life would, however, be far less likely to be visible to the public eye. As such, the domestic sphere of the Roman family was neither a purely 'private' nor a solely 'public' entity. Thus, the Roman family itself fluctuated between the 'public' realm of the city and the 'private' domain of domesticity where access to, and views of, could be enabled or prevented, whilst all the time being carefully controlled.

Not only did the elite Roman family as a whole oscillate between its position in the public eye and privacy but the place of individual family members likewise could shift regularly between the two fields. A person in the process of transferring between these two zones, from public to private or vice versa, thus found themselves also in a transitional state. The rituals of the *salutatio*, weddings and funerals provide us with excellent examples of the threshold status experienced by individuals during their lives. Whether these rituals occurred on a daily basis, like the *salutatio*, or more rarely, like weddings and funerals, they served to open the house up to the scrutiny of others beyond the household. During ceremonies, not only did the *atrium-tablinum* take on a more 'public' role, the family likewise was placed in a situation of personal and social transition. The liminal situation of both space and owner made negotiation of the circumstances, and thus control of the image being portrayed to others, difficult. As the residence owner displayed his status of *patronus* over his *clientes* during the daily *salutatio*, his persona changed from a 'private' one embedded in the workings of the house to a more 'public' one, seeking to persuade others of his wherewithal. Funerals and marriages also demarcated individual and permanent changes in social status. During the wedding ceremony, a Roman girl left behind her childhood to become a bride,[116] whilst the ritual of the funeral was a transitional process as an individual changed from a living being residing in the home, to a skeleton placed in a family tomb and a celebrated ancestor that became part of the family's history. These life and end-of-life events emphasize instances whereby the social categorization of the individual in question altered either temporarily, as in the case of the *salutatio*, or permanently, in the case of the wedding and funeral.

Moreover, the *salutatio*, wedding and funerary rituals launched the rest of the household members into the limelight, since the *atrium-tablinum* became accessible, thus making members of the household visible to visitors or *clientes* as they, too, partook in the ceremonies; particularly during weddings and funerals family members took part in elements of the ceremonies and street parades. The catapulting of the bride and her family, the corpse's relatives and, arguably to a lesser extent, the *patronus* and his household into the public eye potentially presented significant anxieties to the respective individuals, because of their changed social positions now in public view. For the deceased, change in status was naturally of no concern, but for the bride, the *patronus* or the family members who were brought to public attention there was an unfamiliar or, in the case of the *patronus*, a different status on show: in the *atrium*, in the street procession to the groom's house, to the burial or the *forum*, and finally in the *atrium* of the groom's family dwelling, at the tomb or in the *forum*.

During the wedding or funeral, families were in unaccustomed roles, although other relatives would have married or died previously. There is every likelihood that each wedding and funeral differed in some ways, just as there would also be important ways in which these ceremonies would reflect past examples.[117] The *salutatio* presented a different set of circumstances, albeit ones that posed concern to those involved. As a daily fixture in the calendar, the *salutatio* was a ritual to which those involved theoretically became accustomed. In practice, however, just as weddings and funerals would differ in terms of experiences, the same might be suggested of the *salutatio*. Aspects of wedding, funeral or *salutatio* rituals were paraded before witnesses and thus open to unpredictable and uncontrolled praise or censure from onlookers. Potential risks of these rites for negatively affecting carefully constructed images of the family were significant. The unfamiliarity of the bride to her position, for example, the ways in which the corpse might be affected by environmental factors, the possibility of unwanted smells or sounds dissipating into the *atrium-tablinum* during the *salutatio*, or the unwanted arrival of householders or family to the ritual, were all aspects that presented possible anxieties over potential damage to the family image.

Fear of disorder and possible chaos affecting those situations in the *atrium-tablinum* where Rome's elite traditionally paraded their standing to peers and rivals meant careful management was required. This was done as auditory, olfactory, visual, haptic and kinetic experiences bombarded guests and onlookers with displays of wealth and opulence. Yet, as well as providing clear symbols of prosperity, the physical experiences of visitors as they stepped into the *atrium-tablinum* during these ceremonies served another purpose, which was to control the full bodily experience of visitors. By so doing, the house owner aimed to persuade them of his high personal and familial standing in society's hierarchy.

The salutatio

Let us consider the *salutatio*, the daily ritual of reciprocity whereby *clientes* visited their *patronus* to receive *sportulae* of food or financial support. The more dependents awaiting admittance to the *atrium-tablinum*, the more it presented an important means of social display and high status of its owner to contemporaries. Numerous literary references to this ritual emphasize its importance within Roman society.[118]

> Do you behold yonder homes of the great, yonder thresholds uproarious with the brawling of those who would pay their respects? They have many an insult for you as you enter the door, and still more after you have entered. Go past the steps of rich men's houses and their lofty vestibules with their huge horde. Pass

by the steps that mount to rich men's houses, and the porches rendered hazardous by the huge throng; for there you will be standing, not merely on the edge of a precipice but also on slippery ground.[119]

Seneca emphasizes how the gathering of *clientes* outside a residence's entrance sitting on benches as they awaited the start of the *salutatio* would be a highly sensory experience for those waiting for entry, surrounded by peers and rivals.[120] Similarly for members of the household, from slaves or doorkeepers who permitted the *clientes* access to the dwelling's interior, to the owner and family and other slaves or regular household inhabitants, this was an important process whereby social hierarchies were corporeally asserted.

To gain an understanding of the physical experience of the *salutatio*, it is important to note that *clientes* were required to wear togas during the ceremony.[121] This in itself would have a significant impact upon an individual's corporeal experience of the process. Whilst no recognizable examples survive of what we would today describe as togas, making it difficult to reconstruct what they looked like, we do have literary accounts of toga wearing at the *salutatio* and in other circumstances.[122] We also have numerous depictions of men wearing the toga in statues, mosaics, frescoes and funerary reliefs. From this evidence it has been suggested that the toga measured perhaps around 10 foot in width. Made of wool, these garments were not only heavy to wear but were cumbersome to drape around the body, took considerable effort both to put on and keep in place, and restricted considerably the movement of the wearer.[123] Juvenal and Martial regale us with accounts of the physical impact of being obliged to wear such clothing. Trekking sometimes considerable distances around the city through dirt and waste to visit their patrons in their *atrium-tablinum* was uncomfortable, often resulting in clients arriving sweaty at the *salutatio*.[124] Indeed, although it would appear the material used varied between summer and winter with heavier weight wool being used in the winter, and lighter in summer, the physical exertion of walking in the toga whilst trying to keep it in place combined with the material itself would most likely result in clients perspiring uncomfortably, irrespective of the season, and would have made for an unpleasant haptic sensation.[125] The mixture of togas, their colours, quality, age and ways of wearing would provide both varied visual display and serve to demarcate hierarchical levels: poorer individuals would have struggled with the expense of the toga, keeping it clean and in good condition.[126] Likewise, the gathered crowds with relatively unclean bodies smelling of stale sweat and old, threadbare togas dirtied with mud and waste from the streets cannot have provided an agreeable olfactory experience either for those gathered at the door or a residence's inhabitants.[127] Benches and welcoming mosaics located outside residences, opulent frescoes at the mouth to the *fauces*, imposing entrance doors and grand porches would have served to accentuate yet further the social standing of the owner.[128] The full corporeal experience to be had at the threshold of the residence, then, served to emphasize the status discrepancy between all those involved.

Only those who were Roman citizens were permitted to wear the toga. All others, such as slaves and foreigners, had to wear an alternative.[129] For slaves wearing tunics, seeing *clientes* and the *patronus* wearing the formal clothing of the toga, served to highlight the status gap. The more opulent the toga and the more complicated their displayed folds and fastenings, the bigger the visual differentiation between slave and free.[130] For the *clientes* and *patronus*, the toga emphasized status, allowing *clientes* to look down on slaves but equally secured their respect for those above them in society.[131] It is, however, worth bearing in mind the ease of wearing some sort of tunic rather than a toga might have made the process of the *salutatio* a more pleasant corporeal experience for household slaves than for *clientes*.[132] Indeed, here we might also point out a further status distinction of an olfactory nature that served to emphasise the various hierarchies at play in the *salutatio*. The *patronus*, in clothes that were neither dirty nor smelly from trudging through the city's streets to the another's home, would probably smell better than a number of the *clientes* he welcomed into his dwelling. Moreover, whilst any slaves involved in this ritual were clearly dressed differently from the freeborn individuals, that they too had not had to walk through the jostling, hot and dirty city streets would perhaps also mean they provided less of a stench than some of the visitors gathered at the threshold and in the *atrium*. This in turn highlights further the wherewithal and abilities of the *patronus*, for even his slaves are demonstrably well-kept.[133]

As well as providing important olfactory, ocular and haptic experiences for many, the crowds gathered outside the residences of the elite provided additional corporeal experiences for city inhabitants, *clientes*, the *patronus* and other household members. Returning to Seneca's passage about the *salutatio*, we see the auditory impact of such groups of people as they wait for admittance. Not only would the size of the group emphasize the importance of the patron inside, but the loudness of the gathering would also act as a demonstration of his significance, both to those involved in the ritual, and also to the household. The larger the group awaiting their *sportulae*, the louder its decibel level would be, thereby ensuring further display of an owner's status by tapping into an additional bodily sensation.

Whilst texts complain about the issues relating to the *salutatio* in Rome, similar concerns about travelling around Pompeii or Herculaneum, and similar corporeal experiences of the *salutatio* would also be present there. The lack of substantial underground drainage in Pompeii, which necessitated the placement of stones across roads to help pedestrians avoid the waste that flowed through the city streets, supports the notion that walking through the streets of Pompeii would have been smelly and dirty.[134] To arrive at the *atrium-tablinum* of one's patron and mingle with numerous others who had undertaken similar journeys, among whom some (perhaps many) were unable to afford entrance fees or take the requisite time from work to bathe, would ensure pungent, unpleasant bodily smells among the crowd at the entrance. Added to this the halitosis caused by poor dental hygiene and diet, and the smells of the gathered group for the *salutatio* would impact upon those involved in the ritual.[135] For those walking around the city and not involved in *salutatio* rituals, daily gathering of crowds outside residences, sitting on benches, queuing along the pavement, perhaps spilling out into the road, would provide substantial obstructions to movement throughout the city.[136] As well as providing obstacles to movement, groups gathered for *salutationes* would have caused a visual, noisy, pungent experience for all in the city, whether or not involved in the ritual.

A further sensory experience between street and *atrium-tablinum* for consideration is that of touch. From sitting on benches outside houses to the process of stepping across the threshold and the jostling of *clientes* as they mingled in the *atrium-tablinum* in order to be received by their *patronus*, multiple sensory experiences occurred and could be manipulated in the course of vital power plays. Hartnett's examination of street benches considers the process of putting up benches outside houses as possible acts of *euergetism*, helping people to avoid the sun at the hottest part of the day.[137] As Hartnett points out, 'we see bench building as an act aimed simultaneously outward and inward: it considered the comfort of people but with an eye to how an owner might gain'.[138] Crucial to this notion of comfort provision, and what can be developed further is the question of just what the owner sought to gain. I would suggest that this was not just about treating his *clientes* or visitors well (although this certainly was part of the process). Embedded within this display of *euergetism* was a demonstration of the owner's capacity to control (either improving or not) the corporeal experience of those waiting to speak to him by providing (or not) sheltered seats.

Seneca's description of the *salutatio* presents further insight into the haptic (tactile) experiences to be had between home and street. He advises Lucilius to move past the motley gathering in order to avoid the precarious, even dangerous, moral situation in which he might place himself. This includes the haptic experience of both the 'porches rendered hazardous by the huge throng' and the physical process of stepping from a rough pavement surface across a slippery marbled threshold into the mosaic *fauces* of the Roman house. As such, haptic, together with auditory, kinetic and visual experiences of the domestic yet civic process of the *salutatio* mingle around the threshold between the world of the home and the world of the street beyond.

These multisensory experiences served to emphasize social hierarchy, to remind *clientes*, city inhabitants and visitors and household slaves, of recognized signs of wealth through displays of patronage and dependence. The daily hubbub of noise and bodily odour combined with the visual and kinetic messages of the *salutatio* both outside the dwelling and within the *atrium-tablinum* itself highlighted the patron's social dominance to all by emphasizing, via multiple senses, divisions between Rome's elite and lower classes and his ability to control the bodily experiences of those who came into contact with him for the purpose of the *salutatio*. The more he was able to control the physical experience of his visitors and household slaves, the more power he seemingly wielded. As a result, guests would have to accept display of social standing as they visited his domain, and the more widely acknowledged and accepted his status would become.

Weddings and funerals

There has been increasing research into Roman rituals of weddings and funerals, in particular focusing on the wedding as a means of parading elite status and the funeral as a way of delineating individual and collective identities.[139] Examination of aspects of the multisensory realm of these ceremonies, particularly in Graham's and Hope's funerary studies, has helped develop considerably insight into these rites of passage. It is, however, worth revisiting some of the multisensory experiences to be had within both funerals and weddings that occurred in the *atrium-tablinum* of the Roman house before moving on to examine how and why these embedded multisensory characteristics of weddings and funerals were controlled.

The wedding ritual could be divided into three sections: at the *atrium-tablinum* of the bride, the procession of the wedding party to the house of the groom, and at the *atrium-tablinum* of the groom.[140] The literary and material culture evidence concerning the ceremony of the Roman wedding has some contradictions, but what can be seen from many sources are detailed descriptions of the multisensory experiences to be had. Visually the preparation of the bride, and the wedding and its procession through the city streets from the bride's home to the groom's, were all spectacles. In particular, the bride was a sight to behold, wearing her orange-yellow *flammeum* and an ornate hairstyle, called *sex crines*, decorated with flowers and grasses.[141] Together with other sights, sounds, smells, tastes and haptic experiences, the wedding and its associated procession served as an opulent multisensory extravaganza for those involved and for mere onlookers. The wedding entailed the seeking of auspices for the future, the sounds of instruments and voices making invocations, the bride's cry, as she was physically seized from her mother, the torches which lit the way to the groom's house, the nuts thrown to onlookers for eating, and the celebratory feast when the wedding party arrived at the groom's house. All of these sensory experiences and more, accompanied the ritualized movement of the bride from her natal home through the streets to her new abode.[142]

Key to considering potential worries posed to the family by the bride was that she was the focus of the ceremony.[143] So, the experiences for the bride herself of the *sex crines* hairstyle, the orange *flammeum*, the leaving of her childhood toys at her family's *lararium*, the musicians, cheering and jibes celebrating her changing status – all provided new, possibly scary or uncomfortable sensory experiences and emotions that perhaps sought to emphasize to her specifically the importance of the event for securing the family's reputation amongst its peers. They reminded her that she was marked out from the rest and emphasized that all eyes were on her: in her father's *atrium*, during the procession and as she arrived at the groom's house. Her hairstyle, clothing and actions were judged to be a display of what she brought to the union – essentially her virginity and the promise that all offspring from her would be legitimate heirs to further her new family's name.[144] Moreover, as a bride on show she provided an example for other girls to imitate.[145] Prior to this event, however, ideally she would have led a protected existence in her father's home, surrounded and guided by female relatives, disciplined by the *paterfamilias*. Her responses throughout the ritual, particularly displays of reluctance, embarrassment,[146] fear,[147] possibly even tears,[148] served to assure witnesses of her modesty and her innocence.

> There seems to have been a grain of reality in the descriptions of lamenting brides. At whatever age a girl first married, the shock of the wedding day may have been terrible. Rich or poor, few girls would have been the centre of a very public display (and perhaps rude remarks), the end of which resulted in an abrupt separation from her family and sleeping in an unfamiliar bed, for the first time, with a man.[149]

The bride's actions presented both an example to which to aspire and evidence of her own modesty, the nature of her upbringing and the values and morals of her relatives, particularly the *paterfamilias*; hence criticism of her family, were her behaviour perceived not to be 'ideal' by onlookers, was a risk. Indeed, the entire public nature of the wedding ritual and that the celebration revolved around the transition of an inexperienced girl towards womanhood posed significant anxieties for the families concerned. Given her lack of experience of events where she was the focus of attention, being watched and judged, the possibility that her actions might engender disapproval could not be foretold with any degree of certainty. The need to control the situation and ward off unwanted criticism would surely have been significant; thus the colour of her *flammeum*, the flowers in her hair, her cry and/or tears when seized showed the control wielded by the *paterfamilias* over his family, as well as his ability to influence the experiences of onlookers and guests.

As well as the changes to the bride, and how these were perceived by others, we might also consider how the procession through the different spaces connected with the wedding ritual would also have encouraged a variety of sensory experiences for the bride and guest. These in turn would have required careful control, after all, not only was the transition of girl to bride potentially problematic but the movement of the bride from the paternal home to the groom's was likewise a required, yet risky, part of the ceremony where families opened themselves up to possible criticism from onlookers and guests.

The start of the wedding, at least for the bridal party, began in the *atrium-tablinum* of the bride's father's house and moved to its finale in the *atrium-tablinum* of the house of the groom. In essence these *atria-tablina* were the spatial representation of the respective families and as such they represented focal points of the wedding. Here, for example, family records were stored in the *tablina* and the *lararia*, with the household gods and the wax masks of ancestors, were often found displayed in the *atria*.[150] At the same time as being focal points for these rituals, where family traditions, ancestry and wealth were paraded however, these spaces were themselves also liminal zones where the bride underwent significant societal and status change as she transitioned from a girl to a woman. Not only, then, did aspects around the bride, such as her clothing and her hair, need careful regulation, but these two *atria-tablina* spaces likewise required organization on the part of the families involved.

At a superficial level, these two spaces would have had numerous similarities between each other. This in turn would have engendered recognizable physical experiences for all involved including the bride for example, the sound of rain falling into the *impluvium* in the centre of room or the smell of candles as they burned or flowers decorating the spaces. Yet for those moving between these homes, the bride in particular, the two *atria-tablina* would have also looked, smelled, sounded and felt very different from each other and these diverse corporeal experiences would have necessitated monitoring for fear of encouraging the critique of others.

The procession through the streets itself again would have encouraged very different corporeal experiences from those had in the comparatively more sheltered spaces of both *atria-tablina*. The bridal party moved from the relative 'privacy' of the paternal home, processing through 'public' streets before once again reaching the comparatively more 'private' sphere of the groom's domain. As a sphere through which the bride processed, transitioning in her status from girlhood to matronhood, the street represented an even more liminal, and dangerous, space than either of the *atria-tablina* during the wedding ritual. As such the choreography and control of various sensations in the street procession; the throwing of nuts, the lighting of torches, the singing of offensive rhymes, the visible distress of the bride and the sounds of instruments, would have been both particularly important and especially difficult to manage.

Similar points to the discussion of weddings above can be made regarding the public nature of Roman funerary ceremonies and the potential problems that the extraordinary nature of the event and its control posed for relatives, particularly the *paterfamilias*. As with the wedding, so too during the funeral the *atrium-tablinum* became a challenging space to manage as it was both a focal point and a liminal zone where the living transitioned to the dead and a family took on the status of being in mourning. Indeed for some, if the deceased was the current *paterfamilias*, his newly made replacement now tasked with charge over the family would find himself in an especially difficult and unfamiliar situation that required particular care.

Death meant a family became *familia funesta*. This status ensured that the relatives of the dead were obliged to undertake the funeral and, because of the presence of the corpse in the house, were to an extent polluted. Consequently, they were not permitted to undertake certain duties until rituals had been performed to rid the house and family of the contamination.[151] Maintaining respect for society's perception of their uncleanness was crucial but complex, since methods of dealing with the dead not only varied significantly between different families but also **within** individual families, depending on who had died. This served to ensure that each death and its associated funerary ritual could vary considerably from another, thus complicating how deaths were dealt with and meaning that a significant element of unpredictability could be associated with dealing with death in ancient Rome.

In general terms, following a death there were some conventions adhered to by most households. For members of Rome's elite at least, certain preparations were required for the corpse prior to it being laid out for display in the *atrium* of the house.[152] As mentioned earlier, one recognizable sign of a house in mourning was probably the closure of the front doors; which closed off the *atrium-tablinum* from the street outside. There is good evidence to suggest that after bereavement doors to dwellings were closed, for example Tacitus' account following the death of Germanicus:

> The announcement of his death inflamed this popular gossip to such a degree that before any edict of the magistrates, before any resolution of the senate, civic life was suspended, the courts deserted, houses closed (*clauderentur domus*). It was a town of sighs and silences, with none of the studied advertisements of sorrow.[153]

Similarly, in Ovid's *Consolation to Livia* we read about the closure of houses following the death of her son Nero Claudius Drusus. 'In uncertainty they close their houses (*clauduntque domos*) and tremble throughout the city; hither and thither they go in fear, openly and in secret they make moan.'[154]

These two extracts require closer examination in terms of the context in which the 'closure' of houses occurred and what the authors meant in terms of the multisensory, in particular the auditory, impact of closing the entrance doors of a dwelling. Of utmost significance here is that both texts recount Rome's reaction to the deaths of members of the Imperial family. These are not deaths experienced in ordinary Roman families, or even in ordinary **noble** Roman families. These deaths are unusual. As deaths of individuals from the Imperial family, the city as a whole reacts. It is the halting of all aspects of civic life in response to these deaths that is worthy of record. Both passages clearly stress the 'closure' of the city itself because of mourning. Thus, not only do houses close (*claudere*), but everything else stops. Tacitus refers to the suspension of civic life, the desertion of the courts and the silence shrouding the city, and Ovid likewise echoes this when he goes on to state, 'the Courts are silent, and the laws unchampioned are mute and still; no purple is seen in all the Forum.' ('*Iura silent mutaeque tacent sine vindice leges; Aspicitur toto purpura nulla foro*').[155] These two references to the 'closing' of houses do not specifically mention the shutting of doors *per se*, but refer to houses as a whole being closed. Whilst this would, presumably, mean entrance doors were closed to the street outside, 'closing' the house equally could be a term for suspension of typical, daily activities that were ceased at this time of civic grief.[156]

As well as 'closing' the house, implying the cessation of household chores and stopping the public activities of *atrium-tablinum*, there would, of course, be important corporeal implications behind the actual action of shutting of a dwelling's entrance doors and separating the *atrium-tablinum* from the world beyond. Whilst such an action cuts out visual access into the heart of the home, indicated in these two passages, what Tacitus and Ovid underscore is the silence ensuing from 'closing' a house in mourning. Tacitus writes of the sighs and silences of the town 'with none of the studied advertisements of sorrow' (*passim silentia et gemitus, nihil compositum in ostentationem*), while Ovid refers to the 'mute' unchampioned laws. The effect of mourning on the visual experiences of town and dwellings is unquestionable, but sight is not the only sense affected.

Lucan's *Pharsalia* presents a depiction of mourning in ancient Rome similar to those of Tacitus and Ovid, but his description of mourning benefits from analysis. Started in AD 61 and dedicated to the emperor Nero, *Pharsalia* is an epic poem narrating the civil wars between Julius Caesar and Pompey in the latter years of the Republic. The extract with which we are particularly concerned comes from the beginning of book II. Book I ended with the city of Rome in despair following ominous portents of impending disaster.[157] Book II continues to present the gods' anger at Rome, questioning the gods' reasons for giving Romans omens which warned of approaching doom.[158] In particular Lucan compares Rome's reaction to the prescient portents to that of a house in mourning.

> Therefore, when men perceived the mighty disasters which the truthfulness of the gods would cost the world, all business ceased and gloom descended on Rome. The magistrates disguised themselves in normal dress, and no purple accompanied the lictors' rods. Mourning was silent though, for a profound voiceless grief pervaded the people. Thus at the moment of death, before the corpse is laid out, the whole household is stunned and speechless, (*sic funere primo/attonitae tacuere domus*) and before the mother with dishevelled hair summons her attendants to beat their breasts with cruel hands: she still embraces the limbs stiffening with life's departure, gazes on the inanimate features, on eyes fixed in death. Apprehension she feels no longer and as yet no grief, but robbed of thought she hangs there, stunned by loss.[159]

In Lucan, there is no specific reference to the house in mourning closing its doors to the world outside. Rather, the similarity of this passage to those of Tacitus and Ovid is the distinctive effect of grief on auditory experience of the city or home. When Rome faced a situation of trepidation, perhaps from civil war or the death of a member of the Imperial family, or when a house faced a change in circumstances because of an inhabitant's demise, the immediate impact was auditory, not just visual, change. Civic activities stopped and the city anticipated its fate during civil war or after the death of a member of the Emperor's family; in other families the mother in the early stages of bereavement stands still and silent awaiting the start of very public displays of grief through wailing, breast beating and hair-pulling ('*necdum est ille dolor nec iam metus: incubat amens/miraturque malum*').[160] These three authors emphasize not just the visual impact of death, but the uneasy quiet shrouding the expectant city or house as the normal sounds of daily life, of voices chatting in houses and of laws being promulgated in the senate house and courts, are silenced and all await the commencement of the formalized grieving process.

These passages on household reactions to death in Rome present intriguing, albeit in some cases ambiguous, evidence for the closure of houses following bereavement and also comment on the multisensory impact and sensory control that such closure brings.[161] Shutting up a dwelling's front entrance will clearly block, and thus regulate, possible views into a residence from the street and *vice versa*. What is also drawn out, however, is the perceived cessation of noise that such actions encouraged and thus the ability to control the aural landscape of the home and the extent to which this could be experienced beyond the dwelling.

It is also important to remember that in addition to these references to the auditory and visual impact of closing the house in mourning, elite funerals were similarly imbued with the colour of other multisensory experiences. Aural, haptic, olfactory, gustatory, visual and kinetic characteristics of these ceremonies were manifold, and like those connected with the infrequent event of the wedding, many of the associated multisensory experiences of occasional funerals would likewise require careful management.

Just as the bride was the focus of the Roman wedding, the corpse was the focus of the Roman funeral. The physical changes the body underwent following death, however, were even more difficult to control than those perceived to be experienced by the bride as she went from girlhood to womanhood.[162] There could be very little control over the time of death and, without modern refrigeration, little ability to prevent the processes of decay that the corpse would undergo. The length of time bodies were displayed in the *atrium* varied considerably, with some sources suggesting that it could have been laid out for up to a week.[163] The closure of the door to the house at the time of mourning together with the placing of cypress trees outside the residence's entrance served not only to control auditory and visual access into the house, but also protected against the possible seepage of unwanted smells to the outside and acted as a multisensory warning that the house was now in mourning during this time of contamination. As well as offering the *paterfamilias* some ability to control the sensory experiences of his household in the surrounding environs, the closure of the door protected the rest of society from uncontrolled contact with the stigma brought about by death by providing an obvious visual, auditory, olfactory and kinetic alteration to the normal daily calendar of an elite residence's daily *salutatio*.

The impact of displaying the body on the physical experience of the *atrium-tablinum*, where the body was located, could be substantial, since bodies start to decompose immediately upon death. Cause of death and the build of the corpse were both factors that could speed up or slow down the decomposition process, while all processes of decay are quickened by hot temperatures.[164] In the height of summer in Rome, a dead body displayed in the *atrium-tablinum* for a week would probably smell considerably and the need for spices and burning incense throughout the house, especially around the body, is obvious.[165] Together with the flowers and torches that surrounded the body these also, perhaps, helped cover further unpleasant smells emanating from the decomposing body. Ancient authors revealed the need to attempt camouflage of the putrid and unsightly factors of bodily decay. Powder was applied to the face of the deceased by *pollinctores* to conceal the colour of decay, and as Lucian of Samosata, a satirist writing in the second century AD, observes, 'the corpse is next washed, anointed with the choicest unguents to arrest the progress of decay, crowned with fresh flowers, and laid out in sumptuous raiment'.[166]

The last kiss, closing of the eyes at death and transfer of the body to the ground involved haptic and kinetic bodily experiences, whilst washing, anointing, binding and dressing the corpse with flowers had the olfactory effect of trying to control and disguise the stench of rotting flesh and escaping gases as decomposition began.[167] The display of the deceased in the *atrium*, perhaps in finery, would have provided a visual spectacle to visitors and inhabitants.[168] Added to these various sensory spectacles, professional mourners could be hired to sing dirges accompanied by musical instruments, wail in grief and praise the life that had passed. Perhaps encouraged by heralds announcing the death in the streets, people would come to pay their respects.[169] The auditory and other sensory experiences of guests and onlookers would have been significant, and if we add to this the similarly numerous and varied corporeal experiences of the funerary procession to the tomb itself and the accompanying feast, we can see how the funeral as a whole became a great display of wealth and wherewithal.[170]

Actions by the possibly new *paterfamilias* to influence the corporeal experiences of the *atrium-tablinum*, its inhabitants and guests during this transitional time of mourning would demonstrate his ability to control a potentially dangerous time in the family's life which projected them all into the precariously liminal position of being part of a *familia funesta*, when the actions of all inhabitants would be closely monitored and judged by society. As weddings and the *salutatio* posed possible problems of unpredictable factors that required careful control, so too did funerals. This is less surprising than we might imagine, particularly since these rituals all took place, at least in part, in the *atrium-tablinum*, itself a space that oscillated between a 'public' sphere of display and a realm of 'private' and mundane activity. There were distinct variables for all three ceremonies that could not be predicted. Just as weddings and the *salutatio* were a means by which families and individuals presented themselves to the world and were criticized or praised by witnesses and onlookers, the same was true of funerals. Lucian emphasized that many of the activities undertaken during the funeral process were done in the full knowledge that they were not for the benefit of the body but for those watching.

> Now the afflicted senior, in delivering the tragic utterances I have suggested above, and others of the same kind, is not, as I understand it, consulting the interests of his son (who he knows will not hear him, though he shout louder than Stentor), nor yet his own; he is perfectly aware of his sentiments, and has no occasion to bellow them into his own ear. The natural conclusion is, that this tomfoolery is for the benefit of the spectators.[171]

Even at a time of personal and familial grief, an individual would be aware of potential criticisms to be faced if the funeral ceremony went wrong, even though some physical factors and experiences of these rituals were virtually unavoidable.

Conclusion

This chapter has considered the role of the *atrium-tablinum* in the Roman home as well as the bodily and kinetic experiences to be had within it. Various human and architectural impediments and a mixture of activities within served to complicate further the notion of the *atrium* as a 'public' hall constantly physically accessible and dominated by open sightlines and vistas across the space into the centre of the *domus*.[172] Rather they combine to suggest a space that could, and needed to, be carefully controlled in terms of accessibility, and its 'public' or 'private' image and roles. With this more nuanced picture of a greater mix of 'public' and 'private' activities occurring within the *atrium-tablinum* than previously imagined, the question of the physical experience of the space and the role it played in terms of personal display becomes further complicated. Even the process of walking into the *atrium* from the street outside and proceeding across it to the *tablinum* emphasizes the liminal position of this architectural complex as the journey within it moves from the public realm of the street and deeper into the more 'private' realm of the dwelling. Similarly, the further up the *fauces* and the deeper into the *atrium-tablinum* one progressed, the less impact sensory experiences from the street outside had within the dwelling and the less dissipation of sounds and smells from within the house to the street outside would occur. Indeed, corporeal experience of and relationship with surroundings, both the street outside and the rest of the house, depended on one's position within the *atrium-tablinum* complex and the closing or opening of entrance doors. The *atrium-tablinum* complex was, then, a space of great change, varied use and physical experience, and yet it was also situated in a hazardous position, given its proximity to the street.

A house's boundary with the civic world beyond is where street life and domestic life, and the inherent and multiple sensations of both, mingle. Here, multiple sensory experiences filter in from the world outside and vice versa, presenting a precarious, even dangerous, realm where the residence owner parades his ability to control his household and the environment within to the world beyond. Literary references to the impact of shutting the entrance doors upon multiple senses demonstrates the permeability of the house to its surroundings, and the problems the 'leaky' nature of the home posed for a residence owner's ability to display control over their domain. With their various entrances, windows, and the activities that went on within them, homes were unavoidably 'leaky'. Ensuring certain sounds, smells or views were filtered out or in to the home was complicated and uncertain.

As Wolf has highlighted, controlling the environment and action, or movement, of others serves to play a vital role in terms of display of personal power. What mattered for the *paterfamilias*, was the ability to manage the multiple sensory ways in which these spaces were accessed, by whom and when, and how they were experienced, both inside and out. Yet, as a space between the street and the inner confines of the home, the *atrium-tablinum* sat in a particularly precarious location precisely because its liminal positioning in the Roman house meant it presented a potentially uncontrollable space within the house for the owner. The consequence of this was that it was a space that needed careful monitoring and management, whether via opening or closing entrance doors, the existence of secondary entrance doors or the use of lengthy *fauces* or human doorkeepers. All served as a means of controlling access, as well as managing the dissipation of the multisensory experiences from activities that occurred in the *atrium-tablinum* from filtering into the world beyond and *vice versa*.

The home presented a vehicle by which Romans judged themselves and their peers highlighting the importance of getting such multisensory displays 'right', according to time, event, status and individuals involved. Management of the space, of the physical and corporeal experience within it, and of the image it presented to the world outside, was therefore crucial and explains why such care was taken by house owners to manipulate the multisensory environment in and around the entrance to their homes. The ability to distance and close off or open up the front hall of the Roman *domus* allowed the owner an element of control over the image he portrayed to the outside world. Temporally restricted activities and the presence of doors and the *fauces* served to control the image of the day-to-day house. Likewise, additional features to control physical experience when the house and its inhabitants were that much more open, accessible and on show during the rituals of the *salutatio*, weddings or funerals, served to protect further the house and the household as they themselves embarked on a journey of transition.

5

'Public' and 'Private': Multisensory Perception and the Roman *Cubiculum*

Introduction

At the far end of the terrace and portico is a garden suite of rooms, my favourite spot and well worthy of being so. I had them built myself. In this is a sunny chamber facing the terrace on one side, the sea on another, and the sun on both. There is also an apartment which looks onto the portico through folding doors and onto the sea through a window. In the middle of the wall is a neat alcove, which by means of glass windows and curtains can either be thrown into the adjoining room or be cut off from it. It holds a couch and two arm-chairs, and as you lie on the couch you have the sea at your feet, the villa at your back, and the woods at your head, and all these views may be looked at separately from each window or blended into one. Next to it is a bedroom for use at night or taking a nap, and unless the windows are open, you do not hear the sound either of your slaves talking, the murmur of the sea, or the raging of a storm; nor do you see the flashes of the lightning or know that it is day. This deep seclusion and remoteness is due to the dividing passage which separates the wall of the chamber from that of the garden, and so all sound is lost in the empty space between. A tiny heating apparatus has been fitted to the room, which, by means of a narrow trap-door, either circulates or retains the hot air as may be required. Adjoining it is an anteroom and a second bedroom built out to face the sun and catch its rays as soon as it rises, and retains them after midday although by then at an angle. When I retire to this suite, I seem to be quite away from my villa, and I find it delightful to sit there, especially during the Saturnalia, when all the rest of the house rings with the merriment and shouts of the festival-makers; for then I do not interfere with their amusements, and they do not distract me from my studies.[1]

Pliny the Younger's *Letter* to Gallus describes the *cubicula*, or bedrooms, in his Laurentine villa. Describing the corporeal experiences to be had within these spaces, Pliny emphasizes the importance for him not just of pleasant views, but that they were sensorially comfortable, particularly in terms of the quiet peace and the feeling of warmth on the skin. We must remember who Pliny was, and for whom and why he wrote. As a member of Rome's elite, Pliny wrote letters about the pleasures of his various residences throughout mainland Italy, which were an important way of extolling publicly the glories of his home, and his other successes and achievements.[2] Little is known of Gallus, who is not a regular contact within Pliny's *Letters*.[3] It might be that Pliny was introducing his dwelling to someone unfamiliar with it, yet without knowing more, we cannot confirm whether Gallus had ever visited Pliny's residence or was a regular visitor. Irrespective of who Gallus was, however, we know that Pliny wrote his letters for publication to a wider audience, not all of whom would be familiar with his villa.[4]

The quoted passage raises significant questions regarding the *cubiculum* in the Roman house. Scholars have been unable to locate Pliny's Laurentine residence, so attempts to reconstruct the dwelling must consequently remain speculative, although even without actual archaeological finds, Pliny has provided a vibrant account.[5] That account highlights the desire of Pliny to manipulate the embodied area of the *cubiculum* in terms of sights, sounds and temperatures. By closing or opening windows or doors, and through the use of furnaces, curtains and passageways which act as a sensory 'buffer' zone between spaces, Pliny could achieve the required peace and solitude from the rest of his house.

It is this question of solitude or 'privacy' in the bedroom that this chapter explores. Like Pliny, Vitruvius regarded the *cubiculum* as part of the 'private' realm of the house, 'for into the private rooms no one enters, unless invited [*nisi invitatis*], such as the bedrooms'.[6] We should compare this with the discussion in the previous chapter of the 'public' status of the *atrium*. In that chapter we considered the issues that the focus on vision in current scholarship poses in terms of enabling deeper understanding of the complex multisensory relationships that existed in the front section of the house.[7] Moving to the *cubiculum* as a 'private' space, yet one in close proximity to the 'public' areas of the *atrium* or peristyle, this chapter offers further consideration of Roman perceptions of 'public' and 'private', the relationship between such spaces within the domestic realm, and the extent to which a space's perceived 'public' or 'private' nature was impacted not just by visual relationships, but also by the interplay between multiple senses. By highlighting the broader questions of multisensory experiences in the *cubiculum* and their impact upon both the use and interpretation of a room's role, this chapter reaffirms again that the concepts of 'public' and 'private' in Roman terms did not merely revolve around the sense of sight. Other sensations, such as smells and sounds, produced within a space or leaking in from surrounding areas, influenced the perception of an area's 'public' or 'private' nature. Just as Pliny's letter reflects his desire for privacy and isolation and therefore his removal from various sensations, the manner in which corporeal experiences from within *cubicula* filtered into neighbouring spaces and how they might be manipulated to impact their diffusion beyond the bedroom helps us understand more clearly the complexities in understanding 'public' and 'private' in Roman society and the relationship between these spaces within the Roman home.

Identifying and labelling the *cubiculum* in the Roman house: Just a room for sleeping?

> Around the inner court (*cavum aedium*) the house was divided by walls, making rooms useful for different purposes: where they wished something to be stored away, they called it a *cella* 'store-room', from *celare* 'to conceal'; a *penaria* 'food-pantry', where *penus* 'food' was kept; a *cubiculum* 'sleeping-chamber', where they *cubabant* 'lay down' for rest; where they *cenabant* 'dined', they called it a *cenaculum* 'dining-room'.[8]

Just as the word *atrium* presents issues of definition, so too does *cubiculum*. Dwellings of Pompeii and Herculaneum often had numerous small and closed rooms that led off from both or one side of the *atrium*.[9] The tendency of scholars for much of the nineteenth and twentieth centuries has been to describe these rooms as *cubicula*, which according to Varro are rooms for sleeping, yet there is a problem in identifying the use of rooms adjacent to the *atrium*.[10] As Varro outlines above, rooms around the inner court are of mixed function, and might be used as bedrooms, storerooms, pantries or dining-rooms.[11] There is no further clarity in the identification or use of *cubicula* in Vitruvius, since he assigns no particular label to these spaces around the *atrium*. His only reference to *cubicula* in his description of Roman houses, as already discussed, is to state that they are spaces which people are not allowed to enter, unless if invited.[12]

Whilst the interpretation of rooms in Roman houses as having singular uses is not supported in either literary or archaeological evidence, it is nevertheless only relatively recently that scholars have begun to move away from this assumption and towards interpreting rooms as multifunctional.[13] Thus Riggsby details the various literary references to *cubicula* that outline a range of uses for this space, including sex, rest, adultery, receiving guests, displaying art and murder/suicide.[14] Similarly in her examination of the archaeological finds and fixtures of rooms/spaces in the Roman house, Allison identifies the multiple uses of many areas, including *cubicula*, which demonstrate not only evidence of sleeping in the form of bedding remains but also different types of storage and personal activities such as ablutions, ritual activity and cloth working.[15]

This flexibility of the *cubiculum* needs examination in terms of its impact on both the space itself as either 'public' or 'private' domain, and the multisensory experience of this part of the home. Not only is it important to be aware that *cubicula* had various uses aside from sleeping, but it should be noted that even the process of sleep in antiquity was not as straightforward as we sometimes understand it today. The notion, in modern Western societies, of the 'ideal' amount of uninterrupted sleep being 7–8 hours a night is a recent phenomenon.[16] Prior to the early modern era, it appears that sleep, for many Western Europeans, was divided into two main parts interspersed with a period of being awake. Textual remains provide evidence that similar sleeping patterns were followed by the Romans. Throughout the works of Roman authors, references to a first quiet (*primus quies*), first sleep (*primus somnus*) or first night (*primus nox*), suggest that night-time for Romans was likewise divided into phases of slumber and wakefulness.[17] Assuming that night time for many Romans was subdivided with people going to sleep at nightfall, waking around midnight 'for a while (perhaps an hour or two) to talk, write, do chores, have sex, and so on,' and then going back to sleep to awake at dawn, these nocturnal behaviour patterns unfamiliar to today's western societies are likely to impact upon how the *cubiculum* was perceived in antiquity compared with how it is understood today.[18] Depending on the activities which occurred during the period of wakefulness between bouts of sleep, and whether these activities remained in the bedroom, required illumination, occurred in silence or produced sound, these activities would alter the relationship of the *cubiculum*, and its inhabitants, to the rest of the dwelling.

In Quintilian's *Institutio Oratoria*, a work on the theory and practice of oratory that was published in AD 95, he advises on the importance of working at night in the bedroom with illumination from a single lamp.[19] Written at a similar time, Pliny the Younger's letters echo this idea of working at night by candlelight, for he claims both his uncle and the Emperor Vespasian would regularly work in this manner.[20] Similarly, he outlines his own daily practices whilst at his villa.[21] During summer Pliny the Younger states that he woke by the first hour of the day, and between then and the fourth or fifth hour of the day when he got out of bed, he would contemplate the work he needed to do and then dictate passages to an amanuensis.[22] Whilst we cannot be sure where in their dwellings the toil of Pliny the Elder and Vespasian took place, these examples highlight that work, particularly in the wintertime when the hours of daylight were fewer, would regularly occur during hours of darkness, thus requiring illumination, and that work, including dictation, could occur in the *cubiculum*. This is further supported by finds of possible inkwells and a bronze lampstand in house VIII.2.14–16 at Pompeii, and the excavation of a chest with wax-tablets in a room which also housed a bed and a bench from a first-floor room of the house of the Wooden *Sacellum* at Herculaneum.[23]

Together these texts and material finds serve to define the *cubiculum* as a multifunctional area where work as well as sleep was undertaken. As such, we should be aware that even during the hours of night time, when today we might expect most people to be quiet and asleep in the dark of their bedrooms, the same cannot be assumed of Romans. Depending on when people stirred from their first sleep, what they did in their waking hour(s) and where, how long they remained awake, and who else was awake at the same time, the activities in the *cubiculum*, and the individuals performing them, during night time might became more sensorially 'public' and so more complex than we might otherwise imagine. Hence it should be emphasized that whilst this chapter retains use of the term *cubiculum*, this does not assume that this space is merely used for sleeping, instead this term acknowledges flexible use both throughout day and night time.

The physical relationship between *cubicula*, *atria* and *peristylia*

Understanding the physical relationships between rooms within the Roman house requires us to think beyond two-dimensional plans of dwellings that depict open and unobstructed routes between spaces. Rather, standing in a room populated with furniture, plants, textiles, storage cupboards, lamps and people encourages different perceptions of the space and its surrounding environment. Just as Roman house floor plans rarely depict furniture and artefacts, a further absence from them is the presence of doors within thresholds. As Pliny shows, however, the ability to open up or separate and close off neighbouring spaces from each other played an integral part in how a room could be articulated and altered according to the requirements of its owner. 'In the middle of the wall is a neat alcove, which by means of glass windows and curtains can either be thrown into the adjoining room or be cut off from it'.[24] By opening or closing the folding doors of one of his *cubicula*, Pliny altered a room's ability to connect with the nearby arcade, the sea and neighbouring villas. As Pliny highlights, such actions have substantial sensory implications. Just as closing the shutters of a bedroom window blocked out views, light, noise or the heat of the sun, doors worked similarly and could also be used to impact the physical experience of a space as well as its relationship to its surroundings.

Evidence for door architecture in *cubicula* thresholds suggests that most of these rooms could be closed off from neighbouring *atria* and *peristylia*. Archaeological remains suggestive of the presence of doors are substantial. According to Taylor Lauritsen, as well as the remnants of doors, hinges, locks, handles, wooden jambs and cardines (into which pivots at the top and bottom of doors were inserted), we can also look for cuts made in thresholds to hold door architecture, including cuts for cardines and wooden jambs, holes for drop bolt bars and scratches or wearing on the doorsill plate from repeated opening and closing of doors, or stepping into rooms. He goes on to point out that, since doorjambs were often plastered or wood lined, where wooden doorjambs have degraded the gaps they leave behind end suddenly and with straight lines on either side of the doorway.[25] Thus, by examination of a room's wall painting and where it starts and ends in relation to thresholds, we can start to understand whether or not doors could be employed to close off or open up a room to neighbouring spaces.

There is a further matter regarding barriers in thresholds. Whilst doors leave remains that are relatively easy to record, less permanent or durable obstacles to movement and/or dispersal of multisensory experience were also employed between rooms. The insubstantial nature of curtains or screens is that as mobile and/or lightweight items, they often leave behind less evidence of existence: to repopulate a house with them is often contentious.[26] An instance of such barriers can be found in Pliny's letter to Gallus, where he refers to the use of curtains as well as doors between rooms.[27] One less durable means of separating spaces is the partition screen, perhaps the best known example of which was found in the house of the Partition in Herculaneum where it was used to separate the residence's *tablinum* from its *atrium* (Fig. 5.1).[28] As well as being used within wide doorways to separate spaces, such as between the *atrium–tablinum*, partitions were also employed in narrower doorways, as the find of a simple wooden partition screening off a *cubicula* in the *atrium* of the house of the Bicentenary in Herculaneum demonstrates.[29] Use of screens, fixed or mobile, to

Figure 5.1 View from the end of the *fauces* (a) across the *atrium* (b) and towards the *tablinum* (e) in the house of the Wooden Partition (Ins III, 11), Herculaneum. Note the wooden partition used to separate the *atrium* and the *tablinum*. Photo: Hannah Platts.

section off various parts of houses highlights the complexity and changeable nature of the spatial organization of rooms in dwellings.

The partitions used in ancient Rome varied in style from those that were lattice grills (similar to that from the *atrium* of the house of the Bicentenary) to those that were solid (such as the example from the house of the Wooden Partition). The type and size of screen employed determined how far its use affected the relationship between the rooms concerned, in particular the extent to which various sensory experiences could travel between them. In the same way that Pliny describes how closed doors inhibit the transmission of multiple sensory experiences between rooms, partitions act similarly to reduce the dispersal of noise and smell, and the views and movement between the spaces concerned. It is worth noting, however, that whilst when in place both solid and lattice-grill partitions will impinge upon movement between spaces, the effect of partitions with lattice grills in reducing the dispersal of other sensory experiences between rooms such as sight, smell and sound is diminished by their less solid construction. The height of a screen would also affect its impact upon multisensory experience between spaces. If it does not cover the full height of a doorway, for example the screen in the house of the Wooden Partition, it might block out views and certainly movement between rooms but sounds and smells would be less impeded.

Curtains at thresholds further complicate our understanding of possible multisensory relationships between rooms within residences. Their less durable nature means evidence is even less than that for partitions. We rely on finds of bosses, hooks or rings, and poles to suggest the use of curtains in houses.[30] Whilst the passage from Pliny highlights the use of curtains in the context of a *cubiculum*, none of the archaeological evidence so far discovered has been in the proximity of *cubicula* entrances, but rather has been connected with wider thresholds, such as that between *atrium* and *tablinum*.[31]

Allison defined *cubicula* as small and closed rooms that led off both or one side of the *atrium* and/or peristyle. Using this definition of *cubicula*, in July–August 2017 I surveyed the thresholds of these spaces in twenty-nine houses from Pompeii and Herculaneum, looking for visible evidence of door architecture.[32] Where remains of door architecture of the types identified above were found, these were noted as displaying evidence of doors that could be used to close off these small rooms from larger reception spaces and were recorded as 'Present' (see Table 1). Where remains were not seen in thresholds there were two main reasons. The first is that the state of preservation of the evidence in and around the threshold was poor and did not permit accurate assessment of the presence of doors. The second reason was that no evidence of door architecture was detected. Since it was not always possible to distinguish between these explanations, where door evidence could not be verified, such thresholds were marked as 'Unknown'.

The survey demonstrated that in thresholds situated between *cubicula* and *atria* and between *cubicula* and *peristylia*, a higher percentage of doorways had

Table 1 Presence of doors in *cubicula* leading off *atria* and *peristylia*[33]

Threshold location	Doors present	Doors unknown	Percentage of *cubicula* thresholds with doors
cubicula-atria	128	16	89
cubicula-peristylia	51	39	57

evidence of varying types of door architecture than those that did not. In the case of the doorways between *cubicula* and *atria*, an overwhelming proportion of excavated doorways (89 per cent) displayed evidence of door architecture. Between *cubicula* and *peristylia*, fewer doors were uncovered, although the 57 per cent of doorways displaying door architecture still highlights a substantial proportion of door remnants in these thresholds.

A cursory comparison between the total number of doorways around *atria* and around *peristylia* highlights a substantial difference. Around the *atria* the total number of doorways examined was 144, whilst around the *peristylia* it was 90. This discrepancy, however, is not necessarily explained by the fact that there were fewer doorways surrounding *peristylia*, but rather that some houses surveyed lacked a peristyle garden, for example the house of the Bear and the house of the Neptune Mosaic, whilst other houses boasted garden spaces that were either enclosed or lacked surrounding ambulatories from which connecting rooms might lead. Examples of these include the house of the Garden of Hercules, the house of Queen Margherita and the house of the Gem. Irrespective of this discrepancy, what is clear is that whilst doors were regularly employed to partition off *cubicula* from these larger spaces, the percentage of doors being used to provide a barrier between *atria* and *cubicula* is substantial and appears greater than the percentage use of doors in thresholds between *peristylia* and *cubicula*. This perhaps recognizes the central role of the *atrium* within the domestic rituals of wedding, funeral, assumption of manhood and *salutatio*, which meant more doors were required in this part of the house in response to the likelihood that greater numbers of people would enter here than the peristylia at the back. Doors to *cubicula* leading onto the *atrium* could be closed as and when necessary, especially during rituals in the *atrium*, thereby allowing some level of sensory privacy for any continuing activity within the *cubicula* whilst the rituals themselves occurred.

The transmission of multisensory experiences between *atrium* and *cubiculum*, and between *cubicula*

Understanding the impact of doors on multisensory relationships between spaces is complex. Whilst doors can act as a buffer for the transmission of sensory experiences and movement between spaces, the extent to which they affect relationships between rooms depends on numerous factors, including their type, thickness and material, and whether they are open, closed or ajar. With regard to types of internal doors, in general those preserved by Vesuvius are solid wooden bi- or tri-leaf panel doors (Fig. 5.2). Similarly doors depicted in wall paintings tend to be solid, for example those depicted in the *tablinum* wall paintings of the house of Marcus Lucretius Fronto, or the painted door in the entrance area to the house of Julius Polybius (Fig. 5.3).[34] Such doors when fully closed would not only completely prevent visual and physical access into or out of a *cubiculum*, they would also reduce the dispersal of smells or sounds between the spaces concerned.

Beyond the question of doors in thresholds and their impact upon the multisensory experience of one space in relation to another, we should also consider neighbouring rooms separated by walls. The sensory relationships between two neighbouring *cubicula*, and between *atrium* and *cubiculum* are likely to be substantially different. In particular, auditory relationships between the different spaces will probably vary considerably.

Let us consider the potential auditory experiences to be had between *atrium* and *cubiculum* as well as between *cubicula*. We discussed in Chapter Three the nature of sound waves and the way in which they travel losing energy, and thus decibel level, as they hit various materials. When we apply this to possible transmission of sounds from *atrium* to *cubiculum* and between neighbouring

Figure 5.2 Tri-fold doors from the villa of the Mysteries, Pompeii. Photo: Hannah Platts.

Figure 5.3 Fresco of bi-fold doors from the *tablinum* frescoes at (e) in the house of M. Lucretius Fronto (Reg IX.13.3), Pompeii. See fig 5.8 for floor plan of house of M. Lucretius Fronto. Photo: Hannah Platts.

cubicula, we can start to consider how the closing of doors and the presence of partitions between spaces might impact upon the auditory experience of the spaces. With *cubicula* doors open, sound made in the *atrium* will travel relatively unimpeded into the *cubicula* and little will be reflected back into the *atrium*. With a wooden solid panel *cubiculum* door shut, lower pitched sounds in the *atrium*, such as men talking, will be more easily absorbed than the sounds of children squealing or high-pitched musical instruments. Conversely there will be less transmission loss as the sound passes through the wood, because lower frequency sounds travel more easily through it. In terms of sounds being heard between neighbouring *cubicula* in a residence (and depending on the material of the walls in question, since concrete walls have a greater transmission loss), it would only be loud sounds (over 80 decibels) that would be heard between rooms. So the extent to which noises between *cubicula* would be heard would depend on the nature of the activity occurring in the respective rooms. We might suggest, then, that subject to the *cubiculum* doors being closed, there is the potential for some auditory transference from *atrium* into *cubiculum*. In terms of hearing activities occurring in neighbouring *cubicula*, however, it is less likely that quieter sounds will transmit between these spaces due to the denser materials through which the sounds must travel.

When considering the possible transmission of smells between the *atrium* and the *cubiculum*, not only must we bear in mind the presence and type of doors, but airflow also has a particular impact on the transmission of smell, even in relatively small spaces.[35] In the example of the *atrium* of the Roman house, not only might open entrance doors and doors between the peristyle garden, *tablinum* and *atrium* impact upon the dispersal of smell throughout the dwelling, including into *cubicula*, but the *compluvium* (hole) in the *atrium* roof will also play some part in the transmission of odours, since these openings to the outside will permit air flow through the residence.[36] Depending on wind direction or whether fans are being used, smells created in the *atrium* might travel more towards the front entrance of the dwelling, or towards the rear.[37] In contrast, given the closed nature of the *cubiculum*, smells produced there will be more likely to linger and disperse more slowly into the *atrium*, unless the door to the *cubiculum* is open and/or there is a window to the outside in the *cubiculum*, both of which will permit a through-breeze to help shift the odorous molecules.

Irrespective of whether a smell-source originates in the *atrium* or the *cubiculum*, the closure of doors in the thresholds between these spaces will provide substantial barriers to the transmission of smells, assuming the doors fill the width and height of the threshold, are solid and close completely. By comparison, the use of lattice partitions will allow permeation of smell through the holes in the grill-like structure, thereby permitting odours to diffuse in the air.[38] Similarly, doors left ajar will allow odours to permeate more easily from *atrium* into *cubiculum* or vice versa than if the door was fully closed.

Returning to our example of multisensory relationships between *atria* and *cubicula* and between *cubicula*, when considering the possible sensations transmitted between these spaces, we must review the activities we know to have occurred within these rooms, using both archaeological finds and textual evidence. Comparing the sensory experiences filtering from *cubiculum* into *atrium*, with those from *atrium* into *cubiculum*, it is probable that given the *atrium*'s ritual function and often public role, greater levels and variety of odours would diffuse from *atrium* into *cubiculum* than the other way. Before we explore what sensory experiences travelled between these spaces, a word of caution is needed regarding, in particular, archaeological remains. As discussed above and demonstrated in Allison's survey of Pompeian households, the movability and fragility of artefacts, for example lamps, candles, tables, lampstands, ink-wells, braziers, water heaters, jugs and crockery make it difficult to be sure whether items found within a space were utilized, or merely stored there.[39] These issues can impact substantially upon how we might understand the multisensory relationships between household spaces.

The previous chapter considered in depth the physical experiences of *atria*, and given the amount of activity these spaces saw, both in terms of rituals such as weddings or funerals, as well as daily undertakings of domestic life, the dispersal of corporeal experiences from here into neighbouring spaces, such as *cubicula*, was likely to be a regular occurrence. Not surprisingly, the vibrant sounds of the *atrium*, from the noises of children, the click-clack of weaving looms and the hubbub of conversation at the *salutatio*, or the smells of incense and flowers employed at rituals and the glow of lamps or sunlight through the *atrium* roof, were all likely to filter into surrounding bedrooms especially when their doors were open.

Rather more complicated to reconstruct and thus worth considering in some depth, are the possible corporeal experiences that might have filtered from *cubicula* into *atria*. Literary and archaeological remains show the regular presence of lit oil lamps and wax candles in *cubicula*. From *cubiculum* (c) in the house of the Vettii (Fig. 3.14), two bronze lamps were discovered.[40] Similarly in house VIII. 2.26, and house VIII.2.29–30 in three rooms identified as *cubicula* lighting equipment was found, whilst in house VIII. 2. 14–16, in addition to a bronze lamp stand were also excavated two small bronze vases which have been suggested to have been inkwells.[41] Literary evidence also reflects the use of lamps and other forms of lighting equipment in the *cubicula* of the Roman house. Not only have we already seen this from Quintilian's treatise on oratory, but Martial's *Epigram* 'Bedroom Lamp' [*lucerna cubicularis*] written from the point of view of a bedroom lamp, 'I am a lamp, confidante of your sweet bed. You may do whatever you will, I shall be silent' also shows the use of lamps in the bedroom.[42] Likewise in the *Metamorphoses* of Apuleius there are accounts of 'wax candles, sparkled with brilliant light and whitened the night's darkness for us', as the story's protagonist Lucius is wooed by a rich lady.[43] Assuming any windows and doors to the *cubiculum* were open or ajar, smells and light from lamps, candles or wicks would pervade surrounding spaces, and given that frescoes had wax applied to them for protection and to improve their lustre, flickering flames would also have given painted walls a shimmering quality.[44]

The scent and sight of candlelight is not the only sensory experience that might filter between bedrooms and *atria* and between *cubicula*. Evidence for the use of oils, unguents and perfumes in bedrooms can be identified in texts. From the poems of Catullus we hear of Flavius' bed 'perfumed as it is with garlands and

Syrian scent', whilst from Apuleius' account of the wooing of Lucius, not only do we read of candles which 'sparkled with brilliant light', but his paramour rubs herself with pungent balsam oil [*oleo balsamino*].[45] In the archaeology, as well as lighting apparatus being discovered in *cubiculum* (e) of the house of Trebius Valens, for example, two *unguentaria*, which could have held ointments or oils used for personal hygiene were found (Fig. 5.4).[46] Similar finds including small bottles, jars and a small amphora probably for toilette or personal cleanliness were also excavated in room (i) of the house of the Prince of Naples (Fig. 5.5).[47] In addition to the finds of unguent bottles in Roman *cubicula*, there are numerous other references to the use and production of perfumes in houses, albeit not just in *cubicula*. From *cubiculum* (e) of the Villa Farnesina at Rome is a small wall painting of a woman concentrating as she decants perfume into a small bottle, whilst in the *oecus* at (h) in the house of the Vettii are depictions of cupids making perfume at a press and a woman trying the scent being produced

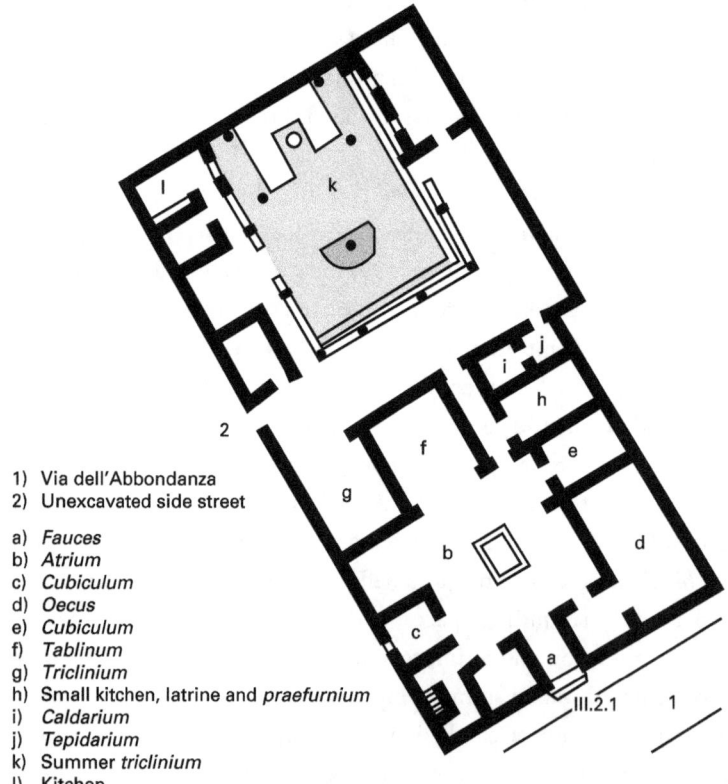

1) Via dell'Abbondanza
2) Unexcavated side street

a) *Fauces*
b) *Atrium*
c) *Cubiculum*
d) *Oecus*
e) *Cubiculum*
f) *Tablinum*
g) *Triclinium*
h) Small kitchen, latrine and *praefurnium*
i) *Caldarium*
j) *Tepidarium*
k) Summer *triclinium*
l) Kitchen

Figure 5.4 Floor plan of the house of Trebius Valens (Reg III.2.1), Pompeii. © Bloomsbury Academic.

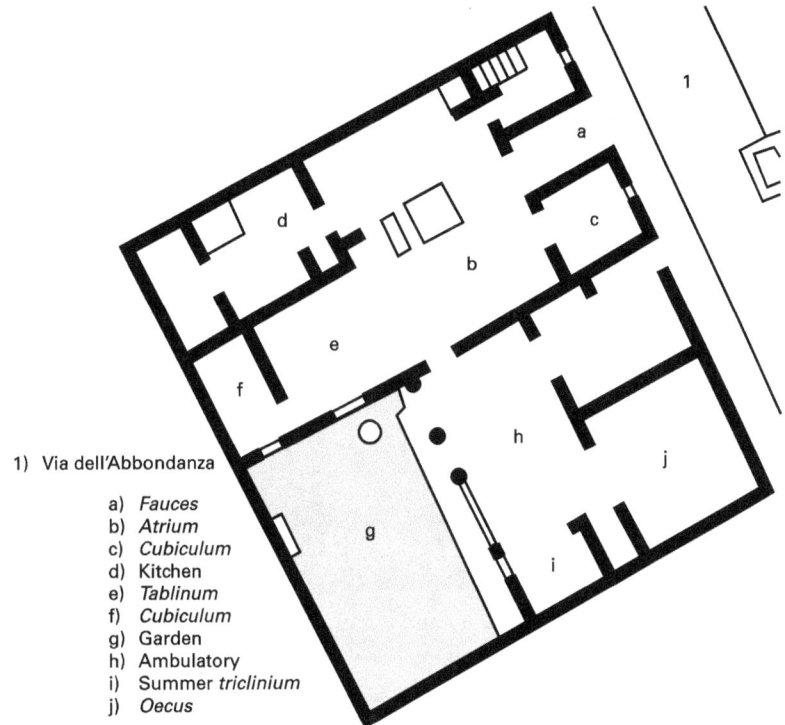

Figure 5.5 Floor plan of the house of the Prince of Naples (Reg VI.15.8), Pompeii. © Bloomsbury Academic.

(Figs 5.6 and 3.14).[48] Tombstones and epitaphs to women also regularly depicted the accoutrements of the female toilette.[49] It is possible the application of perfumes and unguents occurred behind closed doors in the bedroom, thereby reducing the extent to which the scent of perfumes or oils spilled out into surrounding spaces. Once applied and the door reopened, however, depending on the amount of perfume or scent applied to body and clothes, the more chance there was for this to waft beyond the confines of the *cubiculum* and the immediate vicinity of the person wearing it.[50] Roman writers particularly criticize those who use excessive amounts of perfume and cosmetics and spend too much time beautifying themselves.[51]

Perfumes were not the only scent that might emanate from the bedroom. Vessels for eating and drinking were also found in *cubicula* at Pompeii, and whilst some of these were, perhaps, located in *cubicula* for storage purposes, that eating also occurred on occasion in bedrooms should not be ignored. Allison's examination of Pompeian households showed that bedrooms of numerous

Figure 5.6 Fresco of cupids making and selling perfume from *oecus* at (h) in the house of the Vettii (Reg VI.15.1). © De Agostini/Archivio J. Lange/Getty Images.

dwellings when excavated housed vessels for eating and drinking and some showed evidence of cooking. The house of the Menander has a number of such examples. Room (c) has been identified as a *cubiculum* that later became a corridor and stairwell to the upstairs of the residence (Fig. 5.7).[52] Ceramic dishes, some of which displayed evidence of burning, were found here at some distance from the identified kitchen area – this has been understood to suggest that these vessels might have been used for warming and serving food, rather than cooking in ovens or on hearths.[53] Likewise, room (o), again from the same residence, has been identified as either a *cubiculum* or a storeroom.[54] Finds in this room consist of items that were possibly part of a woman's toilette, as well as a tripod, a cooking pot and two lamps. Whilst Allison is unconvinced that these latter four items for cooking were used in this room, unless the house had been divided up into smaller dwellings, this cannot be proved. A similar selection of artefacts was excavated from the house of M. Lucretius Fronto (Fig. 5.8). The mixture of finds from room (j), which included furniture, an amphora, animal bones, ceramic lamps and a stand for either a brazier or a lamp, have led to the room being interpreted as being used for either sleeping, dining or both.[55] A final example from house VI.16.26 serves to highlight the complex nature of interpreting possible activities associated with *cubicula* (Fig. 5.9). In room (d),

'Public' and 'Private' 147

Figure 5.7 Floor plan of the house of the Menander (Reg I.10.4), Pompeii. © Bloomsbury Academic.

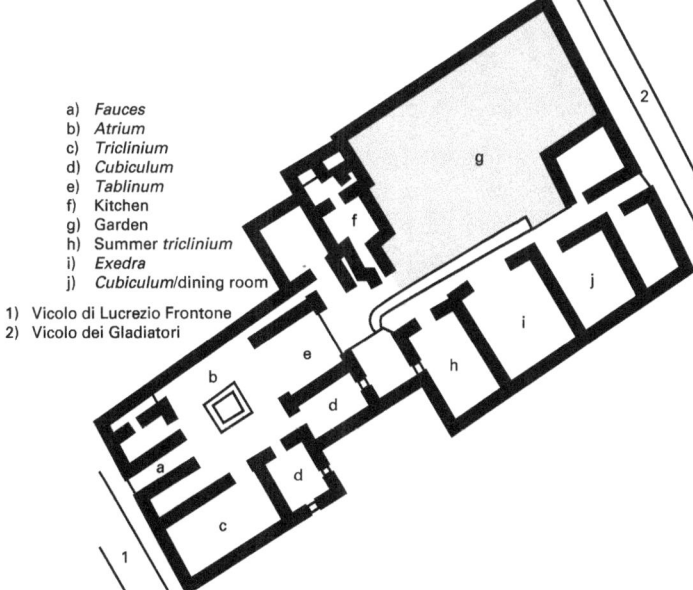

Figure 5.8 Floor plan of the house of M. Lucretius Fronto (Reg IX.13.3), Pompeii. © Bloomsbury Academic.

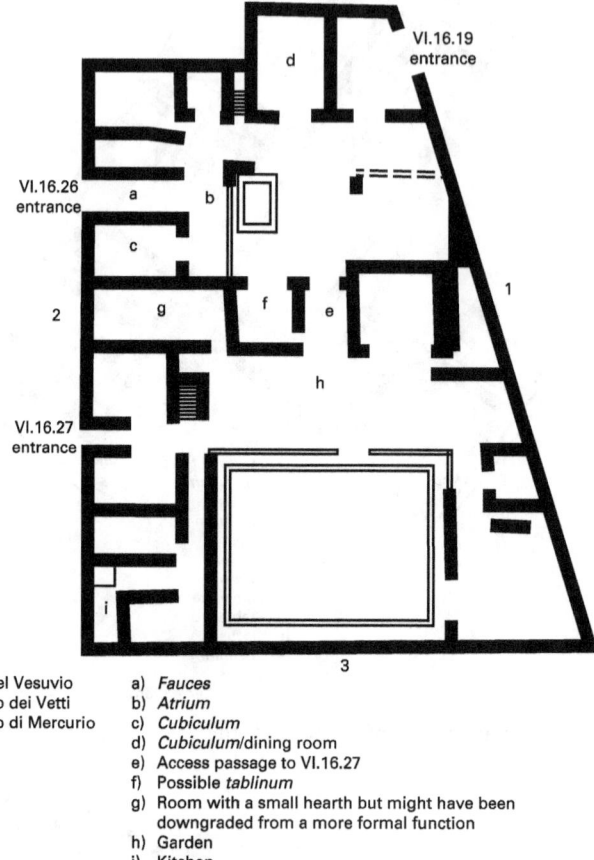

Figure 5.9 Floor plan of house VI.16.26, Pompeii. © Bloomsbury Academic.

decorated in the fourth style, the partial remains of a bed were discovered and wooden furniture together with a bronze cooking pot, a bronze *situla* (a bucket-shaped vessel with a handle) and a spherical bronze vase. The mixture of opulent décor and the finds suggesting cooking and preparing of food implies this was a space used both for sleeping and dining.[56]

This array of artefacts from *cubicula* highlights how complicated it is to delineate exactly which spaces were bedrooms and what activities occurred within them. In Pliny the Younger's Letter on his Laurentine villa, he highlights how *cubicula* might have alternative purposes when he comments: 'On the other side of the building there is ... another chamber which would serve either as a large bedroom or a moderate sized dining-room as it enjoys plenty of sunshine and an extensive sea-view'.[57] It would seem that some of the desirable criteria for bedrooms and dining rooms, at least for Pliny, are comparable, thereby perhaps explaining some of the difficulties of identification.

Activities too pose problems, in view of evidence for eating, food preparation and warming within the *cubiculum*, as well as beds and lamps. Allison comments in her analysis of the combination of finds in room (d) of house VI.16.26, 'The [room's] decoration might not seem to suit that activity [food preparation], although we may be less conversant with types of cooking areas in Pompeian houses than we believe'.[58] Indeed, if we look to literary remains, we do find some evidence of dining occurring in bedrooms. In Apuleius' *Metamorphoses*, Lucius' account of his night with Photis demonstrates that banqueting in the bedroom could occur. 'With that I left and headed for my room [*cubiculum*]. There I discovered quite elegant arrangements for a banquet ... Beside the bed stood a little table displaying some fine leftovers from supper, and generous cups already half full of poured wine awaiting a little water'.[59] Likewise in his *De Ira*, Seneca recalls an account of his friend Caelius dining in his *cubiculum* with a client, whilst in his *Consolation to Marcia* and his account of the suicide of Cordus, he refers to Cordus' retreat to his bed-chamber [*cubiculum*] 'on the pretence of having a meal there'.[60] Since portable braziers were employed regularly in *triclinia* to keep food warm for diners as we hear from Seneca, for example, it is not impossible that they might also be employed for similar purposes in the *cubiculum* when individuals wished to dine there.[61] In order to avoid problems of smoke in these confined spaces, one might imagine such *cubicula* might require either open windows or doors, which in turn would result in the spread of warm food smells dispersing further throughout the dwelling.

As well as possible olfactory experiences from *cubicula* of warming food, oil lamps and perfumes and the visual impact of light pervading both *atria* and neighbouring *cubicula*, we should not forget the potential auditory sensations that might filter from the *cubicula* into surrounding spaces. This would occur particularly if bedroom doors were left open or ajar, which at least on occasion they were, if only to allow a through-flow of air.[62] Auditory interruptions outside residences which reached into the *cubiculum* regularly occurred, according to literary sources. Martial, for example, bemoans the problems of the passing crowd and noisy school teachers disturbing his sleep.[63] Within the home, too, we should also be aware of sounds from the bedroom being heard in the vicinity. Thus Apuleius' protagonist, Lucius, in the *Metamorphoses* recounts the miller's wife shouting from the bedroom before dawn for him to be whipped, whilst elsewhere he refers to the 'nocturnal chatters' [*nocturni gannitus*] of his night with Photis.[64]

This examination of the multisensory relationships between *atrium* and *cubiculum* is not meant to be comprehensive, but provides examples of possible experiences and affecting factors. A similar investigation of the multisensory situation between peristyle and *cubiculum* would provide different conclusions, particularly in terms of the transmission of smell and sound as the spaces in which they occur are dissimilar: the more open nature of the peristyle would certainly impact upon transmission of sounds and smells generated. Equally, given the survey results indicating fewer doors in the peristyle spaces of the *domus*, there would also be an effect upon how sounds and smells travel into the *cubicula* and indeed dispersal from *cubicula* into peristyle.

The impact of multisensory experience on 'public' or 'private' relationships between the *atrium* and *cubiculum*

Vitruvius lists the *cubiculum* as being in the 'private' section of houses, whilst the *atrium* he presents as being 'public'.[65] As considered throughout this book, the terms 'public' and 'private' are complicated particularly since their meanings today differ from those of antiquity. Just as we have seen the relative location of one room to another within the house has an impact upon the perception of a space as 'public' or 'private', we have also seen additionally that the interpretation of a space as 'public' or 'private' varies according to the activity occurring in the room. A further layer of interpretation to the terms 'public' and 'private' might be added: not just the position of a room or space in the dwelling, but also the extent to which levels of sensory and physical accessibility into a space from outside might affect how far it is perceived to be 'public' or 'private'. We have already seen how levels of sensory and physical access from the street into the house might have had an impact upon the 'public' role of the *atrium*, as well as how such access might be reduced by doors and other partitions. Similar questions may also be raised regarding the opportunity for physical and multisensory access to the *cubiculum* from the *atrium* and peristyle, and the impact this might have had upon the 'public' or 'private' roles of these spaces.

In Riggsby's detailed examination of the roles of 'public' and 'private' in Roman culture, he explores the relationship between *atrium* and *cubiculum*.

> the characteristic location of *cubicula* seems to have been immediately off the *atrium* and/or peristyle. Even *cubicula* which did not open directly onto one of these large halls often belonged to small suites which themselves opened onto those same spaces. Large open halls allow for panoptic surveillance of all the

attached small rooms ... They are arranged so as to constrain the effects of the secrecy they produce and hence to reduce their power as sites of resistance to behavioural norms.[66]

Riggsby's suggestion that earmarking specific locations for every behaviour enables a society to judge the activities of its inhabitants without the need to impose a set principled stance on what is or is not acceptable, which in any event could not be enforced, is not doubted.[67] What is problematic, however, is his overriding emphasis upon the role of sight and vision in Roman perceptions of 'public' and 'private' space. Given the examination above of the role of doors between *atria* and *cubicula* as a multisensory barrier between these spaces, his focus on vision when he comments that 'large open halls allow for panoptic surveillance of all the attached small rooms' becomes difficult to uphold. When a barrier, such as a door, is placed within a threshold between rooms, questions of public and private, of sensory and physical access become contentious and Riggsby's hypothesis that the *atrium* works as a means for 'panoptic surveillance' fails.

By closing a door, pulling across a partition or drawing a curtain, to varying extents 'panoptic' surveillance of these smaller spaces becomes difficult. Petronius' description of the actions Quartilla needed to undertake in order to watch a young couple in the bedroom highlights well just how difficult the presence of doors made attempts at voyeurism. 'And so, when they lay there, the door locked, we stood at the chamber threshold, and Quartilla, first naughtily opening a crack in the wood, diligently applied an inquisitive eye to watching their childish passions.'[68] Through the introduction of these barriers at thresholds, the organization and use of the space becomes more complicated since they are no longer permanently open for complete viewing. Similarly, recent developments in viewshed analysis demonstrate that whilst a door might be open, the location of the viewer outside the room and the width of the door through which the view is taken affects how much of the room can be seen.[69] Even with the door open and depending on threshold size and the size and layout of the room in question, one might still be able to hide from surveillance in the room's corners.

We should also bear in mind the role of light in illuminating activities and making them visible. Trying to understand the role of lighting in houses from Pompeii or Herculaneum is difficult today since, as a result of the destruction of upper floors, ceilings, walls, curtains and doors, the remains of residences are generally more open to natural light than they would have been when inhabited; accordingly visitors receive an unrealistic impression of the extent of illumination in these dwellings.

Taking advantage of natural light where possible, at least for certain activities such as weaving, must have been imperative.[70] Whilst lamps of clay and bronze, lamp-stands and candle holders are prolific throughout Pompeii, as Allison's survey of the finds from the *Insula* of the Menander shows, the remains excavated do not even amount to one lamp per room.[71] The consequence of this, as Allison points out, must be that 'buildings must have been poorly lit after dark, with lamps used only in certain parts of the house, as required.'[72] When considering the provision of light in *cubicula*, even with possible small high-up windows in the exterior walls to provide some lighting and airflow or the presence of small windows above thresholds to provide clerestory lighting into the chamber, much of the provision of light into *cubicula* would come from the entrance.[73] Even during daylight hours then, as a consequence of the 'closed' nature of *cubicula*, activities in these rooms must have been in relative darkness, at least in comparison to those in the brightly lit neighbouring spaces of *atrium* or peristyle.

As we have seen, darkness did not mean inactivity in Roman houses, since access to artificial lighting would have enabled activities to continue within a household long after sunset and in rooms without access to much natural light in daytime. It is worth noting, however, that lit lamps were rarely left unattended in rooms but would move with the individual using them, as is suggested by the distribution of lamps in the *Insula* of the Menander.[74] At night, then, without lamps permanently lighting rooms, views into them must have been virtually impossible. Indeed, even with a lamp carried into a *cubiculum* by an individual, the view into the room and clear sight of any activity being undertaken, would have been restricted since the light given by a single-wicked lamp would have been weak and the room, with relatively little ventilation from windows, would have been made darker, by smoke and shadow.[75] Significant contrasts between light and dark causes problems for vision. As Boman points out

> In a room with few light sources (window and door openings or artificial light equipment), the light sources will appear in sharp contrast to the dark surroundings. If the eye is directed straight into the unprotected flame or bright light, the dazzling effect is prominent; the area around the light source appears to be in darkness. This illustrates that, if the light source is too bright in contrast to the surroundings (*dominance of luminance*) the areas around will appear darker.[76]

According to Boman various architectural and decorative methods were undertaken in the Roman home to reduce the dazzling effect of light sources in otherwise dark rooms, thereby creating ambient lighting and visual comfort. These included splaying windows and placing them at a high level in the room to increase the light falling into the room from outside, and the use of wax in wall painting, which would help to reflect light in several places across a wall. These numerous reflections reduced the contrast between the light of the flame and the darkness of the room.[77] Yet whilst Boman's discussion of manipulation of light and shadow in the Roman house is plausible in daytime, where there is more natural light available for use, and indeed for people **within** a room at night-time where they can see the flickering light of candles on the waxed walls, how successful such artifices might be in eliminating contrast between light and dark for someone looking from **outside** into a dim candlelit room and onto the activities within is questionable. Ellis's discussion of lighting and the presence of darkness in the Roman home remains pertinent:

> Romans did not have our concept of 'blanket' lighting. This is primarily a result of the limitations of their artificial light. In modern times we suffer from the fluorescent 'tube' light, which from one source 'floods' the room with a uniform level of lighting. This 'flooding' of a room was not available from the low strength of Roman lights. The way that the Romans also controlled natural light suggests that they did not wish to 'flood' a room with daylight either.
>
> If this is the case it is interesting to reverse the picture and ask about darkness rather than light ... perhaps darkness was seen as the norm. This could lead to the idea that darkness, or shadow, was desirable in some places in the house.[78]

Lighting in Roman houses together with the presence of doors, partitions and curtains at the entrances to many *cubicula*, particularly those leading off the *atrium*, further raises questions as to the 'public' or 'private' nature of these spaces and the extent to which they really could be subject to surveillance at all times. Doors, partitions and curtains could be employed to restrict multisensory and physical access to these spaces. With the entrance to a *cubiculum* open at night-time, the dim glow of a candle might demonstrate a *cubiculum* to be in use, but how far the activity being undertaken could be clearly seen by those outside is questionable. As such, the limited nature of Roman lighting further enabled levels of 'privacy' in the *cubiculum*.

The ability to close doors, or pull partitions or curtains across thresholds, however, does not just impact upon the visual relationship between spaces. Such barriers also affect the transmission of other sensory experiences between rooms and can serve to limit awareness of activities occurring within the spaces in question. To close the door leading from the *cubiculum* into the *atrium* may help prevent conversations being overheard or prevent olfactory intrusions from rituals spreading from one space into another.

Literary evidence supports this notion that 'privacy' is not just about withdrawing from certain eyes.[79] Rather, to achieve 'privacy' and isolation one must also seek freedom from other corporeal experiences, such as sound and smell, as well as sight. We saw above references to the use of oils, unguents and perfumes in bedrooms. The examples of Flavius' perfumed bed and the balsam oil in Apulieus highlight the use of oils and scents particularly in pursuit of sexual gratification. Whilst perfume was used on a daily basis it was regularly associated with sexual liaisons within literature.[80] This, in turn, implies such activities would probably occur behind closed doors, thus preventing dispersal of odour from the erotic use of oils or perfume into surrounding spaces. This allowed a further level of sensory privacy particularly around sexual activity within the bedroom. Indeed, both Apuleius and Catullus suggest an element of desire for distance from their surroundings by the parties involved. The four eunuchs belonging to Lucius' lover 'did not delay their mistress's pleasure by their continued presence, but closed the bedroom door and went away',[81] whilst Catullus criticizes Flavius specifically because Flavius wishes to keep quiet about his sexual conquests.[82]

Sensory withdrawal, and the inherent privacy this brings, is likewise sought through quiet. In Quintilian's reference to working by lamplight in his *cubiculum* discussed above, what is of particular significance is his emphasis on the importance of silence whilst working.[83]

> The mind cannot honestly devote its whole attention to several things at once; and in whatever direction it looks, it ceases to have its eye on its appointed work ... Demosthenes had a better idea: he used to hide away in a place where no sound could be heard and no prospect seen, for fear that his eye might force his mind to wander. So, when we work by lamplight, let the silence of the night, the closed room [*cubiculum*], and the single lamp keep us on our toes ... working by lamplight, when we come to it fresh and rested, gives the best kind of privacy.[84]

Just as we saw at the start of this chapter that Pliny desired relief from the multiple sensory experiences of his slaves enjoying the Saturnalia, or from the sounds and sights of a storm so too for Quintilian, working in a closed bedroom by the light of a single lamp ensured freedom, and therefore privacy, from both auditory and visual stimuli that might otherwise distract him from his work.[85] It would seem then that Roman notions of privacy were not just about the avoidance of being seen and withdrawal from visual stimuli, but also entailed avoidance of other sensory experiences such as smells and sounds.

Conclusion

As we have seen, notions of 'private' and 'public' space in the Roman home are complicated and the applicability of these terms to various places, such as the *cubiculum*, at different times depending on location and activity emphasizes this. Additionally, however, when we consider the built environment of the Roman home, and the varying hierarchies of 'public' and 'private' space within it, we must also consider levels of access, both physical and multisensory, to understand the full fluidity of these terms. Rooms are not just seen: they are smelt, they are heard, they are felt. By permitting or preventing various modes of physical and sensory access through the closing or opening of partitions, I argue that a room's multisensory relationship with neighbouring spaces becomes increasingly 'private' or 'public' thereby changing the role or function of the space.

It is this flexibility of the multisensory relationships between spaces that highlights the importance of examining not just two-dimensional plans of buildings, which often lack detailed information on the remains of fixtures and fittings such as doors and partitions. As soon as we start to think about the Roman house as more than a two-dimensional floor plan and consider it populated by people, furniture, artefacts and doors, the theory of the *atrium* working as a space of 'panoptic surveillance' over smaller satellite rooms, such as *cubicula*, becomes increasingly problematic. Not only does this notion over-emphasize the role of vision whilst ignoring other forms of sensory interaction between rooms, but the presence of barriers and the capability to close them across thresholds equally undermines the ability to monitor activities and allows for considerably more multisensory 'privacy' than one might initially imagine.

6

Beyond Taste: The Multisensory Experience of Roman Dining in the Domestic Sphere

Introduction: Dinner with Domitian

[O]n another occasion he (Domitian) entertained the foremost men among the senators and knights in the following fashion. He prepared a room that was pitch black on every side [οἶκον μελάντατον ἀπανταχόθεν], ceiling, walls and floor, and had made ready bare couches of the same colour resting on the uncovered floor; then he invited in his guests alone at night without their attendants. And first he set beside each of them a slab shaped like a gravestone, bearing the guest's name and also a small lamp, such as hang in tombs. Next comely naked boys, likewise painted black, entered like phantoms, and after encircling the guests in an awe-inspiring dance took up their stations at their feet. After this all the things that are commonly offered at the sacrifices to departed spirits were likewise set before the guests, all of them black and in dishes of a similar colour. Consequently, every single one of the guests feared and trembled and was kept in constant expectation of having his throat cut the next moment, the more so as on the part of everybody but Domitian there was dead silence, as if they were already in the realms of the dead, and the emperor himself conversed only upon topics relating to death and slaughter.[1]

On a recent visit to *Dans Le Noir*, a restaurant in Clerkenwell where diners are served in total darkness by waiters and waitresses who are visually impaired, unable to see anything before me and reaching out gingerly for my cutlery and my glass, relying on the sense of touch, rather than sight, I found myself considering Cassius Dio's account of Domitian's 'black' dinner.[2]

My experience of 'dining in the dark' was quite different from that of Domitian's guests. Dio's description of the event presents a chilling account of what could happen when you dined with an emperor. These were senators who were invited to Domitian's palace and forced to feast silently in a darkened room seated on couches shrouded in black, surrounded by tombstones, served black food by slaves painted black while the emperor discussed topics of death. As Cassius Dio comments, this was 'the triumphal celebration, or as the crowd put it, such was the funeral banquet that Domitian held for those who had died in Dacia and in Rome'.[3]

At *Dans Le Noir*, the situation was quite different. Service was welcoming, the food was fabulous and all diners were helped throughout the meal as they felt and fumbled their way around their plates and glasses. The dining experience encourages a complete re-evaluation of the senses.[4] It was, however, disconcerting. Without the help of servers throughout the dinner to direct me how to find my cutlery, to teach me how to top up my glass (and how not to overfill it when you cannot see!), even to guide me to the toilet, the experience would, at the very least, have been challenging. Beyond the ability to choose from either a vegetarian, fish, meat or 'chef's surprise' menu, I had no idea what food I was being served – I could only guess by taste.[5] Neither had I any clue about what the room looked like or those serving me or indeed who else, apart from my husband, was sitting with me on our 'sharing' table. The manipulation of my physical experience of dining in unknown surroundings and my reliance on others throughout the dinner highlighted the impact that control over, and the ability to alter, multisensory experience can have upon an individual. I had chosen this, potentially unnerving, experience specifically because it challenged my understanding of the corporeal world around me. Domitian's diners had no such choice and whilst they were not dining in pitch dark as I had been, what they saw, together with their other sensory experiences, was unexpected and made each guest scared and 'in constant expectation of having his throat cut'.[6]

Contrast Dio's dining anecdote with those *Silvae* from Statius that record his gratitude, again to Domitian, for invitations to feasts.

> Let Saturn join me free of his chains and wine-soaked December and laughing Humour and wanton Jest, as I tell of merry Caesar's joyous day and the tipsy feast. Scarce had Aurora brought another dawn and already dainties rained down—such the dew that rising East Wind poured down: Whichever are the best of Pontic nuts, and dates from Idume's fertile hills, and plums pious Damascus grows upon her boughs and figs Ebusos and Caunos ripen—free of charge the lavish loot descends.[7]

Here we read of vibrant dining, of plentiful, colourful food and wine from all over the Roman Empire and of the noise of people dining and enjoying themselves.[8] Purple plums and figs are served, and later in the poem Statius regales his readers with accounts of other foods such as spiced cakes.[9] In further contrast to Dio's story of dining with death, Statius later records the manner in which Domitian organized lighting for the festivities once the sun had set.

> Here's the only licence Caesar banned: Scarcely had darkness cloaked the world when a flaming ball rose from the centre of the arena shining in the dense gloom, surpassing the light of the Cretan crown. The sky was bright with flames, allowing no license to night's dark shadows. At the sight of it, lazy Rest and Sleep must take off for other cities.[10]

The differences in sensory experience between these feasting events are extreme. Whilst one relays the opulence and extravagance of a public Saturnalian banquet with the emperor, bathed in light and noise with assortments of food, people and entertainment, the other depicts an ominous private dinner where sensory experiences are constrained, shrouded in shadows and quiet. There remain, however, substantial similarities between these episodes, which require careful examination in terms of how multisensory manipulation provides a means for display of standing.

The two accounts were written over a century apart by men from very different backgrounds, whose agendas are embedded within their texts. It is important to note that although Dio wrote in Greek over a century after the death of Domitian, his depiction of dining with the emperor and the fear instilled in those involved substantially reflects other portrayals of life under Domitian.[11] Relatively little is known about Statius. Born in Naples to a family of relatively low social standing, in his early years as a poet he was awarded the gold crown from Domitian at the Alban poetic contest and moved to Rome where he forged connections among Rome's aristocratic and Imperial court circles.[12] Such associations with Rome's elite, together with the fact he was invited to Domitian's public Saturnalian feast, would explain Statius' lavish praise of life under the Emperor, in contrast to the generally negative depictions of other elite sources. Yet, just as Whitby suggests, panegyric could celebrate and praise at the same time as giving criticism and advice, Statius's *Silvae*, including *Silvae* I.6, can be read as offering both ebullient and vibrant hyperbolic praise of a god-like emperor, and subtle expressions of concern about Domitian's powers and the potential threats they pose.[13]

Given the particular situations in which Statius and Cassius Dio were writing – one during the reign of Domitian and the other long after his assassination and ensuing *damnatio memoriae* – both accounts of dining with the emperor raise questions of reliability. Yet, the two anecdotes serve to emphasize the importance to dining of multisensory experience and sensory manipulation and the role this played not just in demarcating social status, but in emphasizing the ability to control the corporeal experience of others in order to make them feel unnerved, fearful and isolated, or socially integrated and relaxed.[14] Embedded in both accounts is the dominant picture of sensory control of others.

Whilst Statius' portrayal shows generosity through taste, smell, sound, sight and touch in the abundant gifts of food and wine, warmth and light, noise and vibrant colours, it also emphasizes Domitian's controlling orchestration of a scene in which he dictates everything, including time, the calendar and meteorological conditions.[15] Darkness is overcome by use of artificial light and Domitian's largesse of gifts rains down from the heavens onto the diners.[16] These bodily pleasures given by the emperor to his subjects display his power over others in a variety of ways. On a basic level, the provision of such gifts of corporeal delight tie his subjects to him.[17] We see from Statius' encomiastic praise ('They raise countless voices to the stars, sounding the Emperor's Saturnalia, and acclaim him Lord in loving favor.') the emphasis upon loyalty that Domitian's patronage demands.[18] The provision of such multisensory experiences to his people, however, can be read as a rather more complex display of Imperial power for they serve to emphasize Domitian's control over his subjects' physical experiences. As well as dominating their bodily experiences of eating, drinking and intercourse through the delicacies of food and wine that flow freely for all, Domitian also dictates what they see, hear and feel throughout their whole bodies.[19] He permits them to feel warmth from artificial light on their skin, to taste ripe dates, plums and figs, to munch on pastries and drink mellow wine. He allows them to see and feel the excitement of entertainment from fighting women and dwarves.[20] The performance of this Saturnalian feast, then, is not merely about the spectacle of gift-giving and patronage as a means of showing status and commanding loyalty. Rather, through such displays, Domitian demonstrates his ability to dominate the whole panoply of the corporeal reactions of his audience to his largesse. It is the total submission of one's full body experience to an emperor's whim that, where Statius offers praise, also underpins expressions of concern about Domitian's reign.[21]

Statius also acknowledges the Emperor's command over an event that drew different levels of society together to feast under his auspices.

> Freedom has relaxed reverence. Why, you yourself (which of the gods could thus invite, which accept invitation?) entered the feast along with us. Now everyone, be he rich or poor, boasts of dining with the leader.[22]

Domitian's capabilities extend not just to dominating people's physical experiences, but by drawing everyone together he can dissolve society's boundaries. All Romans, irrespective of status, sit and feast as one, united under his leadership. Different social levels become obsolete, as the only important differentiation to be made is between ruler and ruled. Whether senator or plebeian, all are subordinate to Domitian in the guise of Jupiter. He is 'Jove' who 'sends us downpours' of gifts.[23] Essentially, individual standing, wealth and social roles are reduced merely to being under Domitian's control and experiences happen at the emperor's behest. Perceived delineations that separate or group individuals together become irrelevant, for all are now reduced to Imperial subjects and all experience the same events according to the emperor's wishes.

The subsuming of recognized social hierarchies and complete control over corporeal experience of surroundings and situation also underpins Dio's anecdote of the 'black dinner' with Domitian. Whilst those involved here were elite, their standing as senators or knights (γερουσίας καὶ τῶν ἱππέων) did not protect them from suffering the indignities and fear of dining in the dark, sensorially dominated by the emperor. Once again, the emperor's control over their bodily experiences – what they tasted, saw, heard, touched and smelt – served to emphasize their insignificance when compared with him. Indeed, should he see fit, their entire existence could be stopped, and they would have no ability to prevent it. The emperor had the wherewithal to control, and indeed end, all physical experiences irrespective of the status of his subject.

In both accounts there is no detailed description of Domitian, apart from reference to his talk of death at the 'black dinner'. He is not the visible focus of proceedings. The concern of both Dio and Statius is to depict Domitian as a shadowy figure who controls all aspects of the diners' experiences, whether good or bad. His power is emphasized by these authors not via an appearance of Imperial authority through clothing, wreaths and other recognized accoutrements of status. Rather Dio and Statius concentrate on Domitian's ability to command all aspects of every individual's corporeal experience, whilst he himself remains in the background. Domitian's ability to control the physical experience of others emphasized his superior power and undermined existing social hierarchies thereby removing individual feelings of belonging and group identity. Whilst such demonstrations might be used for festivities and enjoyment, the emphasis on corporeal experiences being at the behest of another has the ability to disconcert and engender fear and anxiety irrespective of the nature of the event in question.

These stories of dining with the emperor provide extreme examples of the multisensory nature of the Roman dinner experience and the dining room and how these could be manipulated by hosts. As we will see in the remainder of this chapter, however, other literary and archaeological examples of dinner parties and dining spaces demonstrate similar desires to control the corporeal sensations of both guests and the slaves who serve them, albeit on less excessive scales. It will be argued that through control over the bodily experiences of dinner guests, the owners of residences, as hosts of the meal, sought to display overriding capacity to regulate and influence every aspect of their visitors' experiences, from what they heard and saw to what they felt and tasted. No bodily experience was left unaffected. Importantly as we shall also see, this was not without risk of failure particularly when a successful dinner party relied on careful choreography either of guests or attending slaves, both of which could go disastrously wrong, thereby resulting in possible ridicule and the undermining of an owner's display of personal power.

Defining and identifying domestic dining areas

The last thirty years have seen much scholarly interest in the important social and cultural roles that convivial dining played in the Roman world, particularly in terms of social relationships and the symbolic role of food.[24] An important aspect of research has been to identify spaces potentially used for dining from both literary descriptions and archaeological remains. Defining clearly the terms used for dining rooms in Roman literature is complex, since as Foss points out there is an inherent 'linguistic plasticity' behind the terms used.[25] Not only are some spaces for dining used in a variety of ways, but individual rooms may be referred to by more than one term. This can be seen in the *Epistles* of Pliny the Younger where he refers to his dining room, which overlooks the sea as being both a *cenatio* and a *triclinium*.[26] As Foss explains,

> *Cenatio* is the more general term which refers only to function of the room, and the activity of eating that defines that function. A *triclinium*, however, implies the furnishing of three couches. In first century A.D. literature, all *triclinia* are *cenationes*, but not all *cenationes* are *triclinia*. Clearly, terminology for rooms of a house was not indelibly fixed, but rather overlapped.[27]

The words typically used by modern scholars to denote Roman spaces for dining are *triclinium*, *oecus* or *exedra* and *cenaculum*. Of these, *triclinium* was used most commonly in ancient literature to identify dining areas.[28] By the second century BC the term could refer to either the three couches used in the dining room or the room itself.[29] The term *oecus* is rather less used in Latin, mostly appearing in Vitruvius' comparison of Greek and Roman houses where he comments that in Greek housing dining occurs in the *oeci*.[30] In his stipulation of specific architectural aspects of Roman houses Vitruvius does outline, however, that, if used, *oeci* are larger spaces than *triclinia*.[31] In terms of the word *cenaculum*, the earliest reference to it comes from a fragment of Ennius, which is recorded and explained in the second century AD by the Christian apologist Tertullian.[32] Contemporaneous with Ennius is Plautus' reference to these rooms as being in the upper floor of houses.[33] Following this and evidence from Varro, modern scholars have generally understood that the *cenaculum* was situated upstairs.[34] Due to the specific difficulties of understanding the fragmentary remains of the upper floors of dwellings, and the focus of this book on the downstairs parts of the Roman house, examples of the *cenaculum* are not considered here.

The difficulties with clearly defining dining rooms linguistically are echoed in problems faced trying to identify them in material remains. In terms of archaeological identification of ground floor dining areas, Allison highlights three spaces that have typically been understood as having been used for eating, namely 'rooms off the corners of front halls', 'rooms off gardens or terraces without good views' and 'rooms off gardens or terraces with windows or wide entranceways giving views of gardens or lower floors'.[35] Generally scholars have identified the first two types of area as *triclinia*.[36] These room types have been further defined by scholars who have classified the first as winter dining rooms (*triclinium hibernum*) and the second as summer *triclinia*.[37] According to Allison these architectural subdivisions have stemmed from ancient authors identifying winter *triclinia* and advising different dining areas according to the season.[38] Examples of the third type of space have variously been labelled *oeci*, *exedrae*, and sometimes *triclinia*.[39] These spaces differ from 'the rooms off the front halls' and 'gardens or terraces without views' as they are usually larger and more open.[40]

Whilst typically the spaces outlined above have been labelled as having a dining room function, Leach argues that in fact *triclinia* had neither specific structural forms nor fixed locations in the Roman house.[41] Rooms with squarer measurements labelled as *oeci* by modern scholars have been found in Pompeii, Herculaneum and Rome.[42] Whether these would have been labelled as *oeci* by their owners, given the relatively rare use of the term in literature, however, is perhaps open to question.[43]

A further significant problem in identifying dining spaces is that clear identification of rooms for dining is only possible when excavation of fixtures or fittings provides evidence – these might include masonry couches and floor mosaics.[44] Moreover, as with other rooms in houses, artefact distribution remains a contentious means of identifying room use.[45] As Allison has demonstrated in many houses of Pompeii and Herculaneum, finds including braziers, couch remains and crockery in rooms and *peristylia* complicate our understanding of where food consumption might have occurred, and emphasize the likelihood that rooms and spaces in many dwellings were utilized in a variety of ways.[46] A good example of this problem is evident from the room traditionally known as the *tablinum* (f) from the house of the Menander (Fig. 5.7). The finds of couches probably used for either reclining or eating, suggest this room might have been employed for food consumption, whilst the finds of a marble table and folding stools in the western side of the peristyle garden again indicate eating in this part of the house.[47] Additionally, braziers found in the peristyle (h) of this house might have been employed to keep dishes warm, boil water or provide warmth, and also suggest the possible complexities of classifying dining spaces in houses.[48]

Whilst décor presents a possible way of identifying dining rooms, Foss states that couches present the only secure way of defining them, although very few wooden examples exist today.[49] As Allison has pointed out, couches can also have uses other than dining (such as sleeping) and thus we should be aware that although their presence might suggest food consumption occurring in the room, other activities might also take place.[50] In this chapter, classification of dining rooms (*triclinia*, *biclinia*, *oeci*) stems from traditional interpretations from excavation reports of finds and décor and explores evidence for sensory manipulation when or if a space is used as a dining area. Spaces might have alternative or additional uses, or their uses might have changed over time, but for the purpose of this part of the chapter, which explores an approach to interpretation of manipulation of multisensory experience in dining spaces, this is of less concern.[51] Given the difficulty in locating and defining dining rooms in Roman houses, the examples focused on in the rest of this chapter are from inside houses and from gardens and have been securely identified from excavated remains.[52]

Enargeia and the *convivium*: The multisensory dinner in text and archaeology

For most within Roman society, communal dining occurred in a variety of settings and on differing occasions. From the feasts that followed weddings and funerals, to public and domestic banquets associated with Roman festivals such as Saturnalia, the *convivium* was a deeply embedded feature of Roman social and cultural life.[53] Written evidence of communal dining in the Roman world is plentiful and varied. In Pliny's *Epistles*, Martial's *Epigrams*, Juvenal's *Satires* and Dio's *Roman History*, we read colourful accounts of dinner party experiences, whilst from *Apicius* we gain an insight into gustatory experiences of the Roman banquet.

It is important to remember that all these literary dinner descriptions have a male focus, the authors generally being men of elite standing.[54] Much of our written evidence for Roman dinners can be divided into accounts where in-depth descriptions of food are left out or minimized, or those which revel in detailed descriptions of the opulent (or disgusting) food being served.[55] Given these contrasting portrayals of either highly extravagant or meagre dinners, it is important to bear in mind the messages or social commentary that writers were trying to get across to their audiences.

The extent to which texts recount standard daily meals in a Roman household is questionable. Horace's descriptions, for example, of his meal of oil-cake, chickpeas and leeks served in cheap Campanian-ware vessels, and dinners of the simple fare of Lucrine oysters, turbot or scar fish, or of kid or pullet followed by figs, raisins and nuts, seek specifically to emphasize the frugality of his repast to readers.[56] Similarly, Suetonius relays Augustus' meagre fare, and from Juvenal we learn of the farm-reared kid served alongside wild asparagus, eggs, pears and apples.[57] In contrast to these simple meals, we also read of tables over-loaded with pickled fish, meats, turnips, lamprey and prawns, cranes' legs and fattened goose liver,[58] or dormice sprinkled with poppy-seeds and honey served with sausages, damson plums and pomegranate seeds.[59] Such descriptions either of excess or paucity in relation to food at the dinner table served to reflect the mix of Rome's past and present together; Horace paraded adherence to rustic customs and simple repasts and harked back to the traditions of Rome's early years as a small hill-top settlement, while others, like the representation of Trimalchio, sought to display access to the urbane culture of Rome's burgeoning Empire. As Gowers points out, 'Rome was large enough to allow images of simple and luxurious eating to coexist.'[60] As we see so clearly from Horace's satirical critique of those who favour gourmet food such as peacock over simpler repasts such as pullet, how an author chose to write about food was often laden with comment on social or individual gluttony or self-control.[61]

One particularly intriguing collection of textual sources that gives a more nuanced insight into Roman communal dining practices and their spaces is the

Colloquia. The *Colloquia* are part of a substantially larger collection of bilingual teaching materials known as the *Hermeneumata Pseudodositheana* written for those learning Latin and Greek. Originally made up of two separate parts that were later amalgamated, it is the second section with which we are particularly concerned, since this details some of the activities an adult might undertake across the day and evening.[62] Dated to the second century AD, the adult section of the *Colloquia* comes from the eastern half of the empire and was composed in order to help Greek speakers to learn Latin.[63] Yet, although written by and for those living in the Greek-speaking east of the Empire, significantly they recount daily life in the Latin West, giving insight into how to borrow money, a visit to the baths, going shopping and, importantly for us, preparing for lunches and dinners. As such, these texts are not dissimilar to 'modern foreign-language textbooks which reflect the culture of the language being taught rather than that of its learners.'[64] Their role as Latin language learning tools means they are not without problems for scholars trying to use them as sources for Roman life. Their composite nature means that some individual scenes are probably the result of a number of similar events combined and described. Likewise, their use as teaching aids perhaps means extra vocabulary is listed in order to teach more words to students rather than reflecting exactly what might occur at any particular scene.[65] They are, however, less likely to pose concerns about moralizing than other literary sources on food and dining; as such, they present an alternative written insight into Roman dining experiences that we can use. In the following paragraphs, all these disparate sources will be drawn together.

Starting first with literary accounts of the *convivium*, let us explore the multisensory experience of dining in the Roman world. Visual aspects of the Roman dinner party have been well established in scholarship, and Jones and D'Arms have examined the theatricality of its entertainment and representation in literary accounts of feasts.[66] The rich ocular aspects of the *convivium* are often understood as encapsulated by the word *enargeia*, a term employed in rhetorical handbooks to refer to 'the means or strategy by which the art of bringing a described object to the mind's eye is effected.'[67] In essence, *enargeia* refers to the 'vividness' of a description and an author's ability 'to involve the audience emotionally, to seduce them, to stimulate the imagination (*phantasia*) of readers or listeners in such a way that they see the object before their inner eye as if it were right in front of them physically'.[68] Since *enargeia*, or the vividness of written or spoken depictions, was not just used for objects, but was also employed to bring to life accounts of people, places and events, the application of the term by D'Arms to the colourful descriptions of the *convivium* is unsurprising.[69] In his use of *enargeia* to explain the vibrant portrayals of the Roman dinner party, however, D'Arms focuses mainly upon the visual aspects of these displays whilst brushing over other important sensory experiences to be had at the *convivium*.[70] Yet, whilst ancient sources often emphasize visual descriptions within their explanations of *enargeia*, the importance of drawing on other senses to develop a reader's or listener's mental image of objects, people or events and to draw them in emotionally is also understood.[71]

The specific words often employed to describe such feasts unquestionably show the importance of visual experience, but also that of other senses. According to D'Arms, terms such as *spectabilis, speciosus, mirari, mirabilis* and *ostentus* emphasize the visual aspects of Roman dining.[72] Certainly *spectabilis* and *speciosus* translate generally to mean 'that may be seen, visible' or 'worth seeing' and 'good-looking, showy, handsome, beautiful, splendid, brilliant' respectively and therefore emphasize the importance of sight in the opulent banquets they describe.[73] Closer examination of some of the other terms often used to describe Roman banquets, however, show that vision was not the only sense emphasized or drawn on in literary accounts of feasts and the spaces in which they occurred. Instead, much of the language used to describe banquets and dining rooms drew upon multiple sensory experiences and often can be understood as emphasizing not just visual exhibitions but other forms of sensory engagement. Whilst the terms *mirari, mirabilis* and *ostentus*, for example, can refer to sight, this is not the only way they might be interpreted. *Mirabilis* and *miror* come from the verb *mirari* meaning to wonder, marvel, be astonished, be amazed or admire.[74] As such they are regularly applied to describe other sensory experiences including sound and speech, for example Vergil's phrase '*mirabile dictum truditur e sicco radix oleagina lingo*' when he discusses Nature in the *Georgics*. Here, as well as referring to the wondrous sight of the olive tree growing roots from where it has been cut, he specifically refers to speech and sound in his phrase '*mirabile dictu*' (wonderful to relate).[75] Similarly whilst *ostentatio*, meaning 'a showing, exhibition or display', has visual connotations, it is also a term that can be used to highlight other sensory references, particularly that of sound.[76] In his account of Nero's behaviour at the funeral of Claudius, Suetonius writes, 'Then beginning with a display of filial piety he gave Claudius a magnificent funeral, spoke his eulogy, and deified him'.[77] The pious display here encompasses the senses of sight and sound in the form of the funeral and the eulogy. Likewise, from Cicero's *Ad Herrenium* again the term *ostentatione* is employed with reference to sound, this time in his criticism of boastful speech 'Such is the character of the man that what he effects by empty boasting and showing-off [*gloria atque ostentatione*] in one day I could hardly recount if I talked a whole year.'[78]

It is not just the broader sensory emphasis behind many of these terms that suggests a possible manipulation of the human sensorium as a whole when at the *convivium*. When combined with detailed authors' descriptions of the somatic experiences occurring, the varied and numerous references to bodily immersion at the Roman dinner party emphasize both the importance of multisensory experiences of dining and the broader ways in which the term *enargeia* might be applied to ancient literary evidence. By considering the multiple sensory aspects embedded in the word *enargeia*, and not only focusing on its ocular connotations, this will allow us to comprehend more fully the importance of the 'vividness' of descriptions of the Roman banquet.

Having explored already some of the dining events of Domitian, let us consider another example of a Roman *convivium*, this time from Martial, describing the highly opulent dinner party of Zoilus, a freedman who had climbed the social ranks to become an equestrian.[79]

> Up for an evening with Zoilus? ... He flops in his green suit on a crowded couch, elbowing his neighbours on each side, and props himself up on purple coverlets and little silk cushions. A strapping young fellow stands at attention and passes him red feathers and mastic-wood toothpicks when he belches, and a jumped-up concubine wafts a cool breeze at him with a leek-green fan when he starts sweating; a boy shoos the flies away with a switch of myrtle. A masseuse works him over with quick, skilled moves, pattering her trained hands over every part of his body; a eunuch notes when he snaps his fingers and teases out the shy urine, steering his tipsy penis even as their master continues drinking.
>
> He himself, meanwhile, twists round towards the crowd at his feet; surrounded by lapdogs that are licking at goose-livers, he portions out goujons of boar to his wrestling-coaches and treats his boy-toy to the rumps of turtle-doves. While *we* are served up the rocks of Liguria or unaged wines scorched in the smoke-rooms of Marseilles, *he* toasts his home-born slaves with Opimian nectar served in crystal and murine glasses. His own complexion is darkened out of Cosmus' little bottles, but he doesn't blush as he issues us – from a gilded murex-shell! – the hair-oil of a slutty pauper. Then, wasted from all those half-pints of wine, he starts snoring; and we lie there on our couches, under orders to hush when he snorts, and toast each other with nods of the head. That's the kind of ill-treatment we put up with from the vicious bastard, and we can't pay him back, Rufus: he *likes* the taste of cock.[80]

Although far removed from Domitian's status of emperor, there are distinct similarities between how dinner with Zoilus and dinner with Domitian are portrayed. As with the accounts of dining with Domitian, the multisensory experiences of eating with Zoilus are manifold. From the descriptions of vibrant colours and soft fabrics to the cool crystal or myrrhine glasses of wine and the opulent morsels of food served, the sounds of slaves being summoned by the clicking of fingers and the contrasting haptic sensations of warm bodies being cooled by fans, no physical experience has been neglected. Smells of meats and wine blend with the scents of the unguents with which Zoilus drenches himself or gives to his guests and the pine-like aroma of the mastic-wood tooth picks. Bodily motion as well as physical sensations are likewise described. Zoilus elbowing his guests on the couch, the movement of slaves as they fan hot bodies, scare away flies and help the inebriated Zoilus urinate into a pot.

In a similar way to Domitian's control of his diner's full bodily experience, Zoilus too is concerned with controlling the sensory realms of his guests. From what they smell and hear to what they taste, touch and see, their entire sensory-scape of the events of *convivium* and the space of the *triclinium* itself is controlled by the directions and actions of their host, even when he passes out in a drunken stupor. Once again, however, it is not merely the owner's control over the corporeal experiences of his guests that is crucial here; rather, both hosts use bodily sensations as a means to undermine or (re)order social hierarchies.[81] Just as dining with Domitian dissolved the boundaries of the social spectrum, so that those under him were brought together with the same experiences irrespective of status, Zoilus too used bodily sensations to play with, and indeed assert, a social standing to his diners that he saw fit. Thus, he gave his 'home-born slaves', 'wrestling-coaches' and young boyfriend the finest foods, wines and scents, whilst the rest of his diners suffered the indignities of poorer quality fare. Controlling what guests ate, drank, felt, smelt, saw and where they sat at a *convivium*, then, presented a variety of ways in which one could parade control over one's guests.[82] Not only was it a way by which the full bodily experience of others was organized, but the physical experience that the *convivium* provided afforded a means to demonstrate social status and one's own personal domination over and (re)interpretation of society's hierarchies, giving an individual the power to undermine rivals or promote friends through the full corporeal experience of dining. Of course, whilst Zoilus displays astonishing vulgarity, Domitian represents absolute superiority. Both are (potentially) awful, but it is only Domitian who has control over the diner's life.

It was not just the activity of specific feasts themselves that our sources describe using multisensory terminology. Literary portrayals of the dining rooms for such parties and the general corporeal experiences that could be had by those when dining within them are likewise imbued with bodily sensations. Pliny's accounts of the famous plane trees of Lycia and Velletri, that were used as dining places, are filled with descriptions that demonstrate how these spaces impacted the entire bodily experience of those within them.[83] The Lycian plane tree, located by a cool spring with soft moss covered pumice-stones and branches that formed a shady grove, provided both a leafy dining room for eighteen and a sheltered space for sleeping, away from wind but where one could still hear the sounds of the falling rain. Likewise, Caligula's dining room in a tree could house fifteen as well as their slaves in shade on benches formed from its branches. Both depictions demonstrate particular emphasis on multiple sensations beyond that of sight. In this vein, we might also explore the potential somatic experiences that diners might have in Domitian's dining room called 'The Crumb'.

> I am called 'the Crumb.' You see what I am, a small dining hall. From me (see!) you look out on the dome of the Caesars. Pound the couches, call for wine, take roses, soak in nard. The god himself bids you remember death.
>
> '*Mica vocor: quid sim cernis, cenatio parva: ex me Caesareum prospicis ecce tholum. frange toros, pete vina, rosas cape, tinguere nardo: ipse iubet mortis te meminisse deus.*'[84]

Whilst Martial is not recounting a particular dining event in this epigram, the possible experiences to be had in Domitian's 'Crumb' are again multisensory. There are three references to vision in this epigram: '*cernis*', '*prospicis*' and '*ecce*', which clearly suggest the role of sight in the emperor's dining room.[85] Yet sight is not the only sense explored: there are also three words that suggest the importance of noise in this room, either in the form of speech or sound from hitting an object: '*vocor*', '*frange*' and '*pete*'. In addition, words reflecting olfaction, '*rosas*' (roses) and '*nardo*' (a perfumed oil), and taste, '*vina*' (wine) similarly draw on other aspects of the bodily experience of dining.

Further descriptions that give insight into corporeal experience of unspecified dinner parties and lunches can be found in vignettes from the *Colloquia of the Hermeneumata Pseudodositheana*. Not only are the scenes which portray banquets filled with descriptions of the sensations to be had, but those which explain preparation processes of the dinner or lunch party are particularly pertinent when thinking about how Romans sought to manipulate multisensory experience in dining areas, especially during the *convivium* and other such events.

A passage in the *Colloquium Celtis*, which uses a scene of preparing for a dinner party as a tool for language teaching, is worth quoting in depth.

> Set out a kettle and lots of pots, make dinner, put coals in the dining room brazier, sweep the house, bring water. Set up the couch and put the coverings on it. Open up the store-room and bring out wine, oil, fish-sauce, and beer; for spices pepper, silphium juice, cumin, mixed spices, salt; onion and garlic, cabbages and leeks, beet greens and mallows, eggs and asparagus, nuts and beans, plums and pears, fruits and lupins, artichokes and hyacinth bulbs, radishes and turnips, salad and salted fish, rice and barley-gruel, porridge and peas, beans; vinegar and unmixed wine, fish and gourds, a bit of pork and of suckling pig, salted meat, a little bit of bacon, little fruits, sea-kales, a jug full of absinth-flavoured wine, and another jug of spiced wine. Bring out cups, a bowl, and a candlestick; decorate the three-legged table, sprinkle flowers in the dining room, put out coals and incense, have everything ready. Tell the other servants that they should make tasty foods, since my guests are distinguished men and foreigners.[86]

Here we read of the desire of the house owner to provide a sensory experience worthy of distinguished visitors. Whilst not all of the foods listed necessarily came from a single dinner party, it is likely that such foods typically featured on dinner party menus.[87] Not only does this text probably reflect some of the gustatory experiences of the 'typical' Roman dinner party, but the references to other olfactory, tactile, haptic and visual experiences are also likely to echo those regularly had at the *convivium*.

By examining feasts and dining as a multisensory experience, then, we are starting to develop an understanding of their role in the Roman world. Rather than perceiving dining events as mere visual shows through which elite Romans exhibited standing, authorial use of oratorical techniques of *enargeia* that draw on multiple sensory and emotive experiences shows these eating events to be multisensory displays. The language of feasting was not only visual. It was fully corporeal and drew in readers or listeners through embodied descriptions that allowed them to imagine themselves taking part and ensured the recognized role of dining as a vehicle through which Romans paraded standing to others.

This full body experience of dining is likewise echoed when we explore the material remains of the *triclinium*. When we look beyond written descriptions of the foods consumed and accounts of the spaces where this occurred to the material remnants surrounding feasts, including silverware, frescoed depictions of banquets and architecture or furniture, we observe further evidence for the multisensory experience of communal dining in the Roman world. Although such remains often continue to skew our understanding of dining in ancient Rome towards the behaviour of the wealthier members of Roman society, at the very least it helps develop further insight into the mechanics and social significance of communal dining beyond merely the role and perception of what authors choose to describe.

Just as the account of dining with Zoilus refers to the covers draped over the couches, which would have given both a tactile and visual experience, the *Colloquium Celtis* also refers to the process of dressing the furniture of the *triclinium* in readiness for the diners. Whilst remains of cloth surviving from antiquity are unsurprisingly scarce, we can look to numerous wall paintings depicting the *convivium* which confirm the decorating of the *triclinium* and blanketing of furniture in fabrics to provide a softer and more cushioned tactile sensation for guests. A fresco from the *triclinium* of the house of the Chaste Lovers (Fig. 3.17) depicts an outdoor banqueting scene with diners reclining on couches shrouded with textiles and cushions which both brighten up the stone or wooden benches with cloths in vibrant patterns and make reclining for eating a physically easier experience (Fig. 6.1).[88] Similar depictions of cloth covered couches can be seen in the fresco of an indoor banquet from the house of the Triclinium (Fig. 6.2) and from Herculaneum (Fig. 6.3).[89] Significantly such evidence for covered couches contrasts sharply to depictions from Domitian's black dinner, where diners were forced to recline on bare, black couches, thereby making the experience both physically uncomfortable and visually ominous. Both cases demonstrate contrasting ways by which the guests' experience of a dinner party might be manipulated by owners in order to demonstrate dominion over the sensory environment of others.

As well as fabrics affecting a visitor's sense of touch, artificial cooling or warming of a room via fans or braziers could improve the physical experience of guests as they dined, or, as with Zoilus being fanned by a concubine whilst fellow diners watched, might be used to demonstrate a guest's inability to secure sensory comfort thereby emphasizing their subservient role. We have already heard above from Seneca and Suetonius that lit braziers were regularly moved to warm up rooms in houses, including the *triclinium*, and this is echoed in the extract from the *Colloquium Celtis*, as well as in finds of portable braziers found throughout the houses of Pompeii and Herculaneum.[90] Indeed, the extent to which hosts sought to impact the haptic experiences of the Roman dinner can be seen in attempts either to cool down or warm up drinks using either ice and snow or heaters respectively. Whilst Seneca criticizes the decadence of such fashions, we can see evidence of them being employed in both the literary and

Beyond Taste 173

Figure 6.1 Fresco of an outdoor banquet from the *triclinium* (f) of the house of the Chaste Lovers (Reg IX.12.6), Pompeii. Naples, Museo Nazionale 9015. © DEA/A. DAGLI ORTI/Contributor/Getty Images.

Figure 6.2 Fresco of an indoor banquet from the house of the *Triclinium* (Reg V. 2.4.), Pompeii. Naples, Museo Nazionale 120029. © DEA/A. DAGLI ORTI/Getty Images.

Figure 6.3 Fresco of a banquet between a young man and *hetaera* from Herculaneum. Naples, Museo Nazionale inv. 9024. © AGB Photo Library/Alamy Stock Photo.

archaeological record. Another fresco of a banqueting scene, this time from the north wall of the *triclinium* of the house of the Chaste Lovers has been understood to show an example of the cooling of wine with snow melt that Seneca so despised.[91] Finds of the remains of water heaters (*authepsa*) and food heaters from Pompeii and throughout the Empire suggest a desire on occasion to warm liquids or food at the table before serving (Fig. 6.5).[92]

A banquet also provided a means by which a house owner could influence and manipulate guests' auditory experiences. From the noise of musicians, actors, comedians, dancers and other entertainment, or even from drunken guests as they sang and laughed together to the sounds of clinking goblets and the pouring of wine, auditory sensations could be brought to diners by the foresight, abilities and wealth of the owner.[93] We might compare such scenes of boisterous revelling with those constructed by Domitian and Zoilus above. In both these examples, the host controlled the noise of his guests, either through fear and by dominating the topics under discussion, as with Domitian, or through sleep and being ordered to be silent by attendants, as is the case at Zoilus' dinner. Both examples highlight that whilst entertainment such as musicians provided one means of displaying wealth and status, alternative ways of manipulating the soundscape of guests could equally offer a means to exhibit power and the ability to control the sensations of others.

Whilst archaeological evidence for dinner party entertainment in the form of dancers, comedians and actors might be difficult to find in the Roman home, some artefacts from residences have been found to demonstrate the presence of music and gaming which might provide some evidence of entertainments provided at the *convivium*. Those items connected with gaming comprise items such as knucklebones, dice, and counters, whilst those associated with music seem to include parts for wind instruments and cymbals.[94] Finds related to these activities are often located around the front part of dwellings, or in storage areas. One such example comes from room (m) of the house of the Vettii (Fig. 3.14) where the remains of a silvered bone mouthpiece, probably from a flute, was excavated. The accompanying finds of a horse skeleton, the remains of a bronze basin and bronze furniture handles from this area suggest that this room in the house was employed for storage, thus undermining any notion that the flute would have been regularly used in this space but was probably employed elsewhere in the dwelling.[95] Similarly the remains of gaming counters and stones found in a chest on the north-east corner of the east wall of the *atrium* of the house of the Cabinet Maker, and a partial bronze musical instrument from a chest situated in the same room emphasize that many items employed in leisure activities of gaming and music making were probably stored there when not in use (Fig. 6.4).[96] Indeed, whilst the discovery of gaming counters inside a jug stored in a cupboard in the ambulatory (i) of the house of the Cabinet Maker near the entrance of the *triclinium* (h) might reflect that gaming took place in the spaces nearby (e.g. in the *triclinium*, the ambulatory or the garden), again they might also have been placed in the jug in the cupboard merely for ease of storage, thus making it difficult to be certain where in the house these items were used. What is important to bear in mind, however, is that whilst we cannot be sure that such items were used at the *convivium* and in the spaces associated with it, the finds of musical instruments among such artefacts in combination with literary references to such dinner party activities supports the notion that the auditory experiences of dinner guests would regularly be manipulated by owners in a variety of ways.

Yet, perhaps a more surprising means by which a house owner might seek to manipulate the sensory experiences of diners was via the olfactory realm. Comparisons between the descriptions of dining with Zoilus, the *Colloquium Celtis* and Martial's *Epigram* from Domitian's banqueting hall called the 'Crumb' demonstrate similar uses of unguents, incense, and roses and flower petals during the *convivium*. Indeed the use of perfume at dinner parties was a well-attested phenomenon from as early as Plautus.[97] Whether perfumes would have

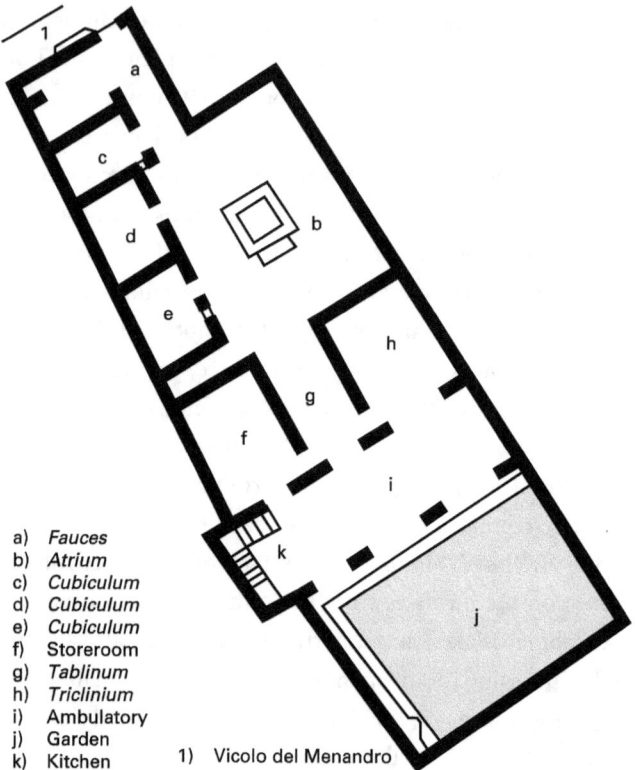

Figure 6.4 Floor plan of the house of the Cabinet Maker (Reg I.10.7), Pompeii. © Bloomsbury Academic.

blocked out all other olfactory experiences is debatable, however the use of unguents or perfumes by diners together with the scent from candles or oil lamps, incense or perfume burners, braziers brought in to heat the room and warm food would have ensured the dining room was filled with a multitude of odours (Fig. 6.5).[98] These in turn would have combined, serving to disguise unwanted smells emanating either from guests as they reclined in close proximity, such as body odour or halitosis, or from the bodily excretions from diners as they gorged on food and wine. Zoilus' dinner party, for example, describes an overindulged Zoilus urinating and vomiting, which is similarly reflected in visual depictions of the *convivium*. Thus, from an indoor banquet scene painted in the house of the *Triclinium* comes the depiction of a slave supporting an inebriated, vomiting guest whilst the banquet continues around them (Fig. 6.2). Indeed, it was not just the mingling of unpleasant reeking bodies and their emissions that owners perhaps sought to camouflage. Rather, as Potter points out, the importance of not smelling the food that was going to be served before

Figure 6.5 Food warmer from the house of the Four Styles (Reg I.8.17), Pompeii. Naples, Museo Nazionale 6798. © DEA/L. PEDICINI/Contributor/Getty Images.

it arrived was key, 'steps were taken to ensure that people would not necessarily know what was coming next'.[99] The use of pungent oils and scents, candles and incense gave dinner party hosts the ability to impact the odours experienced by diners as they mingled, camouflaging those which were unpleasant or which needed to be kept hidden in order to retain the element of surprise for guests was, it would seem, as vital as providing impressive gustatory sensations.

Dining in or near the garden

People used to eat in winter by the hearth, in summer out-of-doors.[100]

The excavation and study of buildings, monuments and artefacts from the Roman world has dominated much of the research into this period, however the last century has seen increasing scholarly attention on Roman gardens. In particular, Jashemski's pioneering archaeological excavations of gardens from Pompeii, Herculaneum and other parts of the Bay of Naples destroyed by Vesuvius have significantly developed our insight into a variety of these spaces.[101] Investigating tree root cavities, pollen samples, carbonized remains, soil contours, furniture, sculpture and fountains in the gardens, together with literary descriptions of the extravagant gardens of men such as Lucius Lucullus and Nero and paintings from residences such as Livia's villa at Primaporta near Rome and the house of the Golden Bracelet at Pompeii, has enabled scholars to recover and understand how gardens were structured and planted, and the ways they might have been used.[102]

In Pompeii and Herculaneum, not all dwellings had gardens and not all gardens were associated with houses. Where there were gardens they were used for various functions, for example in religious activities, cultivation of produce, weaving and spinning and as a play area for children.[103] All of these activities will have had an impact upon the multisensory experience of the garden at a variety of times throughout the day and night, for example the sound of the loom weights and voices chatting as women and, occasionally, men wove cloth either in the portico of a peristyle garden or in the garden itself, combining with the sound of splashing water from fountains, the warmth of the sun or the cool of the evening breeze on the skin and the smell of the flowers, trees or shrubs growing nearby.[104] Just as weaving and children playing did not only occur within the walls of the house, the same is also true of dining, as we can see from the fragment of Varro cited above, and the practice of dining outside arguably presents one of the most complex and layered multisensory experiences associated with the domestic realm. As such rather than focus on gardens and their multisensory experiences as a whole, the rest of this chapter explores gardens which display evidence of dining, either within or overlooking them, in the form of summer *triclinia*.[105]

Throughout Pompeii and Herculaneum there are numerous summer *triclinia* either in rooms or structures overlooking gardens. As such whilst they can take advantage of possible shelter from the elements afforded by their walls, ceilings and doors or curtains across thresholds, they also benefit to an extent from the sensory experiences provided by proximity to the outside, such as the cool summer evening breeze on the skin, wafting the scent of flowers, herbs and shrubs into the dining room.

A particularly good example of a residence with summer dining rooms that take advantage of shelter provided by the house's own structure and yet also have

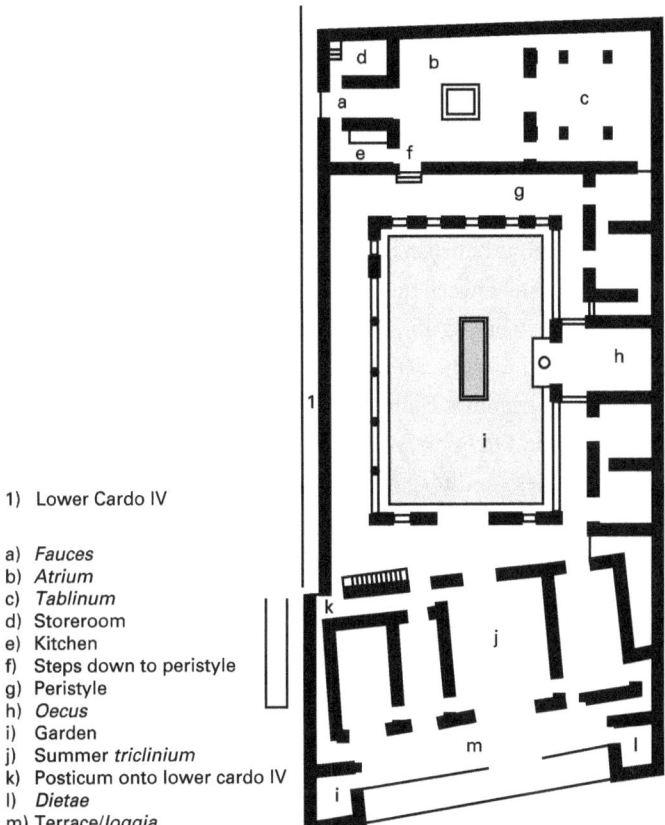

Figure 6.6 Floor plan of the house of the Mosaic *Atrium* (Ins IV, 1–2), Herculaneum. © Bloomsbury Academic.

the chance to use to full effect the sensations provided by the garden can be seen in the house of the Mosaic *Atrium* (Fig. 6.6). Located on the lower half of Cardo IV, a fairly substantial road that runs across the entire width of the excavated site, this dwelling is one of the larger examples from Herculaneum. It boasts a sizeable peristyle garden (i) overlooked by a large *oecus* (h), which could potentially be used for dining, and a summer *triclinium* (j), which also had a panoramic view over the Bay. In the middle of the peristyle garden was a marble-edged rectangular pool at the centre of which was a fountain. Given that the distances from the fountain to the centre of the *oecus* and the centre of the summer *triclinium* was about 7.5 metres and 17 metres respectively, it is likely that the peaceful sounds of water in the fountain would be heard in both areas.[106] When combined with the likely sounds of birds twittering and wind rustling the leaves of shrubs and plants in the garden and on the terrace, these aspects of background noise would serve to mitigate any unwanted auditory commotion from the nearby street that was only about 12 metres from the entrance threshold to the summer *triclinium* and about 18 metres from the entrance threshold of the *oecus*.[107] In addition, the sounds from the fountain, the wind and the birds would disguise or at least divert attention away from any unwanted noises that might emanate from ongoing household activities such as slaves clattering dishes and conversing, as they move between the kitchen (e) and either of the dining areas.[108] The fact that the gaps in between the peristyle columns themselves were windowed on three sides (g),[109] including at least part of the side closest to the street and the whole side closest to the kitchen (e) (Fig. 6.7) but not the side closest to the *oecus* suggests the owner's keenness both to reduce the auditory impact of the kitchen within the dwelling and to boost, where possible, the sounds of the garden realm. We should add to these auditory effects the visual aspects of the garden and its surroundings, both of its water features and flora and fauna. There may have been plants in the low walls of the peristyle on either side of the *oecus* and the painted images of ivy, vines, and oleander in bloom located on the walls under the peristyle windows, on the engaged columns and the doorposts facing towards the garden.[110]

Figure 6.7 Enclosed peristyle colonnade in the house of the Mosaic *Atrium* (Ins IV, 1–2), Herculaneum. Photo: Hannah Platts.

Beyond Taste

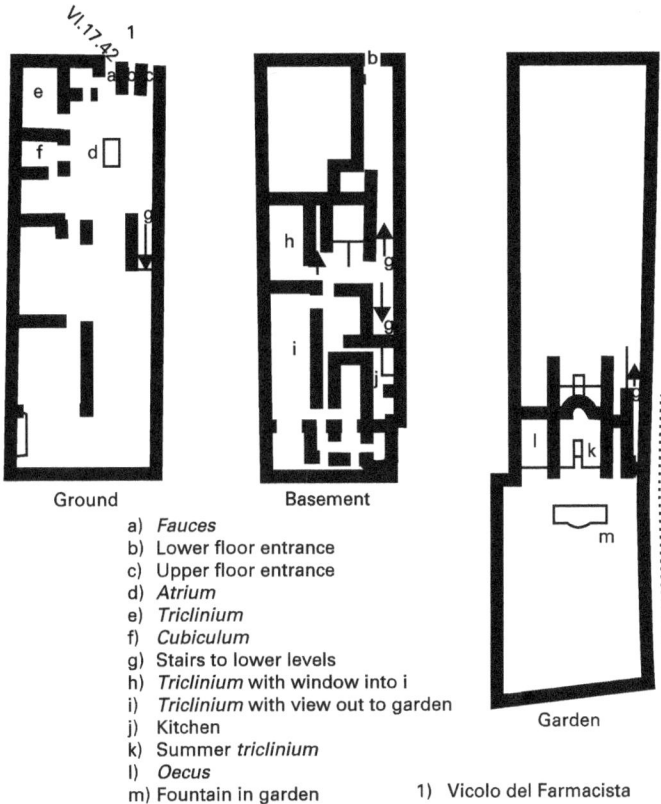

Figure 6.8 Floor plan of the house of the Golden Bracelet (Reg VI.17.42), Pompeii. © Bloomsbury Academic.

All of these would have combined to help foster the visual and auditory suggestion of retreat, away from the distracting sounds and sights of the urban sphere, within a garden that seems to stretch on and on.

Another intriguing residence with a summer *triclinium* situated within the walls of a dwelling, but overlooking a substantial garden, is the house of the Golden Bracelet, Pompeii (Fig. 6.8). To understand the potential sensory experiences of its garden dining area, we need to think in some detail about this residence's particular situation in the city of Pompeii itself, as this would impact upon the potential experiences to be had in the residence's summer dining room.

Located in the *Insula Occidentalis* on the Vicolo del Farmacista and near the junction with the Via Delle Terme, this house was built over Pompeii's western city wall. Like many neighbouring large houses in this part of the city, the owner of this dwelling took advantage of its location on the outskirts of the city both in terms of the extra space that this afforded the residence as well as the city walls and the slope of the hillside on which the city had originally been constructed. As such, this residence was built over three levels.

Although situated on a junction with the Via delle Terme, a relatively main street in Pompeii with two-way traffic, the house of the Golden Bracelet actually opened onto the Vicolo del Farmacista, a considerably narrower street which was served by one-way traffic.[111] In addition to this, the larger Via delle Terme was blocked off some distance in front of this dwelling, making it a no-through road. Such traffic calming measures would have helped to reduce cart and pedestrian noise filtering into this house. Moreover, the nearest workshop of any sort was for metal-working and was located at some distance on the Via Consolare as it forks to the left to meet the Vicolo di Modesto. Between the metal workshop and this house were a variety of other buildings, which would have also reduced the sounds of manufacturing process. There are four taverns of varying sorts located nearby, identified as *popinae* and *cauponae* by Laurence (Fig. 3.2).[112] Whilst literary evidence presents cookshops as smelly and noisy, we need to be aware of the social bias of elite literary authors and their snobbery towards those of the lower orders of Roman society. It was, after all, the lower classes who were understood to frequent taverns for food and accommodation. Moreover, when we consider again the traffic calming measures in the vicinity of this dwelling, it is perhaps not unlikely that these had an impact on the busyness of the area. Although not far from the entrance to the city at the Herculaneum Gate, three of the taverns were situated on a narrow, one-way street, whilst the fourth was located on a two-way main road that was blocked off from access to traffic leading to and from the nearby city gate. As a consequence, it might be argued that these taverns would receive less footfall than others elsewhere in the city, thereby reducing for nearby households the possible sensory nuisances that they produced.

If the Vicolo del Farmacista was a relatively quiet road in the city of Pompeii, it is unlikely that sensory disturbances from the street would filter into the dwelling enough to impact upon diners in the summer *triclinium* at (k), which was housed two floors below, accessed only by a single narrow staircase, and was fully enclosed on three sides whilst overlooking only a garden on its fourth side. Indeed, it might be argued that even feasts occurring in the residence's other *triclinium* at (e) at the front of the dwelling, which backed onto the Vicolo del Farmacista, would probably be relatively undisturbed by noise filtering in from the world outside.

Support for the hypothesis that the street outside this residence was relatively quiet might be gained from the fact that many of the houses on this road have either particularly small, or indeed lack, *fauces* separating their *atria* from the street outside.[113] The owners of the house of the Golden Bracelet were perhaps less troubled by external sensory disruptions, because they were situated in a slightly quieter area of the city. In any event, the outward-looking focus of the house of the Golden Bracelet towards the sea and its three storeys not only took advantage, as much as possible, of views across the Bay of Naples, but also ensured that an important entertaining sector of the dwelling was distanced from the entrance where smells, sounds and sights from outside had the potential to impinge on the owner's attempts at self-display. It might be argued, then, that having access to a substantial terrace and/or a multi-storey, highly opulent dwelling reduced the need for a substantial *fauces* which generally worked to distance the household and its guests from the hubbub and stench outside. Sea breezes across an open terrace or a garden overlooking the coast would dissipate effectively unwanted smells and diminish sounds before they reached inhabitants and visitors, whether they came from outside or whether they were produced within the dwelling itself.[114] Similarly, organizing a dwelling on various levels, ensuring its entrance was located on a different level from at least some of the entertaining rooms, including the summer *triclinium*, would serve to give the owner some control over sounds and smells that might otherwise impinge upon aspects of life and personal display in these residences.

Just as structuring the residence in relation to the street was important in order to avoid unpleasant sensory experiences from the outside world seeping in and disturbing guests, so, too, the internal layout of the residence was vital for ensuring that the owner could control and prevent unwanted sensory distractions produced inside the home from affecting visitors as they dined. Thus both *triclinia* (e) and (k) were situated on different levels from the main cooking area of the house, located in the middle floor of the dwelling at (j), where much of the odoriferous and noisy preparations for banquets would occur.[115] Whilst sounds and smells from this house might dissipate into the Vicolo del Farmacista, in particular from the *triclinium* at (e), in terms of owner display within his dwelling this would surely be of little concern.[116] It might even help parade to the uninvited on the street outside the owner's wealth in the form of entertainment noises and aromas being emitted from the house thereby serving to re-emphasize the social hierarchies of the invited 'haves' and the uninvited 'have-nots'.

In addition to these structural attempts to control the corporeal experiences of diners in the house of the Golden Bracelet, particularly those in the summer *triclinium* (k), we might also consider the role that other factors such as furniture, fountains and vegetation had upon dining next to the garden in this dwelling. The remains of a marble dining couch set out in a 'U' shape are situated in front of a large *nymphaeum* housed in the rear wall of the summer dining room. As well as water tumbling down a central staircase in this *nymphaeum*, a jet of water also spurted up from a fountain situated between the dining couches. The water from these two features finally ended up in a pool, painted blue and situated in front of the *triclinium* (m). At the centre of this pool there was a single jet with twenty-eight further jets located around the edge of the pool.[117] The remains of these three water features with their intricate fountains and jets suggest that the presence of water in this garden would have had a strong sensory impact upon diners in the summer *triclinium*. Not only would the sound of the falling water from the fountains on either side and in front of them impact the diners, but the sight of water falling from fountains into still pools would serve as a useful means of directing the attention of visitors. In addition to the auditory and visual aspects of the water features in this garden and dining area, they would have a cutaneous or haptic impact upon diners as the water would serve to cool the immediate surroundings and guests could wash their hands and perhaps their feet in the central water feature in front of them. These real cascades and pools of water, the summer *triclinium*, as well as the *oecus* to its immediate left, were ornately decorated with frescoes of garden scenes of birds, shrubs and fountains, reflecting pictorially some of the real features of the setting itself. When viewed together with the *tesserae* of the mosaic apse of the *nymphaeum* by the light of flickering candles, the lustre of paintings and the glittering of the water and the mosaics must further have served as either a talking point of the guests or at least a distraction as they were served.

As well as the water impacting the corporeal experiences to be had in this part of the residence, the dining area's proximity to the rest of an ornately planted garden is also important in terms of its aesthetic and olfactory impact upon diners and the sound of wind rustling through the hedges and vines.[118] The remains of shells, and animal and fish bones in the garden near the house are probably evidence of the meals that occurred in the summer *triclinia*. Cow, pig, sheep or goat, chicken bones, fish vertebrae and the remnants of a dormouse excavated in this garden suggest the relatively varied and, as suggest by the dormouse bones, occasionally luxurious diet of the residence's owners and their guests.[119] As such, they give some insight into the gustatory and olfactory experiences to be had here as roasted meats and fish were brought into and consumed in the room.

Summer *triclinia* were not just located within the confines of the house but could also be found at some distance from the dwelling itself. Examples of gardens

Figure 6.9 View of summer dining area (n) and fountain (m) (fig. 3.20) in the large peristyle of the villa of Diomedes, Pompeii. Photo: Hannah Platts.

which offered alfresco dining have been uncovered in residences of varying sizes, from relatively modest examples such as house I. XIV.2, the house of Trebius Valens ((k) on Fig. 5.4) and the house of the Garden of Hercules ((h) on Fig. 3.12) to those in the more substantial dwellings of the house of the Silver Wedding and the villa of Diomedes ((n) on Fig. 3.20 and Fig. 6.9). The dining couches of these outside areas were generally organized in the same u-shaped *triclinia* arrangement often employed within dwellings and thus demonstrate how the outside garden areas of some dwellings could be employed as an extension to the rest of the residence.[120]

Many outside spaces specifically used for dining had masonry couches, thus making them relatively easy to identify and Soprano's catalogue of 1950 lists thirty-nine such *triclinia* in Pompeii.[121] Yet it was not just permanent stone couches that show how garden spaces could be employed for dining parties. Given that archaeological techniques have developed to the extent that we can now detect the imprints left on soil by wood long since destroyed, the actual number of outside dining areas in Pompeii was probably significantly higher.[122] Furthermore, in a similar way to which houses today bring out temporary furniture and gazebos for barbeques in gardens in summer months, wall paintings from houses reflect that this happened also in ancient Roman times. We have already looked at the depictions of dining scenes occurring in internal *triclinia* of Roman houses, but there are also a number of examples of wall paintings that appear to show banquets occurring outside. In the *triclinium* of the house of the Chaste Lovers (Fig. 6.1.) and the house of the *Triclinium*, frescoes display outdoor banquets, whilst a third likewise shows an outside dining scene.[123] Although these scenes are slightly damaged, the outdoor and temporary nature of the setting is highlighted by the flimsy awnings that are either tied to trees or portico columns. Canopies are used both to denote visually an outside space, but they also suggest a means by which to protect diners from the excesses of the elements. That the fresco from the house of the *Triclinium* seems to depict one of these banqueting scenes occurring under a colonnaded portico emphasizes further the use of temporary furniture for the dinner party, since stone couches are unlikely to have been placed within a colonnaded portico. As we have seen with the *Colloquium Celtis*, coverings, cushions, braziers are moveable and so too are the three-legged wooden tables that feature in indoor and outdoor dining scenes. Locating furniture outdoors helped to construct an external summer dining experience under the shelter of a decorative awning.

Just as the house of the Golden Bracelet took advantage of its location on the edge of the city to obtain spectacular views over the Bay of Naples, the house of the Garden of Hercules utilized its position within the city to its own benefit (Fig. 3.12). Identified by Jashemski as a commercial flower garden and perfumery, its position on the Via di Nocera, the main route into the city from the Noceran Gate, and at the junction with the Via della Palaestra, its location close to the city's Noceran Gate was ideal for taking advantage of traffic and the resultant trade that would have passed the residence's entrance on the way into and out of the city.[124] Similarly, the garden's proximity to the palaestra and the amphitheatre, public buildings and spaces that were likely to be decorated with garlands on festival days, further highlights the advantageous situation of the residence, given its associated commercial enterprise.

The garden (g) connected to this dwelling is sizeable and has revealed a fixed masonry *triclinium* (h) situated at some distance from the house itself.[125] Nearby was situated a masonry *lararium* (i) dedicated to the worship of Hercules. Whether or not the outside dining area was utilized merely by the inhabitants and workers of the dwelling, or was also used by other members of Pompeii's flower and perfume trade, the corporeal experiences to be had whilst reclining in the garden would have been significant.[126] Firstly, in addition to the large *triclinium* excavated, a masonry serving table with an arched niche underneath for the storage of fuel was excavated. The storage of fuel in such close proximity to the dining area suggests there would have been some element of heating taking place here, whether for food, similar to today's barbeques, or for warming and lighting the immediate vicinity after sunset, again rather like the wood-burning patio heaters that can be purchased today.[127] Whatever the reason for lighting the fuel, it would have impacted on both the cutaneous, olfactory and auditory experience of the setting as the burning fuel crackled and warmed the surroundings and, perhaps, food.

There are other factors from within and outside the garden that would have affected diners in the garden. To the south of the *triclinium* was discovered a doghouse made from part of an old terracotta *dolium* raised up on a masonry base.[128] The discovery of dog bones suggest that the auditory landscape of this residence and its associated summer *triclinium* would have been disrupted at times by the sounds of barking, but since Jashemski excavated dog bones in all large gardens, the auditory landscape of Pompeii as a whole would clearly have been punctuated with noise from guard, and pet, dogs.[129]

Given the garden's proximity to the city's palaestra and amphitheatre, the noise at peak times, from both traffic entering and leaving the city and the large amount of footfall when the leisure areas of the palaestra and amphitheatre were in use, must have been considerable (Fig. 3.9).[130] Additionally it has been suggested that the palaestra itself was used by Pompeii's youths for exercise and competitive sports, which would have made it a focus for the substantial noise and bustle of many people taking part and cheering on competitors at certain times. Furthermore, the finds of a couple of painted notices on one of the columns of the Large Palaestra indicate that this area might have housed a school. If this is the case, we are reminded of the complaints of Martial who implored his neighbour, a loud schoolmaster, to start classes later in the day, so that they did not disturb those in neighbouring properties who were still sleeping.[131] The plantings of tall plane trees and the construction of walls and porticoes on the three sides of the palaestra that do not back onto the amphitheatre would have helped reduce auditory disturbances filtering into the garden. The rustling of tree leaves in the palaestra would have helped disguise sounds and the presence of the garden's own substantial wall would have further helped to block unwanted noise.[132] That the *triclinium* itself was situated only 3 metres from the garden's east wall, which backed onto the palaestra, but around 25 metres from the west wall, which was next to the Via di Nocera, perhaps suggests that the sound of traffic on the road was more problematic for the owner when using the garden. In practice, the palaestra and amphitheatre were used for loud festivals at times throughout the day and night, but the movement of cart and pedestrian traffic via the Noceran Gate probably had a more consistent impact on those dining and relaxing in the garden.[133]

A final aspect of this garden of particular note is its plantings, which would have impacted upon the corporeal experiences to be had there in a number of ways. The house of the Golden Bracelet showed evidence of a small amount of species in the garden and surrounding the pool, but excavations from the house of the Garden of Hercules provides much information as to the possible plantings of this outside space.[134] Not only were remains of olive found in this garden, suggesting that numerous olive trees had once grown there, but finds of vine root cavities and post holes over the *triclinium* indicate that diners would have been shaded from the sun by a vine-covered pergola. Further finds from this garden include carbonized cherries and possibly lemon trees. As with the plane tree plantings from the palaestra itself, the sound of rustling leaves, particularly from the larger trees in the garden would have helped distract diners from undercurrents of cart traffic and human voices. Similarly the finds of lemon and cherry trees together with vegetation remains from a variety of other plants suggest that further sounds to be heard regularly by reclining diners would have been that of bees and other insects pollinating the surrounding vegetation; this would have acted as a pleasing distraction for diners, albeit an irritation as well when the insects were attracted by any foodstuffs being served! Where bees and insects appear, they also attract birds and these, as noted above, can have a significant effect on a garden's auditory landscape.[135]

A final corporeal experience stemming from the garden's plantings would have been the smell emanating from the flowers and shrubs. In addition to the remains of lemon and cherry trees planted here, the spores of other highly scented plants, including lilies and roses, typically employed in the perfume industry, have been found in this garden.[136] In the warmth of the sun, the aroma from these plants would have been particularly heady, competing with the smells of cooking food and burning fuel to make a cacophony of olfactory experiences for diners. Perhaps these helped overpower some of the rather more unpleasant odours emanating from diners as they belched, vomited, farted or just sat in such close proximity that the reek of their halitosis and body odour was unavoidable? Or perhaps the smells were cleverly organized to ensure that when attempting to create a showy and opulent dining experience at the house of the Garden of Hercules, until the food appeared, the gustatory experiences to be had were truly unpredictable.

Conclusion

> Men say, 'Poor sick fellow!' But why? Is it because he does not mix snow with his wine, or because he does not revive the chill of his drink – mixed as it is in a good-sized bowl – by chipping ice into it? Or because he does not have Lucrine oysters opened fresh at his table? Or because there is no din of cooks about his dining-hall, as they bring in their very cooking apparatus along with their viands? For luxury has already devised this fashion – of having the kitchen accompany the dinner, so that the food may not grow luke-warm, or fail to be hot enough for a palate which has already become hardened.[137]

In his *Moral Letters* to Lucilius, Seneca bemoans the new multisensory fashions of cooling wine with snow and ice and the theatre of opening and serving oysters at the dining table and cooking foods at the table. For him such practices symbolized the increasing opulence of Rome's elite as they sought innovative ways to astonish their dining guests by influencing and manipulating sensory experiences at the table. Frescoes of dinners excavated at Pompeii and Herculaneum further endorse the plethora of sensory experiences to be had whilst dining. Thus, in the house of the *Triclinium* we see an indoor banquet with wine flowing freely, where slaves support vomiting diners and remove their shoes, whilst from the house of the Chaste Lovers we have a similar depiction, this time of women and men reclining together and being attended by slaves (Figs 6.1, 6.2, 6.3).[138]

As a form of theatre, the Roman *convivium* in the home provided a variety of sensations for guests. The owner used surroundings and slaves to highlight his wealth and status to all. This would involve, for example, the visitors themselves, the order in which they sat, the finery in which, and on which, they were draped, and the silverware and unguents used during the dinner. Perhaps the host would also choose to undermine the standing of invited diners, as the example of Domitian's black dinner at the start of this chapter demonstrates.[139]

Control of a guest's gustatory experience at the dinner table was key. Petronius's *Cena Trimalchionis* presents an account of the dinner party of a freedman and provides a mocking view of how Rome's vulgar *nouveaux riches* sought to present themselves through the parties and fare they offered. That picture is supported by still-lifes of food on platters from Pompeian and Herculanean residences and the famous *asarotos oikos* or 'unswept room' mosaic from Rome, depicting chicken and fish bones, lobster claws and other debris thrown by diners to the floor whilst eating.[140] All serve to emphasize the attention paid to the theatre of taste that could be offered to guests. To be able to offer visitors adventures in taste, presented an excellent means of displaying wealth, and visual representations of the food of dinner parties could be used by the owner to present visual memories of experiences past and a tantalizing promise of banquets and taste sensations for those lucky enough to be invited in future.

The banquet itself presented a vital way in which house owners could parade themselves before others: the food, drink and entertainment offered, the lavish surroundings in which it occurred and the extent to which slaves were carefully controlled and choreographed as a display of power and wealth, whilst ensuring the actual workings of the banquet remained unobtrusive.[141] The manipulation of the multisensory experiences to be had by guests during the banquet demonstrated an individual's ability to influence the full body experience of others whilst at home. Yet, the very process of inviting others into one's domain to partake in a *convivium* presented a significant risk to the residence owner; after all one could not be certain that guests would subscribe to displays of rank and status put on for their enjoyment. As Horace's satirical account of the failure of Nasidienus' banquet and Petronius' mockery of Trimalchio's *cena* show, guests at the *convivium* could easily deride their host's attempts at self-display.[142] It was, however, a key means by which Rome's elite presented themselves to others, so much so that, as D'Arms points out, we see a '"trickle-down effect" of Roman culinary luxury' being imitated across mainland Italy as members of the lower classes sought to utilize the well-recognized method of social display that the *convivium* offered.[143]

Despite the risk of mockery and criticism, the reward of praise and admiration that the multisensory display of the Roman banquet offered hosts encouraged them to continue in this opulent pastime. As we explore the household layout and location of the *triclinium* as well as its immediate surroundings, however, we can see the lengths to which owners would organize their houses in order to maintain as much control as possible over the multisensory experience of their dinner guests. The question is why it was necessary to control the multisensory experience of the *convivium* to the extent that houses were often spatially organized to reflect this desire? The answer is hinted at by Potter who comments: 'The cooks were slaves, and steps were taken to ensure that people would not necessarily know what was coming next.'[144] As already discussed, to Potter the importance of not smelling the food, before it arrived was key.[145] Yet what this chapter has suggested was that the critical consideration was not just about hiding or controlling the smells of the food so that diners did not know what to expect and were thus beholden to their host, but was about keeping as much as possible hidden or controlled: sights, sounds, smells and tastes were all to be 'regulated' and, where necessary, concealed or disguised from the guests' perception until the exact moment that ensured the utmost level of surprise and display. Not only did the trappings of the banquet itself help to ensure this control, but the spatial organization and architectural structure of the house likewise served to ensure controlled choreography of the slaves who were themselves both 'the human props essential to the support of upper-class convivial comforts', as well as a vital display of an owner's wealth.[146] Guests judged all aspects of the banquet: food and wine, décor, entertainment and even the slaves. Careful regulation of all aspects, using all means possible enabled owners to make the most of controlling, and ultimately securing, successful personal display whilst dining at the banquet.

7

Housing the Foul: Kitchens and Toilets in the Roman Home

Introduction: Identifying the kitchen and the toilet in literature and archaeology

People who are fed on this diet can no more be sensible than people who live in the kitchen [*culina*] can smell good.[1]

Apollinaris, the doctor of the emperor Titus, defecated well here.[2]

This is Martha's dining room [*triclinium*], as she shits in this dining room.[3]

In most houses, the kitchen and the dining room are intrinsically linked, not necessarily physically, but because of the activities taking place within these spaces.[4] The dining room is where food is consumed, but it is in the kitchen, and perhaps connected larders, pantries or utility areas, where the meals are cooked and foodstuffs stored. This was certainly the case in the elite Roman *domus*.[5] Although innately connected, within the Roman dwelling there existed socially constructed boundaries between these spheres that served to demarcate and clearly emphasize the unequal status of their inhabitants, irrespective of whether the individuals concerned were members of the household or visitors. As diners were seated on banqueting couches and often served differing foods according to perceived social rank, there was also an order of precedence among slaves, with those serving food being seen as more suitable for flaunting to guests in terms of attractiveness and perhaps body odour, given the sentence from Petronius about the bad smell of kitchen slaves.[6]

Given the connections between dining room and kitchen, this chapter builds on the conclusions of the previous chapter, but where Chapter 6 focused on the sensory experiences within the *triclinium* during a banquet and the means by which household owners sought to regulate them in order to control their image, Chapter Seven considers the relationship between kitchen and *triclinium*, and the means by which food, noises and smells of food production in the kitchen were directed away from dining areas. This final chapter accordingly studies the typical sensorially unpleasant domestic offices of the house and examines their location in and relationship to other parts of the residence, particularly the *triclinium*, and the evidence of attempts to reduce transmission of unwanted sensations elsewhere within the dwelling. Key to understanding how potentially 'foul' the stench from the kitchen was, is to realize that domestic toilets were also often situated within them, hence the reason for exploring both kitchens and toilets together within this chapter.[7] Although there are examples of separate rooms used as latrines, as is demonstrated by the graffiti from the lavatory in the house of the Gem at Herculaneum, this was not typical.

Identifying cooking areas in literary evidence is complicated: whilst there are many different words, such as *focus* and *furnus*, which were applied to the cooking area it was only the word *culina* that referred to a specific room used for food preparation.[8] A similar issue revolves around identification of cooking areas in archaeology; whilst fixed hearths and ovens are readily identifiable in the extant remains of many houses in Pompeii and Herculaneum, examples of moveable cooking apparatus, such as braziers, show that cooking could have occurred in areas other than the *culina*.[9] Given the multi-use nature of rooms and the difficulty of identifying areas of houses used for specific purposes, this chapter only looks at kitchens (*culina*) that have been identified definitively thanks to finds and/or hearth remains, benches or ovens.[10] Dining rooms are not considered any further here, but their proximity and routes to them from the kitchen are key in thinking about transmission of sensory experiences between the spheres.

With regard to toilets, this chapter will focus both on designated rooms that show evidence of housing toilets, for which the Latin terminology is either *latrina* or *lavatrina*, and kitchens that also display archaeological evidence for housing latrines within them.[11] When it comes to archaeological evidence for latrines, extant remains are often found in a range of conditions, and thus locating toilets in a dwelling can revolve around identification of a number of features. Many wooden toilet seats were placed upon vertical masonry posts and so, whilst the wood has often long ago decayed, the posts remain, allowing clear evidence of the location of toilets. Additionally, in many examples, these posts were placed on tiled flooring that sloped down towards the wall and the drain thereby facilitating relatively easy removal of excreta.[12] In some instances, long cuts can be found which were made in walls to house horizontal toilet seats which often made unnecessary the use of vertical posts as support; such cuts provide good evidence of latrines.[13] In others, existence of toilets is less obvious and an amalgamation of evidence, including room size and location within the house, drains and windows in rear walls next to the street, or remains of stone seats, has also been employed in identifying latrines.[14]

The sensory experiences of the kitchen

Obtaining literary evidence for sensory experiences of the kitchen is problematic, given which members of the household spent most of their time working there. Kitchens were an area mainly for slaves, a group of Roman society which left very few clear material remains and even less textual evidence about their lives; we are mainly reliant therefore on graffiti and brief comments from Roman authors, both of which are often criticisms of those who spent much of their lives toiling to satisfy the gustatory whims of their owners. As a result, most of the evidence we can use to develop understanding of the multisensory realm of the kitchen stems from archaeological remains, from hearths, cooking utensils and remains of food waste.

As the part of the house where most food preparation, storage and cooking occurred, as well as where waste, human, animal, and food were disposed of, the kitchen in a Roman house would have provided a multitude of powerful sensory experiences, many of which would have been, unsurprisingly, particularly unpleasant. As Martial shows in his *Epigrams*, the activities undertaken in the kitchen often resulted in the slaves involved smelling repulsive to others.

> Who was so unfeeling, may I ask, who so arrogant, as to make you Theopompous, a cook? Does anyone have the heart to defile this face with a sooty kitchen or pollute these locks with a greasy flame?[15]

For slaves working in the kitchen, the experience would have been hot and uncomfortable, as they cooked using hearths or ovens. Hearths in Roman kitchens were masonry platforms on top of which fires were lit for cooking.[16] From Green's survey of the height of kitchen hearths, most stood between 0.5–0.75 metres high, with the average measuring 70.88 centimetres.[17] Not only would these emit heat next to the cook with resultant profuse sweating, sticky and dirty skin, as soot became ingrained in the pores, and body odour that would become embedded in clothing, hair and skin, but since flames were often open and unprotected, a regular experience would be that of pain, as cooks burned arms and fingers.[18] Additionally, according to Green's study, the height of many kitchen hearths would require cooks to hunch uncomfortably over the

Figure 7.1 Window above masonry hearth in kitchen at (i) (fig. 7.7) in the house of the Tragic Poet (Reg VI.8.3), Pompeii. Photo: Hannah Platts.

pots and pans, which in turn would probably result in aching joints.[19] Although many kitchens had windows to provide ventilation, allow smoke to escape and provide some daylight, most were of small size, so kitchens would often have been dark and relatively airless. This would have exacerbated the smell of smoke and persistent odours of the foods they cooked for the slaves that worked there (Fig. 7.1).[20]

In the often cramped and poorly ventilated kitchen, it would not just be the slaves who stank. The odour in the room would have been an assortment of the smells of cooking food, much of which would be pleasant, for example the scent of herbs and spices, fruit and cooking meat, fish and vegetables, but intermingled with that of the cloying and sickly-sweet scent of rotting food waste and human excreta. Remains of foodstuffs from the sewer excavated in Herculaneum's Cardo V demonstrate the wide variety of items that made up the Roman diet. These include fruit and vegetables – such as pears, apples, celery and olives, meat and fish – including eel, sheep, pig, seabream, mussels, limpets, haddock and pilchards, and herbs and spices – such as fennel, mint, dill and coriander.[21] When cut up and cooked, smells from these and other foodstuffs would have mingled to make the kitchen pungent, and if not properly closed off from the rest of the house could have filtered into the other parts of the residence.[22]

It is not just the smell of the kitchen that would have been a substantial sensory experience for those within it and possibly outside it. The sounds of the kitchen, with the clattering and banging of pots and pans, the shouting or talking of the cook(s) and other slaves, the crackle of the fire and the sizzle of cooking meats, and the grinding of the herbs and spices in the pestle and mortar equally served to make this room a noisy space. In Plautus, we find a number of references to the noisiness of the kitchen.

> the old man's shouting in the kitchen, urging on the cooks. And the cooks for their part take care ever so charmingly that the old man won't get his dinner; they knock over the pots and extinguish the fire with water.[23]

Again, depending on the proximity of other rooms to the kitchen and whether the kitchen could be closed off from surrounding spaces and *vice versa*, it is possible that some of the sounds of food production in the kitchen would be heard elsewhere in the dwelling.[24]

One of the key sensory experiences for the cook would have been the gustatory experience of textures and flavours of the food as he tasted his concoctions. Whilst other slaves working in the kitchen might also have had the chance to grab food as they worked, it was the cook's key role to make appetizing meals for the master of the residence and his visitors. That the cook would be testing the meals he produced is made clear by Martial's wish that a cook should have the taste (*gulam*) of his master, not the palate (*palatum*) of a slave.[25] As the cook blended the pungent herbs, perhaps the aniseed flavour of dill or fennel, checking the food for the right balance, we should note his concern or fear, should the dishes be perceived negatively.[26]

These are just some of the multisensory experiences to be had in the kitchen of the Roman home. Not all aspects of the kitchen would have been undesirable, working near a warm stove or oven on a cold winter's day would have provided relief, but as Joshel and Petersen point out, these spaces were not only cramped and dark, but the small windows, whilst giving some element of ventilation and natural light, would have cast even more shadow on kitchen workbenches.[27]

Such working, possibly also sleeping, conditions would have had a lasting impact upon the corporeal experiences of the slaves working there.[28] That slave owners would likely want their most aesthetically and sensorially pleasing slaves on show and waiting at table is unsurprising; the alternative was that guests would be repulsed by the physical condition of kitchen slaves.[29] According to Joshel and Petersen, even bringing food from kitchen to dining room presented a need to organize carefully how the slaves moved between these spaces, and to reduce where possible the extent to which routes were observed by guests.[30] For example, by moving the kitchen in the house of the Ceii from the back of the residence at (i) to the front at (d) (Fig. 3.18), and arranging placement of guests so that they faced the garden in the back of the residence, would have helped reduce for diners unappealing visual nuisances of kitchen slaves.[31] Such actions would help solve ocular concerns raised by slaves being seen in and around the kitchen and bringing food to the tables. There has been, however, little consideration of how other methods of household organization, such as the location of kitchens and toilets in houses, the presence of doors and other architectural obstacles, might have helped shroud the mechanics of the dinner party in mystery, ideal for any host, as well as conceal or disguise the repulsive sight, sounds and smells that might emanate from the kitchen. As we shall see below, the architectural layout of many houses went well beyond planning how to avoid visitors seeing slaves making their way from the kitchen. Rather there was an attempt, through the use of barriers such as doors, the locating of kitchens and toilets on other levels and near roads where necessary, the use of physical distance and/or gardens between kitchens and dining rooms, to ensure that all physical processes of preparing and delivering the *convivium* remained imperceptible to invited guests.

Controlling the transmission of multisensory experiences from kitchens to dining rooms

As we saw in the previous chapter, manipulation of the multisensory experiences of the *triclinium* and related dining activities is widely demonstrated in literature and archaeology. Assertion of effective control over corporeal engagement with the *convivium* starts with the kitchen; its location, surroundings and relationship to the dining room were carefully organized to help reduce the diffusion of sensory nuisances from where food is prepared into where it is consumed. The rest of this chapter seeks to explore methods employed by house owners to separate kitchens which, as we have just seen, were particularly sensorially rich parts of the dwelling, from the rest of the house and especially the *triclinium* where, ideally, food and entertainments should remain a mystery until served.[32]

Locating kitchens and combined toilets in residences of Pompeii and Herculaneum: Data and discussion

> [J]ust as architects relegate the drains of houses to the rear, away from the eyes and nose of the masters, since otherwise they would inevitably be somewhat offensive, so nature has banished the corresponding organs of the body far away from the neighbourhood of the senses.[33]

Olfactory sensations are highly complex experiences that may be either negative and foul or positive and intoxicating as shown by Martial's contrasting epigrams on the stench of an old woman called Thais and the scent of his slave-boy's morning kisses.[34] For those that were disgusting, as Cicero highlights, it was important that they, and the items or people that produced them, were kept at a distance. Thus, Cicero advised that household drains, which remove excreta and other waste with their inherently unpleasant smells and sights, should be situated at the rear of residences.

Penelope Allison's survey of thirty Pompeian houses together with a detailed analysis of their artefact assemblages presents an excellent means by which to develop our understanding of life and activity within the domestic realm. Some of her conclusions, however, would benefit from further examination in terms of the location of rooms within a dwelling and the layout of the residence as a whole. By understanding, for example, the location of a kitchen and toilet area in relation to the layout of the house in general we can start to understand not just rooms as separate spaces within a dwelling, but also attempt to comprehend their role and situation within the functioning house. According to Allison, whilst the materials for cooking and food preparation were not usually stored towards the rear of residences, the actual activities of food preparation were generally located at the back of the residence.[35] If this is the case, then it would appear from the archaeology that Pompeian houses reflected the guidance of Cicero, so that those places which gave off disgusting smells, including kitchens and toilets, should be located at the back of dwellings. When reviewing her selection of residences from her database of rooms and labels given in excavation reports and the analysis of whether kitchens situated in the front, middle or rear part of the house, a rather surprising picture emerges.[36] In this set of thirty-eight kitchens from thirty houses, 26 per cent were found at the front of residences, 50 per cent were situated in the middle and 24 per cent were identified at the rear.[37] Despite her assertions, Allison's survey showed the largest number of fixed food preparation areas to be located in the middle of houses.

A further qualification of Allison's results can be observed when we focus on the locations of these thirty residences within Pompeii. In particular, when we look at the residences of *Insula* VIII we can see that five of the residences are located very close to each other and take advantage of their location next to the city walls, having terraces overlooking the Bay of Naples rather than gardens: all have a fixed food-preparation area situated in the front part of the residence's ground floor and located in close proximity to the road outside.[38] Where they have additional kitchen spaces in other parts of the dwelling, as is the case with houses VIII.2.26 and VIII.2.29–30, these are situated on the lower levels of the dwelling. This suggests a clear concern with separating food preparation facilities from those ground floor terraces which would probably have been used for entertaining important guests and which were at some remove from the *atrium* (or front reception part) of the house. Not only would the physical distance between the kitchen and the terraces serve to reduce the transmission of sounds, smells and sights from the kitchen to the rear part of the house, but the fact that terraces were open to the elements would have served also to reduce sensory impact from the service quarters.

The question of a kitchen's location in either the front, middle or rear section of a house, as well as its relationship to the road outside and the dwelling's *atrium*, raises further interesting questions. I prepared a survey of fifty-five kitchens from fifty-one houses from Pompeii (some of which were included in Allison's earlier survey), and sixteen kitchens from fifteen houses from Herculaneum that enabled comparisons to be drawn between the dwellings from both sites.[39] The data is presented in Table 2 below.

Table 2 Pompeii: kitchen location and proximity to road outside and internal *atrium*. For location of residences, see fig 3.5.

House	House size bracket (no. of rooms)	Kitchen location in house	Immediately off *atrium*	Next to road outside
I.7.19	10–19	MIDDLE and REAR	NO	NO and YES
Ara Maxima	10–19	FRONT	YES	NO
Cabinet Maker	10–19	MIDDLE	NO	NO
Casca Longus	10–19	MIDDLE	NO	YES
Ceii	10–19	FRONT	YES	YES
Figured Capitals	10–19	REAR	NO	NO
Fronto	10–19	MIDDLE	NO	NO

House	House size bracket (no. of rooms)	Kitchen location in house	Immediately off *atrium*	Next to road outside
Lararium	10–19	MIDDLE	NO	NO
Large Fountain	10–19	REAR	NO	YES
Lovers	10–19	REAR	NO	YES
Orchard	10–19	REAR	NO	YES
Prince of Naples	10–19	REAR	YES	NO
Queen Margherita	10–19	REAR	NO	YES
Ship of Europa	10–19	MIDDLE	YES	YES
Sulpicius Rufus	10–19	REAR	NO	NO
Wild Boar	10–19	MIDDLE	NO	YES
Tragic Poet	10–19	REAR	NO	NO
Priest of Amandus	10–19	FRONT	YES	NO
Paquius Proculus	10–19	MIDDLE	NO	NO
Apollo	20–29	REAR	NO	YES
Bronze Bull	20–29	REAR	NO	NO
Diadumeni	20–29	MIDDLE	NO	NO
Dioscuri	20–29	REAR	NO	YES
Ephebus	20–29	REAR and FRONT	NO and NO	YES and NO
Epigrams	20–29	REAR	NO	YES
Fortuna	20–29	REAR	NO	YES
Gavius Rufus	20–29	REAR	NO	NO
Golden Cupids	20–29	REAR	NO	NO
Holconius Rufus	20–29	MIDDLE	NO	NO
Moralist	20–29	MIDDLE	NO	YES
Restaurant	20–29	MIDDLE and MIDDLE	NO and YES	YES and YES
Surgeon	20–29	REAR	NO	YES
Trebius Valens	20–29	MIDDLE and REAR	NO and NO	NO and NO
Venus	20–29	REAR	NO	YES
Vetti	20–29	MIDDLE	YES	NO
Zephyr & Flora	20–29	MIDDLE	NO	NO
Epidius Sabinus	30–39	MIDDLE	NO	YES
Golden Bracelet	30–39	REAR	NO	NO
M. Lucretius	30–39	FRONT	NO	YES
Pansa	30–39	REAR	NO	YES

House	House size bracket (no. of rooms)	Kitchen location in house	Immediately off *atrium*	Next to road outside
Silver Wedding	30–39	MIDDLE	NO	NO
Siricus	30–39	MIDDLE	NO	NO
Coloured Capitals	40–49	MIDDLE	NO	NO
Faun	40–49	MIDDLE	NO	YES
Labyrinth	40–49	MIDDLE	NO	YES
Meleager	40–49	REAR	NO	NO
Obellius Firmus	40–49	REAR	NO	NO
Centennial	50+	REAR	NO	NO
Citharist	50+	MIDDLE	NO	NO
Diomedes	50+	FRONT and FRONT	NO and NO	YES and NO
The Menander	50+	MIDDLE and MIDDLE	NO and NO	YES and NO
TOTALS:	10–19: 19/51 20–29: 17/51 30–39: 6/51 40–49: 5/51 50+: 4/51	FRONT: 7/57 MIDDLE: 25/57 REAR: 25/57	YES: 7/57 NO: 50/57	YES: 26/57 NO: 31/57

This can be expressed as percentages as shown in Table 3.

Table 3 Pompeii: kitchen location in residence and proximity to *atrium* and road, expressed as percentages

Kitchen location	FRONT: 12%		MIDDLE: 44%		REAR: 44%
Directly off *Atrium*	YES: 12%		NO: 88%		n/a
Next to Road	YES: 46%		NO: 54%		n/a
House Size	10–19: 37%	20–29: 33%	30–39: 12%	40–49: 10%	50+ 8%

Table 4 Herculaneum: kitchen location and proximity to road outside and internal *atrium*. For location of residences, see fig 3.6.

House	House size bracket (no. of rooms)	Kitchen location in house	Immediately off *atrium*	Next to road outside
Beautiful Courtyard	0–9	FRONT	YES	YES
Carbonized Furniture	10–19	MIDDLE	NO	NO
Corinthian *Atrium*	10–19	FRONT	YES	YES
Double *Atrium*	10–19	FRONT	YES	YES
Gem	10–19	FRONT	NO	YES
Grand Portal	10–19	REAR	NO	NO
Neptune Mosaic	10–19	FRONT	NO	YES
Samnite	10–19	MIDDLE	NO	NO
Tuscan Colonnade	10–19	REAR	NO	YES
Wooden Sacellum	10–19	FRONT	YES	YES
Wooden Partition	10–19	REAR	NO	YES
Alcove	20–29	FRONT and FRONT	NO and NO	YES and YES
Black Hall	20–29	FRONT	YES	NO
Deer	20–29	FRONT	NO	NO
Mosaic *Atrium*	20–29	FRONT	YES	YES
TOTALS:	0–9: 1/15 10–19: 10/15 20–29: 4/15	FRONT: 11/16 MIDDLE: 2/16 REAR: 3/16	YES: 6/16 NO: 10/16	YES: 11/16 NO: 5/16

This can be expressed as percentages as shown in Table 5.

Table 5 Herculaneum: kitchen location in residence and proximity to *atrium* and road, expressed as percentages

Kitchen location	FRONT: 69%	MIDDLE: 12%	REAR: 19%
Directly off *Atrium*	YES: 37%	NO: 63%	
Next to Road	YES: 69%	NO: 31%	
House Size	0–9: 7%	10–19: 67%	20–29: 26%

Examination of this data demonstrates thought-provoking trends for further consideration. Firstly, comparing figures for kitchen location in the rear, middle and front of these residences from Pompeii and Herculaneum, we can see the percentage with kitchens in the front of dwellings is considerably different. In Pompeii only 12 per cent of houses had kitchens in their front section whilst in Herculaneum it is 69 per cent. When we compare the percentage of houses from Pompeii with kitchens in their middle or rear sectors, we find an equal percentage of 44 per cent for both. Once again in Herculaneum the figures vary considerably from Allison's analysis. Here, 19 per cent of houses have food-preparation areas in the rear of the dwelling and only 12 per cent have kitchens in their middle part. In addition to this comparison, we might also consider how many kitchens are located backing immediately onto the road outside: here again we can observe some different figures. Whilst 46 per cent of kitchens from Pompeian houses back immediately onto a road outside and 54 per cent do not, in Herculaneum 69 per cent of house kitchens back onto the road outside and only 31 per cent do not. Thus, substantially more houses in Herculaneum had their kitchens located close to the road, either to the front or rear of the dwelling, compared with those that did not.

The final comparison to be made concerns the number of residences that have kitchens located immediately off the *atrium*, in other words with no rooms or spaces situated as a 'buffer zone' between kitchen and *atrium*. We can also add to this comparison the size of houses in question to develop the discussion further. Thus, from Pompeii, 12 per cent of houses have kitchens situated immediately next to the *atrium* and 88 per cent of kitchens are located at varying distances. In Herculaneum, the first percentage is larger at 37 per cent, whilst 63 per cent of kitchens are placed at varying distances from the *atrium*. It is only a minority of houses that have their kitchen located in the immediate proximity of the *atrium*. The size of the houses surveyed in Herculaneum was generally smaller than from Pompeii but we can see with the figures from Pompeii that most of the houses with kitchens situated immediately off their *atria* were of the smallest size in the survey. Five out of seven of the houses that had a kitchen located immediately off the *atrium* were in the 10–19 room bracket, and the two larger houses (in the 20–29 room bracket) to have their kitchens sited immediately off the *atrium* were the house of the Vetti and the house of the Restaurant, both of which have two *atria*. The second *atrium* from the house of the Vettii has been generally interpreted as part of the slave/working section of the dwelling (Fig. 3.14) whilst the second *atrium* in the house of the Restaurant, is understood to have been part of a connected *popina* or *lupanare*.[40] It is next to this *atrium* that the kitchen in the house of the Vetti is located. From Herculaneum a slightly different set of results can be seen. Unlike at Pompeii, the two houses that fall into the 20–29 room bracket do not have two *atria*, and the only dwelling in the results to have two *atria*, the house of the Double *Atria*, falls into the 10–19 room bracket and thus is one of the smaller residences in the cohort.

The data from the kitchens which generally were also the location of the residences' toilets encourage interesting theories as to why there were substantial differences between the way in which many residences treated and located their fixed food-preparation areas. Whether organization of combined kitchens and toilets owed anything to hygiene and health concerns is difficult to ascertain. According to Reimers, for any organized society to avoid the rapid growth and spread of disease, the efficient and fast removal of waste is vital.[41] As Hobson rightly points out, however, such a statement risks making inaccurate assumptions and imposing modern perceptions onto Roman ideas and understanding of health, hygiene and the spread of disease.[42] Thus, whilst clothes infested with lice being burnt was perhaps some attempt at personal hygiene, Trimalchio's act of washing and then drying his hands on the hair of a slave after urinating in a chamber pot whilst at the dinner table hardly implies a concern for personal health and cleanliness.[43] Indeed, the widespread presence of *Trichuriasis*, or whipworm eggs, at a variety of sites throughout the Roman Empire, including the cesspits of house I *Insula* IX at Silchester and numerous downpipes from Pompeii, as well as the finds of whipworm larvae together with tapeworm and roundworm eggs from the excreta of a Roman centurion in Alphen aan den Rijn in the Netherlands, indicates that parasitic infestation was common throughout the Empire and suggests a lack of knowledge about the spread of disease and the role of human waste within it.[44] Lack of knowledge about disease and its spread suggests personal hygiene was unlikely to be a concern in the organization of kitchens with toilets located within them at both Pompeii and Herculaneum, but literary evidence, combined with the archaeology and topography of Pompeii and Herculaneum, perhaps presents an alternative corporeal explanation for the data outlined above.

In his *Moral Letters* Seneca bemoans the stench of the city and the fact that the country offered an opportunity for olfactory relief, thereby improving his health.

> As soon as I escaped from the oppressive atmosphere of the city, and from that awful odour of reeking kitchens, which, when in use, pour forth a ruinous mess of steam and soot, I perceived at once that my health was mending.[45]

For Seneca, desire to flee from the miasma of the city and improve his personal health was bound up with sensory experience in the city and the opportunity of freedom from its stench, rather than avoiding the diseases spread by personal contact with raw sewage. Moreover, if we return to Cicero's discussion about the location of drains in houses, or Columella's discussion of where wine rooms and beehives should be situated, we see an overriding emphasis on avoiding repulsive odours: 'It [the wine room] should be far removed from the baths, oven, dunghill and other filthy places which give off a foul odour'.[46] In a similar example from Varro, we are told of Lucullus' aviary which sought to combine two different types of bird coop: those for pleasure and those for the purposes of productivity.[47] Here, diners ate in the aviary alongside the birds as they flew around. Although this aviary was perceived to be unserviceable (*inutile*), this was not because of the potential health implications as we would understand it, but rather because of the unpleasant sensory experiences it engendered.[48] Indeed, that one of the symptoms of the whipworm parasite in humans is diarrhoea (often bloody) and that faecal incontinence was likely to ensure that the excrement of those infected with it would be particularly pungent, messy and voluminous, perhaps explains further the above emphasis on the disgusting aroma of settlements and residences, as well as the desire to avoid it.[49]

In Bradley's recent collection of essays on smell in the ancient world, the chapters by Morley and Koloski-Ostrow present different interpretations of the experience of smell in the ancient city. Koloski-Ostrow emphasizes its noxious aroma for all, while Morley highlights the possibility that sensitivity to smell and consciousness of filth vary over time, rather than being a universal experience.[50] Both arguments present a fascinating approach to the olfactory experience of the ancient past. The question of habituation to smell raised by Morley is key and evidence shows long-term exposure to strong odours impairs ability to smell and that living around odoriferous surroundings leads to olfactory habituation.[51] If we combine literary evidence with archaeological evidence of Pompeii's and Herculaneum's kitchen locations and the different drainage/sewage systems of these settlements, however, we can see perhaps at least a desire to use a dwelling's spatial layout to control smells and the connected sights and sounds within the home.

As a result of their topography, Pompeii and Herculaneum needed to employ different means by which to remove water and waste. Pompeii sat on a layer of porous and permeable subsoil, which enabled toilets to be connected to cesspits.[52] Herculaneum, however, was built on a more compact tuff subsurface that had poor permeability, which meant that cesspits connected to latrines did not work well and required regular emptying.[53] Consequently, many toilets in Herculaneum were connected to the town's sewer system situated beneath Cardo III and Cardo

V: and both Maiuri's excavation of Herculaneum and the excavation of Cardo V as part of the Herculaneum Conservation Project have found that many houses were connected to these sewers.[54]

The diverse topography and soil structures of Pompeii and Herculaneum explain the varied means of waste removal employed and, looking at the data outlined above, this is further echoed in the varying locations of combined kitchens and toilets within houses. In Herculaneum, where toilets were often connected to the main sewer system, proximity to the main road and the sewer underneath, was preferable, thereby enabling more efficient removal of urine, excreta and food waste disposed of in kitchen toilets.[55] Likewise, given the general use of the sewage system in Herculaneum, this also explains the preferred locations of kitchens and combined toilets in the front of the house (thus facilitating access to the sewer under the road). The second choice of location was at the back of the house, which again could take advantage of the proximity to the road and the sewage system. Of the two kitchens and combined toilets located in the middle of houses from Herculaneum, graffiti from the house of the Black Hall demonstrates epigraphic evidence of the need, and associated cost, of emptying the residence's required cesspit.[56]

Conversely, in Pompeii the location of kitchens and combined toilets varied considerably. From my survey of houses, the favoured places for siting the rooms were the middle and rear of houses, whilst the front of the dwelling was by far the least preferred location for situating a kitchen with a toilet. From Allison's collection of Pompeian houses, we see also that the placement of kitchens and toilets differed from that of Herculaneum, but her findings indicate the middle of the house was the preferable place for siting kitchens and toilets, and the back and front of the house were less popular. Similarly, fewer houses in Pompeii situated their toilets in close proximity to the road. From this we can observe how the use of cesspits in Pompeian houses offered considerably more freedom in locating toilets and kitchens. For Herculaneum, the situation was more restricted as efficient removal of waste and effluvia generally required access and use of the town's sewage system. Given that these rooms were likely to be producing the most odours, not to mention sounds, it is perhaps unsurprising that we can note a concerted effort to locate them within residences according to the quickest and most efficient means of removing waste.

Additionally, we see from both Pompeii and Herculaneum a desire to place kitchens and combined toilets at a distance from *atria*. In Herculaneum the cohort of houses surveyed is smaller than that of Pompeii, but the percentage of houses that place their kitchens immediately off *atria* is comparable, even though many of the houses in question have less available space.[57] Thus, in Pompeii only 12 per cent of houses locate their kitchens and combined toilets immediately off the *atrium*, whilst 88 per cent do not. In Herculaneum, a higher percentage house these rooms off *atria* (37 per cent), but it is still a considerably lower percentage than those that do not (63 per cent).

The presence of doors in kitchens and dining areas: Data

Let us start by examining how far my survey of houses of Pompeii and Herculaneum demonstrates evidence for modifying transmission of sensory experiences from kitchens into dining areas via the ability to close or open doors.[58] I undertook a survey of twenty-three residences from Pompeii and ten from Herculaneum in order to establish the presence of doors around kitchens and their architectural relationship particularly to dining rooms.[59]

Of the twenty-three houses examined for door architecture in thresholds either in or leading into kitchens and dining-rooms, fifteen residences showed clear remains of door architecture in rooms used for food preparation and also those used for food consumption. Four residences showed evidence of doors in thresholds around kitchens, but no clear evidence of door architecture around dining rooms and three residences displayed clear evidence for door architecture around dining rooms but not kitchens. Only one residence showed no clear evidence of doors in thresholds in or near either dining rooms or kitchens. The houses have also been categorized into groups according to the number of rooms they have. The groups for room numbers are 1–9, 10–19, 20–29, 30–39, 40–49, and 50 or more rooms on their ground floor. The data is displayed in the Table 6.

Table 6 Pompeii: door architecture in dining room and kitchen thresholds

House name in Pompeii	House size bracket (no. of rooms)	Evidence of door architecture around dining rooms	Evidence of door architecture around kitchens
Ara Maxima	10–19	Yes	Yes
Cabinet Maker	10–19	Yes	Unclear
M. Lucretius Fronto	10–19	Yes	Unclear
Paquius Proculus	10–19	Yes	Yes
Priest of Amandus	10–19	Yes	Unclear
Prince of Naples	10–19	Yes	Yes
Queen Margherita	10–19	Yes	Yes

Housing the Foul 209

House name in Pompeii	House size bracket (no. of rooms)	Evidence of door architecture around dining rooms	Evidence of door architecture around kitchens
Ship of Europa	10–19	Unclear	Yes
Tragic Poet	10–19	Yes	Yes
Bronze Bull	20–29	Unclear	Yes
Golden Cupids	20–29	Yes	Yes
Gavius Rufus	20–29	Unclear	Yes
Venus in the Shell	20–29	Yes	Yes
Vetti	20–29	Yes	Yes
Zephyr and Flora	20–29	Unclear	Yes
Pansa	30–39	Unclear	Unclear
Siricus	30–39	Yes	Yes
Coloured Capitals	40–49	Yes	Yes
Labyrinth	40–49	Yes	Yes
M. Obellius Firmus	40–49	Yes	Yes
Centennial	50 or more	Yes	Yes
Citharist	50 or more	Yes	Yes
Diomedes	50 or more	Yes	Yes

Table 7 Pompeii: door architecture in dining room and kitchen thresholds expressed as percentages

	Number of houses	Percentage (%)
Houses with clear evidence of door architecture in dining room and kitchen thresholds	15	65
Houses with clear evidence of door architecture in dining room but not kitchen thresholds	4	18
Houses with clear evidence of door architecture in kitchen but not dining room thresholds	3	13
Houses with no clear evidence of door architecture in either dining room or kitchen thresholds	1	4

When expressed in percentages, this data highlights the prevalence of houses that show clear evidence for door architecture in thresholds either in or leading into dining rooms and kitchens. Very few houses show no clear evidence of door architecture in the thresholds of dining rooms or kitchens.

A smaller survey of ten houses was undertaken at Herculaneum, again following the constraints of focusing on rooms identified with some certainty as dining rooms and kitchens due to finds and/or décor.[60] The results are listed in Table 8. Once again, these results have been expressed in percentages in Table 9.

Analysis of door architecture data shows some interesting trends. In both Pompeii and Herculaneum a high percentage of rooms for dining and cooking display evidence of door architecture in thresholds, indeed the figure for

Table 8 Herculaneum: door architecture in dining room and kitchen thresholds

House name in Herculaneum	House size bracket (no. of rooms)	Evidence of door architecture around dining rooms	Evidence of door architecture around kitchens
Black Hall	10–19	Yes	Yes
Corinthian *Atrium*	10–19	Yes	Unclear
Gem	10–19	Yes	Yes
Great Portal	10–19	Yes	Yes
Neptune Mosaic	10–19	Yes	Yes
Samnite	10–19	Yes	Yes
Tuscan Colonnade	10–19	Yes	Unclear
Alcove	20–29	Yes	Yes
Deer	20–29	Yes	Yes
Mosaic *atrium*	20–29	Yes	Yes

Table 9 Herculaneum: door architecture in dining room and kitchen thresholds expressed as percentages

	Number of houses	Percentage (%)
Houses with clear evidence of door architecture in dining room and kitchen thresholds	8	80
Houses with clear evidence of door architecture in dining room but not kitchen thresholds	2	20
Houses with clear evidence of door architecture in kitchen but not dining room thresholds	0	0
Houses with no clear evidence of door architecture in either dining room or kitchen thresholds	0	0

Herculaneum reaches 80 per cent with evidence of door architecture in thresholds to or leading into rooms identified as dining or kitchen spaces. In both Pompeian and Herculanean houses, then, a clear propensity has been shown for the presence of doors around either kitchens or dining rooms, and often both. Indeed, it is only one house in Pompeii that does not display clear evidence for door architecture around either its kitchen or dining room.

If we subdivide this information further by grouping houses according to number of rooms, from Pompeii we see a relatively broad spread of houses that have door architecture around both kitchens and dining rooms. Thus, five houses categorized in the 10–19 rooms bracket have door architecture around their kitchens and dining rooms and six houses at the top end of the spectrum (i.e. comprising over 40 rooms) likewise demonstrated evidence of door architecture around their cooking and food consumption areas. In the middle, four houses classed as having between 20–39 rooms demonstrate door architecture for both spaces. Herculaneum has comparatively smaller dwellings since there are no residences with over 30 rooms in the dataset. Once again, however, the evidence for doors in kitchens and dining rooms is well spread between houses with 10–19 rooms (five houses demonstrated this) and those with 20–29 rooms (three houses showed this). Moreover, if we focus specifically on the results of evidence of door architecture in kitchen and combined toilet thresholds, from a survey of 23 houses of Pompeii and 10 houses of Herculaneum, I found that the percentage of kitchens with evidence of door architecture was relatively consistent between the sites with Pompeii showing 78 per cent and Herculaneum displaying 80 per cent. Since the activities in these spaces were likely to be the most odoriferous and noisy, the ability to control the transmission of sensory experiences from this room to others throughout the property via the opening or closing of doors was key in a large percentage of properties.

Other architectural features separating kitchen and dining areas

It was not just doors or curtains that could be employed to separate the kitchen spaces from dining areas. Whilst doors in the thresholds of kitchens and *triclinia* and *oeci* provided the ability to close off or open up rooms as and when desired, there were many other possible architectural means by which either distance or obstacles could be placed between these rooms. These varied considerably according to house and some pertinent examples from Pompeii and Herculaneum are outlined below.

a) Corridors, spaces or rooms between kitchens and dining areas

As Pliny mentions in his Letter on his Laurentine Villa, corridors presented a good means by which to buffer sensory disturbances between two spaces. For him, judicious use of passageways in domestic architecture permitted 'deep seclusion and remoteness'.[61] In addition to corridors separating cooking and eating areas, the use of intervening rooms or spaces between them would also act to diminish the seepage of unwanted sensory experiences between areas, which might particularly include auditory, olfactory and visual interruptions.

Examination of the plans of houses from Pompeii and Herculaneum suggest that spaces, passageways and rooms were often placed between kitchens and dining areas. Perhaps the best examples of locating intervening spaces between kitchens and dining areas can be found when these rooms are situated on opposite sides of *atria* or peristyle gardens. Such organization of domestic spaces ensures a substantial gap between these rooms, which in turn can act to diminish sensory disturbances. Moreover, we find this approach to spatial organization being employed in houses of various sizes. In the relatively small house of the Ara Maxima, which falls into the 10–19 room classification listed previously, room (f) has been identified as the food preparation area, whilst on the other side of the *atrium* is situated the *triclinium* at (e) (Fig. 4.16).[62] Similar patterns of dining and kitchen location being on either side of *peristylia* or *atria* can likewise be found in the houses of the Ceii, Pansa, the Citharist, M. Lucretius Fronto, the Ship of Europa, Gavius Rufus, Coloured Capitals (see Figs 3.18, 4.1, 5.8). That these houses can be categorized into different size brackets suggests that this means of architectural organization was employed in dwellings of modest and opulent means.[63]

The house of the Neptune mosaic from Herculaneum presents another clear example of food preparation and dining areas being separated by large circulation areas (Fig. 7.2). In this dwelling, the kitchen at (c) is located at the front whilst the winter and summer *triclinia* (f) and (g) respectively are at the back, across the *atrium* and down a long corridor.

It is not just locating kitchen and dining areas on either side of *atria* or *peristylia* that separates these spaces and presents a sensory 'buffer' zone between them. Any rooms could be sited in this way, and the space and any walls in between would help to reduce transmission of sights, sounds and smells. A good example of this type of architectural arrangement can be found in the house of the Priest of Amandus (Fig. 7.3). Here, the kitchen at (c) is situated on one side of a passageway and the *triclinium* at (d) is found on the other. The intervening

Housing the Foul 213

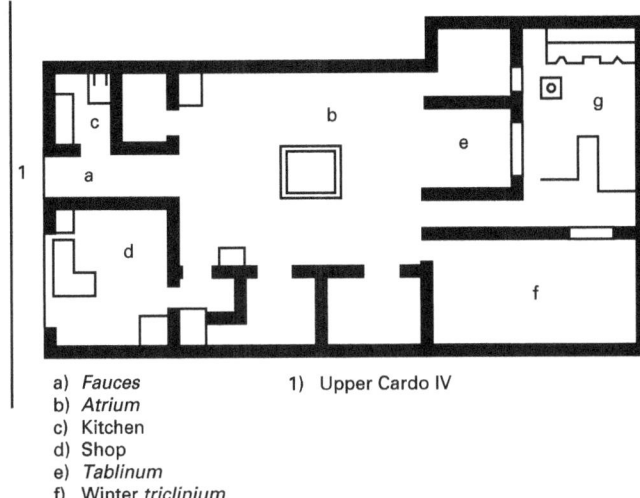

a) *Fauces*
b) *Atrium*
c) Kitchen
d) Shop
e) *Tablinum*
f) Winter *triclinium*
g) Summer *triclinium*

1) Upper Cardo IV

Figure 7.2 Floor plan of the house of the Neptune Mosaic (Ins V, 6-7), Herculaneum. © Bloomsbury Academic.

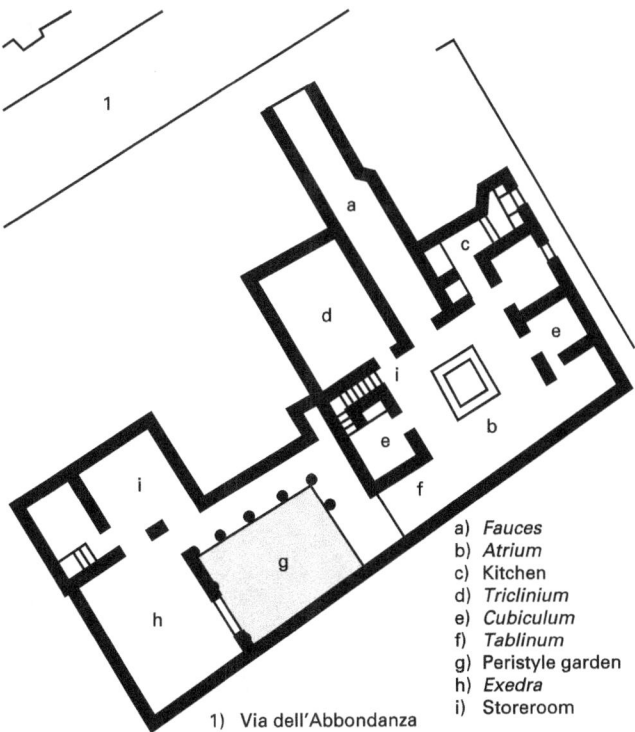

a) *Fauces*
b) *Atrium*
c) Kitchen
d) *Triclinium*
e) *Cubiculum*
f) *Tablinum*
g) Peristyle garden
h) *Exedra*
i) Storeroom

1) Via dell'Abbondanza

Figure 7.3 Floor plan of the house of the Priest of Amandus (Reg I.7.7), Pompeii. © Bloomsbury Academic.

space and walls of the corridor between the dining and kitchen spaces would have reduced the transmission of sensory experiences. Other examples of rooms placed in between kitchens and dining areas and acting as zones for absorbing leakage of sounds or smells and serving to block any unwanted sights can be found in the house of the Golden Cupids where the kitchen at (l) is situated on the rear right corner of the peristyle garden, and the residence's main *triclinium* at (k) is further along the dwelling's back wall overlooking the peristyle garden (Fig. 7.4). A *cubiculum* (j') and a corridor leading to the *posticum* at (n) are placed between these dining and food preparation spaces. Likewise, in the large house of the Centennial, the *triclinium* at (g) is spatially separated from the kitchen at (i) by an intervening room. Similarly, the large *triclinium* at (l) is not only separated from the nearby bath suite (m–q) by a corridor and the substantial walls of the bath suite backing onto the passageway, it is also a substantial distance from the kitchen at (i) and a latrine at (q) (Fig. 7.5).[64]

1) Via del Vesuvio
2) Vicolo dei Vetti

a) Fauces
b) Atrium
c) Cubiculum
d) Tablinum
e) Exedra
f) Peristyle
g) Garden
h) Storeroom
i) Previously used as a latrine
j and j') Cubiculum
k) Triclinium
l) Kitchen
m) Latrine
n) Posticum

Figure 7.4 Floor plan of the house of the Golden Cupids (Reg VI.16.7), Pompeii. © Bloomsbury Academic.

Housing the Foul 215

a) *Fauces*
b) *Atrium*
c) *Tablinum*
d and d') *Exedra*
e) *Peristyle garden*
f) *Exedra*
g) *Triclinium*
h) *Nymphaeum*
i) Kitchen
j) *Cubiculum*
k) Reception room
l) *Triclinium*
m) *Apodyterium*
n) *Tepidarium*
o) *Caldarium*
p) *Frigidarium*
q) Latrine with graffiti

1) Via di Nola
2) Vicolo del Centenario
3) Unnamed road

Figure 7.5 Floor plan of the house of the Centennial (Reg IX.8.6), Pompeii. © Bloomsbury Academic.

An example of the use of rooms as buffer zones between kitchens and dining areas can also be found in the house of the Corinthian *Atrium* from Herculaneum (Fig. 7.6). Here the kitchen has been identified as being in room (d), whilst an *oecus* has been identified at (e). In between these rooms was a small room, which would have helped to reduce some of the kitchen heat, smells and noise from seeping into the dining area.

In larger dwellings, of course, the number of rooms that could be located between a kitchen and any dining areas could be substantially greater than was possible in smaller dwellings. The house of Paquius Proculus presents one such example (Fig. 4.7). The plan of this dwelling suggests yet a further example of

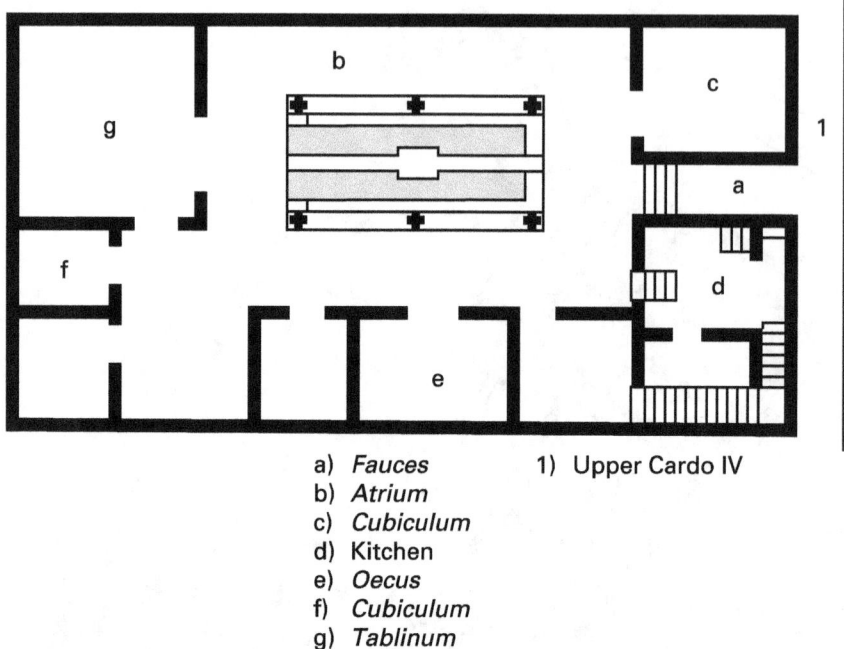

a) *Fauces*   1) Upper Cardo IV
b) *Atrium*
c) *Cubiculum*
d) Kitchen
e) *Oecus*
f) *Cubiculum*
g) *Tablinum*

Figure 7.6 Floor plan of the house of the Corinthian *Atrium* (Ins V, 30), Herculaneum. © Bloomsbury Academic.

rooms being used as intervening spaces between food preparation and food consumption areas. Thus, the *triclinium* at (g) sits at some distance from the kitchen at (i). A further *oecus* (f) sits at an even greater distance from the kitchen, with three rooms located in between them. Such a location of these food consumption and preparation rooms would certainly help alleviate concerns of unwanted sensations. The location of the room entrances facing towards the peristyle garden would provide light to the activities taking place here and allow for breezes from the garden to help reduce more quickly any unwanted smells, excessive heat or other sensory discomforts: the presence of door architecture in the entrances to these three spaces show that these rooms might be further closed off from the peristyle as required.[65]

b) *Walls, obstacles and raised or lowered floors between kitchens and dining spaces*

We also find walls and other obstacles cleverly situated between kitchen and dining areas. These could have helped reduce transmission of unwanted sensory experiences. The house of the Tragic Poet presents an excellent example of how walls have been employed for this purpose (Fig. 7.7). The main *triclinium* at (h) and the cooking area at (i) of this house were situated next to one another on the northeast side, facing the peristyle garden (j). The thresholds of both rooms demonstrated evidence of door architecture, which gave the ability to close off or open up these spaces from the peristyle as need arose, whilst the kitchen hearth and latrine were located at the end of a long corridor, so that sounds and smells would have had further to travel (and greater chance to reduce) before reaching the peristyle garden. Furthermore, the substantial wall between these rooms would have helped diminish noises of cooking activities being heard by diners in the *triclinium* and ensured that diners had no view of cooking taking place.[66]

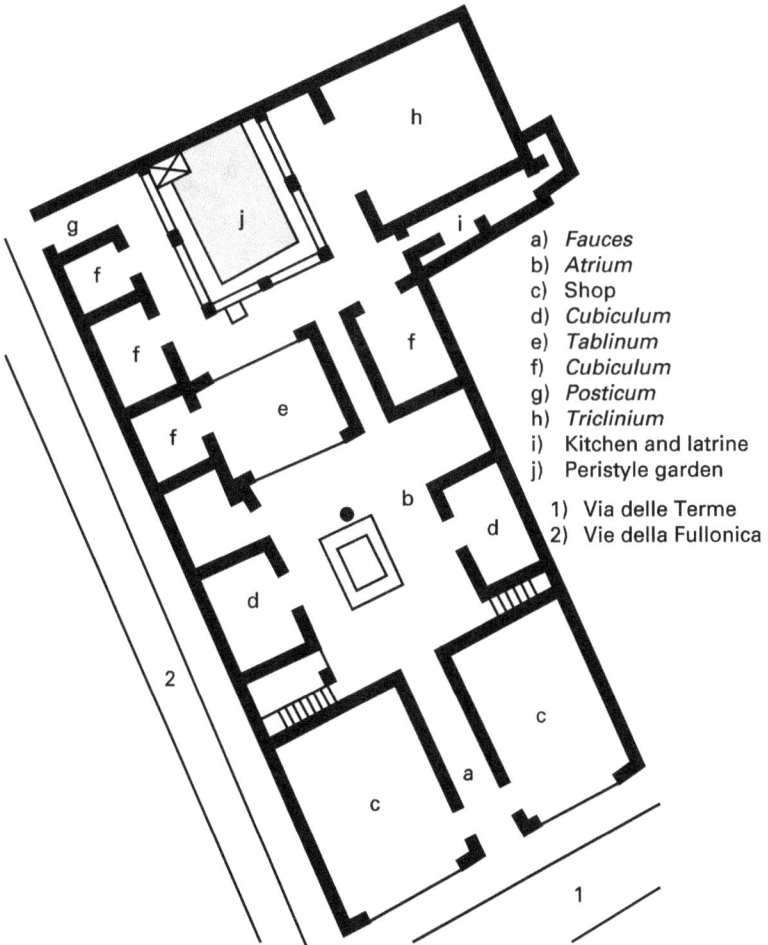

Figure 7.7 Floor plan of the house of the Tragic Poet (Reg VI.8.3), Pompeii. © Bloomsbury Academic.

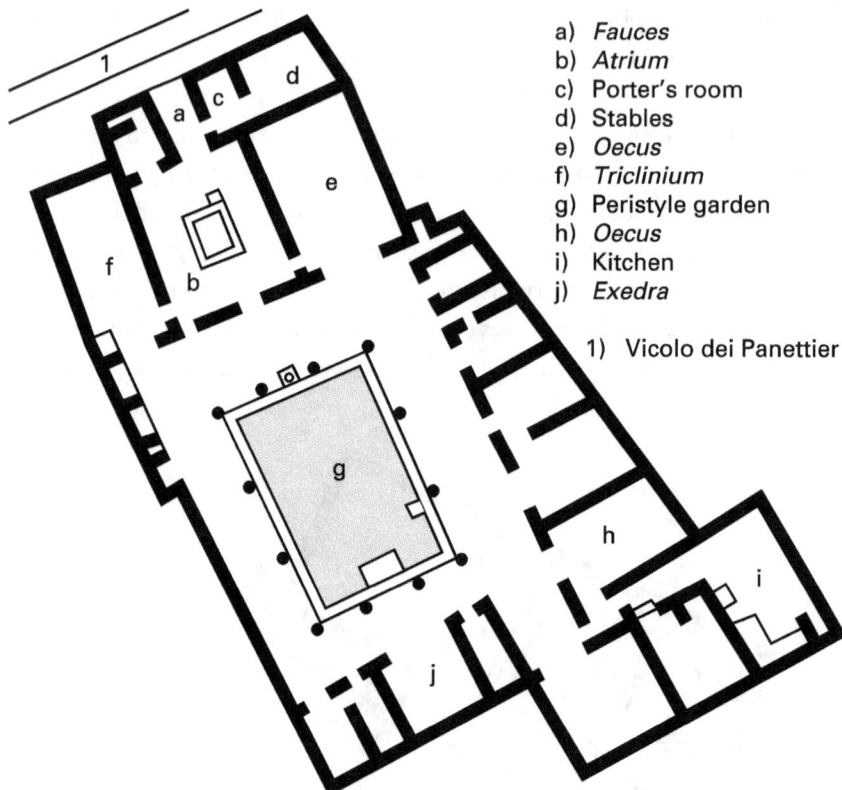

Figure 7.8 Floor plan of the house of Gavius Rufus (Reg VII.2.16), Pompeii. © Bloomsbury Academic.

A similar kitchen and dining area layout can be seen in the house of Gavius Rufus (Fig. 7.8). As a relatively sizeable residence that falls into the 20–29 rooms bracket, this dwelling is a little larger than the house of the Tragic Poet and boasts a number of clearly identified dining rooms. Whilst two of these (e) and (f) are situated near the entrance and on the opposite side of the peristyle garden from the kitchen, a further *oecus* at (h) has been identified next door to the kitchen at (i). Not only is the kitchen situated in a room located down a corridor measuring 4 metres, which would help to dissipate unwanted sensory interruptions, but there is clear door architecture both in the threshold connecting this corridor to the peristyle garden (g), and in the doorway that connects the *oecus* at (h) to the corridor. Thus, whilst proximity between these two areas would make delivery of food easier, there were clear ways by which the sensory experiences of these parts of the house could be controlled if required.

The house of the Ceii presents an equally intriguing example whereby as well as situating the kitchen on the opposite side of the *atrium*, architectural obstacles and alterations were organized between kitchen and dining area in a manner that would have helped reduce sensory impact (Fig. 3.18). According to Michel, this residence underwent substantial renovation in the third style after the earthquake of AD 62 and it was at this stage that the kitchen, which had been at the back of the dwelling at (i), was moved to the front at (d).[67] Once at the front of the residence, this kitchen was on the other side of the *atrium* at (b) from the *triclinium* (f) and room (e) which has been identified as both a *tablinum* and a *triclinio estivo* (summer dining room) on account of its layout.[68] Moreover, the floor of the kitchen (d) was lowered to house the latrine whilst the floor of the *triclinio estivo* (e) was raised up two steps (Fig. 4.18). Even with the door to the kitchen closed, the alteration of the floor levels of both these rooms would have impacted upon the views between them as it would have been harder to see activities in the kitchen when reclining in a dining room situated on a slightly higher level. Joshel and Petersen suggest that diners would have sat with their backs to the kitchen as they dined facing the garden at (h) and its back wall painted with a large hunt scene. Whilst such a positioning would have ensured that diners could not have seen slaves at work in the kitchen, this arrangement of diners is not entirely certain. According to Foss, diners would have been arranged facing into the *atrium*, however the clever arrangement of the columns around the *impluvium* in the *atrium*, one of which was situated directly in the line of sight between the *triclinium* window and the kitchen entrance, would have resulted in diners only glimpsing slaves as they moved between kitchen and *triclinium*.[69]

A substantially larger example of a house that also demonstrates use of spaces between the food production and service area of the residence in combination with interesting uses of wall positioning to reduce the impact of service areas on areas used for dining is the house of Siricus (Fig. 7.9).[70] From its entrance on the Vicolo del Lupanare, a doorway on the left-hand side of the *atrium* (b), with evidence of door architecture, leads onto a narrow corridor (h) and then to an oven with a millstone and catallus at (i).[71] A further means of access to this service and productive part of the dwelling leads from a small doorway in the garden *ambulatio* (m) into (k). Room (k) itself seems to have been divided into two with a raised level in the floor, the remnants of which are visible today (Fig. 7.10). It is possible that this change in flooring height demarcates where a partition existed to separate the room in two. If so, one part of room (k) formed a small space accessed by a single door that led out onto the peristyle at (m). The other

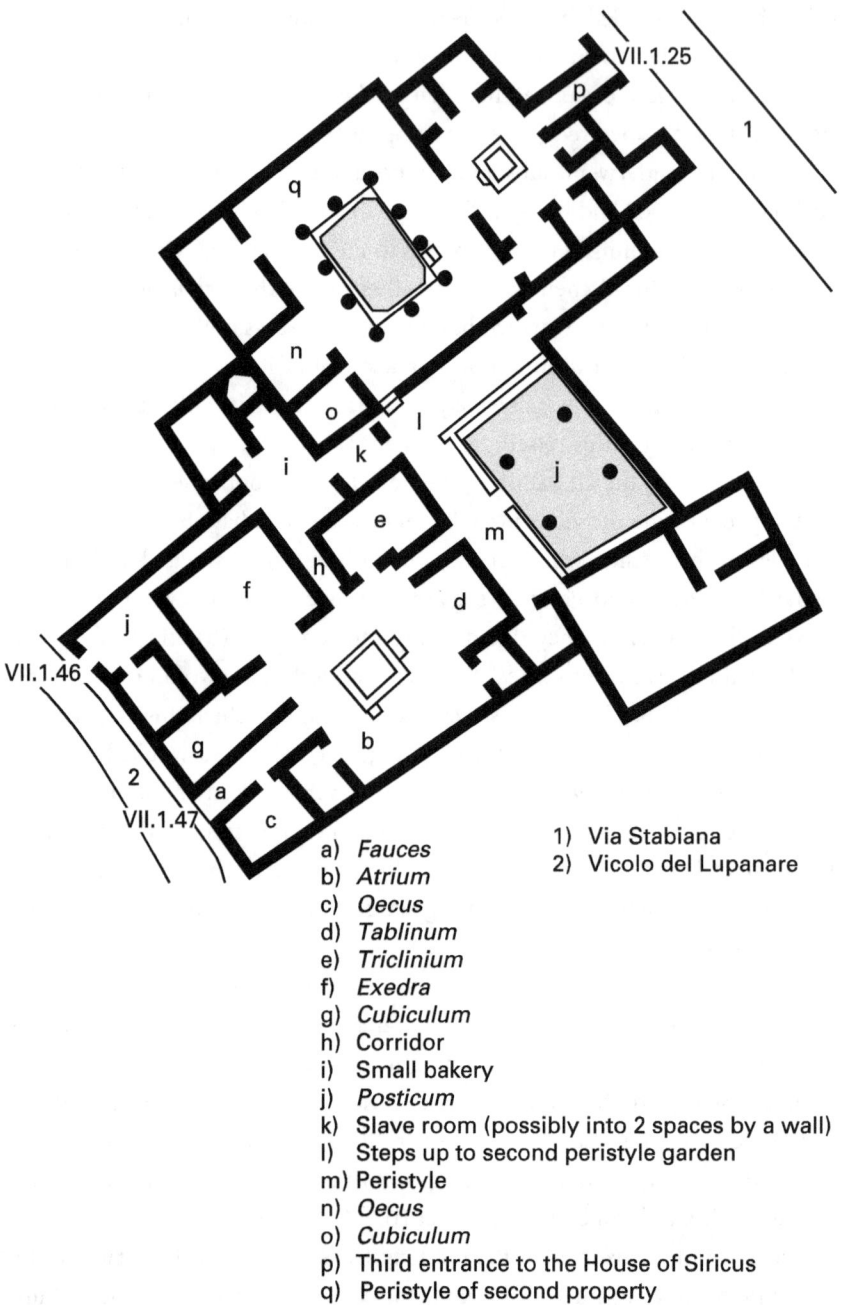

a) *Fauces*
b) *Atrium*
c) *Oecus*
d) *Tablinum*
e) *Triclinium*
f) *Exedra*
g) *Cubiculum*
h) Corridor
i) Small bakery
j) *Posticum*
k) Slave room (possibly into 2 spaces by a wall)
l) Steps up to second peristyle garden
m) Peristyle
n) *Oecus*
o) *Cubiculum*
p) Third entrance to the House of Siricus
q) Peristyle of second property

1) Via Stabiana
2) Vicolo del Lupanare

Figure 7.9 Floor plan of the house of Siricus (Reg VII.1.47), Pompeii. © Bloomsbury Academic.

Figure 7.10 Room (k) of the house of Siricus (Reg VII.1.47) showing uneven floor layers and location of possible partition wall dividing room in two. Pompeii. Photo: Hannah Platts.

part of room (k) made a corridor that led directly into the service section of this dwelling at (i).[72] The presence of a thin narrow corridor here would have acted as a buffer zone between the service section of the dwelling at (i) and the peristyle at (m). Additionally, the service section of the house was also separated from the *oecus* at (n) in a number of ways. Not only was *oecus* (n) situated at a higher level above the service section of the dwelling, but the walls of the service area lacked connecting entrances or windows. This would also mean that transmission of sounds and smells would be substantially reduced and in addition there would be no views between the production area for those dining in *oecus* (n).

The house of the Bronze Bull presents an amalgamation of methods to distance food production areas from dining spaces (Fig. 7.11). The kitchen at (k)

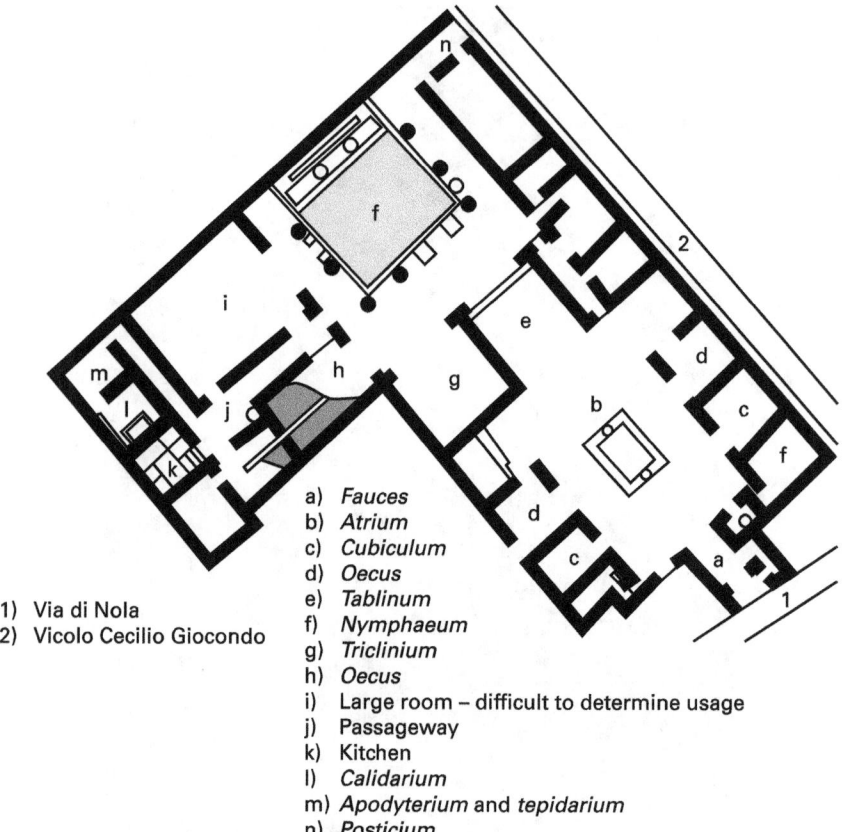

Figure 7.11 Floor plan of the house of the Bronze Bull (Reg V.1.7), Pompeii. © Bloomsbury Academic.

is located at the end of a corridor and circulation area (j). The entrance threshold to the kitchen at (k) shows evidence of door architecture (Fig. 7.12). In addition to the corridor and circulation area measuring in excess of 6 metres in length, which would have helped reduce sensory impact from the kitchen into the *oecus* at (h) and the *triclinium* at (g), the strategic positioning of the walls and narrow side door into the *oecus* at (h) at the furthest distance from the kitchen shows concern with reducing multisensory impact of the food production area on the dining space, but also enabling easy delivery of food to waiting guests.

The houses of the Deer and the Mosaic *Atrium* from Herculaneum both demonstrate imaginative methods of spatial organization of food consumption and food preparation areas, and appear to be ordered with a view to being able to manipulate the sensory interactions of the spaces. Firstly, the house of the

Figure 7.12 Steps from kitchen at (k) up to corridor (j) in the house of the Bronze Bull (Reg V.1.7), Pompeii. Photo: Hannah Platts.

Deer has its kitchen located at (j) behind its main *triclinium* at (c) (Fig. 7.13). Not only did the kitchen threshold display evidence of door architecture, thereby indicating that the space could be closed off from the rest of the house, but it opens on to a narrow corridor at (i) which abuts the *triclinium* on two and a half sides. Additionally, three of the four thresholds of the *triclinium* display clear evidence of door architecture, whilst the fourth and widest threshold, which overlooked the residence's garden at (e), suggests the presence of door architecture although this was difficult to ascertain due to damage. The rooms are organized so that not only is there intervening space between them, but there are substantial walls and numerous doors that could be closed to separate the dining area from the kitchen. The house of the Mosaic *Atrium* not only demonstrates the use of the peristyle garden as an intervening space through which to distance the house's kitchen at (e) from its main dining areas at (h) and (j),

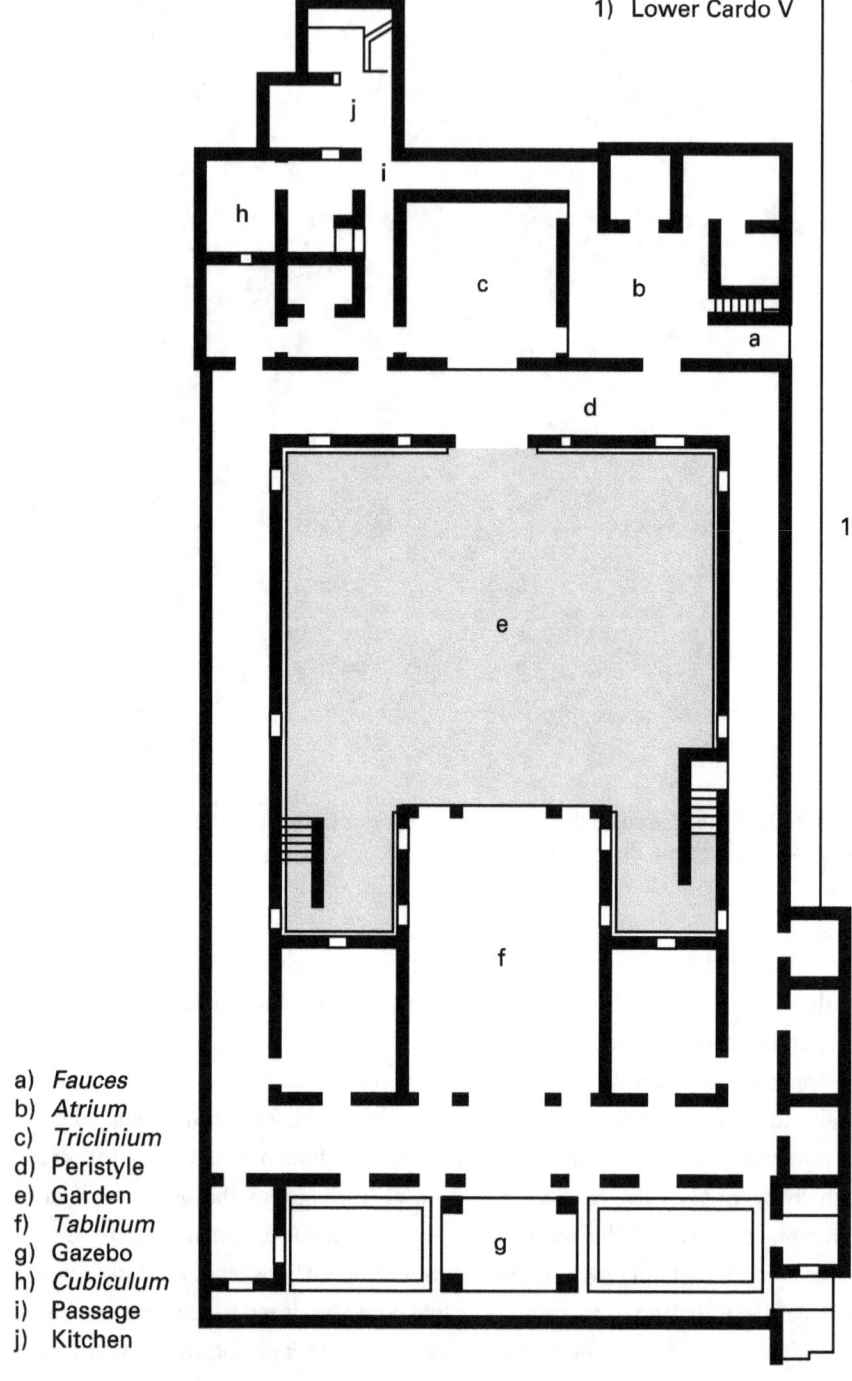

a) *Fauces*
b) *Atrium*
c) *Triclinium*
d) Peristyle
e) Garden
f) *Tablinum*
g) Gazebo
h) *Cubiculum*
i) Passage
j) Kitchen

Figure 7.13 Floor plan of the house of the Deer (Ins IV, 21), Herculaneum. © Bloomsbury Academic.

but also has windows within the peristyle's colonnade at (g) close to the kitchen area at (e) (Fig. 6.6). These would have helped not only to reduce further the smells and sounds from the kitchen travelling across the garden to the dining area, but also to reduce the visibility of slaves bringing food to the back of the house from the kitchen at the front. The fact that the partitions in the colonnade are situated between those columns near the kitchen that are directly in view of the dining area at the opposite end of the garden indicates the wish of the owner to bring foods to guests with little visual or, indeed, other sensory distraction. That slaves would be able to walk from the kitchen at (e) down the steps at (f) in the *atrium* (b), along the ambulatory at (k) or (g) and into either the *triclinium* at (j) the *oecus* at (h) is surely a consequence of careful organization to control the potential sensory experience of guests as they dined overlooking either the sea or the fountain and garden.

c) *Locating cooking and/or storage areas on different storeys from dining areas*

Another means of separating dining areas from cooking and/or storage areas in the Roman house was by locating the productive and/or storerooms on different, often lower storeys, of the dwelling. Perhaps the best example of this can be found in the villa of Diomedes, where a narrow stairway at (g) is located immediately to the righthand side of the entrance, which leads to the residence's main productive and storage area ((j) and the surrounding rooms on Fig. 3.20). Although today this part of the residence is in ruins and overgrown with vegetation, during its excavation in 1773 numerous hearths were discovered here in the large court area at (j), as well as smaller hearths in some of the rooms adjoining area (j).[73] A possible hearth was also further identified at (j).[74] In addition to these stoves, cooking vessels including pans and cauldrons were found both within these rooms and also in situ on the hearth in area (i), which further highlight the fact that part of the function of this section of the dwelling was food production.[75] This part of the villa was not merely used for cooking and storing produce and housing slaves. The very wide and high threshold in area (h) indicates that this area was also used as a cart entrance for the delivery of goods to the villa, which further emphasizes just how noisy and smelly this section of the dwelling might have been.[76] Its location on a lower level from the reception area of the residence demonstrates, therefore, a desire to control unwanted sensory disturbances from filtering into the rest of the villa whilst still permitting easy communication via the stairwell at (g) into the small peristyle and around the rest of the home.

That different levels were used for service, storage and transporting goods to and from a dwelling can also be seen in the house of the Golden Bracelet (Fig. 6.8). It is only, however, when we consider the different levels of this house that we can really start to comprehend the complexity of its organization. Walking in from street level, visitors would find themselves on the same level as room (e), one of the dwelling's *triclinia*. Descending two floors to the level of the garden, once again guests would be in close proximity to another dining room, this time situated at (k). Importantly for our considerations, the main cooking and food preparation area in this residence in the kitchen at (j) has been located on neither of these floors but rather is situated between them on the basement level. The positioning of the kitchen on neither of the levels which houses dining rooms suggests a desire to separate the main food preparation and consumption spaces, thereby reducing sensory disturbances between them. That the kitchen is positioned close to the stairs that lead up to the street level and down to the garden level, however, indicate a desire to retain relatively easy communication between the spaces.

d) Locating kitchens or dining areas near or in gardens

One of the best ways of reducing transmission of smells and sounds from kitchen to dining area would be to ensure the location of the kitchen or dining area in or near outside spaces. In examples of dwellings of a variety of sizes, examination of the positioning of kitchens and dining rooms in relation to external spaces suggests this may have been a possible concern behind their positioning. In the small house of Queen Margherita, not only is the kitchen at (f) situated down a narrow corridor that is separated from the main circulation area (c) by a threshold that holds evidence of door architecture, but the dining area at (d), which also demonstrates door architecture in its threshold, is on the other side of the house (Fig. 7.14). Access to the *triclinium* from the kitchen requires walking past a garden, across which breezes might blow, helping to dissipate lingering food smells and to have impact upon any noise made in the vicinity.

In another relatively small residence, the house of the Cabinet Maker, the kitchen at (k) is separated from the rest of the large circulation area by a partition wall of wood and brick (Figs 6.4 and 7.15). The room next door to it at (f), which might have been employed at times for dining, shows evidence of door architecture,[77] whilst the clearly identified dining space at (h) is situated at some distance from the food production area and overlooking the garden.[78] At the threshold to this room, the discovery of an iron rod seems to suggest a curtain

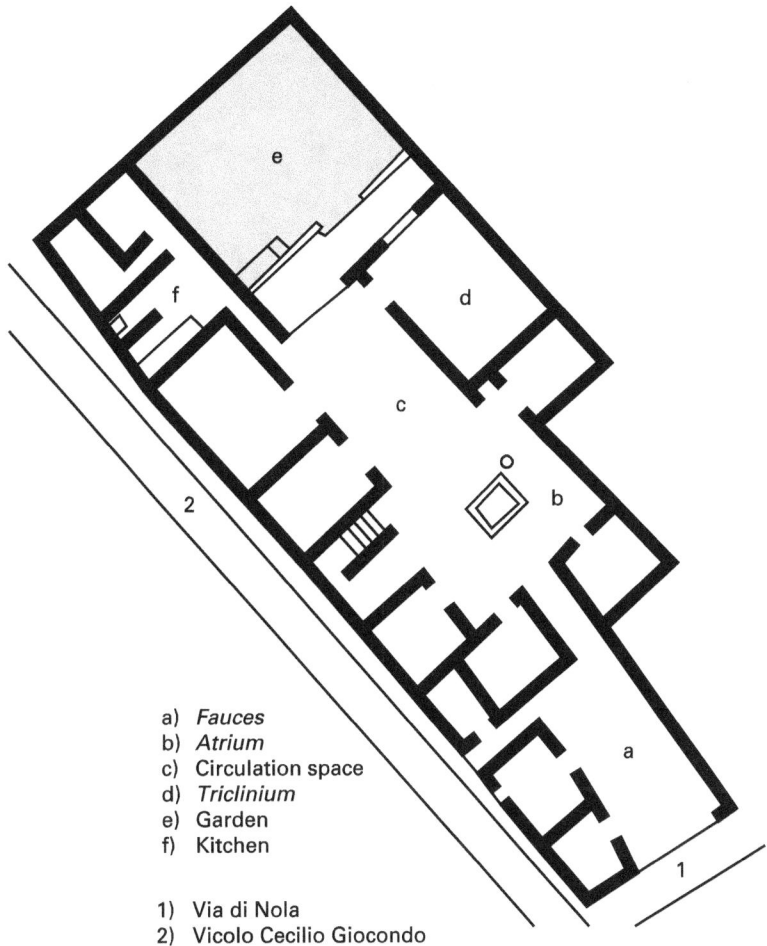

Figure 7.14 Floor plan of the house of Queen Margherita (Reg V.2.1), Pompeii. © Bloomsbury Academic.

could be drawn across the wide entrance to this room; the narrow doorway in the room's west wall showed evidence of door architecture. Both the door and curtain when shut would have cut off views across the circulation space at (i) and the curtain in particular would have helped protect diners from inclement weather as they ate. Since food preparation occurred in the kitchen at (k), which itself was next to the garden at (j), this might also have helped to dissipate further unwanted smells of the cooking process travelling to the diners in (h).

A further means by which dining areas were clearly separated from food production can be found in the examples of summer *triclinia* located in gardens.

Figure 7.15 Kitchen at (k) in the house of the Cabinet Maker (Reg I.10.7), Pompeii. Note the partition wall used to separate this space of from the rest of the ambulatory at (i) (fig. 6.4). Photo: Hannah Platts.

Once again, houses of varying sizes seem to employ this mode of architectural organization, from the relatively modest house of Trebius Valens (which can be classified as having between 20–29 rooms) to the much larger villa of Diomedes (which boasted over 50 rooms) (Fig. 3.20).[79] At the house of Trebius Valens, two kitchens have been identified, one at (h) and the other at (l) (Fig. 5.4).[80] The location of the kitchen at (l) is especially interesting since there seems to have been a small serving hatch between the kitchen and the dining room for serving food to diners in the garden. The wall in which this serving hatch was sited would have blocked views into the kitchen and over the processes of food preparation, and would have reduced transmission of some smell and sound, but it also would have meant that serving hungry diners was relatively easy. Indeed, that the house had two kitchens meant large scale dishes that required complicated preparation could occur in the kitchen at (h), at some distance from the diners in the garden, whilst less complicated activities (or indeed sensory preparations) such as boiling water might have taken place in the smaller, nearer garden kitchen. Thus, the ability to use two kitchens, together with the proximity of one to the garden, might have been organized specifically with an ability or desire in mind to manipulate the sensory experiences of visitors reclining in the summer *triclinium*.[81]

One further point to add to this discussion of the location of kitchens and dining rooms in relation to one another is the extent to which different methods explored above not only created distance between kitchen and dining areas but also had an impact upon the ease with which slaves were able to deliver food to diners. As pointed out with the example of the house of Paquius Proculus, whilst storage and toilet, and dining facilities were situated on different levels, the presence of a ramp would have helped ease communication, especially for slaves carrying produce to kitchens (Fig. 4.7). For those residences, such as the house of the Tragic Poet, which located kitchen and dining room close to one another and relied on walls, doors and small intervening spaces for separation, close proximity would facilitate speedy delivery of food to waiting guests (Fig. 7.7). Where corridors were used to distance kitchens from dining rooms, such as the houses of the Bronze Bull, Queen Margherita, Trebius Valens, Gavius Rufus and the Deer, these demonstrate an interesting means of facilitating the communication between these spaces since the corridor's narrowness would act as an architectural guidance to visitors and slaves alike that it led to a service sector of the house (Figs 5.4, 7.8, 7.11, 7.13, 7.14). Visitors would therefore be discouraged from wandering away from entertainment spaces into the corridor and thereby avoid both obstructing the vital service route between dining and kitchen areas as well as the risk of getting too close to the unpleasant sensory realm of food production areas.[82]

Conclusion

Unpleasant and offensive smells were perceived as evidence of disgusting habits and those who produced them were likewise understood by Rome's elite as belonging to the lower orders of society.[83] Thus for Horace, Juvenal and Lucilius, brothels and prostitutes were seen as places and people of ultimate pollution and stench.[84] Seneca's desire to flee the city, Columella's advice about the spatial organization of the villa and Cicero's need to distance parts of houses that produced malodourous smells demonstrate both a level of concern about noxious smells pervasive in life in the ancient city and at home as well as emphasizing a wish, at least within elite writings, to reduce where possible interaction with such odours. Thus, whilst excessive and continuous contact with strong smells lead both to olfactory habituation and sensory impairment, examination of the archaeological layout of the houses of Pompeii and Herculaneum demonstrates

Roman concern with where these rooms should be situated and a desire to block them off or distance them from the rest of the dwelling, where possible. That many kitchens with combined toilets show evidence of windows to the outside not only demonstrates a desire to light these spaces, but also suggests a concern with reducing smell.[85] Furthermore as Hobson points out, the finds of wooden pegs for hanging up herbs in some toilets, and the facts that cooking and burning of herbs might disguise offensive smells whilst disposal of burning charcoal would seal the content of toilets and burn off excess methane also suggests a desire to reduce transmission of unpleasant smells in the home.[86] Moreover, locating the stench-producing rooms of kitchens and toilets together, or at least near one another, offered a means by which smelly parts of the house might be concentrated into a small area.[87] This in turn might make more possible an owner's ability to control or prevent the transmission of pungent smells throughout the dwelling as well as perhaps infestations of flies and vermin such as rats in the parts of the house that were open to guests.

Yet the architectural organization of the Roman home was not just about eliminating unpleasant smells that emanated from the latrines and kitchens. If the ideal elite *convivium* expected food to appear mysteriously as a surprise for those dining, then controlling all aspects of production and presentation of the meal was crucial for any self-respecting host who sought admiration of contemporaries. Hence careful configuration of the Roman home also sought to conceal or disguise, in a variety of ways, unwanted sounds and sights both from disturbing the experience of diners and making a host look incompetent by diminishing his ability to display power and control over the sensory realm of others.

8

Conclusion: Sensing Status – Approaching a Lived Experience of the Roman House

We think ourselves poor and mean if our walls are not resplendent with large and costly mirrors; if our marbles from Alexandria are not set off by mosaics of Numidian stone; if their borders are not faced over on all sides with difficult patterns, arranged in many colours like paintings; if our vaulted ceilings are not buried in glass; if our swimming-pools are not lined with Thasian marble, once a rare and wonderful sight in any temple pools into which we let down our bodies after they have been drained weak by abundant perspiration; and finally, if the water has not poured from silver spigots. I have so far been speaking of the ordinary bathing-establishments; what shall I say when I come to those of the freedmen? What a vast number of statues, of columns that support nothing, but are built for decoration, merely in order to spend money! And what masses of water that fall crashing from level to level! We have become so luxurious that we will have nothing but precious stones to walk upon.

In this bath of Scipio's there are tiny chinks – you cannot call them windows – cut out of the stone wall in such a way as to admit light without weakening the fortifications; nowadays, however, people regard baths as fit only for moths if they have not been so arranged that they receive the sun all day long through the widest of windows, if men cannot bathe and get a coat of tan at the same time, and if they cannot look out from their bath-tubs over stretches of land and sea.[1]

In his *Moral Letters* to Lucilius, Seneca was writing in the first century AD and looking back some three centuries to the life and death of Scipio Africanus, a hero who, disillusioned with his beloved Rome, ended his days living in self-imposed exile in his villa at Liternum. The core of Seneca's letter is his emphasis on the importance of being content with a simple life: how noble Scipio compared to the lesser men of Seneca's own time. This comparison encapsulates much of the paradox behind the lives of elite Romans and the residences in which they lived: the house presented a clear statement of power, influence and wealth to visitors, whether they were equals who came to conduct business or politics, or clients who approached their superiors for favours – in each case the house served to make an impact. At the same time the house was perceived as offering the owner a sanctuary from the bustle of the city, thus there was a dual role for the house as both a public and private building.

What constituted the public and private areas of a house and the ways in which these could be altered has been extensively discussed in this book, and what emerges is the central function of the whole range of senses employed in a variety of ways within the elite Roman dwelling. It was through the varied manipulation of embodied experience in the home that Rome's elite sought to control their display of personal standing to others. For Seneca, whilst his sense of moral outrage at contemporary living and lifestyles permeates his letter to Lucilius, the important role of manipulating multiple senses in the home is also emphasized. The luxury to which he refers so disparagingly is aimed at all the senses – statues and columns one can touch, luxurious baths with views over sea and land, masses of water crashing down and even precious stones to walk on – an elite house was certainly prepared in order to make a multisensory statement.

When we look at ancient literature and physically engage with space and surroundings, the importance of multisensory experience in ancient Rome is evident. The Greek myths, which were well known to Romans, relied on stories of the manipulation of the senses. Odysseus made the Cyclops, Polyphemus, drunk and blinded him to escape, his men were fed by Circe and turned into swine, it required wax in the ears to escape the alluring song of the Sirens, and when the disguised Odysseus returned to Ithaca it was only his dog who was able to recognize him. The widespread and traditionally held belief that sight is the principal sense has until now, however, dominated attempts to understand the Roman home and its role in society. Most scholarly attention to sensory understanding of life in the Roman home has revolved around sightlines and views into houses as well as movement and vistas once inside. So, whilst much of the evidence on Roman houses explored in this book is well known and has been examined by others, the multisensory approach to the Roman domestic realm suggested here, exploring it as a lived and embodied environment, develops new insights into how to understand ancient domestic space and its role in the Roman world.

This book argues that although the sense of sight and the way in which it engages visitors and inhabitants with the home is key, placing it in a dominant role wrongly implies that other senses were less important in understanding and experiencing the Roman house. The focus on sight, and visually analysing the Roman home creates a blind spot within the scholarship on the Roman domestic realm which risks giving only a partial understanding not only into how Romans lived within their dwellings but also as to how they used their homes as part of their arsenal of resources for personal status display. Whilst concentrating on plotting vistas across gardens or views into rooms, we may overlook the other bodily experiences that household inhabitants and visitors would have had as they stood within and wandered around the Roman *domus*: the sound of rain, for example, falling into the *impluvium* and the smell of smoke from oil lamps lighting dark corners on a winter's morning in Pompeii, or the intoxicating aroma of roses and lilies punctuated with the unpleasant waft of body odour and halitosis as a neighbouring diner in the summer *triclinium* turns to strike up conversation.

The perceived dominance of sight, and the resultant subordination of other bodily experiences, is not only an issue for studying the ancient Roman home. Rather, as modern and ancient scholars exploring the topic of blindness have demonstrated, removal of the visual encourages a more detailed investigation of the other senses of the western sensorium. Lucien Descaves in his novel *Les Emmurés*, following a group of blind adults in Paris, sought to 'create forms of nonvisual expression from within the confines of ocularcentric language', through which visual words were transformed into a multisensory world of textures, sounds, smells and tastes.[2] As such, the other lesser or 'baser' sensations of human life and interaction were brought to prominence.[3] In the same way, scholars of Roman housing should likewise re-place sight amongst the rest of the human sensorium thereby enabling other sensory experiences of touch, smell, sound and taste within the home to come to life, opening up a whole new insight into how the Roman home might have been employed as a vehicle of status display.

When we allow other senses to share equally in our 'reading' of the multisensory experiences that were essential to daily life and the Roman home, we gain a far greater understanding of that life and the ways all senses were manipulated by owners for the purposes of their personal display. In the same way that when standing in a space, we do not just see that which is around us, we also hear it, smell it, feel it and taste it; we might look to Pliny's descriptions of his Laurentine and Tuscan villas where he seeks to do likewise, bringing to life the splendours of his domestic realm in all physical ways possible. He tells his reader of the fragrant violets and soft acanthus leaves, the sounds of the marble fountains, the silence provided by glazed windows in the cloisters during storms, the rooms with windows that allow the warmth of the sun's rays from sunrise to sunset and the foods he can get from the nearby seas or pastures.[4] His villas are at once places of aromatic scents, delicious flavours and textures, discreet and unobtrusive sounds, inviting temperatures and picturesque scenes, all of which combine to make a beguiling display of his wealth and sophistication. Moreover, throughout these letters Pliny emphasizes his personal role in the construction and organization of these dwellings. He explains that his detailed description of his Tuscan home is because he is 'indulging the affection I have for all the places I have mostly laid out myself or where I have perfected an earlier design', whilst he says of his garden suite of rooms in his Laurentine villa that they are 'my favourite spot and well worthy of being so. I had them built myself'.[5] All the pleasant corporeal sensations to be experienced whilst at his home were a consequence of his capabilities and resources which he brought together to create a scene of domestic physical bliss that exuded messages of his power and ability to control both the natural world outside and the sensory realms of those within.

As we have seen, these messages from Pliny that the Roman home was a vehicle by which an owner's wealth, social standing and dominion was displayed through controlling the complete bodily experience of others are echoed in other literary texts and throughout the archaeological remains. Whether such manipulation occurred through the use of doors to close off rooms from the sensory nuisances of the kitchen, through the use of unguents and flowers to conceal the stench of a rotting corpse in the *atrium*, or the use of fountains to distract from the shouts in the street outside, all such actions within, and configurations of, the Roman house sought to show the owner at his best. Thus as we have seen, still and flowing water might freshen the sticky summer air and provide reassuring sounds, sweet smelling plants and trees reduce the stench of street and latrine, roasting meat excite the taste buds, statues and art works divert the eye, the cool touch of marble or silverware at the *convivium* suggest wealth, and curtains and doors ensure privacy.

When we look at descriptions of Roman houses and we examine the remains of their dwellings, then, we must recognize the importance of the full range of senses in the ownership, appreciation and manipulation of the Roman house. For many Romans, particularly Rome's elite, power and its articulation was all-important, and houses formed a backdrop to the display of that power. It was in their houses that leading Romans entertained their equals, patronized their clients, intrigued with their political allies and rivals and lived their family lives. This book has demonstrated that Romans of varying levels of wherewithal recognized the power of multiple senses and exploited this knowledge to greater and greater effect to build and decorate their residences. Whilst Seneca might outwardly deplore such decadence, comparison of his house descriptions with those of other Roman authors such as Pliny the Younger, Statius or Martial together with archaeological remains of dwellings from Pompeii and Herculaneum emphasize equally the concerns of owners to manipulate the full bodily immersion of inhabitants and visitors alike and thereby to intensify displays of power and control over the physical experience and environment of others.

Notes

Chapter 1

1 Hor. *Sat.* II.VI. 79–117, trans. H. Rushton Fairclough.
2 This famous story originates from one of Aesop's earlier fables written between the seventh and sixth centuries BC. As well as being retold by Horace, later versions of the story have been retold for example in Marcus Aurelius' *Meditations* (XI. 22), and the canonical Scottish poet, Robert Henryson's *The Taill of the Uponlandis Mous and the Burges Mous* written around 1480.
3 Pallasmaa 2012: 68.
4 For recent examinations of the complex relationship between text and physical remains see, e.g., Storey 1999; Allison 2001; Sauer 2004; Laurence 2012.
5 Arist. *De Anima*, 429a on sight as the chief sense. On his dealing with the senses in order of their hierarchy see Arist. *De Anima*, 418a. 9ff.
6 For chronological accounts and explanations behind the phenomenon of ocularcentrism in the West see e.g. Synnott 1991; Classen 1993: 15–36, 1997; Howes 2003; Jütte 2005; Smith 2007b: esp. 19–21; Hamilakis 2013a: 24–34.
7 Jütte 2005: 69.
8 Day 2013: 4.
9 Howes 2003: 5; cf. Day 2013: 4.
10 Oken 1847. The remaining senses were perceived as follows: Asian men were connected with the sense of sound, native-Americans with smell and Australians with taste.
11 Merleau-Ponty 1945. Merleau-Ponty (esp. pp. 230–232), aimed to respond to theories of Cartesian dualism that proposed a division between mind and body and placed greater importance onto the role of the mind and its perception of the world over that of the body's experience. For Descartes, the fallibility of the senses meant only the mind's perception of the world could be understood as accurate. On Merleau-Ponty as a response to Descartes see Synnott 1991: 70; cf. Hamilakis 2013a: 28.
12 Howes 2005: 1–2. Proponents of the linguistic turn include Merleau-Ponty 1945; Ricouer 1970; Barthes 1982.
13 Serres with Latour 1995: 131–2.
14 Day 2013: 5. Cf. Evans and Lawlor 2000: 15 on the logocentricity of Merleau-Ponty's philosophy.
15 Serres 1995: 70–84.

16 In particular see e.g. Day 2013; Hamilakis 2013a; cf. Howes 2005 for general bibliographies into sensory studies. For specific focus on individual senses, see the volumes from the Sensory Formations series, e.g. Bull and Back 2005; Classen 2005; Korsmeyer 2005; Drobnik 2006; Edwards and Bhaumik 2008; Howes 2009.

17 On housing in Dura-Europos see e.g. Baird 2014; on housing in Africa see e.g. Thebert 1987. On housing of Egypt, see e.g. Alston 1997; on houses of Ephesus, see e.g. Krinzinger 2010, cf. Ellis 1997 who also considers houses of Halicarnassus, Sardis and Aphrodisias. Different housing types from Britain and mainland Italy have received considerable attention. On dwellings in Roman Britain see e.g. Percival 1976; Smith 1997; Perring 2013. For studies exploring a range of housing types of residences either in mainland Italy or across the Empire see e.g. McKay 1975; Wallace-Hadrill 1988, 1994; Clarke 1991; Ellis 2000; Hales 2003.

18 On studies with a particular focus on elite residences and palaces see e.g. Wallace-Hadrill 1988, 1994; Clarke 1991; Nielson 1994; Bodel 1997; Gros 2001; Lafon 2001; Begović and Shrunk 2002, 2003, Begović-Dvoržak and Shrunk 2004; Hales 2003; Marzano 2007; Platts 2011, 2016, 2018, 2019 (forthcoming); Zarmakoupi 2014. For studies into especially lower class *insula*-style housing, see e.g. Packer 1971; Meiggs 1973; Hermansen 1982; Delaine 1999, 2004; Storey 2002, 2004. For studies focusing on rural housing see e.g. Percival 1976; Smith 1997; Mulvin 2002; Marzano 2007; Bowes 2010; Zarmakoupi 2014; Marzano and Metreaux 2018. For studies with a focus on housing of the Later Roman Empire see e.g. Mulvin 2002; Lavan, Özgenel, Sarantis 2007; Bowes 2010.

19 See e.g. Clarke 1991; Grahame 1997 and 2000; Bergmann 2002; Klynne 2003, Leach 2004; Platts 2011. On the movement and location of slaves as well as possible attempts to avoid monitoring by supervisors or owners within the house and the villa, see Joshel and Petersen 2014.

20 See e.g. Grahame 1993, 1997, 1998, 2000; Laurence 1997; George 1999.

21 Hillier and Hanson 1984. For scholarship which employs Hillier and Hanson's justified access diagrams see e.g. Stöger 2011 on the analysis of the distribution of *scholae* using justified access-maps within ancient Ostia; Grahame 1993, 1997, 1998, 2000 on spatial analysis of Pompeian residences using justified access-maps.

22 Cf. Williams 2013: 208, citing Lefebvre 1991: 39. For criticisms regarding Hillier and Hanson's space syntax analysis see Lawrence 1990: 75.

23 It is important to note, however, that Grahame 2000: 98 does note the usefulness of exploring other aspects of the built environment including decoration and artefacts in order to gain further understanding of houses.

24 Grahame 2000: 24.

25 Grahame 2000: 27, cf. 3–4, 24–26, 28.

26 Grahame 2000: 27. For a more detailed discussion of Grahame's concept of 'contextuality' of space, see ibid., 11.

27 Grahame 2000: 27.

28 Grahame 2000: 28.

29 The interpretation of context here means the location, time and person reading the text in question. If any of these aspects alter, then the way in which the text is understood equally can change. Thus, even being read by the same person at different times or in different locations can affect how the text is interpreted.
30 Grahame 2000: 28.
31 See e.g. Nevett 2010 on the role of changes in time and season in Pompeian houses for affecting room use; cf. Foxhall 2000, 2007 on changes in time and season in Greek housing. On the marking and measuring of time in the Greco-Roman world, see Hannah 2009.
32 On criticisms of Grahame's space syntax analysis study of Pompeian residences see George 2002: 239.
33 Hanson 2003: 109.
34 The need to look beyond the architecture of a site and consider simultaneously its artefacts has been pointed out by Allison 1997a: 81; cf. Ault and Nevett 1999: 51–52.
35 Wallace-Hadrill 1988. Cf. Wallace-Hadrill 1994.
36 Wallace-Hadrill 1988: 77, cf. Wallace-Hadrill 1994: 37.
37 Hanson 2003: 54.
38 On views into the centre of a house from the street through its open entrance, see Wallace-Hadrill 1988: 46, 82–4 citing Drerup 1959: 147–74; cf. Wallace-Hadrill 1994; Clarke 1991.
39 On the possible impact of gender see Henshaw 2014: 27 citing Synott 1991 on survey results of over 1.5 million participants. On the impact of age, see Kivity et al. 2009: 241 cf. Larssona et al. 2000.
40 Henshaw 2014: 29, cf. Corwin et al. 1995.
41 Hamilakis 2013a: 4.
42 Increased awareness of sensory sensitivity has encouraged cinemas to host autism friendly screenings whereby adjustments to films, including volume reduction, lights left on low and the freedom to move, seek to 'reduce over-stimulation and create a welcoming place for people with autism'. See https://www.dimensions-uk.org/families/autism-friendly-environments/autism-friendly-screenings/, date accessed 26.8.16. On the sensory sensitivity of individuals with autism and the way in which it makes sufferers see, hear and feel the world differently from others see http://www.autism.org.uk/about/what-is/asd.aspx, date accessed 26/8/16. Cf. Odeon cinemas statement on accessibility options for visually and hearing-impaired customers, http://www.odeon.co.uk/accessibility/, date accessed 26/8/16.
43 Howes 1991, 2003, 2005, 2009; Classen 1993, 1997.
44 Bull and Back 2005 on sound; Korsmeyer 2005 on taste; Classen 2005 on touch; Drobnik 2006 on smell; Edwards and Bhaumik 2008 on sight.
45 Hamilakis 2013a: 4.
46 Tilley 1994 presents a particularly good example of where initial attempts at exploring sensory archaeology and the landscape resulted in significant criticism for focusing too much on the role of vision. On the ocularcentric nature of Tilley's approach see, for

example, Day 2013: 7; Hamilakis 2013a: 98. On Tilley's attempts to address and rectify these criticisms of a visually dominant approach see, Tilley 2004, 2010: 471–481.
47 Day 2013: 5–6. Cf. Betts 2011.
48 See e.g. Goldhahn 2002; Rainbird 2002; Boivin 2004.
49 For important edited volumes of collected papers on various topics of sensory archaeology see e.g. Hamilakis, Pluciennik and Tarlow 2002; Day 2013; and the volume by Betts 2017 which focus on multisensory approaches to Roman culture.
50 On archaeoacoustics see Lawson and Scarre 2006. On the archaeology of smell see Insoll 2007.
51 Hamilton and Whitehouse 2006a: 159–184; Bradley 2015.
52 On the sense of taste in archaeological studies, see Hamilakis 1998, 1999, 2008, 2012; Fox 2008; Hopwood 2013; Rudolph 2018.
53 See Houston and Taube 2000 on sight, smell and sound in Mesoamerica. For broad overviews into full sensory responses to archaeological sites see e.g. Hamilakis 2013a on imagined multisensory reconstructions of Bronze-Age Crete and Skeates 2008: 207–238, 2010 for a multisensory reconstruction of pre-historic Malta.
54 Favro 1996; Purcell 1987; Vout 2007; Betts 2011; Hartnett 2017.
55 Betts 2011; Butler and Purves 2013; Hamilakis 2013a; selected papers in Day 2013; Bradley 2015; Squire 2015; Purves 2017; Butler and Nooter 2018; Rudolph 2018.
56 E.g. Wallace-Hadrill 1988, 1994; Clarke 1991; Grahame 1997, 1998, 2000; Bergmann 2002; Leach 2004; Klynne 2005; Platts 2011.
57 The literature on the problems of defining the villa is too extensive to cite here in depth. Not only is the early history of these dwellings debated, but their relationship to Greek antecedents has likewise raised substantial questions, as has the issue of how to differentiate between villas and farmsteads. On these topics see e.g. Terrenato 2001; Becker 2003; 2006, 2012; Attema and de Haas 2005; Torelli 2012; Volpe 2012. For a short but clear summary of the issues faced defining the villa, see Percival 1976: 13, Dyson 2012; and on the value of attempting to define it see Terrenato 2012: 2. Regarding definitions of the *domus* see e.g. Wallace-Hadrill 2003: 7–10.
58 Compare, for example, the house of the Ceii and the house of the Citharist. The latter is considerably larger however both are traditionally defined as a *domus* and boast many similar architectural features, including an *impluvium* in the *atrium*, columns, garden spaces and kitchen areas as well as clear evidence of décor including mosaics and wall painting. On the problems of assuming that only large dwellings have magnificent décor, see Hodske 2007: 61–62.
59 Mayer 2012: 172–4 and n. 22.
60 On the difficulties of understanding the social status of many house owners from Pompeii and Herculaneum, see Mayer 2012: 171–172.
61 On 'public' and 'private' in the Roman house see e.g. Wallace-Hadrill 1988: 43–97, 1994: esp. 10–11, 17–37; Gazda 1994; Riggsby 1997; Grahame 1997; Treggiari 1998;

Zanker 1998; Burkhardt 2003; Zaccaria Ruggiu 2005; Cooper 2007; Anguissola 2012; Tuori and Nissin 2015.

62 Riggsby 1997: 49, cf. Tuori 2015: 10.
63 Numerous multiseater toilets which could accommodate upwards of six to eight individuals have been found at Pompeii. See Koloski-Ostrow 2015a: 7–8.
64 Koloski-Ostrow 2015: 84–85, 96, at least in terms of the Western world. Cultural values regarding personal toilet habits and hygiene cannot be assumed to be universal. A recent story regarding a woman's embarrassment at her faeces that 'would not flush' leading to her needing to be rescued by the fire brigade as she became stuck after having thrown it out of a window to get rid of it, highlights, in a rather extreme fashion perhaps, Western modern sensitivities to toilets and excrement, see http://www.bbc.co.uk/news/uk-england-bristol-41167296, date accessed 6/9/17. That this story was also reported by the BBC and became the 'Most Read' story on the BBC website on the day it was reported, perhaps also demonstrates Western toilet humour. I am aware that as a woman brought up in the UK, my own perceptions of the openness of Roman toilet habits are subjective. Other readers might respond to such behaviours with different preconceptions.
65 Lewis and Short 1879: 1447 *s.v. 'privatus'*; 1487 *s.v. 'publicus'*.
66 Koloski-Ostrow 2015: 95, her reference, however, to the relocation of such actions 'in controlled secrecy', highlights further the issues we face when trying to identify the meaning of 'public' and 'private' in Roman terms, since although the act was no longer in full view of all, it was not hidden in the same way that the word 'secrecy' implies. Indeed, if we compare Riggsby's account (1997: 44) of the term 'secrecy' in his discussion of the *cubiculum* as a 'place for secret activity', the examples given of Cremutius Cordus' suicide (Sen. *Marc.* XXII. 6), Martial's lamp promising silence (XIV. 39) about sexual activity in the bed, Pliny the Younger talking with a friend away from the earshot of the friend's wife (I. 12. 7), these examples would suggest that secrecy in Roman terms is rather different from privacy and perhaps cannot be used as a means for explaining the Roman mindset when it comes to perceptions of bodily functions in the multiperson latrine.
67 Vitr. *De arch.* VI. V. 1, trans. Granger 1934. This passage is discussed in depth with relation to the 'public' access into the *atrium* in Chapter 4 and the *cubiculum* in Chapter 5 below.
68 See Clarke 1991: 1–2; Wallace-Hadrill 1994: 10–11, 45; Balch 2008: 35–38, 43 citing Wallace-Hadrill 1994: 45; Russell 2016: 13.
69 *Communis* for Vitruvius is a 'near synonym' with *publicus,* Riggsby 1997: 48. Cf. Tuori 2015: 10 who also implies the synonymous meaning of *communia* and *publicus* when he comments 'Vitruvius uses the terms *communia* and *propria*, which are rather, though not completely, different from our terms "public" and "private".'
70 Vitr. *De arch.* VI. V. 2, trans. Granger 1934.
71 Wallace-Hadrill 1994: 17.

72 Wallace-Hadrill 1994: 17.
73 Wallace-Hadrill 1994: 11.
74 Wallace-Hadrill 1994: 17.
75 On entertaining friends in the *cubiculum* see e.g. Tac. *Dialog*. 3. 1, 14. 1; Sen. *De Ira*, III. 8. 6; Plin. *Ep*. V. 3. 11; Suet. *Vesp*. XXI. On business and trials taking place in the bedroom see Cic. *Verr*. III. 79; Cic. *Ad Q. F.* I. I. 25; Plin. *Ep* V. 1. 5. On Imperial trials occurring in the *cubiculum* see Sen. *De Clem*. I. IX; Tac. *Ann*. XI. 2; Plin. *Pan*. LXXXIII.1 emphasizing the open nature of Trajan's *cubiculum*, cf. Wallace-Hadrill 1994: 219 n. 2. On the bedroom being used for the more 'private' or intimate activities of sleeping, rest and sex, see Riggsby 1997.
76 On the establishment of a city and the typical buildings to be found within Roman cities see e.g. Vitr. *De arch*. I.7.1. cf. Philo *On Creation*, 17; Aelius Aristides, *The Roman Oration*, 97–98 and the regionary catalogues (made up of the *Notitia Regionum XIV* and the *Curiosum Urbis Regionum XIV*) from the fourth century AD, which list the buildings, monuments and amenities within each of Rome's fourteen regions. For archaeological evidence of city buildings and structures see, for example, the so-called Avezzano relief (discussed in Wallace-Hadrill 1991: x; Goodman 2007: 32–33; Kaiser 2011: 9), which appears to depict a bird's-eye view of a generalized cityscape and the fresco from the Oppian Hill under Trajan's Baths, Rome (Van der Meer 1998; Caruso and Volpe 2000; La Rocca 2000; van Tilberg 2007: 156–157). According to Kaiser 2011: 9–10 whilst the Avezzano relief appears to focus upon depicting the city wall, gate, wide streets and private buildings of the city, the focus of the Oppian Hill fresco is not the city gate, but the public buildings within the city wall.
77 On Rome's regionary catalogues see Meiggs 1973: 238.
78 Hales 2003: 97. Cf. Mayer 2012: 171 on the problems of assuming that Pompeii's domestic décor neatly echo the lifestyles of the elite of Rome or that it can be seen as merely 'aping the fashions of the Imperial aristocracy'.
79 Both Pompeii and Herculaneum have early foundation dates. Pompeii was founded by the Oscans in about the seventh or sixth centuries BC. It came under Roman domination by the fourth century BC and was made a Roman colony in 80 BC. Herculaneum was founded in the sixth century BC and after periods of Greek and Samnite control was made a Roman *municipium* in 89 BC.
80 Vitr. *De arch*. VI. V. 1.

Chapter 2

1 Plin. *Ep*. V. 6. 20–25, trans. Firth 1900 (abridged). From http://www.attalus.org/old/pliny5.html#6, date accessed 1/5/18.
2 Plin. *Ep*. II. 17.

3 There have been significant debates as to whether these residences were real, e.g. Sherwin-White 1966; Förtsch 1993. For a useful summary of these debates, see Bergmann 1995: 406–420. For various attempts to find Pliny's Laurentine villa see Ramieri 1995 who identifies it as being either villa Plinio or Palombara at Castel Fusano, and Salza Prina Ricotti 1985 who argues for Pliny's Laurentine villa as being either villa Grotte di Piastra or villa Magna at Castelporziano. Similar interest in locating Pliny's Tuscan villa can be found, see Braconi & Uroz Sáez 1999 who identify the archaeological remains at San Giustino as being Pliny's famous residence. On the enduring interest in recreating Pliny's villas on paper see de la Ruffinière du Prey 1994.

4 Plin. *Ep.* II. 17. 13, 'below is a dining-room where, even when the sea is stormy you hear only the noise of the breakers in dying murmurs', trans. Firth 1900 (abridged). From http://www.attalus.org/old/pliny2.html#17, date accessed 1/5/18. Cf. from later in II. 17. 22–25 'Next to it is a bedroom for use at night or taking a nap, and unless the windows are open, you do not hear the sound either of your slaves talking, the murmur of the sea, or the raging of a storm; nor do you see the flashes of the lightning or know that it is day... When I retire to this suite, I seem to be quite away from my villa, and I find it delightful to sit there, especially during the Saturnalia, when all the rest of the house rings with the merriment and shouts of the festival-makers; for then I do not interfere with their amusements, and they do not distract me from my studies.' Trans. Firth 1900 (abridged). From http://www.attalus.org/old/pliny2.html#17, date accessed 1/5/18.

5 See e.g. Wiseman 1987; Wallace-Hadrill 1988, 1994; Clarke 1991; Hales 2003.

6 Wolf 1990: 586.

7 In Wolf's definitions of the first two modes of power he assigns the first to the person in terms of 'potency or capability' and perceives this as heavily based upon Nietzsche's concept of power. The second he sees as the ability of an individual to impose their will, either in social action or interpersonal relations and revolves around 'interactions and transactions among people', (1990: 586).

8 Wolf 1990: 586.

9 Wolf 1990: 586, citing Foucault 1984: 428.

10 Wolf 1990: 587.

11 Platts 2016, cf. Platts 2019 (forthcoming).

12 Lefebvre 1991, cf. Alston 2002: 35.

13 Plin. *NH* XXXV. 2. 7, trans. Rackham 1938 '*triumphabantque etiam dominis mutatis aeternae domus*'. On the display of triumphal spoils in the Roman home see Rawson 1990: 159–166.

14 On the authority of the father over all members of the household, see Ulpian, *Dig.* L. 60. 195. On *patria potestas* (the power of the father) and the right of the father over the life and death of members of the household, see Gaius, *Inst.* I. 48–9, LII, LV.

15 On the breadth of the power of the *paterfamilias*, see McDonnell 2006: 173.

16 Pallasmaa 2012: 69.
17 Plin. *Ep.* II. 17. 27, trans. Firth 1900 (abridged). From http://www.attalus.org/old/pliny2.html#17, date accessed 1/5/18. Cf. from earlier in the same letter II. 17. 21, 'In the middle of the wall is a neat recess, which by means of glazed windows and curtains can either be thrown into the adjoining room or be cut off from it. It holds a couch and two arm-chairs, and as you lie on the couch you have the sea at your feet, the villa at your back, and the woods at your head, and all these views may be looked at separately from each window or blended into one prospect.' Trans. Firth 1900 (abridged). From http://www.attalus.org/old/pliny2.html#17, date accessed 1/5/18.
18 Plin. *Ep.* II. 17. 5., trans. Radice 1969.
19 Plin. *Ep.* V. 6. 7., trans. Radice 1969.
20 Plin. *Ep.* V. 6. 13., trans. Firth 1900 (abridged). From http://www.attalus.org/old/pliny5.html#6, accessed 1.5.18.
21 Plin. *Ep.* V. 6. 14., trans. Radice 1969.
22 Plin. *Ep.* V. 6. 19., trans. Radice 1969.
23 Bergmann 1994, 2002 on the importance of views within villas.
24 Plin. *Ep.* II. 17. 7., trans. Radice 1969. Cf. n. 32.
25 Plin. *Ep.* II. 17. 23, trans. Firth 1900 (abridged). From http://www.attalus.org/old/pliny2.html#17, date accessed 1/5/18. From the remains of residences, we can likewise see the use of such sensory 'buffering' spaces as a means of influencing the potential experience to be had in a residence's environs, see for example the service corridors in the house of the Menander. As well as serving to demarcate visually the working, and thus more humble, sectors of the house from its parts used for the opulent show of status (Wallace-Hadrill 1994: 39–40), they also served to dampen the dispersal of unwanted odours and sounds from these parts of the dwelling into the main arenas of personal display, see Platts 2016, 2019 (forthcoming) and Chapter 7 below.
26 Plin, *Ep.* V. 6. 21., trans. Radice 1969.
27 Plin. *Ep.* V. 6. 23., trans. Radice 1969.
28 Plin. *Ep.* II. 17. 17–20., trans. Radice 1969.
29 Plin. *Ep.* V. 6. 34, V. 6. 11, V. 6. 33, trans. Radice 1969.
30 Plin. *Ep.* II. 17. 12., trans Radice 1969.
31 Plin. *Ep.* V. 6. 8, trans. Firth 1900 (abridged). From http://www.attalus.org/old/pliny5.html#6, date accessed 1/5/18. Cf. Plin. *Ep.* II. 17. 28. The sense of taste is also implied in Pliny's references to the garden, which he says 'is thickly planted with mulberries and figs, trees which the soil bears very well.' Trans. Radice 1969.
32 Plin. *Ep.* V. 6 26–27, trans. Radice 1969. Cf. Plin. *Ep.* II.17.10 for rooms that can be used in summer and winter.
33 Plin. *Ep.* II. 17. 16, trans. Radice 1969.
34 Plin. *Ep.* V. 6. 21. Similar references to parts of his Laurentine villa which was protected from noise or the sun can be found in *Ep.* II. 17. 4, 10, 22.

35 On ekphrasis in Plin. *Ep.* V. 6 see Chinn 2007, cf. Platts 2019 (forthcoming) on ekphrasis in Plin. *Ep.* II. 17. Whilst vision and the visual is a key sensory experience in the production of ekphrastic descriptions, as Elsner (2007: ii) points out 'even at its most visual—it [ekphrasis] finds itself straying to the evocative resonances of the other senses: sound, smell, taste, and touch'.
36 Plin. *Ep* II. 17, V. 6. On the multisensory experience of Pliny's Laurentine villa see Platts 2019 (forthcoming).

Chapter 3

1 Sen. *Ep.* LVI. 1–2, trans. Gummere 1917. Seneca's letters to Lucilius were all written in the latter years of his life and are therefore dated to *c*. AD 64.
2 Wallace-Hadrill 1988, 1994; Cf. Watts 1987: 187–189; Clarke 1991: 2–6; Laurence 1994: 88; Zanker 1998: 10.
3 Platts 2016, cf. 2019 (forthcoming). Specifically on auditory experiences in the home from the street and *vice versa* see Hartnett 2016.
4 Mart. *Ep.* XII. LVII, trans. Shackleton-Bailey, 1993 (abridged).
5 One such example of this fusion of commercial and domestic premises within one building is visible in the house of Pansa, Pompeii, where shops including a bakery are located at the front and to the side of the dwelling (see Fig. 4.1).
6 Eschebach 1975: 331–338; cf. Raper 1977. On zoning in Herculaneum see Guadagno 1993: 87–91, Tav. 18. For a concise summary and examination of the use of 'no-zoning' within the modern notion of New Urbanism, see Hartnett 2017: 42–44.
7 Wallace-Hadrill 1994: 136.
8 See Laurence 2007: 58–60, 62–63, 65–66, 77, 82–83 for individual maps locating shops for production and consumption and 'deviant behaviour' throughout Pompeii. These include properties with roles such as taverns, shops, *lanifricariae* and *popinae*.
9 The discovery of donkey or mule remains in a *pistrinum* in Herculaneum's *Insula Orientalis* II (off Cardo V) demonstrates the use of the animals in the workings of bakeries.
10 Hartnett 2008: 94, cf. 2017: Plate I.
11 Wall paintings from the *praedia* of Julia Felix showing scenes from the Roman forum, show wooden stools and benches with figures on them, Nappo 1991, cf. Hartnett 2008: 93.
12 Hartnett 2008: 94, cf. 2017: Plate I.
13 Henshaw 2014: 170.
14 Henshaw 2014: 170, cf. ibid. 187 for a useful diagram on the role of airflow in the transmission of smells.

15 On the smells from butchers see Mart. *Ep.* VI. 6. 18–21; tanners, Juv. *Sat.* XIV. 202; Mart. *Ep.* VI. 93. 4; urinals in the street, Mart. *Ep.* VI. 93. 1–2; Macrob. *Sat.* III. 16. 15. On the smells from fulleries see Bradley 2002, 2015, *contra* Flohr 2003, 2017.

16 Juv. *Sat.* III. 274–277. His complaints about the dangers of walking through the streets of Rome and the risk of faeces being thrown out of house windows are reflected both in legislation from Justinian's sixth-century AD compilation and codification of all Rome's laws (*Digesta* 9. 3) and a painted decree from Herculaneum (*CIL*. IV. 10488, *AE* 1960: 277, 1962: 234) banning the throwing of excrement: *M(arcus) [Alf]icius Pa[ul]lus / aedil(is) / is velit in hunc locum / stercus abicere nonetur n[on] / iacere si quis adver[sus ea] / i(u)dicium fecerit liberi dent / [dena]rium n(ummum) servi verberibus / [i]n sedibus admonentur.* 'Marcus Alficius Paulus, aedile, (declares): whoever wants to throw excrement [*stercus*] in this place is warned that it is not allowed. If someone should act contrary to these orders, let him, if freeborn, pay a fine of [...] denarii, if slaves, let them receive lashes at the place of their infraction.' trans. Cooley and Cooley 2014: 181 (abridged). As Cooley and Cooley point out, the punishment stipulated in this decree depends according to status, and the level of fine owed by freeborn individuals has not been preserved.

17 Cormack 2007: 586.

18 Scott 2013: 89. On the publications for the Noceran Gate necropolis see e.g. Mau 1888 vol III: 120–149, 1908: 450–454, figs. 265–7. Ambrosio and De Caro 1983, 1987; Kockel 1985. For publications on the Herculaneum Gate necropolis see Kockel 1983, 1985.

19 Permanent examples of *ustrina* have been discovered in urban cemetaries (Polfer 2000: 31). No *ustrina* have been identified as yet at Pompeii, (Kockel 1983: 39).

20 For examples of cremations in private tomb enclosures see the finds of bone, carbon and ash in the tomb of Marcus Obellius Firmus in Cormack 2007: 592 cf. 603 n. 27. On pyres at burial sites see Weekes 2005: 22–25. As Weekes points out, however, it is important to note direct archaeological evidence for this latter practice is rare, however see the example of Marcus Obellius Firmus above.

21 On the smell of burning flesh and corpses see Morley 2015: 114. According to smell experiments, the smell of fire and cooking meat travels further than many other smells. According to Whitehouse and Hamilton 2006: 178, in an enclosed outdoor setting the smell of cooking meat can travel a minimum of 17 metres and a maximum distance of 122 metres.

22 Bodel 2000: 130, cf. Hope 2009: 69–70, 157.

23 Suet. *Vesp.* V.5; Suet. *Nero*, XLVIII.2.

24 Oros. *Adv. pagan.* VII. 4. 1–2. Mart. *Ep.* X. V, trans. Shackleton-Bailey 1993 (abridged). Cf. Scobie 1986: 418–419.

25 Varro, *Ling.*, V. 25; cf. Hor. *Sat.* I. 8. In the nineteenth century, excavations led by Lanciani found pits filled with animal and human remains, see Lanciani 1888;

Hopkins 1983: 208–9; Bodel 1994: 40; Graham 2006a, although whether these were the *puticuli* that Varro described is debatable, see Coarelli 1999. That they may not be *puticuli* is also possible, see Graham 2006a.

26 Bodel 2000: 131–132. Bodel does note the difficulties of ascertaining the number of dead bodies in the Roman burial pits, since Lanciani's excavations uncovered both human and animal remains together with other bits of rubbish.

27 Bodel 2000: 132.

28 Plut. *Pub.* 20. 2. According to Plut. *Pub.* 20. 3. this situation of doors opening immediately onto streets was also seen in Greek housing.

29 Juv. *Sat.* III. 236–238, trans. Braund 2004. As Braund notes, it is believed that Juvenal's reference to Drusus here is probably alluding to the emperor Claudius (Tiberius Claudius Drusus) who was renowned for his drowsiness. We also learn of the bodily impact of a busy pedestrianized area; the jostling and bustling, the muck and the possible injuries one suffers as one journeys through the city: 'As I hurry along, the wave ahead gets in the way and the great massed ranks of people behind me crush my kidneys. One pokes me with his elbow, another with a hard pole. This guy bashes my head with a beam, that guy with a wine cask. My legs are caked with mud. Soon I'm trampled by mighty feet from every side and a soldier's hobnail sticks into my toe.' Juv. *Sat.* III. 243–248, trans. Braund 2004.

30 Martial appears to have obtained the status of *eques*, which required a wealth in excess of 400,000 sesterces see Mart. *Ep.* V. XVII. Cf. Williams 2011: xii. There is more debate about Juvenal's wealth. Whilst some scholars (e.g. Green 1998: 23–24) suggest Juvenal came from a fairly wealthy family, Barr 1999: xiii is more cautious: 'We have insufficient evidence to enable us to pinpoint with anything like accuracy Juvenal's position in the echelons of the Roman class system'.

31 Whilst Juvenal's work clearly emphasizes its satirical nature in its title *Satires*, identifying exactly what epigrams comprise is more difficult to ascertain. According to Watson 2005: 201 (cf. Puelma 1996) even to identify epigram as a specific 'genre' is difficult, as 'the term "epigram" did not come into currency as the designation for a recognizable literary form until the 1st century AD'. By the time Martial was composing his *Epigrams* however, these poems had 'become in [Martial's] hands a vehicle for witty satire' (Watson 2008: 209). As such I have classed the texts of both Juvenal and Martial as satirical in subject matter and consider above the significance of this for judging the reliability of their presentations of life in Rome.

32 Griffin 1994: 1. Cf. Barr 1999: xvii, Quintero 2007: 2–6.

33 Mart. *Ep.* XII. 18, trans. Shackleton-Bailey 1993. Cf. Juv. *Sat.* III. 236–238. Martial (*Ep.* XII. 18.) goes on to provide an important comparison of noisy Rome with his somnolent and peaceful birth place of Bilbilis in the province of Hispania Tarraconensis.

34 For an excellent summary of recent scholarship on journeys through the city of Rome see Kaiser 2011: 2–7 citing the work of scholars including Corlàita 1979, MacDonald

1986, Zanker 1987, Favro 1996 and Malmberg and Bjur 2011. On the cultural importance of walking in Roman culture see O'Sullivan 2011, cf. Östenberg, Malmberg and Bjørnebye: 2015. A relatively early example of how people might have experienced Pompeii as they moved around it is Gesemann's research of 1996 into how building façades might have been seen from the city's streets.

35 Pompeii is currently about two-thirds excavated, however substantial sections of *regiones* I, III, IV, V, IX remain unexplored.

36 On wear of roads, kerbstones and stepping stones as evidence of levels of traffic density, see Poehler 2017: 124–137. On cart ruts see Tsujimura 1991; Poehler 2006, 2017. On two-way and one-way traffic and vehicular impediments see e.g. Poehler 2006, 2017; Kaiser 2011.

37 For maps of Pompeii's cart rut depth, see Tsujimura 1991, cf. Poehler 2017: 9, fig. 1.3. For maps of Pompeii's two-way and one-way streets see Kaiser 2011: 94, map 3.6; cf. Poehler 2017: 172–173, figs: 6.5–6.8 for maps detailing the evolution of Pompeii's traffic systems.

38 Whilst Kaiser (2011a: 178, fig. 7.1 cf. 2011: 94, Map 3.6) locates traffic blocking stones throughout Pompeii and emphasizes changes that had been made to the city's traffic patterns, Poehler 2017: 18 and n. 65, 67 highlights errors in Kaiser's assumptions, the most important being 'the identification of impediments where none exist and claims that ramps specifically designed to permit traffic are impediments'. He goes on (2017: 18) to point out 'Kaiser's own admission that some "impediments" did not actually bar traffic'.

39 Laurence 1995, 2007, 2008. For a brief summary of the means by which Laurence has combined explorations of streets and buildings together at Pompeii, see Kaiser 2011: 6.

40 Kaiser 2011.

41 Hartnett 2017: 29–33. Cf. On Pompeii, see Saliou 1999. On Herculaneum, see Mauiri 1958: 33–42; Pagano 1993: esp. 597.

42 Hartnett 2017: 29–30 and n. 4 for measurements of Pompeian and Roman streets. For Pompeii measurements see, Gesemann 1996; Kaiser 2011: 71–74 as well as Hartnett's measurements. For Rome's measurements (from both actual remains and extrapolation from the *Forma Urbis Romae*), see Quilici 1990; Macaulay-Lewis 2011: 266–270. On Herculaneum's street widths, see Hartnett 2017: 31.

43 Mouritsen 1988: fig. 3 focuses specifically on electoral notices; Laurence 2007: 109–113, maps 6.5–6.8. On studies of graffiti in Pompeii see Milnor 2014. On general studies into graffiti see Baird and Taylor 2011. For The Ancient Graffiti Project for mapping and studying the graffiti of Pompeii and Herculaneum, see http://www.ancientgraffiti.org/Graffiti/, date accessed 5/4/19.

44 Laurence 2007: 89. On measuring street activity in Pompeii, see Laurence 2007: 88–103 cf. maps 6.1–6.4 and 6.5–6.8.

45 Laurence 2007: 100.

46 Hartnett 2017: 32.
47 Laurence 2007: 100.
48 Laurence 2007: 98–99.
49 On one-way traffic on the Vicolo del Lupanare see Poehler 2017: 173.
50 Laurence 2007: 98–99.
51 Poehler 2017: 173 suggests that one-way traffic systems were employed on both roads, but that the specific direction of northbound and southbound that traffic was permitted to travel changed between the late republican period and the time of Pompeii's destruction. Kaiser 2011: 94 Map 3.6 agrees that these roads only held one-way traffic, however he also located an impediment to cart traffic at the entrance to Vicolo dei Lucrezio Frontone from Via di Nola. See n. 37, p. 248, however, for possible issues regarding Kaiser's interpretation of traffic impediments as raised by Poehler.
52 According to Baird and Taylor 2011: 3–4, graffiti in ancient Rome was not perceived as uniformly negative in the same way as it is today. Finds of inscriptions such as *CIL*. XI.575, (Baird and Taylor 2011: 16), which sought to dissuade people from scrawling in some places, however, suggest that there were places where graffiti was discouraged. Similarly, examples of graffiti occurring under cover of darkness again suggest that at times there was an illicit and anonymous element to graffitiing. In particular, see Plut. *C. Gracc.* XVII. 9, trans. Morstein-Marx 2012: 198 on the event of Lucius Opimius overseeing the construction of the Temple of Concordia following the murder of Gaius Gracchus. 'So at night some people wrote in below the dedicatory inscription of the temple this line: "an act of madness made the Temple of Concordia."' If we apply, to examples of Pompeian graffiti, the possibility that at least some instances of the act might have been poorly regarded, this suggests that using graffiti in Pompeii as an indicator of social activity in Pompeii's streets should be considered together with detailed insight of other specific characteristics of the street in question.
53 For details on studies of cart ruts in Pompeii, see n. 35 and 36 above.
54 Poehler 2017: 54. For detailed discussion of the methods and materials of road construction in Pompeii, see Poehler 2017: 53–100.
55 On sounds of carts in the street and the disturbances these provide for inhabitants, see Hor. *Epist.* I.XVII.6, cf. Juv. *Sat.* III 236–238.
56 For a detailed discussion of the acoustic properties of spaces see Veitch 2017.
57 For absorption coefficients of material that correlate with ancient building materials see Veitch 2017: 60 drawing on Everest and Pohlmann 2009: Appendix. Note the different frequencies of sound and the impact this has upon levels of sound absorption depending on material. The contents of the spaces will also affect the way in which sound travels.
58 With *cubicula* doors open, most of the sound made in the *atrium* will travel unimpeded into the *cubicula* and will not be reflected back into the *atrium*.
59 Veitch 2017: 62.

60 Veitch 2017: 62.
61 In March 2013 *The Independent* recorded that a Golden Retriever had been added to the Guinness Book of Records for making the loudest ever recorded bark at 113.1 decibels. This is equivalent to a rock concert. See https://www.independent.co.uk/news/world/australasia/meet-charlie-the-golden-retriever-with-a-bark-thats-louder-than-a-pneumatic-drill-8548076.html, date accessed 8/01/18.
62 This ability of birds to sing louder in response to increased background noise is called the Lombard effect, see Gil and Brumm 2014: 72.
63 Plin. *HN*. X. 81–82. On nightingales in the ancient world, see Mynott 2018: esp. 49–60. For examples of nightingales in wall painting from the Bay of Naples see Jashemski and Myer 2002: 383.
64 Gil and Brumm 2014: 72
65 See e.g. Cic. *Rosc. Am.* 134; Prop. IV. 8. 51–62 and Ov. *Met.* XIV. 748–751.
66 Smith 1999: 58.
67 On animal waste, see *Dig* XLIII. 10. 1. 5.
68 On Herculaneum's sewerage system, see pp. 206–207 and n. 53–55, p. 286.
69 For the fewer plotted cart ruts of Ostia, see Kaiser 2011: 130.
70 The literature on Ostia is substantial see, for example Hermansen 1970, 1973, 1982; Meiggs 1973; DeLaine 1999, 2004, 2012.
71 On the impact of cold on smells see Porteous 2006: 99–100. On the varying impacts of rain on smells see Kitchen 1963: 24 (cited in Porteous 2006: 99) and Porteous 2006: 99.
72 Hope 2009: 44. Cf. on the problems of summer and heat see Hor. *Ep.* 1. 7. 2–9.
73 Rolandi et al. 2007: 96. The winds in Pompeii in the autumn and winter period blow towards a north-east and less commonly a south-east direction, whilst in the summer months they tend to blow towards a westerly direction. This data, together with substantial historical evidence, has led to re-dating of the eruption of Vesuvius to an autumn rather than a summer date (as is generally supposed) due to the south-easterly direction in which the volcanic material fell.
74 Smith 1999: 58–59 and citing Crooke 1616: 607 on the effect of wind direction on sound perception.
75 Research comparing temperature change over the last 2,000 years suggests that the period AD 21–80 was substantially warmer than 1971–2000, Ahmed et al. 2013: 342. Di Fusco and Di Caterina 1998: 11 suggest rainfall levels at Pompeii were considerably heavier in the past and have only decreased recently, with levels falling from an average in 1926–50 of 1,000 millimetres to around 550 millimetres today.
76 Smith 1999: 58–59.
77 Decreased activity in the street at night will also mean there is less background noise competing with, and perhaps reducing, potential perception of any loud individual sounds.

78 Lefebvre 2004: 15; Day 2013: 6; Bradley 2015: 3; Morley 2015: 113; Derrick 2017: 72.
79 Derrick 2017: 72.
80 See Cooley and Cooley 2014: 68 for a bar chart plotting half-monthly distribution of games in Pompeii and nearby towns, as advertised on painted notices throughout the city. This data shows that games were not constantly held either in Pompeii or elsewhere.
81 Providing exact comparative measurements for an event in a Roman amphitheatre is challenging especially given the use of loudspeakers at many events today, however recent comparative information on stadium noise suggests decibel levels in excess of 100 decibels, see https://moderngov.lambeth.gov.uk/mgConvert2PDF.aspx?ID=27432, p.1, date accessed 5/7/17.
82 Suet, *Calig.* 18, trans. Rolfe 1913. Cf. Tac. *Ann.* XIV. 20–1.
83 *CIL* X 854; *CIL* X 855 = *ILS* 5653c; *CIL* X 857a = *ILS* 5653a; *CIL* X 857d = *ILS* 5653a cf. Cooley and Cooley 2014: 61–63.
84 Identification of II. 3. 8–9 as a potter's workshop, house and garden has been based on the discovery of a wall painting of a god, (either Vulcanus or Hephaestos) and a potter at his wheel on the entrance doorway to the garden (II.3.9), *SAP* inv. no. 21631.
85 We know processions were often included in relation to games: see the games of Aulus Clodius Flaccus in the early first century AD on his first and second elections as duumvir, *CIL* X 1074d = *ILS* 5053. 4, cf. Cooley and Cooley 2014: 65–66 as did those of Gnaeus Alleius Nigidius Maius, *CIL* X 1074d = *ILS* 5053.4, cf. Cooley and Cooley 2014: 65–66. See also the relief of the different stages of the games from the *MANN* inv. No. 6704.
86 Poehler 2017: 173, cf. Fig 3.2, p. 35.
87 For doorways in the amphitheatre/palaestra district see Laurence 2007: 93. For graffiti in the amphitheatre/palaestra district see Laurence 2007: 98–99.
88 MANN inv. no 112222. Cf. fragments of painted notices discovered by the arched openings of the amphitheatre, which provide further evidence for temporary stalls near the amphitheatre e.g. *CIL* IV 1096 'By permission of the aediles. Gnaeus Aninius Fortunatus occupies (this space)', trans. Cooley and Cooley 2014: 275. Cf. *CIL* IV 1096a–1097b, 2485.
89 Evidence that temporary braziers were regularly used around Pompeii can be seen in the Forum fresco from the *praedia* of Julia Felix, *Le antichità di ercolano esposte*, Vol III, cited in Beard 2010: 74–75. The lack of toilets excavated at the amphitheatre would probably result in people needing to relieve themselves in the surrounding area, see Beard 2010: 264. On the cries of hawkers at a baths disturbing nearby residents see Sen, *Ep.* LVI 1–2, text on p. 31 above.
90 Whitehouse and Hamilton 2006: 178.
91 See n. 69 above.
92 Moeller 1976 suggested they provided the first phase of the wool production industry. Cf. Borgard and Puybaret 2004: 51–52; Robinson 2005: 91; Monteix 2011: 170–171.

93 Flohr 2013b: 59–60, citing the large amount of animal bones found in these buildings, cf. Flohr 2007: 132; 2012: 70. The houses where these manufacturing processes are very clearly separated from the rest of the residences can be found at VII.10, 5. 8. 13, VII 12, 17–21 and VII 12, 22–24, cf. Flohr 2013b: 60, 2007.
94 Flohr 2013b: 59 highlights the clustering of *officiae lanifricariae* in areas that would have been frequented by many people, perhaps to increase sales of goods to customers.
95 Monteix 2010. On the felt-making industry in Pompeii see Flohr 2013b: 64–65.
96 Flohr 2007: 131 categorizes bakeries with no mills as baking shops rather than bakeries. The presence of bakeries with mills has been seen to highlight increased productivity to those that lacked them, Flohr 2007: 132, cf. Monteix et al. 2013: 224. On the evidence of horse or donkeys in bakeries to help grind corn and transport produce see Jashemski 1979: 194–195; La Rocca et al. 1994: 289; King 2002: 425, cf. the finds of mule skeletons in bakeries e.g. in the house of the Chaste Lovers. Visual evidence of how donkeys and horses were used to grid corn in mills can be found in a sculpted relief now in the Vatican, see Vigneron 1968: pl. 71. For literary descriptions see Apul. *Met.* IX. 10–13, cf. Juv. *Sat.* VIII. 66–7; Columella. *Rust* VI. 37. 1
97 Potter 1999; Bradley 2002, 2015; Koloski-Ostrow 2015.
98 Maxey 1938: 37; Wilson 2000: 280; Bradley 2002: 35; Kudlien 2002: 58.
99 Morley 2015; Flohr 2017.
100 This fullery has traditionally been connected with Stephanus due to the discovery of electioneering notices on its façade, which mention him (*CIL* IV. 7172, 7174). As Mourtisen 1988: 18–27; Wallace-Hadrill 1994: 108 and Allison 2001: 57–8 argue, questions can be raised as to how far such notices on a property's façade can be connected with its inhabitants; however, for want of a clearer way to refer to this dwelling, I will continue to use the traditional association of the *fullonica* with Stephanus.
101 Flohr 2011: 89, citing Jashemski 1993: 150; Foss 1994: 221; Bradley 2002: 36.
102 Maiuri 1942: 173; Spinazzola 1953: 765–785, cf. Flohr 2011: 89.
103 Flohr 2011: 90.
104 Flohr 2013a: 206, cf. 2011: 92. Significant also was the fact that there was both a substantial distance of *c.* 30 metres between the shop entrance and the fullery processing section at the back of the premises, and the latter were located out of the direct line of sight from the shop. This will again have helped to diminish some of the leakage of the corporeal aspects of the fulling process into the rest of the dwelling and into the street beyond.
105 On the domestic and personal artefacts found in the *fullonica* of Stephanus, see Della Corte 1912: 248, 283–4, 286, 333, cited in Flohr 2011: 93.
106 The *fauces* of the house of the *Cryptoporticus* measured *c.* 9 metres whilst that of P. Casca Longus measured *c.* 5 metres.
107 In particular smell is impacted by wind speed and direction, which can serve to dissipate odours speedily or encourage them to linger.

108 The house of the Painters at Work abuts onto the house of the Chaste Lovers; however, this is not fully excavated and the location of its main entrance is currently unknown. On the excavation of these two buildings see Varone 1993, 1989, 1990, 1995: 124–136.
109 The house of the Ceii (I.VI.15) in located in the same insula as the house of the *Lararium* of Achilles but opens onto the Vicolo del Menandro.
110 Hales 2003: 105–106.
111 See Proudfoot 2013 on side rooms for doorkeepers, cf. Hales 2003: 36–7 on literary evidence for doorkeepers restricting access to the interior of houses.
112 See e.g. the houses of Marcus Lucretius Fronto, the *Lararium*, the Ceii, the Four Styles, where the traditionally labelled '*triclinia*' are located off and entered from the *atrium* and which lack openings onto the peristyle garden. The presence of high-up small windows in these dwellings would have helped the circulation of air.
113 On curtain architecture see Taylor Lauritsen 2013: 101–103. On its use in later Roman houses, see Stephenson 2014.
114 Flohr 2007: 133, 2017: 46 on the wide openings of workshops. That these wide openings ensured workshops would be reasonably well lit in the day (Flohr 2017: 46) is key, however they also permitted increased views in from the street, as well the seepage of louder sounds and stronger smells into the street beyond.
115 Michel 1990; cf. Foss 1994: 235–240. According to Michel, the smallest and last room of this residence had been used as a kitchen until the earthquake of AD 62, after which the kitchen was moved to the front of the residence.
116 Flohr 2017: 49 on the noise from the fullery of Stephanus, cf. 2017: 45–46, 51–52 on the possible smells produced by fulleries.
117 The villa of the Four Mosaic Columns is the subject of the ongoing Via Consolare project run by San Francisco State University and begun in 2005, which seeks to explore the chronology and stratigraphic record of the villa's environs together with a study of *Insula* VII, 6. See http://www.sfsu.edu/%7Epompeii/index.html, date accessed 20/7/17.
118 On the excavation and reburial, see Dyer 1875: 498.
119 Much of the higher section of the dwelling lies in the unexcavated area of Pompeii making complete understanding of the relationship between villa and landscape difficult.
120 The reburial of the villa of Cicero in 1763 post–excavation makes it difficult to comment in depth on the potential multisensory experiences of its relationship to the street. It is possible to examine more broadly, however, the implications of its position set back from the road.
121 On the burials and cremations outside Pompeii, see pp. 37–38 and n. 19–20 p. 246.
122 *CIL* 7454/ *ILS* 8342; *CIL* V 4489; *CIL* V 7906/ *ILS* 8374; *CIL* VI 9626; *CIL* X 9835; Buonpane 1990: 171–174, cf. Carroll 2006: 42.

123 On the finds of food traces found near cemeteries and graves, see Carroll 2006. Festivals which celebrated the dead included the *Parentalia*, which took place in February and which was the official day for commemorating the deceased. The other was the *Rosalia*, the feast of roses, which occurred in May and June. See Duncan-Jones 1974: 203–206.

124 *CIL* X 1033; Kockel 1983: 109–110 pl. 31. That funerary *triclinia* around tombs for funerary feasts were a well-established phenomenon can been seen in other examples found from Rome (Baldassare 2001: 387), Ostia (Heinzelmann 2000: 69–72, 2001: 380) and Portus (Dunbabin 2003: 128–129 fig. 74), as well as epitaphs referring to them from Italy and Gaul (Carroll 2006: 42 n. 64).

125 In addition to a long *fauces* leading to the *atrium*, this villa also had a long path leading from the road to the villa entrance, which again served to set the dwelling back from the street. According to Dyer (1875: 498) on either side of this path were situated numerous apartments which were 'supposed to have been stables and other offices.' Depending on the use of these rooms, they would also have served to reduce the extent to which activity from the Via dei Sepolchri filtered into the dwelling, although they themselves would have likely provided their own sensory disturbances which would have penetrated the front part of the dwelling.

126 According to Kockel 1983: 191, on either side of the main entrance to the villa of the Four Mosaic Columns, for example, were located shops, a *thermopolium* and possibly a cartwright's workshop. In addition to these shops, there were twelve other shops near this villa which 'structurally supported the upper stories of the villa. In fact, the two are so integrated that parallels could be drawn between this arrangement and the appearance of the *caseggiati* of Ostia in which the lower shops were occasionally located under relatively luxurious living accommodations'. See http://www.sfsu.edu/%7Epompeii/index.html, date accessed 20/7/17. These shops had residential apartments attached that included *cenaculi* (dining rooms).

127 Betts 2011: 125. On outdoor conversations making up a substantial proportion of the auditory landscape of historic sites see Smith 1999: 58, cf. pp. 50–51 above. Typical speech measures around 60 decibels, whilst rainfall is around 50 decibels. When distance is doubled from the source of sound, sound levels drop by 6 decibels. Thus, if a sound is 75 decibels at 1 metre from source, at 2 metres from source the sound will measure 69 decibels and at 4 metres it will measure 63 decibels. Measurements obtained from http://ele.aut.ac.ir/~wind/en/tour/env/db/dbdef.htm, date accessed 1/5/17. Information on the inverse square law obtained from http://www.nonoise.org/hearing/noisecon/noisecon.htm, date accessed 1/5/17.

128 On transmission of sound between street and house see pp. 48–49.

129 Platts 2019 (forthcoming). Shallow cart ruts have been excavated outside this residence (Fig. 3.21). Further excavation along the Via Ercolanense might, of course, uncover further tombs and shops in the vicinity of the Villa of Diomedes.

Chapter 4

1. Vitr. *De arch.* VI. 5. 1, trans. Granger 1934 (abridged).
2. There are considerable debates as to the exact dating of Vitruvius' *De Architectura*, see Baldwin 1990. According to Rowlandson and Howe 2001: 5, the most probable date is before 22 BC.
3. On city design and location see Vitr. *De arch.* I.4, on acoustics of theatres see Vitruv. *De arch.* V.6, on temple building see Vitr. *De arch.* IV. 3, on housing see Vitr. *De arch.* VI. 5. 3ff.
4. Allison 2004a: 161–162.
5. Flower 1996: esp. 185–222 on its history and function and its role as the location for the display of family trophies, portraits and painted family trees. On painted family trees as being a particular feature of elite Roman *atria* see Plin. *HN.* XXXV. 6.
6. Allison 2004a: 161ff.
7. Allison 1993; 2004a; Berry 1997.
8. On the *salutatio* see Goldbeck 2010; on the wedding see, esp. Hersch 2010; on the funeral see esp. Toynbee 1971; Hope 2009, 2017; Graham 2011.
9. Wallace-Hadrill 1994: 5.
10. On Livius Drusus, see Vell. Pat. II. 14. 3. On the visibility of Cicero's house see Cic, *Dom*, 100.
11. Wallace-Hadrill 1988: 46, cf. 1994: 5 and n. 13. Cf. Flower 1996: 92 n. 5 citing Wallace-Hadrill 1988: 46.
12. On the importance of the framing of views into the house from the threshold, and the best standing position for the ideal views into a residence, see Drerup 1959: 156–159. This viewpoint has been followed by numerous scholars including Wallace-Hadrill 1988, 1994; Clarke 1991.
13. Hor. *Sat.* I. 1. 9, trans. Rushton Fairclough 1926.
14. Sen. *Epis.* LXVIII. 10, trans. Gummere 1920.
15. Mart. *Ep.* X. 20, trans. Shackleton Bailey 1993.
16. Sen. *Ep.* VIII. 1, ibid. LXXX. 1, trans. Gummere 1920.
17. Hor. *Carm.*, III. 7. 27, *Carm*, I. 25, trans. Rudd 2004.
18. Gowers 2012; Harrison 2017. Cf. Fraenkel 1957: 74 on the size of Horace's audience.
19. Mart, *Ep.* I. 34, trans. Shackleton Bailey 1993. *At meretrix abigit testem ueloque seraque/ raraque Submemmi fornice rima patet./ A Chione saltem uel ab Iade disce pudorem: / abscondunt spurcas et monumenta lupas./ Numquid dura tibi nimium censura uidetur?/ deprendi ueto te, Lesbia, non futui.*
20. Examples of mechanisms for locking doors e.g. postholes have been found in numerous houses, for example the posthole in the secondary entrance of the house of the Tragic Poet, discussed below pp. 92–93. For details on other aspects of door architecture see p. 136 below citing Taylor Lauritsen 2011: 61–62.

21 Ivanoff 1859. Cf. Greenough 1890: esp. 8-9 'The length, breadth, and height of the *atrium* are given [in Vitruvius] then the right and left appendages [*alae*], which are **never** closed, but form a part of the architectural feature in question; then the *tablinum*, which stands in the same relation at the back; then the *fauces*. The only part that stands in the same relation is the passage at the front, which never has a door, and which being directly opposite the *tablinum* – the pendent to it, as it were – ... It must be remembered that all of these parts are visible to a person standing either at the outer or inner end of the *atrium*, and no others are. All the side passages have, in the Pompeiian houses, thresholds and marks of doors, and must have been closed, so that these rooms could not have formed a part of the *atrium* considered, as Vitruvius evidently is considering it, as an architectural member. It seems impossible to regard the *fauces* as anything else but the front passage'.
22 Lauritsen 2011: 69. For supporting evidence for the apparent open threshold between *fauces* and *atrium* in the Roman house see Ivanoff 1859: 82 who specifically notes the presence of a secondary door as being unusual (ungewöhnlich) and cites only two examples where it does occur, in the houses of Marcus Asellini and L. Caecilius Jucundus. Greenough 1890: 8-12; Smith et al. 1890: 669.
23 Ivanoff 1859: 82 '[I] moderni autori i quali pongono in mezzo altre porte oltre [delle ianuae principali], sia tra le ante della strada, sia tra le ante dell'atrio, cadono manifestamente in errore'.
24 Mazois 1822: 288-289, plate III. Cf. ibid., 1824, vol 2: 18-19; Gell 1832: 146 cited the presence of a door in the *fauces* of the house of the Tragic Poet. A useful summary of this secondary door of Pompeian houses debate can be found in Proudfoot 2013: 92, 94.
25 Proudfoot 2013. As well as outlining the four different forms of entrances: direct entrance, entrance vestibule (with subsequent entrance passage), entrance vestibule with side room/passage and entrance passage, of particular value is his list of Pompeian entranceways with inner closures at the rear of the *fauces*.
26 On partitions and curtains in houses see Taylor Lauritsen 2011, 2013 and 2015 and Chapter 5. For a good example of a partition found in an *atrium* see the partition found in the house of the Wooden Partition, Herculaneum, fig. 5.1.
27 Proudfoot 2013: 107.
28 Laurence 2007: 102.
29 See e.g. Apul. *Met.* 3. 5; Fronto, *Ep.* V. 1; Plaut. *Asin.* 273; Ovid, *Fast.* 1. 135.
30 Livy *Ab urbe condita*, V. 41, trans. Foster 1924 (abridged).
31 Livy, *Ab urbe condita,* Praef; Aug. *RG:* 8. This perception of a moral and social decline is likewise echoed in other late Republican authors e.g. Sallust, Horace. It is worth noting that Livy does not make the dating of his preface clear.
32 E.g. Suet. *Aug.* XXXIV, XL. 5, XLIV. 2, XLIII; Dio XLIX. 16. 1, LII. 42. 1-4, LIV. 16. 1, Suet. *Aug.* XL; Plin. *HN.* XXXIII. 2.

33 A comparison might be drawn here between Livy's account of the actions of Rome's elite during trouble with the Gauls in c. 390 BC and the later years of the Republic where sources suggest that many of Rome's upper echelons conspired and, when necessary, fled to houses and villas and locked themselves away from dangers. E.g. Cic. *Vat.* 22; Cic. *Mil.* 18; Cic. *Verr.* 2. 69; Cic. *Cat.* 28; Tac. *Hist.* 1. 33.

34 The first passage from Livy (VI. 25. 9) cited by Laurence as evidence for the entrance doors of houses normally being open is problematic since although similar in subject matter to Livy's account of the Gallic invasion, the open houses in question are in Tusculum, not Rome, and thus not directly relevant.

35 Livy, *Ab urbe condita*, V. 13. 6–7, trans. Foster 1924 (abridged). '*Tota urbe patentibus ianuis promiscuoque usu rerum omnium in propatulo posito, notos ignotosque passim advenas in hospitium ductos ferunt, et cum inimicis quoque benigne ac comiter sermones habitos; iurgiis ac litibus temperatum; vinctis quoque dempta in eos dies vincula; religioni deinde fuisse quibus eam opem di tulissent vinciri*'.

36 Hope 2017: 86.

37 It should be noted that in the above passage Vitruvius uses the terms *atrium* and *cavædium* to refer to covered or partially covered courtyards within the house. Citing evidence from Pliny the Younger that suggests some element of differentiation between these two rooms, Allison (2004a: 164, citing Plin. *Ep.* II. 17) argues that the interchangeable nature of these terms cannot be assumed. Indeed, that Vitruvius refers specifically only to *atria* as needing to be 'lofty' and suitable for those of the upper echelons perhaps further highlights a distinction between these spaces – the required opulence, or not, of *cavædium* is not considered. Irrespective of this possible distinction between the spaces, what is significant here is the importance Vitruvius places upon the public nature of both *atria* and *cavædium*, which seems incontrovertible.

38 Vitr. *De arch.* VI. 5. 1 trans. Granger 1934 (abridged), '*namque ex his quae propria sunt, in ea non est potestas omnibus intro eundi nisi invitatis, quemadmodum sunt cubicula triclinia balineae ceteraque quae easdem habent usus rationes. Communia autem sunt in quibus etiam invocati suo iure de populo possunt venire, id est vestibula cava aedium peristylia quaeque eundem habere possunt usum*'.

39 Wallace-Hadrill 1995: 10–11, 45.

40 Sen. *Ben.* VI. 34. 2. See Goldbeck 2010: 147–167, cf. Flower 1996: 219 '[they divided] their callers into three categories of "friends", presumably to make access to themselves seem more important and special. Only their intimates were allowed a private audience, while callers of the second rank were kept waiting in the *atrium*, being admitted only in groups, and the common man might not even get passed the door-keeper.'

41 Hor. *Sat.* I. 9. 53–59.

42 On not getting past the doorkeeper at the *salutatio* see e.g. Cic. *Verr.* II. 3. 8; Epict. *Ench.* XXXIII.13; Luc, *Nigr.* XXII–XXIII; Mart. *Ep.* V. 22; Sen. *Constant* XIV. 1; *Tranq.* XII.6.

43 Speksnijder 2015: 97 n. 76, *contra* Hales 2003: 37.
44 Speksnijder 2015: 97.
45 Vitr. *De arch.* VI. 5. 1, trans. Granger 1934 (abridged).
46 Sen. *Ben.* VI. 34. 1, trans. Basore 1935. 'There are many other doors that will shut out even those who have gained admittance'.
47 Hales 2003: 111. According to Hales (2003: 108–9) these obstacles include doorkeepers, the presence of the *fauces* which acted to provide a physical distance between door and *atrium*, and warning images such as the *cave canem* mosaic discussed above (p. 50) which 'invite the viewer to stop'. We might also add guard dogs to this list given the discovery of remains of numerous dogs around Pompeii. On the evidence for dogs at Pompeii see ch. 6, cf. Jashemski 1979: 103, 283.
48 Wallace-Hadrill 1994: 10–11, 45, citing Vitr. *De arch.* VI. 5. 1. See *contra* Hales 2003: 107–111 who also examines the accessibility of the Roman house to those who were uninvited. She proposes, however, that actual physical admittance to dwellings was controlled via numerous mechanisms including architecture, mosaics and door keepers. As such for Hales (2003: 107) 'the combination of *atrium*, *tablinum*, and so on, as seen from the front entrance, is precisely that – just a view.'
49 Balch 2008: 38.
50 According to Balch, those residences displaying frescoes and mosaics that have injured animals, guarding dogs or boars (for example the house of the Wounded Bear, the house of the Tragic Poet and the house of Paquius Proculus and the house of the Wild Boar respectively) are meant to provide 'warnings to thieves and others, warding off the evil eye' (2008: 37).
51 Balch 2008: 38.
52 Balch 2008: 35.
53 See p. 67 n. 107 p. 252 on discussion of the *fauces* and the use of doorkeepers at the entrance to Roman houses.
54 The *posticum* for the house of the Tragic Poet is doorway #3 on the Vicolo della Fullonica.
55 On this residence see Overbeck and Mau 1884: 282–285.
56 Balch 2008: 36.
57 The exact date of the merging of these two houses has been connected to the Claudian period on account of both dwellings being re-decorated in the third style at around this period, see Mau 1876: 163, 232, 245; cf. Strocka 2007: 307. Third Style, dated approximately to the Claudian period (Strocka 2007: 307; Ehrhardt 1987 and 2012: 103), although see Dexter 1975; Richardson 2000 who attribute the wall paintings in these two houses to the second style.
58 The earliest development phase of this house (V. I. 26) should be attributed to the second century BC, see Mau 1876. Cf. Karivieri and Forsell, 2006–7: 121.

59 For detailed excavation records see Mau 1875: 161–163, 1876: 41–49, 149–152, 161–167, 223–234., *GdSc.* N.S. 1884–1887: 150–153, 169, 174–176, 251–256. Cf. The Swedish Pompeii Project for excavation details of the entire *insula* at V. I. Accessible at http://www.pompejiprojektet.se/project.php, date accessed 22/08/17.
60 Fiorelli 1861: 19.
61 We have some evidence for curtains and partitions being used to separate space within houses and these are explored in later chapters. On the use of curtains in houses see Taylor Lauritsen 2013.
62 On the *salutatio* see Goldbeck 2010; on the wedding see, esp. Hersch 2010; on the funeral see esp. Toynbee 1971 and Hope 2009; on the male coming-of-age ceremony see Dolansky 2008.
63 On issues of understanding the specifics of the Roman wedding see Hersch 2010, for problems with funerals see Hope 2009 esp. ch 3. Other rituals and processions experienced in the Roman world include the triumph, coming of age ceremonies, the *salutatio* and public sacrifices. Problems equally exist when trying to reconstruct these events e.g. see Beard 2007, esp. ch. 3, on the problems of reconstructing the triumph.
64 Wallace-Hadrill 1994: 17.
65 Wallace-Hadrill 1994: 117.
66 Dickmann 2011: 60.
67 Vitr. *De. arch.* VI. 5. 1.
68 Goldbeck 2010.
69 Dickmann 2011: 71. For literary evidence of the *atrium* being employed for domestic and familial usage see e.g. Livy *Ab urbe condita* I. 57 on the working of wool in the *atrium* by Lucretia. On children playing in the *atrium* see Verg. *Aen.* VII, 377–389; Lucr., IV. 400–404. On the temporal division of daily activities for Rome's elite see Laurence 2007: 154–166.
70 Dickmann 2011: 61.
71 Allison 2004a: 69. Cf. Allison 2006: 396–7 on the evidence of weaving found in house I. 10. 1 and house I. 10. 8 in the *Insula* of the Menander. Similar evidence for weaving was found by Berry (1997: 193) in her examination of the finds of the house of M. Epidius Primus.
72 Allison 2006: 397.
73 Aldrete 2004a: 241. According to Aldrete an hour in Roman summer time might measure up to a modern hour and a half, whilst an hour in winter might only reach the length of our forty minutes.
74 These numbers of hours do not take into the consideration the possible impact of overcast days or stormy days, which might further impact upon the amount of sunshine experienced that allowed close work such as weaving without the aid or extra illumination.
75 Allison 2006: 388–389.

76 Varro, *Ling.* VIII. 29; Sen. *Constant.* 4b. 13. 7; Suet. *Tib.* LXXIV refers to the use of coals and embers in the emperor's dining room on Capri in March. In Suet. *Vit.* VIII. 2 he refers to a fire in the emperor's dining room due to an overturned hearth.
77 Wallace-Hadrill 1994: 156. On children in Rome and late antiquity see e.g. Rawson 2003; Laes 2011, 2016. On infants under one year in ancient Rome, see Carroll 2018.
78 Huntley 2011: 71; cf. Huntley 2017: 137.
79 Huntley 2011: 71.
80 On the issues of differentiating between dolls and votive figurines see Shumka 1999: 617. On the issues of identifying the role of miniature pots or tools see Kiernan 2009.
81 Allison 2004a: 80–81.
82 Wallace-Hadrill 1994: 113. In her examination of the finds from 30 houses in Pompeii, Allison (2004a: 155) stipulates 'no recorded artefacts ... could be attributed to children'.
83 Allison 2004a: 156.
84 Huntley 2011: 69–89; 2017: 137–154. According to Huntley 2017: 144 just over 40 per cent of children's graffiti was excavated in 22 domestic buildings.
85 Huntley 2011: 79–83; 2017: 144–145. According to Huntley's results neither were examples of children's graffiti found in kitchens.
86 Huntley 2017: 145.
87 Huntley 2017: 145.
88 Verg. *Aen.* VII. 380–382.
89 Lucr. IV. 400–404, trans. Rouse 1924, rev. Smith 1975.
90 Huntley 2017: 145.
91 On the *cella ostiarius* monitoring the household see Joshel and Petersen 2014: 41.
92 Allison 2004a: 81–82, cf. Allison 2006: 387–8, cf. Allison 2004a: 67 and 81 outlining the houses with evidence of cupboards or chests for storage. According to Allison (2004a: 69), examples of strongboxes (*arca*) as found in the *atrium* of the Vetti were rare. There are some further examples from the house of M. Obellius Firmus and from villa B at Torre Annunziata (Roberts 2013: 84–85). As Mau (1899: 249) points out, these strong boxes were sometimes decorated with reliefs, and some wealthy Pompeian houses had more than one, see Mau (1899: 316) who draws on the example of the house of the Vettii, which had two *arca* in its *atrium*.
93 In particular during the festival of the *Lemuria* (May 9, 11, 13), which commemorated the dead, the *lararium* was the focus of many rituals undertaken by the paterfamilias in order to propitiate the ghosts of the deceased. On the *Lemuria* festival see Ovid, *Fasti*, V. 421ff.
94 For more detailed consideration of extraordinary rituals undertaken in the *atrium*, see pp. 113–127.
95 On the offerings at the household *lararium* and the decoration of these altars see Clarke 1991: 6–12, 2005: 75–81.
96 Allison 2006: 389.

97 Allison 2006: 389, cf. Allison 2004a: 70.
98 On the finds of braziers in the houses of the Menander and of the Cabinet Maker, as well as the house of the Ephebe and house VIII. 5. 9 see Allison 2004a: 102. On the ability to move braziers to different locations around the house, see Dyer 1875: 550–551.
99 Allison 2004a: 70.
100 On the possible use of the house of Stallius Eros see Mauiri 1929: 395–5. He suggests (1929: 430) that the *atrium* might have been employed as a builder's yard. On the use of house I. 6. 8–9 see Mauiri 1929: 394–400.
101 Mauiri 1929: 432.
102 Allison 2004a: 103, citing Foss 1994: 42. For further discussion of visible architectural attempts to prevent the unwanted spread of smells in the *domus* see Chapter 6 below. On the social criticism and judgement of 'bad' smells as evidence of lower standing see Bradley 2015: 4–8; Potter 2015: 127.
103 In this chapter we are only considering the kitchen's location in relation to the *atrium* and the way in which this might affect the sensory experience of the *atrium*. For more detailed discussion on the multisensory experience of the kitchen see Chapter 7.
104 For more detailed discussion of the multisensory experience of the kitchen and its relationship to the rest of the house see ch. 7.
105 For example in the houses of the Mosaic *Atrium*, the Beautiful Courtyard, the Ara Maxima, and the Ceii.
106 Sen. *Ep.* 104.6, trans. Gummere 1925.
107 Petron. *Sat.* II. 1, 70. 11; Mart. *Epi.* I. 92. 9.
108 Juv. *Sat.* V. 162–168; Hor. *Sat.* II. 38. 8, cf. Potter 2015: 127.
109 On the noises of the kitchen see for example Plaut. *Cas.* 763–767, trans. De Melo 2011. 'Everybody's rushing around inside through the entire house. The old man's shouting in the kitchen and urging on the cooks: "Why won't you get on with it today? Why aren't you giving us anything if you are giving us something? Hurry up, dinner ought to be cooked already." ... And the cooks for their part take care ever so charmingly that the old man won't get his dinner; they knock over the pots and extinguish the fire with water.'
110 Petron. *Sat.* 70. 11.
111 On the importance of pleasant smells whilst eating see Juv. *Sat.* V. 149–150 and 161–162.
112 Allison 2006: 389.
113 Allison 2004a: 80–82, cf. Allison 2006: 390.
114 Flower 1996: 199 citing Wallace-Hadrill 1994: 96.
115 Plut. *T. Gracc.* 8. 5. Lack of financial, military or political prowess amongst Roman elite families threatened to cast one's family into political and social oblivion for decades, possibly centuries, to come. See, for example, Caesar whose family (the *Julii*

Caesares) had seen some decline in their political and thus social prominence prior to the first century BC, and Sulla from the patrician clan of the *Cornelii*. His particular branch of the *gens* Cornelia had become impoverished during his youth, leading Sulla to spend his time with actors and musicians, Plut. *Sull* 2. 2.

116 Hersch 2010. I am focusing specifically here on young girls as they marry for the first time. There are, of course, numerous examples of remarriage in ancient Rome, for example Augustus' marriage to Livia, but they are not under consideration here.

117 See Hersch 2010: 17–18, 289–290; cf. Hope 2009 and Hamilakis 2013a: 129–160.

118 Juv. *Sat.* I. 100, III. 127, V. 19; Sen. *Ben.* VI. 33; Mart. *Ep.* X. 74.

119 Sen. *Ep.* 84. 12, trans. Gummere 1920. '*Intueris illas potentium domos, illa tumultuosa rixa salutantium limina? multum habent contumeliarum ut intres, plus cum intraveris. Praeteri istos gradus divitum et magno adgestu suspensa vestibula: non in praerupto tantum istic stabis sed in lubrico*'.

120 It will also provide substantial visual experiences for other inhabitants of the city as they see people queuing.

121 George 2008: 96. See e.g. Juv. *Sat.* I. 96 reference to crowds attending a *salutatio* as '*turbae togatae*' essentially 'togate hordes'.

122 Martial's *Epigrams* (e.g. VIII. 28, XII. 8) and Juvenal's *Satires* (e.g. III. 126–130) provide numerous satirical discussions on the practice and difficulties of wearing the toga at the *salutatio*, whilst Quintilian writes in depth about how orators should wear the toga in order to impress their listeners. See Vout 1996: 210 on the difficulties of identifying remains of togas today.

123 On the possible width of the toga material see Wilson 1924: 71. George 2008: 99 on the weight and material of the toga, and the problems of moving whilst wearing one, dressing oneself and the need for a slave called a *vestipicus* (clothes folder).

124 Mart. *Ep.* V. 22 and XII. 18 on the warmth of the toga resulting in a wearer sweating. Cf. Mart. *Ep.* V. 22 on trekking through the dirt and waste of the city see 'I must ascend the steep path of the Suburan hill, and the pavement filthy with footsteps never dry;' trans. Shackleton Bailey 1993 (abridged).

125 On sweating at the *salutatio* see Mart. *Ep.* XII. 18. On different wools being used for winter and summer see Olsen 2017: 23.

126 On the order in which individuals were admitted into the *salutatio* as a means of visually demarcating *clientes*, see p. 90. On the variety and colours of toga, see Edmondson and Keith 2008, esp. Edmondson 2008: 26 ff.

127 On the threadbare nature of some people's togas and cloaks see, Mart. *Ep.* III. 30, III. 36, IX. 57, IX. 100, XIV. 125; Juv. *Sat.* III. 148–151, III. 180. On filthy togas and cloaks the problems of keeping a toga clean see e.g. Mart. *Ep.* IV. 34; VIII. 28; IX. 49; Juv. *Sat.* III. 148–151. On wearing out four togas during a summer in Rome due the *salutatio* duties see Mart. *Ep.* X. 96. On the role of the toga as a tool for highlighting inferiority see George 2008.

128 Examples of houses with stone benches outside include the houses of the Wooden Partition, Aristeides and the Bronze Herm (Herculaneum) and the houses of the Ceii, the Menander, M. Obellius Firmus and Octavius Quartio (Pompeii). Welcoming mosaics in the pavement outside dwellings can be seen outside the houses of the Faun and the Wild Boar (Pompeii). Opulent *fauces*' mosaics are found at, e.g. the houses of the Bear, the Tragic Poet (Fig. 3.8), the Wild Boar, Paquius Proculus (Pompeii) and the house of the Mosaic *Atrium*, (Herculaneum). Imposing entrance doors are visible e.g. at the house of Octavius Quartio (Pompeii) and other examples of grand entrance architecture are visible at e.g. the house of the Grand Portal (Herculaneum), the houses of the Augustalis (Pompeii). On the methodological issues of studying stone benches outside houses from Pompeii and Herculaneum see Hartnett 2008: 93-95. There is, of course, every possibility that wooden benches and seats might also have been located outside residences, but these no longer survive. Evidence for such use of more perishable street furniture can be seen in frescoes from the *atrium* of the *praedia* of Julia Felix, which depict people sitting on wooden benches and stools, see Nappo 1989: 81-83, 88-89. cf. Hartnett 2008: 93. Three wooden benches have been found in houses at Herculaneum, see Mols 1999: 52-55, cf. Hartnett 2008: 93.

129 Edmondson 2008: 21, cf. 23 for examples of the civic duties that required individuals to wear the toga.

130 On understanding the visual language of the toga see Vout 1996; George 2008.

131 See e.g. Mart. *Ep.* III. 56 V. 22; XII. 18; XII. 82; XIV. 125; IX. 100; Juv. *Sat.* I. 95; III.127 on the *clientes* wearing togas to visit their patronus. Cf. Edmondson 2008: 23.

132 Slaves would have worn clothes that probably reflected their role in the household but since slave voices are not a significant feature in our evidence, it is difficult to know what their outfits might have been. Apul. *Met.* II. 7. describes a domestic slave girl who wore a linen tunic with a red sash, whilst at *Met.* II. 19 we hear of liveried slaves waiting on tables, thereby showing the variety of outfits slaves might be given.

133 It is worth remembering that household slaves had a variety of jobs and those who worked in a dwelling's kitchens, for example, were more likely to be smelly and dirty than those working as a *cubicularius* or as a *nomenclator* given the nature of their jobs. On the perception of kitchen slaves such as cooks being smelly and greasy, see p. 195.

134 On the paucity of underground sewage drainage at Pompeii, see Kaiser 2011: 71. According to Kaiser, where underground drainage did exist in Pompeii, this was probably in order to drain the baths and the forum, rather than remove waste from the streets. On the dangers of walking around the streets of Rome due to chamber pots being emptied from upper stories of dwellings, see Juv. *Sat.* III. 277, cf. p. 37. above. Urinating and defecating in the street were likewise regular occurrences as signs from Rome suggest, (*CIL* VI. 29848: 'Twelve gods and goddesses, and Jupiter, the biggest and the best, will be angry with whoever urinates or defecates here' found

near the Baths of Titus) and Pompeii in *regio* V (*CIL* IV. 7038: 'If you shit against the walls and we catch you, you will be punished') Cf. Hobson 2009: 143–144. These further emphasize obstacles that needed dodging and potential factors that might affect one's bodily smell as individuals traversed city streets.

135 See e.g. *Philogelos* 231; 232–4, 235, 236–40, 242; Petron. *Sat.* IX.
136 Hartnett 2008: esp 108–115.
137 Hartnett 2008: 116.
138 Hartnett 2008: 116
139 Hersch 2010 on the wedding as a means of parading elite status, Graham 2011 on funerals delineating individual and collective identities, and Hope 2017 on mourning behaviours, the senses of the bereaved and the extent to which they impacted upon those not involved.
140 In terms of pre-nuptial rites there are suggestions that prior to the wedding itself, girls would dedicate their childhood clothing (Arn. *Adv. Nat.* 2. 67) and dolls (Pers. 2. 70). According to Dolansky (2008: 60 n. 3), however, we know very little about this rite. Since we cannot be sure when it occurred in relation to the wedding itself, whether it occurred years or days before the wedding, or indeed whether it was a public or private ceremony, I am not specifically considering it in relation to the ritual of the wedding itself.
141 On the bride being bedecked in finery, making her stand out from the rest of the wedding party, see Plaut. *Cas.* 767–768. The ornate bridal hair style was called *sex crines* and involved the hair being divided, perhaps with a spear, into six locks and fastened to the top of the bride's head. On this, see Festus 454L cf. Hersch 73–80. On the flowers and grasses in the hair of the bride, see Festus 56L cf. Apul. *Met.* 4. 27, Stat. *Silv.* I. 2. On the orange-yellow *flammeum*, see e.g. Plin. *HN.* X. 148; Luc. *Pharsalia* II. 360–364; Schol. *Ad Juv* VI. 225.
142 On the seeking of auspices, see e.g. Tac. *Ann.* XI. 27; Plaut. *Cas.* 84–86; Stat. *Silv.* I. 2. 229–230; Sid. Apoll. *Epithal.* XI. 54. For musical instruments, see e.g. Welsch 2010: Figs 1 and 2. On the seizing of the bride and her refusal, see e.g. Catull. LXI. 82–86, Festus, 467L; Juv. *Sat.* II. 119–120. On the torches lighting the way, see Festus, 282, 283L cf. Hersch 2010: 138–140. On the throwing of nuts to onlookers, see Hersch 2010: 151–157. On the feasting at the groom's house, see Catull. 66. 303–306.
143 Hersch 2010: 2.
144 Hersch 2010: 9, 11.
145 Hersch 2010: 13.
146 Reinsberg 2006: 78.
147 Claud. *Epithalamium Palladio et Celevinae* 25. 134–138.
148 Catull. 61.
149 Hersch 2010: 62, but see Catull. 66. 15–17 for the suggestion that tearful bridal reactions to the events of the wedding day were false.

150 On the location of the wax masks, called *imagines*, in the *atrium*, see. Polyb. VI. 53–4.
151 Hope 2009: 71.
152 Hope 2009: 71–72. It is worth remembering here once again the elite bias of our literary evidence which likely skews our understanding of Roman funerary practices.
153 Tac. *Ann.* II. 82, trans. Jackson 1931.
154 Ovid, *Cons. Ad Liv.* 183, trans. Mozley 1929, rev. Goold 1939. Note Wallace-Hadrill (1988: n. 46, cf. 1994: 5 n. 13) incorrectly attributes this text to Seneca. Whilst there is some debate as to authorship of this text, most copies of the work currently associate it with Ovid.
155 Ovid, *Cons. ad Liv.* 185, trans. Mozley 1929, rev. Goold 1939.
156 On the possible figurative nature of Tac. *Ann.* II. 82 see Proudfoot 2013: 103.
157 Luc. *Pharsalia*, I. 584–637.
158 Luc. *Pharsalia*, II. 1–6.
159 Luc. *Pharsalia* II. 15–28, trans. Duff 1928.
160 On female displays of grief at funerals see, e.g., Luc, *Pharsalia* II. 29–43.
161 Wallace-Hadrill 1994: 5.
162 Hope 2009, esp. ch. 3.
163 Servius, *On Vergil's Aeneid*, VI. 218, '*servabantur cadavera septem diebus*', but see Lucian, *On Mourning*, 24 who implies the laying out was for a shorter period of three days.
164 Boddington, Garland and Janaway 1987: 66 state that with deaths from certain types of septicaemia, putrefaction of the corpse might occur virtually the same time as death, whilst the corpse of an obese individual retains heat for longer, thus again speeding up the stages of putrefaction. According to Boddington, Garland and Janaway 1987: 66, between one to three days after death the internal organs begin to decompose, and between three to five days after the body will start to swell and fluids including blood will start to leak from the mouth and nose. During this time the body will also start to bloat with the build-up of gases produced during bodily decay.
165 On the vast amounts of perfumes and incense specifically associated with death being used each year, see Plin. *HN.* 12. 41. 83. In contrast, a corpse on display in the *atrium* for only three days during the winter would start to decompose at a significantly slower speed, and thus the physical experience of proximity to, and movement around, the body could thus be completely different. Whilst embalming did exist, this was perceived to be a foreign and exotic custom and thus rarely occurred in Rome, see Toynbee 1971: 41; Hope 2009: 74.
166 Lucian, *On Mourning*, 11.
167 On the movement of the body to the ground see Artemidorus, *The Interpretation of Dreams*, I.12, cf. Varro, *Ling* V. 64 and Servius, *On Vergil's Aeneid*, XII. 395. On the washing, anointing and dressing of the corpse see Verg. *Aen.* VI. 218–220, 9, 485–90; Luc, *On Mourning*, 11–12.

168 On the body being dressed in finery see Polyb. *Hist.* VI.53.7; Cic. *De Leg.* II. 24. 60; Livy *Ab urbe condita* V. 41; Juv. *Sat.* III. 171. On the specifics of the corpse's display see Plin. *HN.* VII. 46; Pers. III. 105. Cf. the funerary relief from the tomb of the Haterii, now in the Vatican Museums (Cat no. 9997, 9998).

169 See *CIL* XIV 2112 cf. Dutsch 2008. An interesting parallel might perhaps be drawn between *clientes* visiting their *patronus* during the *salutatio* and people coming to 'pay their respects' to the dead. At the very least the main elements of both rituals were focused around the *atrium-tablinum* space.

170 For a visual representation of a funeral procession that highlights the plethora of corporeal experiences to be had during it, see the Amiternum relief dated to the first century BC, now located in the Museo Nazionale d'Abruzzo, Aquila.

171 Lucian, *On Mourning*, 15, trans. Fowler and Fowler 1905. Cf. ibid., 24 where Lucian particularly emphasizes the concern of mourning parents as to how they will be judged by others regarding their behaviour, 'The parents are persuaded, though they go to work [on eating at the burial feast] at first in a somewhat shamefaced manner; they do not want it to be thought that after their bereavement they are still subject to the infirmities of the flesh.'

172 That individuals are also praised for the 'open' and 'public' nature of their dwellings likewise suggests an element of control in terms of access to the *domus*, see Plut. *Cic.* 36. 3 and Cic. *Comment Pet.* 13. 50). Cf. Platts 2019 (forthcoming).

Chapter 5

1 Plin. *Ep.* II. 17. 20–24, trans. Firth 1900 (abridged). From http://www.attalus.org/old/pliny2.html#17, date accessed 1/5/18.

2 See, e.g. Plin. *Ep.* V. 6 and IX. 7.

3 Birley 2000: 50–51 suggests it might have been Clusinius Gallus, who was also the recipient of *Ep.* IV.17, but this cannot be confirmed especially since, as Syme 1968: 148 points out, the name Gallus is relatively common.

4 Plin. *Ep.* I. 1.

5 The difficulties of trying to reconstruct the architectural plan of a residence from text alone has been well demonstrated by the numerous attempts to recreate floor plans of Pliny the Younger's Laurentine and Tuscan villas from the detailed accounts in his letters, see de la Ruffinière du Prey 1994: esp. ch. 3 and 4. On the various attempts to locate Pliny's Laurentine Villa see du Prey 1994: 81–86.

6 Vitr. *De arch.* VI.V.1.

7 See pp. 77–129.

8 Varro, *Ling.* V. 162, trans. Kent 1938.

9. Similarly styled small, closed rooms leading off from peristyle gardens, terraces and lower floors of dwellings have also typically been termed '*cubicula*', Allison 2004a: 94–98.
10. See e.g. McKay 1975: 34; Stroka 1984: 20–21; Michel 1990: 30; Clarke 1991: 3; Seiler 1992: 25, 27.
11. Cf. Plin. *Ep.* II. 17. 10 who refers to a bedchamber in his Laurentine villa which could also be used as a dining-room and p. 148 below.
12. Vitr. *De arch.* VI.V.1. For more detailed analysis of this passage see Chapter Four above.
13. See Allison 2004a, 2006; Dickmann 2011.
14. Riggbsy 1997: 36–43. Leach 1997 also explores the textual references to rooms within Roman houses and considers the impact this might have upon interpreting their decorative features.
15. Allison 2004a: 72–76 on the '*cubicula*' off the *atrium*, 94–98 on the '*cubicula*' off gardens, terraces or lower floors. Allison (2004a: 96) highlights a potentially different pattern of usage in the '*cubicula*' to the back of residences according to increased finds associated with ablutions and cloth working.
16. Ekirch 2005: 300.
17. See e.g. Verg. *Aen.* II. 268, VIII. 407; Ov. *Met.* VIII. 83, both of whom refer to *prima quies*, or 'first quiet'. On sleeping patterns in ancient Rome, see Storey 2018: 328–329.
18. Storey 2018: 328.
19. Quint. *Inst.* X. 3.
20. Plin. *Ep.* III. V.
21. Plin. *Ep.* IX. 36.
22. The first hour of the day during summer in Roman times ran from 4.27–5.42 am. The fourth hour was from 8.13–9.29 am and the fifth hour was from 9.29–10.44 am, see Smith 1875: 614; Storey 2018: 324. On the division of day and night into twelve unequal hours each which varied in length according to season, see Laurence 2007: 122–132.
23. On the identification of room (e) in house VIII. 2. 14–16 as a *cubiculum* see Mau 1892: 9 and on the finds of this room see Allison 2004b: http://www.stoa.org/projects/ph/rooms?houseid=24#521, date accessed 26/8/18. On the house of the Wooden Sacellum, Herculaneum, including its finds, see Maiuri 1958: 252–255; Mols 1999: 129. For similar examples of finds in house V. 22 see Maiuri 1958: 443; Mols 1999: 135, 160–1, 255–6.
24. Plin. *Ep.* II. 17. 21, trans. Firth 1900 (abridged). From http://www.attalus.org/old/pliny2.html#17, date accessed 1/5/18.
25. Taylor Lauritsen 2011: 61–62.
26. See Taylor Lauritsen's (2013: 101–102) discussion of Monnier's 1864 reconstruction of the house of Pansa for an example of the problems of the prevalence of curtains in

popular depictions of Roman houses. Likewise, Alma-Tadema's imagined Roman domestic interiors equally emphasize the presence of curtains and other forms of soft furnishings, which cannot be ascertained from the archaeological evidence.

27 Plin. *Ep.* II. 17. 21.
28 Further examples of evidence for partitions between *atria* and *tablina* including the remnants of cuts in doorjambs have been found in the house of the Menander, Allison 2006: 57; Taylor Lauritsen 2011: 63.
29 *Contra* Taylor Lauritsen 2011: 63.
30 Elia 1934: 286–7 records the remains of a long iron rod in the house of the Cabinet Maker near the threshold to the *triclinium*, which has been interpreted as a curtain rail. In the house of Trebius Valens, five bronze rings were recorded near the entrance to an *ala* and were interpreted as curtain rings (Spano 1915: 419). Similarly, the discovery by Sogliano (1905: 254–6) of two pairs of bronze bosses on either side of the threshold between the *atrium* and the *tablinum* in the house of Obellius Firmus were interpreted as used for tying back curtains that hung here.
31 Taylor Lauritsen 2013: 103.
32 The 29 houses were selected randomly according to ability to gain access to the dwellings and to investigate residences of various size. See p. 285, n. 39 of factors affecting housing selection for this study.
33 Lauritsen 2011: 105 has undertaken a similar survey of thirty-one houses from Pompeii and Herculaneum. The figures he cites in terms of thresholds with doors are comparable, in particular the 90 per cent of thresholds between *cubicula* and *atria* where he found door evidence. His percentage for doors between *cubicula* and *peristylia* is a slightly lower 47 per cent, whilst from the houses I surveyed the percentage of 'present' doors between *cubicula* and *peristylia* is 57 per cent. Irrespective of the 10 per cent discrepancy between our corresponding figures, the overall comparison of relationships between *cubicula* and *atria*, and *cubicula* and *peristylia* in terms of connectivity and potential obstacles impinging on movement and free-flowing multisensory experience between these spaces is clear.
34 Some evidence for lattice grill doors being used around houses highlights that we perhaps cannot assume all doors were made of solid wood. Gusmann's work on Pompeii (1900: 255) mentions the use of a secondary door in the *fauces* of the house of Popidius Priscus that was made of open ironwork. Although this was apparently a door in a *fauces*, it should at least be noted that such lattice-style doors might be employed elsewhere in the home.
35 On measuring smell and the problems of smell-mapping see pp. 37–38.
36 For those residences that lack an *impluvium* and *compluvium*, such as the house of the Moralist, this will not be an influencing factor on the transmission of smell in the space. Similarly, for those residences which feature open areas or gardens close to their entrances, such as the house of the Ship of Europa or the house of Pinarius Cerialis,

once again these will equally impact upon the dispersal of smells around the front section of the dwelling.

37 On the use of fans inside Roman houses see e.g. Mart. *Ep.* III. 82. 11.

38 Since evidence for curtains has not, so far, been found in or near the thresholds of *cubicula*, the impact of these is not considered here.

39 Allison 2004a. On the movability of artefacts and the issues this poses for identifying the role of rooms in houses see pp. 109–110 above.

40 Allison 2004b: http://www.stoa.org/projects/ph/rooms?houseid=18#380, on this room's identification as a *cubiculum*, see Allison 2004b https://web.archive.org/web/20160306034506/http://www.stoa.org/projects/ph/rooms?houseid=18#380, date accessed 1/5/18. cf. Anonymous 1895: 207; Peters 1977: 114.

41 On the identification of room (p) in house VIII. 2. 26 as a *cubiculum* see Mau 1888: 191 and on the finds of this room see Allison 2004b: http://www.stoa.org/projects/ph/rooms?houseid=25#573, date accessed 26/8/18. On the identification of room (l) in house VIII. 2. 29-30 as a *cubiculum* see Mau (1884: 212) and on the finds of this room see Allison 2004b: http://www.stoa.org/projects/ph/rooms?houseid=27#624, date accessed 26/8/18. On the identification of room (e) in house VIII. 2. 14-16 as a *cubiculum* see Mau 1892: 9 and on the finds of this room see Allison 2004b: http://www.stoa.org/projects/ph/rooms?houseid=24#521, date accessed 26/8/18.

42 Quint. *Inst.* X. 3.; Mart. *Ep.* XIV. 39, trans. Shackleton Bailey 1993.

43 Apul. *Met.* X. 20, trans. Hanson 1989.

44 On the wax applied to wall paintings see Vitr. *De arch.* VII. 9. 3-4.

45 Catull. VI. 8, trans. Cornish, 2nd ed. 1995; Apul. *Met.* X. 21.

46 The lighting equipment found here consisted of a bronze lamp, amongst other paraphernalia, see Spano 1915: 341 fig. 6, cf. Allison 2004b: http://www.stoa.org/projects/ph/rooms?houseid=14#284, date accessed 27/8/18. On the unguent bottles see Spano 1915: 340 figs 4-5, cf. Allison 2004b: http://www.stoa.org/projects/ph/rooms?houseid=14#284, date accessed 27/8/18.

47 On the identification of room (m) in the house of the Prince of Naples as a *cubiculum* see Mau 1898: 36, on the finds of items for personal ablutions see Allison 2004b: http://www.stoa.org/projects/ph/rooms?houseid=20#439, date accessed 27/8/18.

48 Pappalardo 2004: 215.

49 Stewart 2007: 67–68.

50 On the use of perfumes behind closed doors, see p. 149. On scent and scented powders being applied to clothes see Stewart 2007: 54–55.

51 See e.g. Mart. *Ep.* III. 55. Cf. Stewart 2007: esp. 134–135 on judgements about excessive quantity of perfume and cosmetics used.

52 Ling 1997: 135–136.

53 See Allison 2004b: http://www.stoa.org/projects/ph/rooms?houseid=9, date accessed 27/8/18.

54 Ling 1997: 114, 314. Possible evidence for shelves has been found here, leading to suggestions that this was a space for storage, however the possibility that this could also have been a *cubiculum* should not be overlooked, cf. Allison 2004b: https://web.archive.org/web/20150711001555/http://www.stoa.org/projects/ph/rooms?houseid=9#176, date accessed 28/8/18.
55 Allison 2004b: http://www.stoa.org/projects/ph/rooms?houseid=17, date accessed 27/8/18.
56 Allison 2004b: http://www.stoa.org/projects/ph/rooms?houseid=23, date accessed 28/8/18.
57 Plin. *Ep.* II. 17. 10, trans. Firth 1900 (abridged). From http://www.attalus.org/old/pliny2.html#17, date accessed 1/5/18.
58 Allison 2004b: http://www.stoa.org/projects/ph/rooms?houseid=23, date accessed 28/8/18.
59 Apul. *Met.* II. 15, trans. Hanson 1989 (abridged).
60 Sen. *De Ira*, III. 8. 6; *Cons. Ad. Marc.* XXII. 6, trans. Basore 1932 (abridged).
61 Sen. *Ep.* 78. 23. The notion of portable braziers that can be transported easily and used in various settings is supported by Juv. *Sat.* III. 249–253 who tells us of clients visiting their patrons accompanied by slaves carrying portable braziers so that they are able to warm the *sportula* they receive.
62 Suet. *Aug.* 82 on Augustus sleeping with the doors of his bedroom open in the summer.
63 Mart. *Ep.* XII.57 on the noise of the passing crowd and IX. 68 on the racket from school teachers in neighbouring schools.
64 On the shouting of the miller's wife, Apul. *Met.* IX. 15. On Lucius' night with Photis, Apul. *Met.* II. 15, trans. Hanson 1989.
65 Vitr. *De arch.* VI. 5. 1.
66 Riggsby 1997: 51.
67 Riggsby 1997: 54.
68 Petron. *Sat.* 25–26, trans. Rouse 1913, abridged.
69 'Viewshed' is the visible area from a specific location. It includes everything that is within line of sight and excludes all that cannot be seen due to being beyond the horizon or obstructed by other features such as trees, walls, buildings. See, e.g. Ellis 2004 on the use of viewshed analysis for understanding the placement of bar counters at Pompeii to enable more unobstructed views of bar counters by prospective customers.
70 See pp. 106–107 above on the location of weaving in the *atrium* because of good natural light.
71 Allison 2006: 390.
72 Allison 2006: 390.
73 Examples of small high up windows in the exterior walls of *cubicula* can be found, for example, in the house of the Bronze Bull. Clerestory lighting above the entrance to

cubicula off *atria* can be found in the house of Trebius Valens, or those above the *cubicula* of the *atrium* in the house of the *Triclinia*.
74 Allison 2006: 391.
75 Although see Bailey 1972: 9 on the ways to reduce smoke from burning oil via the design of lamp nozzles and the positioning of the wick. Cf. Boman 2011: 94. Obviously increasing the number of nozzles and wicks of a lamp will increase the amount of light it can give off.
76 Boman 2011: 90.
77 Boman 2011: 91–93; 97–98.
78 Ellis 1994: 70.
79 It is important to bear in mind that slaves are likely to be in attendance in most 'private' situations as we see, for example, from Apul. *Met.* II. 15 when slaves remain in the room when Lucius sleeps with his lover, Photis.
80 Stewart 2007: 139.
81 Apul. *Met.* X. 20, trans. Hanson 1989. '*Nec dominae voluptates diutina sua praesentia morati, clavis foribus facessunt*'.
82 Catull. VI. 15–17, trans. Cornish 1913, 2nd ed. 1995. '*quare, quidquid habes boni malique,/ dic nobis. volo te ac tuos amores/ ad caelum lepido vocare versu.*' 'Well then, whatever you have to tell, good or bad, let me know it. I wish to call you and your love to the skies by the power of my merry verse.'
83 See p. 134.
84 Quint. *Inst.* X. 3. 23–27.
85 Plin. *Ep.* II.17. For the text see p. 131.

Chapter 6

1 Dio Cass. 67. 9. 1–4, trans. Cary 1925.
2 For further information on the excellent multisensory dinner experience *Dans Le Noir*, visit http://london.danslenoir.com/en/home/, date accessed 10/10/17.
3 Dio Cass. 67. 9. 6, trans. Cary 1925.
4 This is what the website suggests the experience aims for, see http://london.danslenoir.com/en/concept-eng/, date accessed 10/10/17. In particular it suggests the experience will encourage diners to re-evaluate perceptions of taste and smell, but I found myself questioning all sensory experiences whilst there, including sight, hearing and touch as well.
5 Once I got to see the menu at the end of the meal and read what I had eaten, I realized my ability to rely on taste to identify what I had been eating was a rather unreliable way of understanding what I had been served.
6 Dio Cass. 67. 9. 6, trans. Cary 1925.

7 Stat. *Silv.* I. 6. 4–16, trans. Shackleton Bailey 2003 (abridged) cf. ibid., IV. 2 for further gratitude from Statius for Domitian's generosity at feasts.
8 On the noise from people enjoying themselves see lines 51, 70–72. 81–83.
9 Stat. *Silv.* I. 6. 19.
10 Stat. *Silv.* I. 6. 84–92, trans. Shackleton Bailey 2003 (abridged).
11 For highly critical accounts of Domitian and life under his rule see, Suet. *Dom.*; cf. Plin. *Ep.* 4. 11; 4. 22; 10. 2. 3. For detailed examination of Suetonius' account of Domitian, see Jones 1996. In particular, positive accounts of Trajan's reign serve to emphasize the dislike of Domitian, at least by elite circles who provide us with much of the insight on views of his reign. See, e.g. Plin. *Ep.* 3. 18. 7, Plin. *Pan.* 20, 52, 95; Tac. *Agr.* 3. 1–3, 44. 5–46. On Pliny's *Panegyric*, see Radice 1968; Roche 2011. On presentations of Domitian and Trajan in Tacitus and Pliny the Younger, see Dominik 2010.
12 On Statius' career, see Coleman 1988: xv–xx, in particular Coleman's suggestion that Statius' family lost *equestrian* status (xv). On Imperial patronage under Domitian, see Nauta 2002.
13 Whitby 1998: 1, cf. Newlands 2002: 3, 229.
14 There are no other accounts of Domitian's banquet of death, so ascertaining the veracity of this story is difficult, see Schultz 2016: 289. Regarding Domitian's public feast for Saturnalia festivities, we have other accounts of similar public feasts put on by him, see Mart. *Ep.*, VIII. 49; Dio Cass. LXVII.8.4; Juv. *Sat.* I.II.
15 Stat. *Silv.* I. 6. 21–27, 85–90, cf. Newlands 2002: 240–247. The title of the poem, *The December Kalends* suggests Domitian's manipulation of time and the calendar because he has relocated Saturnalian festivities to the *Kalends*, the most important time in the month, thereby ensuring the first day of the last month of the year revolves around himself, see Newlands 2002: 236.
16 See also Stat. *Silv.* I. 6. 16, 20, 27, for further references to the gifts 'raining' down from Domitian to his guests.
17 Newlands 2002: 243.
18 Stat. *Silv.* I. 6. 81–83, trans. Shackleton Bailey 2003.
19 Stat. *Silv.* I. 6. 37.
20 On the artificial light see p. 159 and n. 10 on p. 271. On the references to foodstuffs see e.g. Stat. *Silv.* I. 6. 13–15, 17–18, 32. On the fighting women and dwarves see Stat. *Silv.* I.6. 53–61.
21 As outlined above, p. 159.
22 Stat. *Silv.* I. 6. 43–50, trans. Shackleton Bailey 2003 (abridged).
23 Stat. *Silv.* I. 6. 26, trans. Shackleton Bailey 2003.
24 On the delineation of social relationships through the Roman *convivium*, see, for example, D'Arms 1984, 1990, 1991, 2000; Murray 1990; Dunbabin 1991, 1996, 2003; Slater (ed.) 1991; Goddard 1994 (a) and (b). On the role of food as symbolizing social, cultural and moral values see Gowers 1993; Edwards 1993: 173–206; Dalby 2000.

25 Foss 1994: 84–85.
26 Plin. *Ep.* II. 12–13.
27 Foss 1994: 85. A further issue of defining terminology for dining rooms identified by Foss is that some words for dining rooms change use over time (see Foss 1994: 85 citing Servius Honoratus I. 698 and his discussion of the changing interpretation of the term *triclinium* by the fourth century AD). Given this book's chronological timeframe, this is less of a concern here.
28 See, e.g. Petr. *Sat.* LXXXV. 4; Plin. *HN* XXXIV. 9; Plin. *Ep.* II. 17. 12–13; Sid. *Ep.* II. 2. 11; Varro, *Ling.* V. 162, VIII. 32 and Vitr. *De arch.* VI. 3. 8.
29 Foss 1994: 91–92.
30 Vitr. *De arch.* VI. 7. 4, VI. 7. 5. According to Foss 1994: 90 and Leach 1997: 60 the only other Latin author to use this term was Pliny (*HN*. XXXVI. 60).
31 Vitr. *De arch.* VI. 3. 8–10.
32 Enn. *Ann.* 1. 57 recorded in Tert. *Ad Valent.* 7.
33 Pl. *Am.* 861–864.
34 Varro, *Ling.* V. 162. Cf. Mau 1899: 267–270; Maiuri 1927: 34–35; McKay 1975: 80, although it is worth noting that the term has also been used to identify the entire upstairs of a residence see McKay 1975: 80; Dosi and Schnell 1986b, 12–15; Sutherland 1990: 3–7; Wallace-Hadrill 1994: 108. Furthermore, using an inscription (*CIL* IV. 138) which lists spaces for rent including *cenaculum*, *domus* and *tabernae cum pergolae* in the *Insula* Arriana Polliana (VI, 6) Pirson 1997: 167–173 suggests the use of this term to denote upper floor spaces at Pompeii. Since the inscription does not specifically refer to the location of the *cenaculum* as being on an upper storey, its upper floor location is based on assumption (cf. Holleran 2012: 103 who follows this assumption).
35 Allison 2004a: 168, 170–171.
36 Allison 2004a: 168–170 lists the scholars who have labelled 'rooms off front halls' as *triclinia*, including Mau 1899: 253; Ehrhardt 1988: 32; Michel 1990: 36; Stemmer 1992: 26; Peter et al. 1993: 404; Descœudres et al. 1994: 9, fig. 6, and references scholars identifying *triclinia* as spaces located 'off gardens or terraces without good views', which include Mau 1898: 22; Armitt 1993: 239; Descœudres et al. 1994: 111.
37 See e.g. Richardson 1983: 63–64; Descœudres 1987: 174, fig: 10.13, who see winter *triclinia* as existing off front halls. For examples of specifically allocated summer *triclinia*, see Descœudres 1987: 174.
38 Allison 2004a: 168, 170 citing Varro, *Ling.* V. 162 and Vitr. *De arch.* VII. 4. 4 and Vitr. *De arch.* VI. 4. 2
39 Allison 2004a: 170 suggests the identification of spaces as *oeci* or *exedrae* is more complicated, with rooms being variously labelled as *oeci* (see, e.g., Mau 1899: 259; Maiuri 1933: 57, 160, 175; Strocka 1991: 41, 44; Descœudres et al. 1994: 109; Ling 1997: 272, 301) or as *exedrae* (see, e.g., Mau 1899: 241, fig. 110; Salza Prina Ricotti 1987: 125; Strocka 1991: 35, 37; Seiler 1992: 32; Descœudres et al. 1994: 123). These third room

types are also occasionally described as *triclinia* for example, Maiuri 1933: 168; Strocka 1984: 26, 1991: 38; Seiler 1992: 62; Staub Gierow 1994: 64. The use of the term *exedrae* for these spaces is contentious, for whilst Vitruvius (VI. 3. 8) uses the term in his discussion of *triclinia* and *oeci*, Foss 1994: 84 shows there are no literary examples of dining occurring in spaces labelled as *exedrae*, rather these spaces appear to have been employed for conversing and siestas. Thus, here dining spaces will be called *oeci* or *triclinia* and not *exedrae*.

40 Foss 1994: 91.
41 Leach 1997: 67-68.
42 Maiuri 1952: 1-8; Richardson 1988a: 432. Cf. Leach 1997: 60-1 identifying examples of a tetrastyle *oecus* in the house of the Silver Wedding (Pompeii) and the house of Augustus (Rome), and Egyptian *oecus* is the house of the Mosaic *Atrium* (Herculaneum), and Corinthian *oeci* in the house of the Labyrinth and the house of Meleager (both from Pompeii).
43 Allison 2004a: 170.
44 Dunbabin 1996: 67-68, 2003: 38-42.
45 Allison 2004a: 168.
46 Allison 2004a, 2006.
47 Allison 2006: 390.
48 Dyer 1875: 550-551. Allison 2004a: 89 suggests evidence for braziers was regularly found in or near peristyle ambulatories and cites the houses of Julius Polybius, the Cabinet Maker, the Lovers, the Prince of Naples, VIII. 5. 9, the Ephebe and the Ceii as further evidence of this phenomenon.
49 Foss 1994.
50 Clarke 1991; Dunbabin 1991; Ling 1991; Allison 1992, cf. Vitruv. *De Arch.* VII.3.4–VII. 4. 4, advising dark wall painting for winter dining rooms.
51 Identifications of rooms as dining rooms from the houses listed come from Dyer 1875; Sogliano 1895, 1897, 1898 a and b, 1900, 1901, 1906, 1907, 1908; Mau 1896, 1898, 1901; Maiuri 1927, 1933, 1958; Elia 1934; Bastet 1975; Brunsting 1975; Wynia 1982; Wallace-Hadrill 1988, 1994, 2011; Seiler 1992; Stemmer 1992; Peters et al. 1993; Foss 1994; Cooley 2003; Cooley and Cooley 2014; Allison 2004a, 2006.
52 On the identification of dining rooms according to fixtures, fittings and décor, see Foss 1994: 105–112.
53 On feasting as part of the Roman wedding and funeral see Chapter Four above, see also Hersch 2010 and Hope 2009. On the connections of festivals with banquets see Macrob. *Sat.* I. 16. 2–6, 'Thus on the festival days there are sacrifices, religious banquets, games and holidays ... The celebration of a religious festival consists of the offering of sacrifices to the gods or the marking of the day by a ritual feast', trans. Beard, North and Price 1998: 61. Literary evidence on the saturnalia in particular highlights the importance of communal public and domestic dining as a facet of the festivities Livy

22. 1; Sen. *Ep.* XLVII. 14; Macrob. *Sat.* I. 24. 22–3. On the festival of the *Saturnalia* in particular, see Versnel 1992: 136–227; Dolansky 2011. On festivals in general, see Warde-Fowler 1899; Scullard 1981. On feasting as part of Roman religion see Rüpke 2001: 137–153.

54 Somewhat different from the typical elite male backdrop of much textual evidence is Apicius, since there has been considerable debate over its authorship. According to Alcock 2006: 122 *Apicius* is a collection of Roman recipes thought to have been compiled in the fourth or fifth century AD. Cf. Grocock and Grainger 2006: 13–38, who argue that the recipes were not compiled by a single person, but were gathered and transcribed from the collections of working cooks. Also known as *De re coquinaria* or *De re culinaria*, the work has been erroneously connected with Marcus Gavius Apicius, an infamous gourmand and lover of luxury, opulence and fine dining from Tiberius' reign about whom sources record all manner of anecdotes on his desire for extravagance. See e.g. Plin. *HN.* IX. 30, X. 133, XIX. 137; Ael. *Ep.* 113 and 114; Athenaeus *Deipnosophistae* 1.7a; Sen. *Cons. ad Helv.* X.

55 Gowers 1993: 7.

56 Hor. *Sat.* I. 6. 115–118, *Epod.* II. 53–60, *Sat.* II. 2. 116–25.

57 Suet. *Aug.* 76–77; Juv. *Sat.* XI. 64–76. Cf. Verg. *Ecl.* I. 80; Ov. *Fast.* IV. 545–8, V. 505–22.

58 Hor. *Sat.* II. 8.

59 Petron. *Sat.* XXXI. Cf. Petron. *Sat.* XXX–LXXVIII for the full account of the food eaten at Trimalchio's supper. For further accounts of extravagant, ridiculous and often revolting foods served at some *convivia*, see e.g. SHA. *Heliogab* 19–30; Suet. *Vit.* XIII; Plin. *HN.* X.27; Hor. *Sat.* II.2.23–52.

60 Gowers 1993: 18, citing examples of such co-existence as including the juxtaposition of pontifical banquets, cookshops and tables laid with frugal fare as a commemoration of the past (Dion. Hal. *Ant Rom.* II. 23–5) and the presence of paupers' rooms [*Timoneas cenas et pauperum cellas*] in the houses of the wealthy which allowed rich owners to pretend they were following a paltry and basic diet, cf. Sen. *Ep.* 100. 6; Mart. *Epi.* III. 48.

61 Hor. *Sat.* II. 2.

62 The first part of the *colloquia* describes a schoolboy's day from sunrise to around lunch and dates to at least the first century AD, but it may be much older. Dickey 2017: 3 cites the existence of six different versions of the *colloquia*, which in some places are identical whilst in others are quite different from one another. This probably reflects the different ways in which the texts of the *colloquia* were rewritten by various ancient authors over time. Due to this process of writing and rewriting over time, each *colloquium* should be seen as a composite of texts evolving over a period of time, as parts of each were rewritten by successive teachers in order to make more useful for students.

63 According to Dickey (*pers. comms.* 25. 10. 18) the composite nature of the *colloquia* means that there is no single date to which all the adult scenes of one *colloquium* can

be dated (however none are demonstrably earlier than the second century AD). Particular passages can sometimes be more closely dated, especially in the *Montepessulanum*. Even then, though, it is difficult to be sure that a passage has not preserved some earlier content while being rewritten so that the language is later. With this in mind, then, it is possible to suggest that although written in at least the second century AD, some of the material in the vignettes of life in the Roman West described in the *colloquia* might have pre-dated the time of writing.

64 Dickey 2017: 2.
65 Dickey 2017: 98 suggests both issues are likely to affect the dinner party account of *Colloquium Celtis* 47a–54b.
66 Jones 1991; D'Arms 2000.
67 Elsner 2002: 1 drawing on 'Hermogenes', *Progymnastmata* 10. 49f. For further scholarship on *enargeia* cf. Zanker 1981, 2004: 39–42; Graf 1995; Dubel 1997; Webb 2006: 114–115, 2009: 87–130; Plett 2012; Roby 2016.
68 Borg 2014: 235. See Cic. *Brut.* 188 on the importance of the orator making the audience feel emotionally involved.
69 Borg 2014: 235. On *enargeia* in descriptions of the *convivium* see D'Arms 2000: 302.
70 For example, D'Arms 2000: 302 does suggest both the ocular and aural nature of entertainments at feasts, however he focuses mainly on the visual aspect of most of these displays.
71 On the importance of visual descriptions see Theon, *Progymnasmata* 118. 7–8; ps.-Hermog. *Prog.* X. 2, X. 25. On the important role played by other senses in *enargeia* see Cic. *Part. or.* VI. 20., Quint. *Inst.* VIII. 3. 67–69, cf. on the importance of manipulating the hearing of an audience see, Cic. *Brut.* 192–3.
72 D'Arms 2000: 301–302.
73 '*Spectabilis*' in Lewis and Short 1879: 1737; '*speciosus*' in Lewis and Short 1879: 1737. The etymological backgrounds of these terms come from *spectare* meaning 'to look on, look at, behold, gaze at, watch, observe, inspect, attend' thereby highlighting their visual focus, see D'Arms 2000: 303.
74 '*Miror*' in Lewis and Short 1879: 1149.
75 Verg. *G.* II. 30. For further examples of *mirabile* being connected with sound and speech Cic. *Partor.* V. I. 35 '*Nec hoc tam re est quam dictu inopinatum atque mirabile*' (Nor is this really so startling a paradox as it sounds).
76 '*Ostentatio*' in Lewis and Short 1879: 1283.
77 Suet. *Nero*, IX, trans. Rolfe 1914, rev. 1997, '*Orsus hinc a pietatis ostentatione Claudium apparatissimo funere elatum laudavit et consecravit*'.
78 Cic. *Ad Her.* IV. 51. 64, trans. Caplan 1954 cf. ibid., IV. 50. 63 'In the meanwhile all his conversation is spent in boasting ostentation [*ostentatio*].' trans. Caplan 1954. See also Sen. *Ep.* XL 8 on *ostentatio* in an orator's speech 'Even when the orator is carried away by his desire to show off [*ostentatio*] his powers, or by uncontrollable emotion, even

then he should not quicken his pace and heap up words to an extent greater than the ear can endure.'
79 Mart. *Ep.* III. XXIX.
80 Mart. *Ep.* III. LXXXII, trans. Nisbet, 2015. A similarly critical, albeit longer, account of a dinner party can be seen in Petronius' account of Trimalchio's dinner, Petron. *Sat.* 26-78.
81 See Gowers 1993: 26 on the socially divisive dinner party.
82 On the hierarchies of the seating arrangements of the *convivium* see Dunbabin 2003: 43. These would have served to emphasize visually the perceived social hierarchies of individual dinner parties and the way in which hosts regarded the status of their guests.
83 Plin. *HN.* XII. 9-11 uses '*miraculo*' and '*mirati*' to describe the plane trees of Lycia and Vellitri respectively. Both words come from 'mirari', see discussion above p. 167.
84 Mart. *Ep.* II. 59, trans. Shackleton Bailey 1993.
85 D'Arms examines both Pliny's and Martial's descriptions of these three dining rooms, however his description focuses only upon the visual accounts of these spaces.
86 *Colloquium Celtis* 47a-54b, trans. Dickey 2015; cf. *Colloquium Montepessulanum* 12a.
87 See n. 65 above.
88 *MANN* inv. no. 9015.
89 Banquet scene from the house of the *Triclinium*, *MANN* inv. no. 120029; banquet scene from Herculaneum, *MANN* inv. no. 9024.
90 See p. 107 and n. 76 on p. 259. For portable braziers found in Pompeii for example, see the portable braziers found in the garden of the house of Pinius Cerialis (della Corte 1927: 79) and in the peristyle of the house of the Menander (Allison 2006: 67). Cf. Fig. 6. 5 for an example of a bronze food warmer found in the house of the Four Styles, Pompeii.
91 Dunbabin 2003: 54-55; cf. Sen. *Ep.* 78. 23; *Colloquia Monacensia-Einsidlensia* 11a-e, n-o.
92 The *authepsa* held boiling water and was used by guests at the *convivium* to alter both the temperature and strength of their wine according to taste. On the use of water heaters and coolers at the dinner table see Juv. *Sat.* V. 63; cf. Varro, *Rust.* III. 5. It was not just the practice of cooling or warming water that was perceived to be decadent (see n. 91 above), the *authepsa* itself could be an immense display of wealth, see Cic. *Rosc. Am.* 33.
93 On the singing of drunk guests see the painting from the house of the *Triclinium*, where carved into the fresco of an outdoors *convivium* are the words 'I am singing'. *MANN* inv. no. 120031. On much laughter at the *convivium*, see Hor. *Sat.* I. V. 70. For a variety of types of entertainments at dinner parties including comics, musicians, reciters, clowns, dancers see e.g. Plin. *Ep.* I. 15, III. 1, IX. 17; Mart. *Ep.* V. 78; Plut. *Luc.* 40.

94 Allison 2004a: 142. References to gaming at the Roman dinner party are scarce. Since archaeological remains of gaming boards are lacking from Pompeii, knuckle bones, counters and dice are the main types of evidence that exist today. If, however, we combine the examples of wall paintings depicting gaming found in Pompeian taverns, for example the *Caupona* of Salvius and the *Caupona* on the Street of Mercury both in Pompeii (Joshel and Petersen 2014: 115–117) with the fact that paraphernalia connected with gaming has also been found in substantial residences including the house of the Menander (Allison 2006), it is perhaps not unlikely that games might also occur in the home, including at drinking and dinner parties in the *triclinium*. Mary Beard's reinterpretation of a fresco from the house of the Triclinium which depicts reclining couples supports this suggestion. In her article for the *Times Literary Supplement* written 18/8/13 (https://www.the-tls.co.uk/a-roman-sort-of-word-play-house-of-the-triclinium-pompeii/, date accessed 16/6/18) words on the image could be translated as saying either '*Est ita valeas*', 'Yes, you go for it' or possibly '*est ita v . . . alea*', which translates as 'Let have a game of dice'. The damaged state of wall-painting makes it difficult to be certain exactly what is written, however the presence of knuckle bones and dice found by Allison in *atria* and near *triclinia* of Pompeian residences helps to support Beard's interpretation.

95 Allison 2004a: 142–3. Cf. Allison 2004b http://www.stoa.org/projects/ph/rooms?houseid=18#373, date accessed 13/7/18.

96 On the finds of the gaming counters and stones in the *atrium* of the house of the Cabinet Maker see Elia 1934: 296; Allison 2006: 165. On the find of the remains of a musical instrument here see Elia 1934: 294, 295 (fig.15); Allison 2006: 169.

97 Plaut. *Mostell.* 309 cf. *Bacch.* 1181, *Pseud.* 947 as cited by Potter 2015: 127.

98 The stories of the emperor Nero sprinkling scented water on to his dining guests, (Suet. *Nero* 31. 2) and the emperor Heliogabalus drowning his diners in rose petals (SHA, *Heliogab.* 21. 5) take the desire for the manipulation of the olfactory experience of diners to extremes. Whilst the reality behind such accounts is open to question, they highlight just how far the stories of olfactory manipulation at diners by patrons were seen to go. On the stench from oil lamps see Juv. *Sat.* VII. 226–227, *Sat.* V. 87. Whilst individual lamps are likely to provide some smell, the finds of lampstands that held more than one oil lamp would provide a rather stronger olfactory experience. Burning lamps would also make a large amount of soot which, in turn, would dirty hands, clothes and walls, see Juv. *Sat.* VII. 227–228 and Vitr. *De arch.* VII. 4. 4. On the discovery of portable incense or perfume burners from Oplontis, see Fergola 2016: 98–99. For a particularly excellent terracotta example, and from the house of the Moralist, Pompeii see Spinazzola 1953: 727–62 and Jashemski 1993: 102 on the finds of a bronze incense burner in the shape of a woolly lamb.

99 Potter 2015: 126–7.

100 Varro *ap. Nonius*, cited in Jashemski 1979: 89.

101 Jashemski 1979 and 1993.
102 On the gardens of Lucullus see e.g. Plut. *Luc.* 39. On the gardens of Nero's *Domus Aurea* see Suet. *Nero*, 31. On Livia's villa at Primaporta see Plin. *HN.* XV. 136; Suet. *Galba.* 1. Other ancient Roman gardens that have seen detailed exploration include those from Herodian palaces at Judaea (Gleason 1987–8); houses in Tunisia (Jashemski 1995); Livia's villa at Primaporta (Klynne and Liljenstolpe 2000); the Palatine Hill in Rome (Villedieu 2001); and the city of Petra (Bedal 2002, 2003).
103 Jashemski 1979: 89–140. A recent exhibition at the Wellcome Trust on architecture emphasized the wide variety of uses for the garden in the past and even today when it referred to the lively nature of back gardens of houses which were not quiet but rather were full of children and teeming with life. Wellcome Trust exhibition 'Living with Buildings: Health and Architecture' – visited 28. 12. 18.
104 According to Jashemski 1979: 102 in addition to the loom weights she uncovered in every garden she excavated, two houses (house of M. Terentius Eudoxus and house of the Figured Capitals) also displayed graffiti which suggested the presence of substantial weaving and spinning establishments in their porticoes, see Jashemski 1993: 147, 181. The latter *graffiti* from the house of the Figured Capitals suggests that men used the looms in this dwelling.
105 Jashemski 1979 and 1993 shows gardens were also connected with tombs, public spaces such as temples and theatres, shops, restaurants and taverns. For the purposes of this book we are concerned only with those from the domestic realm. The multisensory experience of gardens as a whole is an area that would benefit from study in the future.
106 The decibel levels from a fountain are affected by many factors including the size of the fountain and the volume of water within it as well as the height from which the water drops. The lower the water volume in the fountain, the lower the level from which it drops and the lower the surface area of the water, the quieter the sound levels will be from the fountain, see Watts, Pheasant, Horoshenkov and Ragonesi 2009; Galbrun and Ali 2013.
107 On the probability of potted plants being situated on the terrace see Jashemski 1993: 262.
108 On the noise from fountains distracting audiences from hearing other nearby unwanted sounds see Watts et al. 2009; cf. Calarco 2015: 37, accessed from http://hdl.handle.net/10399/3084, date accessed 1/10/18.
109 Jashemski 1991: 262.
110 Maiuri 1945: 28–30, 1958.
111 The neighbouring houses of Fabius Rufus and the Library similarly opened onto the Vicolo Del Farmacista and also sought to take advantage of the proximity of the city's walls, its sloping topography and the views from this part of the city over the Bay of Naples.

112 Laurence 2007: 95–6. The four eating establishments defined as nearest this dwelling are located i) diagonally opposite the house of Fabius Rufus, ii) on the opposite side of the Vicolo del Farmacista, iii) at the junction of Vicolo del Farmacista and Via Consolare and iv) at the junction of Vicolo di Modesto and Via delle Terme (Fig. 3. 2).

113 The neighbouring houses of Fabius Rufus and the Library likewise either lack, or have very small, *fauces*. On the role of the *fauces* as a means of distancing a house from the street outside, see Chapter 3 above.

114 For discussion of a similar situation where a residence took advantage of its position overlooking the Bay of Naples in order to reduce the sensory nuisances provided by the main road, see Platts 2019 (*forthcoming*) on the villa of Diomedes which was located on the Via Ercolanense, but which had two belvederes and a promenade situated overlooking the coast, at a substantial distance from the main road.

115 On the sensory experiences of kitchens and controlling it within the house, see Chapter 7 below.

116 On noises from the home spreading into the street beyond see e.g. Cic. *Rosc. Am.* 134; Prop. IV. 8. 51–62 and Ov. *Met.* XIV. 748–751.

117 Jashemski 1993: 166, 356.

118 According to Jashemski 1993: 166–167 the root cavities found in this garden suggest there was a formal garden planted here, possibly in box hedging, with vines situated near the pool in front of the dining area and along the north wall of the garden. Flowers were also probably planted here, which would have had an olfactory impact on the diners' experiences, and although their remains have not been discovered, the excavation of plant remnants such as lilies and roses elsewhere in Pompeian gardens allow us to suggest in general terms the possible plants and their olfactory impact on this space. On the finds of specific flowers in Pompeian gardens see p. 188 below.

119 Jashemski 1993: 167. On dormouse as a particular foodstuff of Romans see Apicius VII. 9, Varro, *Rust.* III. 3. That it was seen as a luxurious item of food is demonstrated by the fact it was served by Trimalchio at his dinner (Petron. *Sat.* XXXI. 10) and criticized by Ammianus Marcellinus as an excessive mark of display (Amm. Marc. *RG* XXVIII. 4. 13) and by the fact that at times the serving of it in dinner parties was prohibited e.g. Plin. *HN.* VIII. 223; XXXVI. 2.

120 Occasionally *biclinium* or *stibadium* couches are used outside. See, for example, in the outside area of the house of Octavius Quartio, where masonry *biclinium* couches are situated next to a fountain and a *euripus* and in the house of Adonis where a semi-circular couch (*stibadium*) was excavated.

121 Soprano 1950: 288–310.

122 Jashemski 1979: 89 n.1. lists the outdoor *triclinia* found after Soprano because of improved archaeological techniques.

123 Fresco from the house of the Chaste Lovers, *MANN* inv. no. 55652. Fresco from the house of the *Triclinium*, *MANN* inv. no. 120031. For the third painting of an outdoors banqueting scene which lacks a clearly recorded findspot, see Dunbabin 2003: 54, cf. n. 42 and Plate II. It is also now located in *MANN* inv. no. 9015. For detailed description of these images see Dubabin 2003: 52–60.
124 On the movement and legislation restricting wagon traffic in the city of Rome see Robinson 1994: 62–63.
125 On the excavation of the Garden of Hercules see in particular Jashemski 1979, 1992, 1993.
126 Given the size of the *triclinium* and *lararium*, Jashemski suggested the garden dining area might have been used for gatherings of those involved in Pompeii's profitable flower and perfume industry. On Pompeii's renown for perfume production see Plin. *HN*. XIII. 26, XVIII. 111. For inscriptions attesting perfume makers in Pompeii see *CIL* IV. 609, 9932a, 2184, X. 892. Frescoes depicting flower garland makers and perfumiers in the guise of cupids have been excavated in the *oecus* (h) of the house of the Vettii, whilst two paintings of flower sellers (now lost) were discovered in the house of the Calpurnii and the *macellum* (Trendelenburg 1873: 44–48, cf. pl. 3, 2a and b; Jahn 1868: pl 6. 4 respectively) and a depiction (now lost) of a customer sampling a perfume was also found in the house of the Calpurnii (Trendelenburg 1873: 44–48, cf. pl. 3. 2b), for discussion of these inscriptions and frescoes see Jashemski 1979: 409; Mattingly 1990.
127 On the niche in the masonry serving table see Jashemski 1979: 404.
128 Jashemski 1979: 103, 283 fig. 422. According to Jashemski, bones of smaller pet dogs were also found in Pompeii, as was evidence of their kennels, see e.g. the remains of a small masonry doghouse discovered in the *tablinum* of a house on the Via di Nola (IX.V. 2).
129 See p. 249, n. 58 on the decibel levels of a dog barking. The presence of depictions of dogs in wall paintings and mosaics such as the *cave canem* mosaic from the entrance to the *fauces* of the house of the Tragic Poet (Fig. 3. 8) and the chained dog mosaic from the house of Paquius Proculus similarly highlights their ubiquity in Pompeii.
130 On the impact of the amphitheatre on the corporeal experiences of the houses in the immediate vicinity see Chapter 3 above. That the palaestra was used on festival days when the amphitheatre hosted games can be seen in the remains of a fresco from the house of Actius Anicetus depicting a riot between the Nucerians and the Pompeians at the amphitheatre and palaestra, which shows temporary stalls in the Large Palaestra, cf. p. 251, n. 84 for evidence for stalls in the amphitheatre's arches.
131 *CIL* IV 8562, 8565. According to Mart. *Ep.* IX. 68, the bellowing and beatings coming from the schoolmaster to his students are louder than the noises of blacksmiths and the roars of the amphitheatre.

132 See Jashemski 1979 and 1993 on the plantings and portico of the *palaestra*. Rustling leaves measure about 20 decibels, see p. 254, n. 123.

133 For discussion of a similar situation where a summer *triclinium* was situated at a distance from a main road into Pompeii and the auditory impact this would have had on those dining outside see Platts 2019 (*forthcoming*) on the summer *triclinium* of the villa of Diomedes which was situated on the Via Ercolanense.

134 On the discussion of the plantings in the house of the Golden Bracelet, see p. 280 and n. 118 above.

135 On the auditory impact of bird song particularly that of nightingales, see p. 249, n. 59 above.

136 Jashemski 1993: 94–95.

137 Sen. *Ep.* 78. 23, trans. Gummere 1920.

138 Dunbabin 2003: 52–60.

139 On the seating order for the Roman *convivium* see Dunbabin 2003: 43. An example of silverware perhaps employed in Roman domestic dinner parties is the Boscoreale Treasure now in the Musee du Louvre (inv. 86EE 1899). An interesting example of the display of opulent silverware to diners comes from the fresco from the tomb of Vestorius Priscus. Here large amounts of silver tableware were depicted on a table situated next to diners, essentially making a great display of wealth. According to Mols and Moormann 1994: 15–52, although from a tomb, this should rather be interpreted as a depiction of a private celebration within the domestic context of the house and the sort of event the Vestorius Priscus himself might have attended or put on when alive.

140 Petron. *Sat.* 26–78. On the still life frescoes from Pompeii and Herculaneum and the *asarotos oikos* see Dunbabin 2003: 64.

141 On the importance of owners controlling slaves in the *triclinium* during the banquet see Joshel and Petersen 2014: 37–40. On the various means by which owners sought to conceal the actual mechanics of the *convivium* from diners including through the location of the kitchen in relation to the *triclinium*, the use of doors, and the siting of slaves nearby, but out of view of guests, see Chapter 7.

142 Hor. *Sat.* II. 8. 63–67, Petron. *Sat.* 26–78. There is substantial scholarship on dinner parties going either well or badly in terms of an owner's attempt at self-presentation see, for example, Bradley 1998; Clarke 2003: esp. 223–227. On the importance of slaves for ensuring the banquet goes well, see Juv. *Sat.* II. 8. 65–74, cf. D'Arms 1991, Joshel and Petersen 2014: 37–40.

143 D'Arms 2000: 311.

144 Potter 2015: 127.

145 Potter 2015: 127, see pp. 176–177 for discussion of Potter's argument on the olfactory manipulation of the dining room.

146 On the vast numbers of slaves see e.g. Petron. *Sat.* 28–33; Sen. *Ep.* XCV. 24, cf. Saller 1987: 65; D'Arms 1991: esp. 172–177.

Chapter 7

1. Petron. *Sat.* II, trans. Rouse 1913, rev. Warmington 1969.
2. Graffiti found in the toilet of the house of the Gem, Herculaneum, *CIL* IV. 10619: *Apollinaris medicus Titi imp(eratoris) hic cacavit bene*, trans. Cooley and Cooley 2014: 110.
3. Graffiti found in the toilet of the house of the Centennial. *CIL* IV. 5244, trans. Cooley and Cooley 2014: 109. In the graffiti, the word used for dining room, *triclinium* is misspelt as *trichilinium*: *Marthae hoc trichilinium est nam in trichilino cacat*.
4. In many modern-day homes where open-plan living occurs, however, examples of combined kitchen and dining spaces are frequently found.
5. In terms of this division of dining room and kitchen in the ancient Roman home, I am specifically referring to examples found within the Roman *domus* where most examples of these types of residences have separate dining and cooking quarters. In other types of Roman domestic realms, such as the *insula*, the division of these spaces is often less assured, with evidence from many examples of multioccupancy accommodation such as the *medianum* suggesting that cooking and eating might occur within the same room. There is a growing amount of scholarship on Roman *insulae* see e.g. Hermansen 1970, 1973, 1982; Storey 2002, 2004.
6. On seating arrangements at the banquet according to status, see p. 276 n. 82. On food being used to differentiate between the standing of guests, see e.g. Mart. *Ep.* III. LXXXII; Plin. *Ep.* II. 6. On the degrading of diners through giving them unattractive slave attendants see Juv. *Sat.* V. 51. On the unpleasant sight and smell of kitchen slaves particularly in comparison with waiting slaves see Mart. *Epi.* X. 66. It is important to note, however, that whilst cooks might be perceived as smelling unpleasant and greasy in many texts, they, together with bakers, carvers and wine waiters, were seen to have a highly trained skill set, e.g. Liv. XXXIX. 6; Mart. *Ep.* XIV. 220; X. 98; Juv. *Sat.* V. 120, XI. 136; Sen. *Ep.* XLVII. 6, *De Brev. Vit.* XII. 5.
7. Jansen 2011: 160–161; cf. Koloski-Ostrow 2015: 94; Potter 2015: 125.
8. For a detailed investigation of the different terms for cooking fires see Foss 1994: 62–74.
9. See e.g. Sen. *Ep.* 78. 23 for his criticism on the developing fashion for cooking in the dining room, discussed p. 189, and p. 281, n. 137 above.
10. Allison 2004a: 172 highlights the issues of conflating the terms *culina* with the modern term 'kitchen' explaining that use of these modern terms means 'it is easy to assume that it performed a function similar to kitchens of the modern world' but that the finds from her sample of houses show that 'food preparation and some cooking could have been carried out in rooms of this type, but that cooking could also have been carried out in closer proximity to eating areas. Assemblages in rooms of this type also indicate a close relationship among food preparation, ablutions, and possibly religious practices within these spaces.' With careful attention to the fact that the *culina* often

demonstrated a range of roles and that cooking could occur away from this space, this chapter will use the terms *culina* and kitchen to refer to rooms that have been clearly identified as having (or being connected with rooms with) static cooking apparatus.

11 On the Latin terminology of *latrina* or *lavatrina* for entire rooms as toilets, see Allison 2004a: 172.
12 Jansen 2002: 59; Hobson 2009: 47–49. Hobson 2009: 49 makes the point that men might have also urinated directly onto the tiled flooring.
13 Hobson 2009: 49, as Hobson points out, not all toilets that had these wall cuts lacked supporting masonry posts.
14 Hobson 2009: 51. The evidence for stone seats in Pompeii is relatively sparse: only one has been recorded and which has now been lost (Mygind 1921: 311). The discovery of a further partial stone toilet seat remains from IX. 3. 15 in Pompeii is equally problematic, given its lack of clear archaeological context, Hobson 2009: 51.
15 Mart. *Ep.* X. 66, trans. Shackleton Bailey 1993.
16 Green 2015.
17 Green 2015: 136–137.
18 Whilst tripods were used to regulate the cooking temperature, see Dosi and Schnell 1986b: 87; Salza Prina Ricotti 1987: 117–120, these would do little to protect the cook from burning themselves on the open flames.
19 Green 2015.
20 It is worth noting that whilst both wood and charcoal were generally employed as fuel in Roman houses, less smoky charcoal might have been the preferred choice for cooking indoors, see Salza Prina Ricotti 1978/80: 252–255. On the types of fuel used in ancient food production see Veal 2017.
21 Robinson and Rowan 2015: 109–111.
22 See Hamilton and Whitehouse 2006 on the distance at which cooking meat can be smelt outside. Cf. Foss 1994: 41 on how far a cooking meal can be smelt within a dwelling.
23 Plaut. *Cas.* 759–779, trans. De Melo 2011. Cf. Plaut. *Pseud.* 889–892.
24 See Foss 1994: 41 on the theoretical sound range of cooking, which was 30.2 metres depending on how loud the food preparation processes were and the acoustics of the rooms concerned.
25 Mart. *Ep.* XIV. 220.
26 See Mart. *Ep.* III.13, VIII. 23; Petron. *Sat.* XLVII. 13 on the punishment of cooks.
27 Joshel and Petersen 2014: 78.
28 Joshel and Petersen 2014: 79 on the possibility of slaves sleeping in a loft in the kitchen of the Caupona of Sotericus, Pompeii.
29 Mart. *Ep.* X. 66.
30 Joshel and Petersen 2014: 41–59. A key part of their argument here, for example is the demarcation of patron and guest routes and those for slaves throughout the house via

varying sized doorways. Such architectural tactics served to reduce the visibility of the slaves by clearly delineating which routes could be used by whom.

31 For detailed discussion of the relocation of this kitchen from the back to the front of the dwelling see. pp. 68–69. On the movement of the kitchen meaning slaves serving from the kitchen will for the most part be invisible, see Joshel and Petersen 2014: 53–55. There is some disagreement about the direction of the guests sitting in this room. Joshel and Petersen believe they would have faced the garden, whilst Foss suggests they would have faced the *atrium*, p. 219. Either way, both demonstrate attempts to ensure slaves working in the kitchen are barely, if at all, visible.

32 On the need for foods to remain a surprise in the elite banquet see pp. 89–91.

33 Cic. *Nat. D.* II. 56. 141, trans. Rackham 1933.

34 For Martial on Thais see Mart. *Ep.* VI. 93 and on his slave-boy's kisses see ibid., XI. 8, cf. Bradley 2015: 6–7.

35 Allison 2004a: 127.

36 Allison 2004b. The analysis of household space as either front, middle or rear section of a dwelling is assigned relative to a dwelling's longitudinal axis directly from its front entrance.

37 Where multiple kitchens were identified in single residences, e.g. house VIII. 2. 29 and the house of the Menander, the location of all recorded kitchens was included in the survey results, hence leading to a final figure of 37 kitchens. In residence I. 10. 8 no separate *culina* space was listed on Allison's *Online Pompeian Companion* database, however the finds of a hearth and downpipe in space 9 (a through corridor), suggests this would have been employed as a fixed food preparation area. The figures are as follows: Kitchens located in the front of dwellings: 10/38 = 26 per cent; Kitchens located in the middle of dwellings: 19/38 = 50 per cent; Kitchens located in the rear of dwellings: 9/38 = 24 per cent.

38 These residences are: VIII. 2. 26, VIII. 2. 28, VIII. 2. 29–30, VIII. 2. 34, VIII. 2. 39.

39 The residences selected were chosen to consider residences of varying sizes from across both Pompeii and Herculaneum and, for those from Pompeii, as a consequence of accessibility restrictions due to house closures in 2016–17 following a substantial grant from the EU for conservation purposes.

40 Clarke 1991: 208.

41 Reimers 1991: 112.

42 Hobson 2009: 105, 147.

43 Scarborough 1980: 37; Hobson 2009: 105 cf. Petron. *Sat.* 27.

44 On the parasite remains at Silchester see Fulford et al. 2011. On the parasite remains at Pompeii see Dubbin 2003: 35–38 and Love 2007. On the various parasite remains from Alphen aan den Rijn see Kuijper and Turner 1992. For further remains of whipworm eggs in faecal matter from Roman sites see Dickson 1979; Hall *et al.* 1983; Jones 1985; Kenward et al. 1986; Maltby 1994; Kenward and Hall 1995; Boyer 1999.

The lack of evidence for handwashing after using latrines (Hobson 2009) as well as the use and sharing of sponge-sticks (Koloski-Ostrow 2015: 86–87) and other items including mosses (Dickson 1979; Kenward and Hall 1995) for wiping in particular emphasizes the lack of understanding about the role of personal sanitation, toilet habits and the spread of disease in antiquity.

45 Sen. *Ep.* 104. 6, trans. Gummere 1941. Cf. Juv. *Sat.* III on the vile odours of the city.
46 Columella, *Rust.* I. 6. 11, trans. Ash 1925. On the location of beehives, see Columella. *Rust.* IX. 5. 1. For Cic. *Nat. D.* II. 56. 41 see p. 146 above.
47 On the two types of aviaries (*ornithon*) see Varro, *Rust.* III. 4. 2.
48 According to Varro, *Rust.* III. 4. 3, trans. Hooper and Ash 1934. 'the birds fluttering around the windows do not give pleasure to the eyes to the same extent that the disagreeable odour which fills the nostrils gives offence.' (*Quod inutile invenerunt. Nam non tantum in eo oculos delectant intra fenestras aves volitantes, quantum offendit quod alienus odor opplet nares.*)
49 Morley 2015: 116 on the increased smell and mess caused by gastric infections and diarrhoea.
50 Koloski-Ostrow 2015: 90–109, cf. Potter 1999:169; Morley 2015: 116–119.
51 Henshaw 2014: 25–26.
52 Jansen 1991, 1997, 2007: 262.
53 Camardo 2006: 204 n. 23.
54 Jansen 2007: 264, cf. Jansen 1991: esp. 155–160. For example, given that toilets were regularly located in kitchens and that finds of kitchen waste have been excavated in the sewer under Cardo V not only does this emphasize the multifunctional role of the toilet downpipe as a disposal route into the sewer for both faeces and kitchen waste, as DeKind 1998: 99–106, 139, 177 highlights, but this further emphasizes the connection of kitchens from private properties to the public sewer, cf. Camardo 2011 90–91; Robinson and Rowan 2015: 113 *contra* Koloski-Ostrow 2015: 93–94; 'We can attest, for Pompeii and Herculaneum, at least, a clear preference for internal cesspit toilets in domestic dwellings and no sewer connections in those dwellings. We must wonder why Romans resisted connecting their toilets to the public sewers to expel this [cesspit] waste from their houses?' On the excavation of the sewers at Herculaneum see Maiuri 1958: 466–469 and the more recent excavation of the sewer under Cardo V, see Robinson and Rowan 2015.
55 On the contents of food remains from the sewers coming both from food preparation and leftovers as well as from human faeces see Robinson and Rowan 2015: 108.
56 Jansen 2002: 110 citing *CIL* IV suppl. 3.4.10606 '*Exemta Tre(r)cora A(ssibus) XI*' translated as 'the cesspit was emptied for eleven asses'. As yet the remains of a sewage system under upper Cardo IV (on which the back entrance of the house of the Black Hall is situated) or under the *Decumanus Maximus* (on which the front entrance to the house of the Black Hall is found) has not been identified, leading Camardo (2011:

90) to suggest that this part of the Cardo IV was not served by a public sewer. Georadar and geoelectrical surveys have, however, identified a further sewer underneath lower Cardo IV, see Camardo 2011: 90–91 for plans of the site of Herculaneum mapping both excavated and hypothesized sewer branches.
57 See pp. 202–203 above.
58 The evidence used here to suggest the presence of doors in thresholds is similar to that employed in Chapter Five.
59 As with the selection of houses made above for locating kitchens, the residences selected here were chosen to provide data for residences of varying sizes from across both Pompeii and Herculaneum. Once again those studied from Pompeii were as a result of access restrictions due to house closures in 2016–17 following a substantial grant from the EU for conservation purposes. I also needed to study houses where I could access both kitchens and dining spaces in order to draw proper comparisons between them in terms of the presence or lack of doors.
60 See p. 283, n. 10 above.
61 Plin. *Ep.* II. 17. 22. trans, Firth 1900. From http://www.attalus.org/old/pliny2.html#17, date accessed 1/5/18.
62 Allison 2004a. For the identification of room (g) as *triclinium* see Stemmer 1992: 26. Next to room (g) is room (f), which has been variously identified as a *triclinium* (Sogliano 1908: 74) or *tablinum* (Stemmer 1992: 23) on account of finds of couch feet. This debated interpretation of room (f) means it is not the focus of discussions in this chapter, but it is worth noting it might have been employed as a space for dining.
63 These dwellings have been variously categorized into the 10–19 rooms classification (Ship of Europa, the Ceii and M. Lucretius Fronto), 20–29 room classification (Gavius Rufus), 30–39 rooms classification (Pansa) and 40–49 rooms classification (the Citharist and Coloured Capitals).
64 This latrine at (q) in the house of the Centennial is where the graffiti cited at the start of Chapter Seven was found. See p. 282, n. 3.
65 It is worth remembering that this residence had a lower level. On this level service rooms and a latrine were situated; Kastenmeier 2007: 121–123. This further suggests a desire to separate domestic/service spaces from the main reception areas of the dwelling.
66 The house of the Great Portal from Herculaneum presents a comparable example of dining room and kitchen organization. Here the kitchen is located in an 'L-shaped' space down a long, narrow corridor measuring 6.4 metres and with rooms located in between the kitchen corridor and the dining room. As such here we see both the use of spaces as buffer zones to separate kitchen and dining areas and large walls without communicating doors. The thresholds to both the dining room and kitchen showed evidence of door architecture.

67 Michel 1990; cf. Foss 1994: 235–240. The movement of the kitchen from the back to the front of the house is discussed in more detail in Chapter Seven below, which explores kitchens and their situation in houses rather than their specific architectural relationship to *triclinia*.

68 Spinazzola 1953, I: 265; Michel 1990: 35; Foss 1994.

69 Foss 1994: 240.

70 When initially excavated it was understood to be two separate dwellings, one with a main entrance at no. 47 on the Vicolo dei Lupanare and a further *posticum* at no. 46 Vicolo dei Lupanare, the other with an entrance at no. 25 on the Via Stabiana, however the discovery of inscriptions to Siricus next to these two entrances together with three steps at (l) linking the garden (j) to the peristyle (q) of the second property, further suggests the possible amalgamation of these two houses at some point during their history. Consequently for this discussion, this house is understood as a single inhabitation. See Dyer 1875: 462.

71 Dyer 1875: 465.

72 Fiorelli 1875: 179–180.

73 Fontaine 1991: 263–266.

74 Fontaine 1991: 263. The finds of many used cooking vessels in room (u) further aid the identification of this room as a housing a stove.

75 Fiorelli 1860 vol. 1: 249–282. Fiorelli's entry for 15 May 1773 reads *'Oltre di queste cose si è trovato in un focolaro del cortile rustico un vaso pure di bronzo, nella parte di sotto affumato, della forma di una porzione di sfera, che ha nella parte piana la sua bocca nel mezzo con un collaro attorno; dal collar pende il manico come quello di un caldaro, ed un coperchio per chiudere la bocca. Ferro.'* On the find of the cauldron on the stove in area (s), see La Vega, n. 72 in Fiorelli 1860 vol. 2: 118–133. *'Nella stessa settimana. Si è trovato un vaso di bronzo (sopra quelle fornacelle), con il coverchio e manico, a figura di tegame, di diam. on. 15, alto on. 4, tutto crepato.'*

76 See Fontaine 1991: 260, on the wide and high threshold in this part of the house.

77 On room (f) being changed from a *cubiculum* into a *triclinium* see Elia 1934:282, although *contra* see Ling 1997: 152.

78 On room (h) as a *biclinium* see Elia 1934: 287, on this room as a *triclinium* see Foss 1994: 299.

79 On the discussion of the summer *triclinium* in relation to the main kitchen area in the villa of Diomedes and the impact the distance and garden might have had upon the transmission of sensory experiences between the two areas see Platts 2019 (forthcoming).

80 On room (h) being identified as a kitchen see Della Corte 1916: 32. Allison suggests this might not have been in use as a kitchen at the time of eruption due to the lack of loose finds here, see Allison 2004b, https://web.archive.org/web/20160402014713/http://www.stoa.org/projects/ph/rooms?houseid=14#299, date accessed 3/5/18. On

room (l) as a kitchen, see Spano 1916: 233. Allison 2004b, https://web.archive.org/web/20160402014713/http://www.stoa.org/projects/ph/rooms?houseid=14#292, date accessed 3/5/18 suggests it might not have been fully functioning as a kitchen at the time of eruption.

81 The location of the *triclinium* at (g) and an *oecus* at (d) in this residence, whilst not discussed in depth here are likewise at some distance and separated from the kitchens of the house by numerous rooms and spaces, which would have served to reduce the transmission of sensory experiences between these areas.
82 On the narrowness of doors and passageways in houses as a visual discouragement to visitors from using these areas, see Joshel and Petersen 2014: 40–44.
83 Bradley 2015: 135, 140.
84 Hor. *Sat.* I. 2. 30; Juv. *Sat.* VI. 132, XI. 172–3; Lucil. XXX. 130.
85 Although the presence of glass in some of these windows raises questions of just how efficient these openings were for reducing the stench of excreta and cooking, Hobson 2009: 106.
86 Hobson 2009: 106–108.
87 Potter 2015: 127.

Chapter 8

1 Sen. *Ep.* LXXXVI, trans. Gummere 1920.
2 Thompson 2017: 58. Descaves wrote Les Emmurés in 1894.
3 Bolt 2014: 72–73. As Bolt explains, the division of the five senses of the Western sensorium into 'contact' and 'distance' sensory experiences stems from Aristotle's *De Anima*. The contact senses of touch and taste can only be perceived via direct bodily contact, whilst distance sensory experience does not require of sight and to an extent hearing can be perceived at a distance and without tangible bodily contact. Smell sits between the two groups, whereby one can smell things at a distance, however, its close connection with taste makes it something of an intermediary between these two groups of senses, see Arist. *De Sens.* 445a4–16, cf. Polansky 2007: 302.
4 E.g. V. 6. 16–23, Plin. *Epis.* II. 17. 21–28.
5 Plin. *Epis.* V. 6. 41, trans. Radice 1969 (abridged), II. 17. 20. trans. Firth 1900. From http://www.attalus.org/old/pliny2.html#17, date accessed 1/5/18.

Bibliography

Translations used

Apuleius, *Metamorphoses*, trans. Hanson, J. A. 1989, Loeb, Cam. MA.
Catullus, *Poems*, trans. Cornish, F. W. 2nd ed. 1995, Loeb, Cam. MA.
Cicero, *Rhetorica Ad Herennium*, trans. Caplan, H. 1954, Loeb, Cam. MA.
Cicero, *De Natura deorum.*, trans. Rackham, H. 1933, Loeb, Cam. MA.
Colloquium Celtis 47a–54b, trans. Dickey 2015, Cambridge University Press, Cam.
Columella, *De Re Rustica*, trans. Ash, H. 1925. Loeb, Cam. MA.
Dio Cassius, *Roman History*, trans. Cary, E. 1925. Loeb, Cam. MA.
Horace, *Odes*, trans. Rudd, N. 2004, Loeb, Cam. MA.
Horace, *Satires*, trans. Rushton Fairclough, H. 1926, Loeb, Cam. MA.
Juvenal, *Satires*, trans. Braund, D. 2004, Loeb, Cam. MA.
Livy, *Ab Urbe Condita*, trans. Foster, B. O. 1924, Loeb, Cam. MA.
Lucan, *Pharsalia*, trans. Duff, J. D. 1928, Loeb, Cam. MA.
Lucian, *On Mourning*, trans. Fowler, H.W. and Fowler, F. G. 1905, Oxford Clarendon Press, Oxford.
Lucretius, *De rerum natura*, trans. Rouse, W. H. D. 1924, rev. Smith, M. F. 1975. Loeb, Cam. MA.
Martial, *Epigrams*, trans. Nisbet, G. 2015. Oxford University Press, Oxford.
Martial, *Epigrams*, trans. Shackleton-Bailey, D. R. 1993, Loeb, Cam. MA.
Ovid, *Consolatio ad Liviam*, trans. Mozley, J. H. 1929, rev. Goold, G. P. 1939. Loeb, Cam. MA.
Petronius, *Satyricon*, trans. Rouse, W. H. D. 1913, rev. Warmington, F. H. 1969. Loeb, Cam. MA.
Plautus, *Casina*, trans. De Melo, W. 2011. Loeb, Cam. MA.
Pliny the Younger, *Epistles*, trans. Firth, J. B. 1900. From http://www.attalus.org/old/pliny2.html#17.
Pliny the Younger, *Epistles*, trans. Radice, B. 1969. Loeb, Cam. MA.
Plutarch, *Life of Gaius Gracchus*, trans. Morstein-Marx, R. Franz-Steiner Verlag, Heidelberg.
Seneca the Younger, *De Beneficiis*, trans. Basore, J. W. 1935. Loeb, Cam. MA.
Seneca the Younger, *De Consolatione ad Marciam*, trans. Basore, J. W. 1932. Loeb, Cam. MA.
Seneca the Younger, *Epistles*, trans. Gummere, R. M. 1917. Loeb, Cam. MA.
Seneca the Younger, *Epistles*, trans. Gummere, R. M. 1920. Loeb, Cam. MA.
Seneca the Younger, *Epistles*, trans. Gummere, R. M. 1925. Loeb, Cam. MA.

Seneca the Younger, *Epistles*, trans. Gummere, R. M. 1941. Loeb, Cam. MA.
Statius, *Silvae*, trans. Shackleton Bailey, D. R. 2015, Loeb, Cam. MA.
Suetonius, *Caligula*, trans. Rolfe, J. C. 1913, Loeb, Cam. MA.
Suetonius, *Nero*, trans. Rolfe, J. C. 1914, rev. 1997, Loeb, Cam. MA.
Tacitus, *Annals*, trans. Jackson, J. 1931, Loeb, Cam. MA.
Varro, *De Lingua Latina*, trans. Kent, R. G. 1938, Loeb, Cam. MA.
Varro, *De Re Rustica*, trans. Hooper, W. D. and Ash, H. D. 1934, Loeb, Cam. MA.
Vitruvius, *De Architectura*, trans. Granger, F. 1934, Loeb, Cam. MA.

Secondary Sources

Ackerman, D. 1990. *A Natural History of the Senses*, Vintage Books, New York.
Ackerman, J. 1995. *The Villa: Form and Ideology of Country Houses*, Thames and Hudson, London.
Adam, C. and Tannery, P. 1964–1976. *Oeuvres de Descartes*, vols. I–XII, Librarie Philodophique J. Vrin, Paris.
Adams, G. W. 2006. *The Suburban Villas of Campania and Their Social Function*, Oxbow, Oxford.
Afzelius, A. 1938. 'Zur Definition der römischen Nobilität vor der Zeit Ciceros' *ClMed* 1: 40–94.
Afzelius, A. 1945. 'Zur Definition der römischen Nobilität vor der Zeit Ciceros' *ClMed* 7: 150–200.
Ahmed, M. et al. 2013. 'Continental-Scale Temperature Variability During the Past Two Millennia' *Nature Geoscience* 6: 339–346.
Alcock, J. P. 2006. *Food in the Ancient World*, Greenwood Press, West Connecticut.
Alfaro, C., Wild, J.-P., and Costa, B. eds. 2004. *Actas del I Symposium Internacional sobre Textiles y Tintes del Mediterráneo en Época Romana*. Purpureae Vestes, Universidad de Valencia, Valencia.
Alföldy, G. 1988. *Social History of Rome*, Routledge, London.
Allison, P. M. 1993. 'How Do We Identify the Use of Space in Roman Housing?' in ed. Moorman, E. M.: 4–11.
Allison, P. M. ed. 1997a. 'Why do Excavation Reports have Finds' Catalogues?' in eds. Cumberpatch, C. G. and Blinkhorn, C.W.: 77–84.
Allison, P. M. 1997b. 'Artefact Distribution and Spatial Function in Pompeian Houses' in eds. Rawson, B. and Weaver, P.: 321–354.
Allison, P. M. ed. 1999. *The Archaeology of Household Activities*, Routledge, Abingdon.
Allison, P. M. 2001. 'Using the Material and Written Sources: Turn of the Millennium Approaches to Roman Domestic Space' *AJA* 105.2: 181–208.
Allison, P. M. 2004a. *Pompeian Households: An Analysis of the Material Culture*, The Cotsen Institute, University of California, Los Angeles.

Allison, P. M. 2004b. *Pompeian Households: An Analysis of the Material Culture*, on-line companion: www.stoa.org/pompeianhouseholds.

Allison, P. M. 2006. *The Insula of the Menander at Pompeii, vol. III.*, Cambridge University Press, Cambridge.

Allison, P. M. 2007a. 'Domestic Spaces and Activities' in eds. Dobbins, J. J. and Foss, P. W.: 269–278.

Allison, P. M. 2007b. 'Engendering Domestic Space' in eds. Westgate, R., Fisher, N. and Whitley, J.: 343–350.

Alston, R. 1997. 'Houses and Households in Roman Egypt' in eds. Laurence, R. and Wallace-Hadrill, A.: 25–39.

Alston, R. 2002. *The City in Roman and Byzantine Egypt*, Routledge, London.

Ambrosio, A. and De Caro, S. 1983. *Un impegno per Pompeii: Fotopiano e documentazione della Necropoli di Porta Nocera,* Touring Club Italiano, Milan.

Ambrosio, A. and De Caro, S. 1987. 'La Necropoli di Porta Nocera. Campagno di Scavo 1983' in eds. Hesberg, H. and Zanker, P.: 199–228.

Andreae, B. and Kyrieleis, H. eds. 1975. *Neue Forschungen in Pompeji*. Aurel Bongers, Recklinghausen.

Andrea di Castro, A. and Hope, C. A. eds. 2015. *Houses and Habitat in the Ancient Mediterranean*, BABesch supplements, Peeters, Leuven.

Anguissola, A. 2012a. 'The Dynamics of Seclusion. Observations on the Casa del Labirinto and the Casa degli Amorini Dorate at Pompeii' in ed. Anguissola A.: 31–47.

Anguissola, A. 2012b. *Privata Luxuria: towards and Archaeology of Intimacy*, Herbert Utz Verlag, Munich.

Anonymous, 1895. 'Pompei – Giornale degli scavi redatto dagli assistenti' *NSc*, Tip. della R. Accademia dei Lincei, Rome: 207.

Armitt, M. 1993. 'La Casa della Venere in Bikini (1 11, 6–7)' in ed. dell'Orto, L. F.: 237–241.

Astin, A. E. 1967. *Scipio Aemilianus*, Oxford University Press: Oxford.

Astin, A. E. 1978. *Cato the Censor,* Oxford University Press: Oxford.

Attema, P. and de Haas, T. 2005. 'Villas and Farmsteads in the Pontine Region between 300BC and 300AD: A Landscape Archaeological Approach' in eds. Frizell, B.S. and Klynne, A.: 97–112.

Attema, P., de Haas, T. and Nijboer B. 2003. 'The Astura project, interim report of the 2001 and 2002 campaigns of the Groningen Institute of Archaeology along the cost between Nettuno and Torre Astura' *BABesch* 78: 107–140.

Attema, P., Nijboer, A. J. and Zifferero, A. 2003. *Papers in Italian archaeology VI: Communities and Settlements from the Neolithic to the Early Medieval Period. Proceedings of the 6th Conference of Italian Archaeology held at the University of Groningen, Groningen Institute of Archaeology, The Netherlands, April 15–17,* ArchaeoPress, Oxford.

Augoyard, J-F. and Torgue, H. 2006. *Sonic Experience: A Guide to Everyday Experience*, McGill-Queen's University Press: Montreal.

Ault, B. A. 2015. 'Kitchens' in eds. Wilkins, J. and Nadeau, R.: 206–211.

Ault, B. A. and Nevett, L. 1999. 'Digging Houses: Archaeologies of Classical and Hellenistic Greek Domestic Assemblages' in ed. Allison, P.: 43–56.

Bailey, D. M. 1972. *Greek and Roman Pottery Lamps*. 2nd edition. British Museum Press, London.

Baird, J. A. 2014. *The Inner Lives of Ancient Houses: An Archaeology of Dura-Europos*, Oxford University Press, Oxford.

Baird, J. and Pudsey, A. 2019 (forthcoming). *Between Words and Walls*. Cambridge University Press, Cambridge.

Baird, J. and Taylor, C. eds. 2011. *Ancient Graffiti in Context*. Routledge, London.

Balch, D. L. and Osiek, C. 2003. *Early Christian Families in Context: An Interdisciplinary Dialogue*. Wm. B. Eerdmans Publishing Co, Ann Arbor.

Balch, D. L. 2008. *Roman Domestic Art and Early House Churches*. Mohr Siebeck, Tübingen.

Balch, D. L. and Weissenrieder, A. eds. 2012. *Contested Spaces: Houses and Temples in Roman Antiquity and the New Testament*. Mohr Siebeck, Tübingen.

Baldassare, I. 2001. 'La Nécropole dell'Isola Sacra' in ed. Descœudres J.-P.: 385–390.

Baldwin, B. 1990. 'The Date, Identity and Career of Vitruvius' in *Latomus* 49.2: 425–434.

Barbet, A. and Miniero, P. eds. 1999. *La Villa San Marco a Stabia*. École française de Rome: Naples, Rome, and Pompei.

Barr, W. 1999. 'Introduction' in *Juvenal: The Satires*, trans. Rudd. N. Clarenden Press, Oxford.

Barthes, R. 1982. *Empire of Signs*, trans. R. Howard, Hill and Wang: New York.

Barton, I. M. 1996. *Roman Domestic Buildings*. Liverpool University Press: Liverpool.

Bartsch, S. and Elsner, J. 2007. 'Introduction: Eight Ways of Looking at an Ekphrasis' *Special Issues on Ekphrasis*, *CP* 102.1. Eds. Bartsch, S. and Elsner, J.: i–vi.

Bartsch, S. and. Elsner, J. 2007. *Special Issues on Ekphrasis*. *CP* 102. No. 1. Chicago University Press, Chicago.

Bastet, F.L. 1975. 'Forschungen im Haus des M. Lucretius Fronto' in eds. Andreae, B. and Kyrieleis, H.: 193–197.

Beacham, R. 1992. *The Roman Theatre and its Audience*, Harvard University Press, Cambridge.

Beacham, R. 1999. *Spectacle Entertainments of Early Imperial Rome*, Yale University Press, New Haven.

Beard, M. 2007. *The Roman Triumph*, Belknap Press of Harvard University Press, Cambridge MA and London.

Beard, M. 2010. *Pompeii*. 3rd ed. Profile Books, London.

Beard, M., North, J. and Price, S. 1998. *Religions of Rome, Vol I: A History*, Cambridge University Press, Cambridge.

Beard, M., North, J. and Price, S. 1998. *Religions of Rome, Vol II: A Sourcebook*, Cambridge University Press, Cambridge.

Becker 2003. 'Investigating Early Villas: The Case of Grottarossa' in eds. Attema, P. A. J. Nijboer, A. J. and Zifferero, A.: 813–21.

Becker, J. A. 2006. 'The Villa delle grotte at Grottarossa and the Prehistory of Roman Villas', *JRA* 19: 213–20.
Becker, J. A. and Terranato, N. 2012. *Roman Republican Villas: Architecture, Context, and Ideology*, University of Michigan Press, Michigan.
Bedal, L.-A. 2002, 'The Petra Garden Feasability Study' in *ADAJ* 46: 381–90.
Bedal, L.-A. 2003. 'The Petra Pool-Complex: A Hellenistic Paradeisos in the Nabataean Capital (results from the Petra Lower Market Survey and Excavation, 1998)' Georgias Dissertations: Near Eastern Studies 4. Gorgias Press, New Jersey.
Begović Dvorzak, V. 1990. 'Antička vila na Brijunima' *VAMZ*, 3.s, XXIII: 97–110.
Begović Dvorzak, V. 1995. 'Rezidencijalni kompleks u uvali Verige na Brijunima: primjer ekstrovertirane maritimne vile harmonično uklopljene u krajolik' *HistriaAntiq* 1: 47–53.
Begović, V. and Schrunk, I. 1999–2000. 'Villae rusticae na Brijunskom Otočju'. *OpArch* 23–24: 425–439.
Begović, V. and Shrunk, I. 2002. 'Roman Villas of Istria and Dalmatia, Part I' in *Prilozi* 19.1: 113–130.
Begović, V. and Shrunk, I. 2003. 'Roman Villas of Istria and Dalmatia, Part II: Typology of Villas' *Prilozi* 20.1: 95–111
Begović Dvorzak, V. and Dvoržak Schrunk, I. 2004. 'Roman Villas of Istria and Dalmatia, Part III: Maritime Villas' *Prilozi* 21: 65–90.
Bek, L. 1980. *Towards Paradise on Earth: Modern Space Conception in Architecture: A Creation of Renaissance Humanism,* Odense University Press, Odense.
Bell, A. 1997. 'Cicero and the Spectacle of Power' *JRS* 87: 1–22.
Bell, A. 2004. *Spectacular Power in the Greek and Roman City,* Oxford University Press, Oxford.
Bergmann, B. 1994 'Painted Perspectives of a Villa Visit' in ed. Gazda, E.: 49–70.
Bergmann, B. 1995. 'Visualising Pliny's Villas' in *JRA* 8: 406–420.
Bergmann, B. and Kondoleon, C. 2000. *The Art of Ancient Spectacle,* Yale University Press, Washington and London.
Bergmann, B. 2002. 'Art and Nature at Oplontis' in eds. McGinn, T. et al.: 87–122.
Bernstein, A. H. 1978. *Tiberius Sempronius Gracchus: Tradition and Apostasy,* Cornell University Press, Ithaca.
Berry, J. 1997. 'Household Artefacts: Towards a Re-interpretation of Roman Domestic Space' in eds. Laurence, R. and Wallace-Hadrill, A.: 183–195.
Berry, J. 2007. *The Complete Pompeii*, Thames and Hudson, London.
Berry, J. and Laurence, R. eds. 2001. *Cultural Identity in the Roman Empire*, Routledge, London.
Betts, E. 2011. 'Towards a Multisensory Experience of Movement in the City of Rome' in eds. Laurence, R. and Newsome, D.: 118–132.
Betts, E. 2017. *Senses of the Empire*, Routledge, Abingdon.
Birley, A. 2000. *Onomasticon to the Younger Pliny. Letters and Panegyric.* K. G. Saur, Munich and Leipzig.

Blom, H. van der 2010. *Cicero's Role Models. The Political Strategy of a Newcomer*. Oxford University Press, Oxford.

Boddington A., Garland, A. N., and Janaway, R. C., 1987. *Death, Decay and Reconstruction: Approaches to Archaeology and Forensic Science*, Manchester University Press, Manchester.

Bodel, J. 1994 [1986]. 'Graveyards and Groves: A Study of the *lex Lucerina*' *AJAH* 11: 1–133.

Bodel, J. 1997. 'Monumental Villas and Villa Monuments' *JRS* 10: 5–35.

Bodel, J. 2000. 'Dealing with the Dead: Undertakers, Executioners and Potter's Fields in Ancient Rome' in eds. Hope, V. and Marshall, E.:128–151.

Bodel, J. 2012. 'Villaculture' in eds. N. Terrenato and J. A. Becker: 45–60.

Boehm, G. and Pfotenhauer, H. eds. 1995. *Beschreibungskunst, Kunstbeschreibung: Ekphrasis von der Antike bis zur Gegenwart*, W. Fink, Munich.

Boivin, N. 2004. 'Rock art and rock music: Petroglyphs in the south Indian Neolithic' *Antiquity* 78: 38–53.

Bokern, A., Bolder-Boos, M., Krmnicek, S., Maschek, D., and Page, S. eds. 2013. *TRAC 2012: Proceedings of the Twenty-Second Annual Theoretical Roman Archaeology Conference*, Frankfurt 2012, Oxbow Books, Oxford.

Bolt, D. 2014. *The Metanarrative of Blindness: A Re-Reading of Twentieth-Century Anglophone Writing*, Michigan University Press, Michigan.

Boman, H. 2011. 'White Light – White Heat: The Use of Fire as a Light and Heat Source in an Atrium House in Roman Pompeii' *Current Swedish Archaeology* 13: 59–75.

Bon. S. E. and Jones, R. eds. 1997. *Sequence and Space in Pompeii*, Oxbow Books, Oxford.

Borg, B. 2014. 'Rhetoric and Art in Third Century AD Rome' in eds. Elsner, J. and Meyer, M.: 235–255.

Borgard, Ph. and Puybaret, M.-P. 2004. 'Le travail de la laine au début de l'empire: l'apport du modèle pompéien. Quels artisans? Quells équipements? quelles techniques?' in eds. Alfaro, C., Wild, J.-P. and Costa, B.:47–59.

Bourdieu, P. 1977. *Outline of a Theory of Practice*, Cambridge University Press, Cambridge.

Boyer, P. 1999. 'The Parasites', in Conner, A. and Buckley, R.: 344–6.

Bowes, K. 2010. *Houses and Society in the Later Roman Empire*. Duckworth, London.

Braconi, P. and Uroz Sáez, J. 1999. *La Villa di Plinio il Giovane a San Giustino: Primi risultati di una ricerca in corso*, Quattroemme, Perugia.

Bradley, K. 1998. 'The Roman Family at Dinner' in eds. Nielsen, I. and Sigismund Nielsen, H.: 36–55.

Bradley, M. 2002. 'It All Comes Out in the Wash: Looking Harder at Roman *fullonica*' *JRA* 15: 21–44.

Bradley, M. 2012. *Rome, Pollution and Propriety: Dirt, Disease and Hygiene in the Eternal City from Antiquity to Modernity*, Cambridge University Press, Cambridge.

Bradley, M. 2015. *Smell and the Ancient Senses*, Routledge, London.

Branigan, K. ed. 1997. *Cemetery and Society in the Aegean Bronze Age*, Sheffield Academic Press, Sheffield.

Brandt, J. R. X. Dupré Raventós and G. Ghini eds. 2003. *Lazio e Sabina 1*, Edizione Quasar, Rome.

Bringmann, K. 1985. *Die Agrarreformen des Tiberius Gracchus: Legende und Wirklichkeit*, Steiner Franz Verlag, Stuttgart.

Broise, H. and Lafon, X. 2001. *La villa Prato de Sperlonga*. Collection de l'École française de Rome 285. l'École française de Rome, Rome.

Broughton, T. R. S. 1951-2, 1986. *The Magistrates of the Roman Republic*, 3 vols. Scholars Press, New York and Atlanta.

Bruhn, J., Croxford, B. and Grigoropoulos, D. eds. 2005. *TRAC 2004: Proceedings of the Fourteenth Roman Archaeology Conference, Durham*. Oxbow Books, Oxford.

Brunsting, H. 1975. 'Forschungen im Garten des M. Lucretius Fronto' in eds. Andreae B. and Kyrieleis, H.: 198-199.

Brunt, P. A. 1971. *Social Conflicts in the Roman Republic*, Chatto and Windus, London.

Brunt, P. A. 1982. 'Nobilitas and Novitas' *JRS* 72: 1-17.

Bull, M. and Back, L. 2005. 'Introduction: Into Sound' in eds. Bull, M. and Back, L.: 1-18.

Bull, M. and Back, L. eds. 2005. *The Auditory Culture Reader*, Berg, Oxford.

Buonpane, A. 1990. 'Nuove iscrizioni di Verona' *Epigraphica* 52: 159-178.

Burckhardt, L. 1990. 'The political elite of the Roman Republic: comments on recent discussion of the concepts Nobilitas and Homo Novus' *Historia* 39: 77-99.

Burckhardt, L. 2003. 'Zu Hause geht Alles, wie wir wünschen: Privates und Politisches in den Briefen Ciceros' *Klio* 85: 94-113.

Butler, S. and Nooter, S., 2018. *Sound and the Ancient Senses*, Routledge, Abingdon.

Butler, S. and Purves A. eds. 2014. *Synaesthesia and the Ancient Senses*, Routledge, Abingdon.

Cadogan, G., Iakovou, M., Kopaka, K. and Whitley, J. eds. 2012. *Parallel Lives: Ancient Island Societies in Crete and Cyprus,* British School at Athens, London.

Calarco, F. M. A. 2015. *Soundscape Design of Water Features Used in Outdoor Spaces where Road Traffic Noise is Audible*, Unpub. Thesis.

Camardo, D. 2006. 'Gli scavi ed i restauri di Amedeo Maiuri. Ercolano el'esperimento di una città museo' *Ocnus* 14: 69-81.

Camardo, D. 2007. 'Archaeology and conservation at Herculaneum: from Maiuri campaign to the Herculaneum Conservation Project' in *Conservation and Management of Archaeological Sites* 8: 205-214.

Camardo, D. 2011. 'Case Study: Ercolano: La riscostruzione dei sistemi fognari' in eds. Jansen, G. M. C., Koloski-Ostrow, A. O. and Moorman, E. M.: 91-94.

Carandini, A. ed. 1985b. *Misurare la terra: centuriazione e coloni nel mondo romano. Città agricoltura commercio: materiali da Roma e dal suburbio*. Panini, Modena.

Carandini, A. 1989. 'Italian wine and African oil: commerce in a world empire' in ed. Randsborg K.: 16-24.

Carandini, A. ed. 1985a. *Settefinestre: una villa schiavistica nell'Etruria romana*, Panini, Modena.

Carratelli, G. P. and Baldassarre, I. eds. 1990–2003. *Pompei. Pitture e mosaici* 9 vols., Instituto della Enciclopedia Italiana, Rome.

Carrington, R. 1931. 'Studies in Campanian "*Villae Rusticae*"' *JRS* 21:110–130.

Carroll, M. 2006. *Spirits of the Dead: Roman Funerary Commemoration in Western Europe*, Oxford University Press, Oxford.

Carroll, M. 2018. *Infancy and Earliest Childhood in the Roman World: 'A Fragment in Time'*, Oxford University Press, Oxford.

Caruso, G. and Volpe, R. 2000. *Preesistenze e persistenze delle Terme di Traiano* in ed. Fentress, E.: 42–56.

Cassola, F. 1988. 'Lo scontro fra patrizi e plebei e la formazione della nobilitas' in ed. Momigliano, A. and Sciavone, A.: 451–481.

Champlin, E. 1982. 'The Suburbium of Rome', *AJAH* 7: 97–117.

Chinn, C. M. 2007. 'Before Your Very Eyes: Pliny *Epistulae* 5.6 and the Ancient Theory of Ekphrasis,' *CP* 102 no. 3: 265–280.

Claridge, A. and Holleran, C. 2018. *Blackwell Companion to the City of Rome*, Wiley-Blackwell, London.

Clarke, J. R. 1991. *The Houses of Roman Italy, 100BC–250AD: Ritual, Space and Decoration*, University of California Press, Berkley.

Clarke, J. R. 2003. *Art in the Lives of Ordinary Romans: Visual Representation and Non-Elite Viewers in Italy, 100BC–AD 315*, University of California Press, California.

Clarke, D. L. 1977. *Spatial Archaeology*, Academic Press, London.

Classen, C. 1993. *Worlds of Sense: Exploring the Senses in History and Across Cultures*, Routledge, London.

Classen, C. 1997. 'Foundations for an Anthropology of the Senses' *International Social Science Journal* 153: 401–412.

Classen, C. 2005. *The Book of Touch*, Berg, Oxford.

Classen, C. 2016. *A Cultural History of the Senses in the Age of Empire*, Bloomsbury, London.

Classen, C., Howes, D. and Synott, A. 1994. *Aroma: The Cultural History of Smell*, Routledge, London.

Coarelli, F. 1981. *Dintorni di Roma. Guida archeologiche*, La Terza, Rome.

Coarelli, F. 1999. 'Puticuli' in ed. Steinby, E. M. *LTUR* 4: 173–174.

Coleman, K. ed. 1988. *Statius IV. Book 4*, Oxford University Press, Oxford.

Conner, A. and Buckley, R. 1999. *Roman and Medieval Occupation in Causeway Lane, Leicester*, Leicester Archaeology Monograph 5: 344–6.

Cooley, A. 2003. *Pompeii*, Duckworth, London.

Cooley, A. and Cooley, M. G. L. 2014. 2nd ed. *Pompeii and Herculaneum: A Sourcebook*, Routledge, London.

Cooper, K. 2007. 'Closely Watched Households: Visibility, Exposure and Private Power in the Roman *Domus*' *PastPres* 197: 3–33.

Corbin, A. 1996. *The Foul and the Fragrant: Odour and the Social Imagination*, Macmillan, London.

Scagliarini-Corlàita, D. 1979. La situazione urbanistica degli archi onorari nella prima età imperiale' in ed. Mansuelli G. A.: 29–72.

Cormack, S. 2007. 'Tombs at Pompeii' in eds. Dobbins, J. J. and Foss, P. W.: 585–606.

Cornell. T. 1995. *The Beginnings of Rome: Italy and Rome from the Bronze Age to the Punic Wars (c. 1000–264 BC)*, Routledge, London.

Cornell, T. and Lomas, K. eds. 1995. *Urban Society in Roman Italy*, UCL Press, London.

Corwin et al. 1995. 'Workplace, Age, and Sex as Mediators of Olfactory Function: Data from the National Geographic Smell Survey', *Journals of Gerontology – Series B Psychological Sciences and Social Sciences*, 50 B.4: 179–186.

Cotton, M. A. and Métraux, G. P. 1985. *The San Rocco Villa at Francolise,* British School at Rome, London.

Crawford, M. 1976. *Roman Republican Coinage,* Cambridge University Press, Cambridge.

Cremin, A. ed. 1988. *The Enduring Past: Archaeology of the Ancient World for Australians*, University of New South Wales Press, Sydney.

Crook, J. A., Lintott, A. and Rawson, E. eds. 1994. *CAH IX: The Last Age of the Roman Republic. 146–43 BC*, Cambridge University Press, Cambridge.

Crooke, H. 1616. *Mikrokosmographia, A Description of the Body of Man*, W. Jaggard, London.

Croxford, B., Goodchild, H., Lucas, J., and Nick, R., eds. *TRAC 2005: Proceedings of the Fifteenth Annual Theoretical Roman Archaeology Conference. Birmingham 2005,* Oxbow, Oxford.

Cumberpatch C. G., and Blinkhorn, P. W. 1997. *Not so Much a Pot, More a Way of Life*, Oxbow, Oxford.

Cummings, V. 2002. 'Experiencing Texture and transformation in the British Neolithic' *OJA* 21 (3): 249–261.

Cunliffe, B. 2013. *The Roman Villa at Brading, Isle of Wight: The Excavation of 2008–10,* Oxbow, Oxford.

Curtis, R. I. ed. 1989. *Studia Pompeiana et classica in Honor of Wilhelmina F. Jashemski*, II. Aristide D. Caratzas Pub, New Rochelle.

D'Arms, J. H. 1970. *Romans on the Bay of Naples,* Harvard University Press, Cambridge MA.

D'Arms, J. H. 1984. 'Control, Companionship and Clientela: Some Social Functions of the Roman Communal Meal' *EchCl* 28: 327–48.

D'Arms J. H. 1990, 'The Roman *Convivium* and the Idea of Equality' in ed. Murray, O.: 308–320.

D'Arms J. H. 1991. 'Slaves at the Roman *Convivia*' in ed. Slater, W.: 171–183.

D'Arms J. H. 2000. 'Performing Culture: Roman Spectacle and the Banquets of the Powerful' in Bergmann, B. A. and Kondoleon, C.: 300–319.

Dalby, A. 2000. *Empire of Pleasures: Luxury and Indulgence in the Roman World*, Routledge, London.

Dalby, A. 2003. *Food in the Ancient World from A–Z*, Routledge, London.

David, B. and Wilson, M. eds. 2002. *Inscribed Landscapes: Marking and Making Place*, University of Hawaii Press, Honolulu.

Day, J. ed. 2013. *Making Senses of the Past: Towards a Sensory Archaeology*, Southern Illinois University Press, Illinois.

De Angelis, F. 2011. 'Playful Workers. The Cupid Frieze in the Casa dei Vettii' in eds. Poehler, E., Flohr, M., and Cole, K.: 62-73.

De Franceschini, M. 1998. *Le ville romane della X regio: Venetia et Histria. Catalogo e carta archeologica dell'insediamento romano nel territorio, dall'età repubblicana al tardo impero*, L' Erma Bretchneider, Rome.

De Franceschini, M. 2005. *Ville dell'Agro romano*, L' Erma Bretchneider, Rome.

de Ligt, L. 2001. 'Studies in Legal and Agriarian History III: Appian and the *Lex Thoria*' *Athenaeum* 89: 121-44.

De Rossi, G. M. 1979. *Forma Italiae. Bovillae*. Olschki, Firenze.

DeKind, R. E. L. B. 1998. *Houses in Herculaneum, a New View on the Town Planning and the Building of Insulae III and IV. J. C.*, Gieben, Amsterdam.

DeLaine, J. 1999. 'High Status Insula Apartments in Early Imperial Ostia - a Reading', *Meded* 58: 175-189.

DeLaine, J. 2004. 'Designing for a Market: *Medianum* Apartments at Ostia', *JRA* 17: -146-176.

DeLaine, J. 2012. 'Housing in Roman Ostia' in eds. Balch, D. L. and Weissenrieder, A.: 327-51.

Della Corte, M. 1911. 'Pompei - Scavi eseguiti durante il mese di settembre', *NSc.* 5. 8.

Della Corte, M. 1912. 'Pompei - Continuazione dello scavo di via dell'Abbondanza', *NSc.* 5. 9.

Della Corte, M. 1913. 'Pompei - Continuazione dello scavo di via dell'Abbondanza', *NSc.* 5. 10.

Della Corte, M. 1914. 'Pompei - Continuazione dello scavo di via dell'Abbondanza', *NSc.* 5. 11.

Della Corte, M. 1915. 'Pompei - Continuazione dello scavo di via dell'Abbondanza', *NSc.* 5. 12.

Della Corte, M. 1916. 'Pompei - Continuazione dello scavo di via dell'Abbondanza', *NSc.* 5. 13.

Della Corte, M. 1919. 'Pompei - Continuazione della esplorazione nella predetta Abondanza. Scavi esegueti nel mese di ottobre 1915', *NSc.* 5. 16.

Della Corte, M. 1927. 'Pompei - Relazione sui lavori di scavo dal marzo 1924 al marzo 1926', *NSc.* 7.3: 3-116.

dell'Orto, L. F. ed. 1993. *Ercolano 1738-1988: 250 anni di ricerca archeologica*, L'Erma di Bretschneider, Rome.

Derrick, T. 2017. 'Sensory Archaeologies: A Vindolanda Smellscape' in ed. Betts, E.: 71-85.

Descaves. L. 1894. *Les Emmurés*, Tresse et Stock, Paris.

Descœudres, J.-P. 1987. 'Rome and Roman Art' in ed. Cremin, A.: 164-209.

Descœudres, J. P. 2001. Ostia: Port et Porte de la Rome Antique, Georg Editeur, Geneva.

Descœudres, J.-P. et al. 1994. 'Tour of the house of the Painted Capitals' in Descœudres J.-P. et al.:57–150.
Descœudres, J.-P. et al. 1994. *Pompeii Revisited: The Life and Death of a Roman Town*, Meditarch, Sydney.
Develin, R. 1985 *The Practice of Politics at Rome 366–167 B.C.*, Latomus, Brussels.
Dexter, C. E. 1975. *The Casa di L. Cecilio Giocondo in Pompeii*, unpub. PhD thesis, Duke University.
Di Fusco, N. and Di Caterina, E, 1998. *Il Vesuvio*, Electa, Naples.
Dickey, E. 2012. *The Colloquia of the Hermeneumata Pseudodositheana*, Vol I. Cambridge University Press, Cambridge.
Dickey, E. 2015. *The Colloquia of the Hermeneumata Pseudodositheana*, Vol II. Cambridge University Press, Cambridge.
Dickey, E. 2017. *Stories of Daily Life From the Roman World: Extracts from the Ancient Colloquia*, Cambridge University Press, Cambridge.
Dickmann, J-A. 2007. 'Residences in Herculaneum' in eds. Dobbins, J. and Foss, P.: 421–434.
Dickmann, J-A. 2011. 'Space and Social Relations in the Roman West' in ed. Rawson, B.: 53–72.
Dickson, J. H. 1979. 'Exotic Food and Drink in Ancient Scotland', *Glasgow Naturalist* 19.6: 437–42.
Dixon, S. 2007. *Cornelia: Mother of the Gracchi*, Routledge, London.
Dobbins, J. and Foss, P. eds. 2007. *The World of Pompeii*, Routledge, London.
Dolansky, F. 2008. '*Togam virile sumere*: Coming of Age in the Roman World' in eds. Edmondson, J. and Keith, A: 47–70.
Dolansky, F. 2011. 'Playing with Gender: Girls, Dolls and Adult Ideals in the Roman World', *ClAnt* 31.2: 125–57.
Dolansky, F. 2017. 'Roman Girls and Boys at Play: Realities and Representations' in eds. Laes, C. and Vuolanto, V.: 116–136.
Dominik, W. and Hall, J. 2010. *A Companion to Roman Rhetoric*, Wiley-Blackwell, London.
Dominik, W. 2010. 'Tacitus and Pliny on Oratory' in eds. Dominik, W. and Hall, J.: 323–338.
Dondin-Payre, M. 1981 'Homo novus: Un slogan de Caton à César' *Historia* 30: 22–81.
Dosi, A. and Schnell, F. 1986a: *Le abitudini alimentari dei Romani* (*Vita e costumi dei Romani antichi 1*), Ed. Quasar, Rome.
Dosi, A. and Schnell, F. 1986b: *Pasti e vasellame da tavola* (*Vita e costumi dei Romani antichi 2*), Ed. Quasar, Rome.
Dosi, A. and Schnell, F. 1986c: *I Romani in cucina* (*Vita e costumi dei Romani antichi 3*), Ed. Quasar, Rome.
Drerup, H. 1959. 'Bildraum und Realraum in der römischen Architektur' *RM* 66: 147–174.
Drobnik, J. ed. 2006. *The Smell Culture Reader*, Berg, Oxford.

Du Prey, P. de la R. 1994. *The Villas of Pliny from Antiquity to Posterity*, University of Chicago Press, Chicago and London.

Dubbin, A. M. 2003. *An Analysis of Faecal Deposits from Pompeii, Italy: A New Source of Evidence for Ancient Diet and Urban Ecology*, unpub. MSc Diss., University of Bradford.

Dubel, S. 1997. '*Ekphrasis et enargeia*: La description antique comme parcours' in eds. Levy, C. and Pernot, L.: 249–64.

Dunbabin, K. M. D. 1991. '*Triclinium* and *Stibadium*' in ed. Slater 121–148, figs 1–36.

Dunbabin, K. M. D. 1996. 'Convivial Spaces: Dining and Entertainment in the Roman Villa' *JRA* 9: 66–80.

Dunbabin, K. M. D. 2003. *The Roman Banquet: Images of Convivality*, Cambridge University Press, Cambridge.

Due, O. S., Johansen, H. F. and Larsen, B. D. 1973. *Classica et Mediaevalia Francisco Blatt Septuagenario Dedicata*, Gyldendal, Copenhagen.

Duncan-Jones, R. 1974. *The Economy of the Roman Empire: Quantitative Studies*, Cambridge University Press, Cambridge.

Dupré y Raventos, X and Remolà, J. A. 1996. *Sorder Urbis. La eliminaciòn des residuos en la ciudad romana*. L'Erma di Bretschneider, Rome.

Dutsch, D. 2008. '*Nenia*: Gender, Genre, and Lament in Ancient Rome' in ed. Suter, A.: 258–279.

Dyer, T. ed. 1875. *Pompeii: its History, Buildings and Antiquities*, G. Bell and Sons, London.

Dyson, S. L. 2002. 'The Excavations at Le Colonne and the Villa Culture of the Ager Cosanus' *MAAR* 47: 209–228.

Dyson, S. L. 2012. 'Concluding Remarks' in eds. Terrenato, N. and Becker, J. A.: 129–136.

Earl, D. C. 1961. *The Political Thought of Sallust*, Cambridge University Press, Cambridge.

Earl, D. C. 1963. *Tiberius Gracchus: A Study in Politics*, Latomus, Bruxelles-Berchem.

Eder, E. ed. 1990. *Staat und Staatlichkeit in der frühen römischen Republik*, Franz Steiner Verlag, Stuttgart.

Edmondson, J. and Keith, A. 2008. *Roman Dress and the Fabrics of Roman Culture*, University of Toronto Press, Toronto.

Edmondson, J. 2008. 'Public Dress and Social Control in Late Republican and Early Imperial Rome' in eds. Edmondson, J. and Keith, A.: 21–46.

Edwards, C. 1993. *The Politics of Immorality in Ancient Rome*, Cambridge University Press, Cambridge.

Edwards, E. and Bhaumik, K. eds. 2008. *Visual Sense: A Cultural Reader*, Berg, Oxford.

Ehrhardt, W. 1987. *Stilgeschichte Untersuchungen an römischen Wandmalereien von der Späten Republik bis zur Zeit Neros*, Philip von Zabern, Mainz am Rhein.

Ehrhardt, W. 1988. 'Casa dell'Orso' *Häuser in Pompeji 2*, Hirmer, Munich.

Ehrhardt, W. 1998. 'Casa di Paquius Proculus' *Häuser in Pompeji 9*, Hirmer, Munich.

Ehrhardt, W. 2004. 'Casa dell Nozze d'argento' *Häuser in Pompeji 12*, Hirmer, Munich.

Ehrhardt, W. 2012. *Dekorations- und Wohnkontext*, Reichert, Wiesbaden.

Ekirch, R. 2005. *At Day's Close: Night in Times Past*, University of Chicago, Weidenfeld and Nicolson, London.

Elia, O. 1932. 'I cubiculi nelle case di Pompei' *Historia* 4. 3: 394–421.
Elia, O. 1934. 'Pompei – Relazione sullo scavo dell'Insula X della Regio I', *NSc* 6.10: 264–344.
Ellis, S. 1997. 'Late Antique Houses in Asia Minor', in eds. Isager, S. and Poulsen, B.: 38–50.
Ellis, S. 2000. *Roman Housing,* Duckworth, London.
Ellis, S. 'Late Antique Houses in Asia Minor', in eds. Isager, S. and Poulsen, B.: 38–50.
Ellis, S. J. R. 2004. 'The Distribution of Bars at Pompeii: Archaeological, Spatial and Viewshed Analyses' *JRA* 17.1: 371–384.
Elsner, J. 2002. 'The Genres of Ekphrasis', *Ramus* 31: 1–18.
Elsner, J. 2007. 'Viewing Ariadne: From Ekphrasis to Wall Painting in the Roman World' in eds. Bartsch, S. and Elsner J.: 20–44.
Elsner, J. and Masters, J. eds. 1994. *Reflections of Nero,* The University of North Carolina Press, Chapel Hill.
Elsner, J. and Meyer, M. 2014. *Art and Rhetoric in Roman Culture*, Cambridge University Press, Cambridge.
Eschebach, H. 1970. *Die städtebauliche Entwicklungen des antiken Pompeji mit einem Plan 1:1000 und einem Exkurs: Die Baugeschichte der Stabianer Thermen nach H. Sulze*, RM, Erganzungsheft 17, Kerle, Heidelberg.
Eschebach, H. 1975. 'Erläuterungen zum Plan Pompejis' in eds. Andreae, B. and Kyrieleis, H.: 331–338.
Eschebach, H. and Eschebach, L. 1995. *Pompeji vom 7. Jahrhundert v. Chr. bis 79 n. Chr.*, Böhlau, Cologne.
Evans, F. and Lawlor, L. eds. 2000. *Chiasms: Merleau-Ponty's notion of the Flesh*, State University of New York Press, Albany.
Evans, F. and Lawlor, L. 2000. 'The Value of Flesh: Merleau Ponty's philosophy and the Modernist/Post-Modernist Debate' in eds. Evans, F. and Lawlor, L. Albany: 1–20.
Everest, F. A. and Pohlmann, K. 2009. 5th edn. *Master Handbook of Acoustics*, McGraw-Hill, New York.
Favro, D. 2006. 'In the Eyes of the Beholder: Virtual Reality Re-creations and Academia' in eds. Haselberger, L. and Humphrey, J.: 321–334.
Favro, D. 1996. *The Urban Image of Augustan Rome*, Cambridge University Press, Cambridge.
Fentress, E. ed. 2000. *Romanization and the City: Creation, Transformations, and Failures*, JRA Suppl. 38: 42–56.
Ferenczy, E. 1976. *From the Patrician State to the Patrician-Plebeian State*, A. M. Hakkert, Amsterdam.
Fergola, L. 2016. *Oplontis and its Villas*, Edizioni Flavius, Pompeii.
Fergola, L. and Pagano, M. 1998. *Oplontis: Le Splendide Ville Romane di Torre Annunziata*, T and M, Naples.
Ferguson, T. J. 1996. *Historic Zuni Architecture and Society: An Archaeological Application of Space Syntax*, University of Arizona Press, Arizona.

Fieller, N. R. J., Gilbertson, D. D., and Ralph, N. G. A. eds. 1985. *Paleobiological Investigations: Research Design Methods and Data Analysis*, BAR-Is 266: 105–17.
Finley, M. I. 1980. *Ancient Slavery and Modern Ideology*, Chatto and Windus, London.
Fiorelli, G. ed. 1860–1864. *Pompeianarum Antiquitatum Historia* I–III, Naples.
Fiorelli, G. 1873. *Scavi*. Tipografia Italiana nel Liceo V. Emmanuele: Naples.
Fiorelli, G. 1875. *Descr.* Tipografia Italiana Liceo V. E al Mercatello, Naples. (reprinted 2013, Cambridge University Press, Cambridge).
Fisher, N. and Van Wees, H. 2011. *Competition in the Ancient World*, Classical Press of Wales, Wales.
Flach, D. 1990 *Römische Agrargeschichte*. C. H. Beck, Munich.
Flohr, M. 2003. 'Fullones and Roman Society. A Reconsideration', *JRA* 16: 447–50.
Flohr, M. 2007. 'Nec quicquam ingenuum habere potest officina? Spatial contexts of urban production at Pompeii, AD 79' *BABesch* 82: 129–148.
Flohr, M. 2011. 'Reconsidering the *Atrium* House: Domestic *Fullonicae* at Pompeii' in Poehler, E., Flohr, M., and Cole, K.: 88–102.
Flohr, M. 2012. 'Working and living under one roof: workshops in Pompeian *atrium* houses' in ed. Anguissola, A.: 51–72.
Flohr, M. 2013a. *The World of the fullo. Work, Economy and Society in Roman Italy*, Oxford, University Press, Oxford.
Flohr, M. 2013b. 'The Textile Economy of Pompeii' *JRA* 26.1: 53–78.
Flohr, M. 2017. 'Beyond Smell: The Sensory Lanscape of the Roman *Fullonica*' in ed. Betts, E.: 39–53.
Flohr, M. and Wilson, A. 2011. 'The Economy of Ordure' in Jansen, G, C. M., Koloski-Ostrow, A. O. and Moorman, E. M. 2011: 147–156.
Flower, H. 1996. *Ancestor Masks and Aristocratic Power in Roman Culture*, Oxford University Press, Oxford.
Fontaine, T. H. M. 1991. *Die Villa di Diomede in Pompeji. Baugeschichtliche, typologische un stilistische Untersuchungen*, unpub. thesis., University of Trier.
Förtsch, R. 1993. *Archäologischer Kommentar zu den Villenbriefen des jüngeren Plinius*, Beiträge zur Erschliessung hellenistischer und kaiserzeitlicher Skulptur und Architektur 13. Zabern, Mainz am Rhein.
Foss, P. 1994. *Kitchens and Dining Rooms at Pompeii: The Spatial and Social Relationship of Cooking to Eating in the Roman Household, vol I.* unpub PhD thesis, University of Michigan.
Foster, S. M. 1989. 'Analysis of Spatial Patterns in Buildings (Access Analysis) as an Insight into Social Structure: Examples from the Scottish Atlantic Iron Age', *Antiquity* 63: 40–50.
Foucault, M. 1984. 'The Subject and Power' in ed. Wallis, B.: 417–432.
Fox, R. 2008. 'Tastes, Smells, and Spaces: Sensory Perceptions and Mycenean Palatial Feasting' in eds. Hitchcock, L., Laffineur, R., and Crowley, J.: 133–140.

Foxhall, L. 2000. 'The Running Sands of Time: Archaeology and Short-Term Time Scales' *WorldArch* 31: 484–498.

Foxhall, L. 2007. 'House Clearance: Unpacking the 'Kitchen' in Classical Greece' in eds. Westgate, R., Fisher, N. and Whitley, J.: 233–242.

Fraenkel, E. 1957. *Horace*, Clarendon Press, Oxford.

Fulford, M. and Clarke, A. 2011. *Silchester: A City in Transition. The Mid Roman Occupation of Insula IX c. AD 125–250/300. A Report on Excavations Undertaken Since 1997*, Britannia Monograph Series 25, Society for the Promotion of Roman Studies, London.

Galbrun, L., and Ali, T. T. 2013. 'Acoustical and perceptual assessment of water sounds and their use over road traffic noise', *The Journal of the Acoustical Society of America* 133: 227–237.

Gazda, E. 1994. *Roman Art in the Private Sphere: New Perspectives on the Architecture and Décor of the Domus, Villa and Insula*, University of Michigan Press, Michigan.

Gell, W. 1832. *Pompeiana: The Topography, Edifices and Ornaments of Pompeii the Result of Excavations since 1819. 2 Vols*, Jennings and Chaplin, London.

Gelzer, M. 1912. *Die Nobilität der römischen Republik*. B. G. Teubner, Berlin.

Gelzer, M. 1969. *The Roman Nobility*, trans. R. Seager, Blackwell, Oxford.

George, M. ed. 1999. *Constructions of Space IV: Further Developments in Examining Social Space in Ancient Israel*, Library of Hebrew Bible and Old Testament Studies 569, T and T Clark International, New York and London.

George, M. 2002. 'Review of Reading Space: Social Interaction and Identity in the Houses of Roman Pompeii by Grahame, M', *JRS* 92: 238–239.

George, M. 2008. 'The "Dark Side" of the Toga' in eds. Edmondson, J. and Keith, A.: 94–112.

Gesemann, B. 1996. *Die Straßen der antiken Stadt Pompeji: Entwicklung und Gestaltung*, Peter Lang, Frankfurt am Main.

Gibson, R. K. and Morello, R. 2012. *Reading the Letters of Pliny the Younger*, Cambridge University Press, Cambridge.

Gil, D. and Brumm, H. 2014. *Avian Urban Ecology: Behavioural and Physiological Adaptations*, Oxford University Press, Oxford.

Giordano, C and Casale, A. 2007. *Perfumes, Unguents and Hairstyles in Pompeii* (2nd ed. revised and undated by Garcia y Garcia, L), Bardi Editore, Rome.

Gleason, K. L. 1987–88. 'Garden Excavations at the Herodian Winter Palace in Jericho,' *Bulletin of the Anglo-Isreal Archaeological Society* 7: 21–39.

GdSc, n.d. 1874–1877. *Unpublished Excavation Reports Held at the Archives of the Soprintendenza archeologica di Pompeii*: 150–153, 169, 174–176, 251–256.

Goddard, J. P. 1994a. *Moral Attitudes to Eating and Drinking in Ancient Rome*, Diss. Cambridge.

Goddard, J. P. 1994b. 'The Tyrant at the Table' in ed. Elsner, J. and Masters, J.: 67–82.

Goldbeck, F. 2010. *Salutationes: die Morgenbegrüßungen in Rom in der Republik und der frühen Kaiserzeit*, Klio, Berlin.

Goldhahn, J. 2002. 'Roaring Rocks: an audio-visual perspective on hunter-gatherer engravings in northern Sweden and Scandinavia' *Norwegian Archaeological Review* 35 (1): 29–61.

Gonlin, N. and Nowell, A. 2018. *Archaeology of the Night: Life After Dark in the Ancient World,* University Press of Colorado, Boulder.

Goodman, P. J. 2007. *The Roman City and its Periphery: From Rome to Gaul,* Routledge, Abingdon.

Gowers, E. 1993. *The Loaded Table,* Oxford University Press, Oxford.

Gowers, E. 2012. 'Introduction' in *Horace: Satires Book I.* trans. Gowers, E. Cambridge University Press, Cambridge.

Graf, F. 1995. 'Ekphrasis: die Entstehung der Gattung in der Antike' in eds. Boehm, G. and Pfotenhauer, H.: 143–155.

Graham, E-J. 2006a. *The Burial of the Urban Poor in Italy in the Late Roman Republic and Early Empire,* BAR-IS 1565, Archaeopress, Oxford.

Graham, E-J. 2006b. 'Discarding the destitute: ancient and modern attitudes towards burial practice and memory preservation amongst the lower classes of Rome' in eds. Croxford, B., Goodchild, H., Lucas, J., and Nick, R.: 57–71.

Graham, E-J. 2011. 'Memory and materiality: re-embodying the Roman funeral' in eds. Hope, V and Huskinson, J.: 21–39.

Grahame, M. 1993. 'Reading the Roman House: The Social Interpretation of Spatial Order' in ed. Leslie, A.: 48–74.

Grahame, M. 1997. 'Public and Private in the Roman House: The Spatial Order of the Casa del Fauno' in eds. Laurence, R. and Wallace-Hadrill, A.: 137–64.

Grahame, M. 1998. 'Material Culture and Roman Identity: the Spatial Layout of Pompeian Houses and the Problem of Ethnicity' in eds. Berry J. and Laurence, R.: 156–78.

Grahame, M. 2000. *Reading Space: Social Interaction and Identity in the Houses of Roman Pompeii: A Syntactical Approach to the Analysis and Interpretation of Built Space,* Oxbow, Oxford.

Green F. M. 2015. 'Cooking Class' in eds. Tuori, K. and Nissin, L.: 133–148.

Green, P. 1998. 'Introduction' in Juvenal. *The Sixteen Satires,* trans. Green, P. 3rd edn. Penguin Books, London.

Greenough, J. B. 1890. 'The *Fauces* of the Roman House', *Harvard Studies in Classical Philology* 1: 1–12.

Griffin, D. H. 1994. *Satire: A Critical Reintroduction,* University Press of Kentucky, Kentucky.

Griffiths, S. and A. von Lünen eds. 2016. *Spatial Cultures: Towards a New Social Morphology of Cities.* Routledge, Abingdon.

Grimal, P. 1969. *Les jardins romains,* 2nd ed. E. de Boccard, Paris.

Grocock, C. and Grainger, S. 2006. 'Introduction' in *Apicius: A Critical Edition with an Introduction and English Translation,* trans. Grocock, C. and Grainger, S. Prospect Books, Devon.

Gros, P. 2001. *L'architecture romaine. Vol. 2. Maisons, palais, villas et tombeaux*, Picard, Paris.

Gruen, E. 1992. *Culture and National Identity in Republican Rome*, Cornell University Press, Ithaca.

Guadagno, G. 1993. 'Eredità di cultura e nuovi "Herculanensium sull'accesso dati"'; in ed. Franchi dell'Orto, L.: 73–98.

Guldager Bilde, P. 2003. 'Nordic Excavations of a Roman Villa by Lake Nemi, loc. S. Maria' in eds. Brandt, J. R., X. Dupré Raventós and G. Ghini: 259–268.

Guldager Bilde, P. 2004. 'Caesar's villa? Nordic Excavations of a Roman Villa by Lake Nemi, loc. S. Maria (1998–2001)', *AnalRom* 30: 7–42.

Guldager Bilde, P. 2005. 'The Roman villa by Lake Nemi: from nature to culture – between private and public Roman villas around the Urbs. Interaction with landscape and environment.' in eds. Santillo Frizell, B. and Klynne, A. 2004. http://www.isvroma.it/public/villa/screen/guldagerbilde.pdf. Date accessed 1.8.17.

Gunther, R. T. 1913. *Pausilypon*, H. Hart, Oxford.

Gusman, P. 1900. *Pompei: The City, its Life and Art*, trans. Simmonds, F. and Jourdain, M. William Heinemann, London.

Haeussler. R. 2013. *Becoming Roman: Diverging Identities and Experiences in Ancient Northwest Italy*, Left Coast Press, California.

Hales, S. 2003. *The Roman House and Social Identity*, Cambridge University Press, Cambridge.

Hall, A. R. and Kenward, H. K., 1990. *Environmental Evidence from the Colonia. The Archaeology of York 14/6*, Council for British Archaeology, London.

Hall, A. R., Kenward, H. K., Williams, D., and Greig, J. R. A. 1983. *Environment and Living Conditions and Two Anglo-Scandinavian Sites. The Archaeology of York 14/4*, Council for British Archaeology, London.

Hamilakis, Y. 1998. 'Eating the dead: mortuary feasting and the political economy of memory in the Bronze Age Aegean' in ed. Branigan, K.: 115–132.

Hamilakis, Y. 1999. 'Food Technologies/Technologies of the Body: The Social Context of Wine and Oil Production and Consumption in Bronze Age Crete', *WorldArch* 31: 38–54.

Hamilakis, Y. 2008. 'Time, performance and the production of a mnemonic record: from feasting to an archaeology of eating and drinking' in eds. Hitchcock, L. A, Laffineur, R. and Crowley, J.: 3–20.

Hamilakis, Y. 2013a. *Archaeology and the Senses: Human Experience, Memory and Affect*, Cambridge University Press, Cambridge.

Hamilakis, Y. 2013b. 'Afterword: Eleven Theses on the Archaeology of the Senses' in ed. Day, J.: 409–419.

Hamilakis, Y. and Sherratt, S. 2012. 'Feasting and the consuming body in Bronze Age Crete and Early Iron Age Cyprus' in eds. Cadogan, G, Iakovou, M, Kopaka, K. and Whitley, J.: 187–207.

Hamilakis, Y., Pluciennik, M. and Tarlow, S. eds. 2002. *Thinking Through the Body: Archaeologies of Corporeality*, Kluwer/Plenum, New York.

Hamilton, S. and Whitehouse, R. 2006a. 'Three Senses of Dwelling: Beginning to Socialise the Neolithic Ditched Villages of the Tavoliere, Southeast Italy' in eds. Jorger, V. et al.: 159–184.

Hamilton, S. and Whitehouse, R. (with Brown, K., Combes, P., Herring, E. and Seager Thomas, M.) 2006b. 'Phenomenology in Practice: Towards a Methodology of a 'Subjective' Approach', *EJA* 9(I): 31–71.

Hannah, R. 2009. *Time in Antiquity. Sciences of Antiquity*, Routledge, London.

Hanson, J. 2003. *Decoding Homes and Houses*, Cambridge University Press, Cambridge.

Harlow, M. and Laurence, R. 2002. *Growing Up and Growing Old in Ancient Rome: A Life Course Approach*, Routledge, Abingdon.

Harrison, S. ed. 2005. *A Companion to Latin Literature*, Blackwell, MA.

Harrison, S. 2017. 'Introduction', in Horace, *Odes Book II.* trans. Harrison, S. Cambridge University Press, Cambridge.

Hartnett, J., 2008. '*Si quis hic sederit*: Streetside Benches and Urban Society in Pompeii' in *AJA* 112: 91–119.

Hartnett, J. 2011. 'The Power of Nuisances on the Roman Street', in eds. Laurence, R. and Newsome, D.: 135–159.

Hartnett, J. 2016. 'Sound as a Roman Urban Social Phenomenon' in eds. Haug, A. and Kreuz, P.: 159–178.

Hartnett, J. 2017. *The Roman Street: Urban Life and Society in Pompeii, Herculaneum, and Rome*, Cambridge University Press, New York.

Haselberger, L. and Humphrey, J. eds. 2006. *Imaging Ancient Rome: Documentation – Visualisation – Imagination, JRA Supp.* 61, RI, Portsmouth.

Haug, A. and Kreuz, P. eds. 2016. *Stadterfahrung als Sinneserfahrung in der römischen Kaiserzeit*, Brepols, Belgium.

Heinzelmann, M. 2000. *Die Nekropolen von Ostia: Untersuchungen zu den Gräberstraßen vor der Porta Romana und an der Via Laurentina*, F. Pfeil, Munich.

Henderson, P. J. 2012. 'The Extraurban Belvedere'. Spaces and Flows: An International Journal of Urban and Extraurban Studies, 2(II): 9–21.

Heinrich, F. B. J. and Hansen, A.M. eds. 2017. *Tidjschrift voor Mediterrane Archeologie, Special Issue: Mediterranean Food Economies* 28 (56).

Henshaw, V. 2014. *Urban Smellscapes: Understanding and Designing City Smell Environments*, Routledge, Abingdon.

Hermansen, G. 1970. 'The *Medianum* and the Roman Apartment', *Phoenix*, 24, 4: 342–347.

Hermansen, G. 1973. 'Domus and Insula in the City of Rome' in Due, O. S., Johansen, H. F. and Larsen, B. D.: 333–341.

Hermansen, G. 1982. *Ostia: Aspects of Roman City Life*, University of Alberta Press, Edmonton.

Hersch, K. K. 2010. *The Roman Wedding: Ritual and Meaning in Antiquity*, Cambridge University Press, Cambridge.

Hesberg, H. and Zanker, P. eds. 1985. *Römische Gräberstrassen – Selbstdarstellung – Status – Standard*, Verlag der Bayerischen Akademie der Wissenschaften, Munich.

Hillier, B. and Hanson, J. 1984. *The Social Logic of Space*, Cambridge University Press, Cambridge.
Hitchcock, L. A, Laffineur, R. and Crowley, J. eds. 2008. *DAIS: The Aegean Feast*, University of Liege and University of Texas at Austin, Liege, and Austin.
Hobson, B. 2009. Latrinae et Foricae: *Toilets in the Roman World*, Duckworth, London.
Hodder, I. 1977. *The Spatial Organisation of Culture*, Duckworth, London.
Hodske, J. 2007. *Mythologische Bildthemen in den Häusern Pompejis*, Franz Philipp Rutzen, Ruhpolding.
Hölkeskamp, K. 1993. 'Conquest, Competition and Consensus: Roman Expansion in Italy and the Rise of the *Nobilitas*', *Historia* 42: 12–39.
Holleran, C. 2012. *Shopping in Ancient Rome: The Retail Trade in the Late Republic and the Principate*, Oxford University Press, Oxford.
Hölscher, T. 1990. 'Römischer nobiles und hellenistische Herrscher' in *Akten des XIII Internationalen Kongresses für klassische Archäologie Berlin 1988*. P. von Zabern, Mainz am Rhein: 351–400.
Hope, V. 2009. *Roman Death: Dying and the Dead in Ancient Rome*, Continuum, London.
Hope, V. 2017. 'Blood, Fire and Feasting: The Role of Touch and Taste in Graeco-Roman Animal Sacrifice' in Betts, E.: 86–103.
Hope, V. and Huskinson, J. eds. 2011. *Memory and Mourning: Studies on Roman Death*, Oxbow, Oxford.
Hope, V. and Marshall, E. eds. 2000. *Death and Disease in the Ancient City*, Routledge, London.
Hopkins, K. 1978 *Conquerors and Slaves*, Cambridge University Press, Cambridge.
Hopkins, K. 1983. *Death and Renewal*, Sociological Studies in Roman History, no. 2. Cambridge University Press, New York.
Hopwood 2013. 'Sustenance, taste, and the practice of community in Ancient Mesopotamia' in ed. Day, J.: 222–242.
Houston, S. and Taube, K. 2000. 'An Archaeology of the Senses: Perception and Cultural Expression in Ancient Mesoamerica', *CAJ 10*: 261–294.
Howes, D. 1991. *The Varieties of Sensory Experience: A Sourcebook in the Anthropology of the Senses*, University of Toronto Press, Toronto.
Howes, D. 2003. *Sensual Relations: Engaging the Senses in Culture and Social Theory*, University of Michigan Press, Michigan.
Howes, D. 2005. *Empire of the Senses: The Sensual Culture Reader*, Berg, Oxford.
Howes, D. 2009. *The Sixth Sense Reader*, Berg, Oxford.
Howes, D. 2016. *A Cultural History of the Senses in the Modern Age*, Bloomsbury, London.
Huntley. K. V. 2011. 'Identifying Children's Graffiti in Roman Campania: A Developmental Psychological Approach', in eds. Baird, J. and Taylor, C.: 69–88.
Huntley. K. V. 2017. 'The Writing on the Wall: Age, Agency, and Material Culture in Roman Campania', in eds. Laes, C. and Vuolanto, V.: 137–154.
Ingold, T. 2011. *The Perception of the Environment*, Routledge, Abingdon.
Insoll, T. 2007. *Archaeology: The Conceptual Challenge*, Duckworth, London.

Isager, S. and Poulsen, B. eds. 1997. *Patron and Pavements in Late Antiquity*, Halicarnassus Studies II, Odense University Press, Odense.

Ivanoff, S. 1859. 'Varie Specie di Soglie in Pompei ed Indagine sul Vero Sito della Fauce'. *Annali dell'Instituto di Corrispondenza Archeologica* 1: 82-108.

Jahn, D. 1868. *Über Darstellung des Handwerks und Handelsverkehrs auf Antiken Wandgemälden*, S. Hirsel, Leipzig.

Jansen, G. C. M. 1991. 'Water Systems and Sanitation in the Houses of Herculaneum' in *Meded* 50: 149-166.

Jansen, G. C. M. 1997. 'Private Toilets in Pompeii: Appearance and Operation' in eds. Bon. S. E. and Jones, R.: 121-134.

Jansen G. C. M. 2000. 'Systems for the Disposal of Waste and Excreta in Roman Cities. The Situation in Pompeii, Herculaneum and Ostia' in eds. Dupré y Raventos, X and Remolà, J. A.: 37-49.

Jansen, G. C. M. 2002. *Water in de Romeinse stad: Pompeji - Herculaneum - Ostia*, Peeters, Louvain.

Jansen, G. C. M. 2007. 'Toilets with a View. The Luxurious Toilets of the Emperor Hadrian at his Villa near Tivoli' in *BABesch* 82: 165-181.

Jansen, G. C. M., Koloski-Ostrow, A. O. and Moorman, E. M. 2011. *Roman Toilets: Their Archaeology and Cultural History*, Peeters, Leuven.

Jashemski, W. F. 1979. *The Gardens of Pompeii: Herculaneum and the Villas Destroyed by Vesuvius, Vol. 1*, Caratzas Brothers, New York.

Jashemski, W. F. 1987. 'Recently Excavated Gardens and Cultivated Land in the Villas at Boscoreale and Oplontis' in ed. E. B. Macdougall: 31-76.

Jashemski W. F. 1992. 'The Gardens of Pompeii, Herculaneum and the villas destroyed by Vesuvius' in *JGH* 12.2: 102-125.

Jashemski, W. F. 1993. *The Gardens of Pompeii: Herculaneum and the Villas Destroyed by Vesuvius, Vol. 2*, Caratzas Brothers, New York.

Jashemski, W.F. 1995. 'Roman Gardens in Tunisia: Preliminary Excavations in the house of Bacchus and Ariadne and in the East Temple at Thuburbo Maius', *AJA* 99: 559-576.

Jashemski, W. F. and Myer, F. G. eds. 2002. *The Natural History of Pompeii*, Cambridge University Press, Cambridge.

Jones, A. K. G. 1985. 'Trichurid Ova in Archaeological Deposits: Their Value as Indicators of Ancient Faeces' in eds. Fieller, N. R. J., Gilbertson, D. D., and Ralph, N. G. A.: 105-117.

Jones, C. P. 1991. '*Dinner*-theater' in Slater, W. J.: 185-98.

Jones, A. and Macgregor, G. eds. 2002. *Colouring the Past*, Berg, Oxford.

Jorger, V. O. et al. eds. 2006a. 'Approaching "Prehistoric and Protohistoric Architectures" of Europe from a "Dwelling Perspective"', *Journal of Iberian Archaeology*, 8, Porto.

Joshel, S. R. and Petersen, L. H. 2014. *The Material Life of Roman Slaves*, Cambridge University Press, Cambridge.

Jung, F. 'Gebaute Bilder' in *AntK* 27 1984: 71-122.

Jurkic Girardi, V. 1979 'Scavi in una parte della villa rustica romana a Cervera Porto presso Parenzo'. *Atti Centro Richerche Storiche di Rovigno*: 427-438.

Jütte, R. 2005. *A History of the Senses from Antiquity to Cyberspace*, Polity, Cambridge.
Kaiser, A. 2011. *Roman Urban Street Networks*, Routledge, New York.
Karivieri, A. and Forsell, R. 2006-7. 'The house of Caecilius Jucundus V. I, 22–27: A Preliminary Report' *Opuscula Romana* 31-32: 119–138.
Kastenmeier, P. 2007. *I luoghi del lavoro domestic nella casa pompeiana*. L'Erma Bretschneider, Rome.
Kent, S. 1990. *Domestic architecture and the Use of Space: An Interdisciplinary, Cross-Cultural Study*, Cambridge University Press, Cambridge.
Kenward, H. K., Hall, A. R., and Jones, A. K. G. 1986. *Environmental Evidence from a Roman Well and Anglian Pits in the Legionary Fortress*, The Archaeology of York 14/5. The Council for British Archaeology, London.
Kenward H. K., and Hall A. R., 1995. *Biological Evidence from Anglo-Scandinavian Deposits at 16-22 Coppergate*, The Archaeology of York 14/7. The Council for British Archaeology, London.
Kiernan, P. 2009. *Miniature Votive Offerings in the North-West Provinces of the Roman Empire*, F. Ph. Rutzen, Wiesebaden.
King, A. 2002. 'Mammals: Evidence from Wall Paintings, Sculpture, Mosaics, Faunal Remains, and Ancient Literary Sources' in eds. Jashemski, W. F. and Myer, F. G.: 401–450.
Kitchen, F. 1963. *Brother to the Ox: the Autobiography of a Farmer's Boy*, Dent, London.
Kivity, S., Ortega-Hernandez, O.D. and Shoenfeld, Y. 2009. 'Olfaction – A Window to the Mind', *IMAJ*, 11: 238–243.
Klynne, A. 2005. 'The Laurel Grove of the Caesars: Looking in and Looking out' in eds. Klynne, A. and Santillo Frizell, B. 167–176.
Klynne, A. and Liljenstolpe, P. 2000. 'Investigating the Imperial Gardens of the Villa of Livia', *JRA* 13: 220–233.
Klynne, A. and Santillo Frizell, B. 2005. *Roman Villas around the Urbs. Interaction with Landscape and Environment. Proceedings of a Conference held at the Swedish Institute in Rome, September 17-18, 2004*, The Swedish Institute at Rome, Rome.
Kockel, V. 1983. *Die Grabbauten vordem Herkulaner Tor in Pompeji*, Von Zabern, Mainz.
Kockel, V. 1985. Review of 'Un impegno per Pompei by Licia Vlad Borelli, Franca Parise Badoni, Oreste Ferrari, Antonio d'Ambrosio, Stefano de Caro'. *Gnomen* 57: 545–551.
Kockel, V. 1985. 'Funde und Forschungen in den Vesuvstädten I'. *AA* 21: 495–571.
Kockel, V. and Weber, B. F. eds. 1983. 'Die Villa delle colonne a mosaico in Pompeji', RM 90(I): 51–89.
Koloski-Ostrow, A. 2015a. 'Roman urban smells: Archaeological evidence' in ed. Bradley, M.: 90–109.
Koloski-Ostrow, A. 2015b. *The Archaeology of Sanitation in Roman Italy: Toilets, Sewers, and Water Systems*, University of North Carolina Press, Chapel Hill.
Korsmeyer, C. ed. 2005. *The Taste Culture Reader: Experiencing Food and Drink*, Berg, Oxford.
Krinzinger, F. 2010. *Hanghaus 2 in Ephesos*, OAW, Wien.
Kroll, W., 1933. *Die Kultur der ciceronischen Zeit*, Dieterich, Weisbaden.

Kudlien, F. 2002. 'P. Patulcius L. f., Walker und Probulos im späthellenistischen Magnesia', *Laverna* 13: 56-68.

Kuhn, C. 2012. *Politische Kommunikation und oeffentliche Meinung in der antiken Welt*, Franz Steiner Verlag, Heidelberg.

Kuier, W. J. and Turner, H. 1992. 'Diet of a Roman Centurion at Alphen aan den Rijn, The Netherlands, in the First Century AD', *Review of Palaeobotany and Palynology* 73: 187-204.

La Rocca, E. 2000. '*L'affresco con veduta di città dal Colle Oppio*' in ed. Fentress, E.: 57-71.

La Rocca, E. de Vos, M., de Vos, A. (co-ordinated by Coarelli, F.) 1994. *Pompeii*, A. Mondadori, Milan.

La Vega, F. 1763-1790. 'Giornali degli scavi di Pompei di Francesco La Vega' in Fiorelli, G. ed. I: 118-133.

Laes, C. 2011, *Children in the Roman Empire. Outsiders Within*, Cambridge University Press, Cambridge.

Laes, C. and Vuolanto, V. 2017. *Children and Everyday Life in the Roman and Late Antique World*, Routledge, Abingdon.

Laes, C. and Vuolanto, V. 2017. 'A New Paradigm for the Social History of Childhood and Children in Antiquity' in eds. Laes, C. and Vuolanto, V.: 1-10.

Lafon, X. 2001. *Villae Maritimae: Recherches sur les Villas Littorales de l'Italie Romaine*, École française de Rome, Rome.

Laidlaw, A. 'Mining the Early Published Sources: Problems and Pitfalls' in eds. Dobbins, J. and Foss, P.: 620-636.

Lanciani, R. 1888. 'La 'Venus Hortorum Sallustianorum', *BullCom* 16: 3-11.

Lange, C. H. and Madsen, J. M. eds. 2016. *Cassius Dio: Greek Intellectual and Roman Politician*, Brill, Leiden.

Larmour, D. H. J, and Spencer, D. J. 2007. *The Cites of Rome: Time, Space, Memory*, Oxford University Press, Oxford.

Laurence, R. 2007. *Roman Pompeii: Space and Society*, Routledge, New York.

Laurence, R. 2012. *Roman Archaeology for Historians*, Routledge, Abingdon.

Laurence, R. 2017. 'Children and the Urban Environment: Agency in Pompeii' in eds. Laes, C. and Vuolanto, V.: 27-42.

Laurence, R. and Newsome, D. eds. 2011. *Rome, Ostia, Pompeii: Movement and Space*, Oxford University Press. Oxford.

Laurence, R. and Wallace-Hadrill, A. eds. 1999. Domestic Space in the Roman World: Pompeii and Beyond, *JRA* Supp. series 22, Portsmouth, RI.

Lavan, L., Özgenel, L., and Sarantis, A. 2007. *Housing in Late Anquity: From Palaces to Shops*, Brill, Leiden.

Laurence, R. 2012. Roman Archaeology for Historians, Routledge, Abingdon.

Lawrence, R. J. 1990. 'Public Collective and Private Space: A Study of Urban Housing in Switzerland' in ed. Kent, S.: 73-91.

Lawson, G. and Scarre, C. eds. 2006. *Archaeoacoustics,* MacDonald Institute for Archaeological Research, Cambridge.

Leach, E. W. 1997. '*Oecus* on Ibycus: Investigating the Vocabulary of the *Roman House*' in eds. Bon S. and Jones, R.: 50–72.
Leach, E. W. 2004. *The Social Life of Painting in Ancient Roman and on the Bay of Naples*, Cambridge University Press, Cambridge.
Lefebvre, H. 1991. *The Production of Space*, trans. Nicholson Smith, D. Blackwell, Oxford, Cambridge, Mass.
Lefebvre, H. 2004. *Rhythmanalysis: Space, Time and Everyday Life*, Continuum, London.
Leveau, Ph. and Garmy, P. 2002. 'Conclusion: La *villa* et le *vicus*. Formes de l'habitat et exploitation domaniale', *Revue archéologique de Narbonnaise* 35: 313–317.
Leslie, A. ed. *TRAC 1993: Proceedings of the Fifteenth Annual Theoretical Roman Archaeology Conference. Glasgow*, Oxbow Books, Oxford.
Levy, C. and Pernot, L. eds. 1997. *Dire l'évidence. Philosophie et rhétorique antiques*, L'Harmattan. Paris-Montréal.
Lewis, C. T. and Short, C. 1879. *A Latin Dictionary; Founded on Andrews' edition of Freund's Latin dictionary*, Clarendon Press, Oxford.
Linderski, J. 1985. 'The Dramatic Date of Varro, *De Re Rustica*, Book III and the Elections in 54', *Historia* 34: 248–254.
Linderski, J. 1989. 'Garden Parlors. Nobles and Birds.' in ed. Curtis, R. I.: 105–127.
Ling, R. 1997. *The Insula of the Menander at Pompeii I: The Structures*, Oxford University Press, Oxford.
Lintott, A. 1972. 'Provocatio: From the Struggle of the Orders to the Principate', *Aufstieg und Niedergang der römischen Welt. Geschichte und Kultur Roms im Spiegel der neureren Forschung*. 1.2: 226–67.
Lintott A. 1994a. 'The Crisis of the Republic: Sources and Source-problems' in eds. Crook, J. A., Lintott, A. and Rawson, E.:1–15.
Lintott, A. 1994b. 'The Roman Empire and its Problems in the Late Second Century' in eds. Crook, J. A., Lintott A. and Rawson E.: 16–39.
Lintott, A. W. 1999. *The Constitution of the Roman Republic*, Oxford University Press, Oxford.
Love, M. 2007. *Analysis of Calcareous Deposits from the Down Pipes of First Century Pompeii*, unpub. diss. Univ. of Bradford.
Macaulay-Lewis, E. 2011. 'The City in Motion' in eds. Laurence, R. and Newsome, D.: 262–89.
MacBain, B. 1980. 'Appius Claudius Caecus and the Via Appia', *CQ* 30: 356–72.
MacDonald, W. L. 1986. *Roman Empire*, vol. II. Yale University Press, New Haven.
Macdougall, E. M. ed. 1987. *Ancient Roman Villa Gardens*, Dumbarton Oaks Colloquium on the History of Landscape Architecture 10, Washington DC.
MacGregor, G. 1999. 'Making Sense of the Past in the Present: a Sensory Analysis of Carved Stone Balls', *WorldArch* 31: 258–271.
MacMahon, A. and Price, J. eds. 2005. *Roman Working Lives and Urban Living*, Oxbow, Oxford.

Maiuri, A. 1927. 'Pompei – Relazione sui lavori di scavo dal marzo 1924 al marzo 1926', *NSc* 6.3: 3–83.

Maiuri, A. 1929. 'Pompei – Relazione sui lavori di scavo dall'aprile 1926 al dicembre 1927', *NSc* 6.5: 354–476.

Maiuri, A. 1933. *La Casa del Menandro e il suo Tesoro di Argenteria*, La Libreria dello Stato, Rome.

Maiuri, A. 1942. *L'Ultima Fase Edilizia di Pompei*, Istituto di Studi Romani, Rome.

Maiuri, A. 1945. *Herculaneum. Guidebooks to the Museums and Monuments of Italy*, La Libreria dello Stato, Rome.

Maiuri, A. 1952. A. *Maiuri*, 'Gli 'oeci' vitruviani in *Palladio* e nella casa pompeiana ed ercolanese', *Palladio* 1–2: 1–8.

Maiuri, A. 1958. *Ercolano: i nuovi scavi (1927-1958)*, Roma: Poligrafico dello Stato.

Maiuri, A. 1973. *Herculaneum: and the villa of the papyri*, Istituto Geografico de Agostini, Novara.

Maiuri, A. 1989. *La villa dei misteri*, Istituto Poligrafico dello Stato, Rome.

Malmberg, S. and Bjur, H. 2011. 'Movement and Urban Development at Two city Gates in Rome: The Porta Esquilina and Porta Tiburtina' in eds. Laurence, R. and Newsome, D.: 361–386.

Maltby, M. 1994. 'The Meat Supply in Roman Dorchester and Winchester' in eds. Hall, A. R. and Kenwood, H.:85–102.

Mansuelli, M. 1979. *Studi sull'arco onorario romano*, l'Erma Bretschneider, Rome.

Marzano, A. 2007. *Roman Villas in Central Italy: A Social and Economic History*, Brill, Leiden and Boston.

Marzano, A. and Métraux, G. P. R. 2018. *The Roman Villa in the Mediterranean Basin: Late Republic to Late Antiquity*, Cambridge University Press, Cambridge.

Matijasic. R. 1982. 'Roman Rural Architecture in the Territory of Colonia Iulia Pola', *AJA* 86.1: 53–64.

Mattingly D. J. 1990. 'Paintings, Presses and Perfume Production at Pompeii', *OJA* 9: 71–90.

Mattingly, D. J. and Salmon, J. 2002. *Economies Beyond Agriculture in the Classical World*, Routledge, London.

Mattusch, C. 2005. *The Villa dei Papiri at Herculaneum: Life and Afterlife of a Sculptural Collection*, J. P. Getty Museum Publications, Los Angeles.

Mau, A., 1875. 'I scavi di Pompei', *BdI*: 161–163.

Mau, A., 1876. 'I scavi di Pompei', *BdI*: 12, 24, 34–35, 149–151, 161–168, 223–234, 243–249.

Mau, A. 1884. 'Scavi di Pompei', *BdI*: 210–216.

Mau, A. 1888. 'Scavi di Pompei 1886–88', *RM* 3: 181–207.

Mau, A. 1888. 'Sepolchri della Via Nucerina', *RM* 3: 120–149.

Mau, A. 1892. 'Scavi di Pompei', *RM* 7: 3–25.

Mau, A. 1896. 'Scavi di Pompei 1894–95', *RM* 11: 3–97.

Mau, A. 1898. '*Ausgrabungen vom Pompeji:* Insula VI,15', *RM* 13: 3–59.

Mau, A. 1899. *Pompeii: its Life and Art*, trans. Kelsey, F. W. Macmillan, New York.

Mau, A. 1901. 'Ausgrabungen vom Pompeji'. *RM* 16: 283–365.

Mau, A. 1908. *Pompeji in Leben und Kunst*, rev. edn.: 450–454, figs. 265–7, Verlag von Willhelm Engelmann, Leipzig.

Maxey, M. 1938. *Occupations of the Lower Classes in Roman Society as seen in Justinian's Digest*, Chicago University Press, Chicago.

Mayer, E. 2012. *The Ancient Middle Classes: Urban Life and Aesthetics in the Roman Empire 100BCE–250CE*, Harvard University Press, Cambridge Mass.

Mayer, J. W. 2005. *Imus ad villam: Studien zur Villeggiatur im stadtrömischen Suburbium in der späten Republik und frühen Kaiserzeit*, Geographica Historica, 20. Franz Steiner, Stuttgart.

Mazois, F. 1822. *Le Palais de Scaurus, ou Description d'une Maison Romaine, Fragment d'un Voyage Fait à Rome vers la Fin de la République*, 2nd Edition, Firmin Didot, Paris.

Mazois, F. 1824. *Les Ruines de Pompéi*. Vol. 2. Firmin Didot, Paris.

Mazzolini, D. 2004. *Domus: Wall Painting in the Roman House*, Getty, Los Angeles.

McDonnell, M. 2006. *Roman Manliness: Virtus and the Roman Republic*, Cambridge University Press, Cambridge.

McGinn, T., Carafa, P. and Bergmann, B. 2002. *Pompeian Brothels, Pompeii's Ancient History, Mirrors And Mysteries, Art And Nature At Oplontis, and The Herculaneum 'Basilica'*, *JRA* Supp. 47.

McKay, A. G. 1975. *Houses, Villas and Palaces in the Roman World*, Thames and Hudson, London.

Meiggs, R. 1973. *Roman Ostia*, 2nd edition. Clarendon Press, Oxford.

Merleau-Ponty, M. 1945. *Phenomenology of Perception*, trans. C. Smith 1962, Routledge, London.

Michel, D. 1990. 'Casa dei Cei (I.6.15)', *Häuser in Pompeji 3*, Hirmer, München.

Mielsch, H. 1987. *Die Römische Villa: Architektur und Lebensform*, C. H. Beck, Munich.

Milnor, K. 2014. *Graffiti and the Literary Landscape in Pompeii*, Oxford University Press. Oxford.

Mitchell, R. E. 1990. *Patricians and Plebeians: The Origin of the Roman State*, Cornell University Press, Ithaca.

Mladenović, D. and Russell, B. eds. 2011. *TRAC 2010: Proceedings of the Twentieth Annual Theoretical Roman Archaeology Conference, Oxford*. Oxbow Books, Oxford.

Moeller, W. O. 1976. *The Wool Trade of Ancient Pompeii*, Brill, Leiden.

Mols, S. T. A. M. and Moormann, E. M. 1994. 'Ex parvo crevit: Proposta per una letturaiconografica della Tomba di Vestorius Priscus fuori Porta Vesuvio a Pompei', *RStPomp* 6:15–52.

Mols, S. T. A. M. 1999. *Wooden Furniture in Herculaneum: Form Technique and Function*, J. C. Gieben, Amsterdam.

Moltensen, M. and Poulsen, B. 2010. *A Roman Villa by Lake Nemi. The Finds: The Nordic Excavations by Lake Nemi, loc. S. Maria (1998–2002)*, Edizione Quasar, Rome.

Mommsen, T. 1887. *Römisches Staatsrecht*, S. Hirzel, Leipzig.

Momigliano, A. and Schiavone, A. eds. 1988. *Storia di Roma I: Roma in Italia*, Einaudi, Torino.

Mongelluzzo, R. 2013. 'Maya Palaces as Experiences: Ancient Maya Royal Architecture and its Influence on Sensory Perception' in ed. Day, J.: 90–112.

Monteix, N. 2010. *Les lieux de métier: boutiques et ateliers d'Herculanum*, Collection du centre Jean Bérard 34, Ecole française de Rome, Rome.

Monteix, N. and Tran, N. eds. 2011. *Les savoirs professionnels des gens de métier études sur le monde du travail dans les sociétés urbaines de l'empire romain*, Collection du Centre Jean Bérard 37, Naples.

Monteix, N., Zanella, S., Aho, S., Macario, R., and Proudfoot, E. 2013. 'Pompéi, Pistrina: Recherches sur les boulangeries de l'Italie romaine', *CEFR*. From https://journals.openedition.org/cefr/1242, date accessed 14.8.17.

Moorman, E. M. 1993. 'Functional and Spatial Analysis of Wall Painting': *Proceedings of the Fifth International Congress on Ancient Wall Painting*, BABesch, Leiden.

Moorman, E. M. ed. 1995. *Mani di pittori e botteghe pittoriche nel mondo romano: Tavola rotunda in onore di W. J. Th. Peters in occasione del suo 75.mo compleanno, RM 54*, Dutch School, Rome.

Moorman, E. M. 2007. 'Villas Surrounding Pompeii and Herculaneum' in eds. Dobbins, J. and Foss, P.: 435–454.

Moretti M. and Sgubini-Moretti A. M. 1977 *La villa dei Volusii a Lucus Feroniae*, Autostrade SpA, Rome.

Morley, N. 2015. 'Urban Smells and Roman Noses' in ed. Bradley, M.: 110–119.

Morstein-Marx, R. 2012. 'Political Graffiti in the Late Roman Republic: Hidden Transcripts and Common Knowledge' in ed. Kuhn, C.:191–217.

Mouritsen, H. 1988. *Elections, Magistrates and Municipal Elites: Studies in Pompeian Epigraphy*, L'Erma di Bretschneider, Rome.

Mulvin, L. 2002. *Late Roman Villas in the Danube-Balkan Region*, Archeopress, Oxford.

Murray, O. 1990. *Sympotica. A Symposium on the Symposion*, Oxford University Press, Oxford.

Mygind, H. 1921. 'Hygienische Verhältisse im alten Pompeji', *Janus* 15: 251–383.

Mynott, J. 2018. *Birds in the Ancient World*, Oxford University Press, Oxford.

Nappo, S. 1989. 'Fregio dipinto del '*praedium*' di Giulia Felice con rappresentazione del foro di Pompei' *RStPomp* 5: 79–96.

Nauta, R. R. 2002. *Poetry for Patrons: Literary Communication in the Age of Domitian*, Brill, Leiden.

Neudecker, R. 1988. *Die Skulpturenausstattung Römischer Villen in Italien*, P. von Zabern, Mainz am Rhein.

Nevett, L. C. 2010. *Domestic Space in Classical Antiquity*, Cambridge University Press, Cambridge.

Newhauser, R. 2016. *A Cultural History of the Senses in the Middle Ages*, Bloomsbury, London.

Newlands, C. 2002. *Statius' Silvae and the Poetic of Empire*, Cambridge University Press, Cambridge.

Newsome, D. 2011. 'Introduction: Making Movement Meaningful' in eds. Laurence, R. and Newsome, D.: 1–54.
Nicolet, C. 1977. *Rome et la conquête du monde méditerranéen 1, les structures des Italie romaine*, Presses Universitaires de France, Paris.
Nielsen, I. 1998. 'Royal Banquets: The Development of Royal Banquets and Banqueting Halls from Alexander to the Tetrarchs' in eds. Nielsen, I. and Sigismund Nielsen, H.: 102–133.
Nielsen, I. 1999. *Hellenistic Palaces: Tradition and Renewal*, Aarhus University Press, Aarhus.
Nielsen, I. and Sigismund Nielsen, H. eds. 1998. *Meals in a Social Context. Aspects of the Communal Meal in the Hellenistic and Roman World*, Aarhus University Press, Aarhus.
Nissin, L. 2015. 'Sleeping areas in the houses of Herculaneum' in eds. Tuori, K. and Nissin, L.: 101–118.
Noy, D. 2000. 'Building a Roman Funeral Pyre' *Antichthon* 34: 30–45.
O'Sullivan, T. 2011. *Walking in Roman Culture*, Cambridge University Press: Cambridge, New York.
Oken, L. 1847. *Elements of Physiophilosophy*, trans. A. Turk, Ray Society, London.
Ogawa. T. ed. 1981. *Public Health: Proceedings of the 5th International Symposium* on the Comparative History of Medicine – East and West, Oct 26th – Nov 1st 1980, Taniguchi Foundation, Tokyo.
Östenberg, I., Malmberg, S. and Bjørnebye, J. 2015. *The Moving City: Processions, Passages and Promenades in Ancient Rome*, Bloomsbury, London.
Overbeck, J. A. and Mau, A. 1884. *Pompeji in seinen Gebäuden, Alterhümern und Kunstwerken dargestellt*, Verlag von Wilhelm Engelmann, Leipzig.
Packer, J. E. 1971. *The Insulae of Imperial Ostia. MAAR* 31, American Academy in Rome, Rome.
Pagano, M. 1993, 'Il teatro di Ercolano', *CronErcol* 23: 121–156.
Pagano, M. trans. Pesce A. 2000. *Herculaneum: A Reasoned Archaeological Itinerary*, T and M, Torre Del Greco.
Pallasmaa, J. 2012. *The Eyes of the Skin: Architecture and the Senses*, Wiley and Sons, Chichester.
Pani, M. 1982. 'Quale Novitas?', *Quaderni de storia* 16: 193–203.
Pappalardo, U. 2004. 'Villa Farnesina' in Mazzolini, D.: 210–241.
Paris, R. 2000. *The Villa of the Quintili*. Electa, Rome.
Parisinou, E. 2007. 'Lighting Dark Rooms: Some Thoughts about the Use of Space in Early Greek Domestic Architecture' in eds. Westgate, R., Fisher, N. and Whitley, J.: 213–223.
Pearce, J. Millet, M and Struck, M. 2000. *Burial, Society and Context in the Roman World*, Oxbow Books, Oxford.
Percival, J. 1976. *The Roman Villa*, Batsford, London.
Perring, D. 2013. *The Roman House in Britain*, Routledge, Abingdon.
Peters, W. J. 1977. 'La composizione delle parete dipinte nella Casa dei Vettii a Pompei', *Meded* 39: 95–128.

Peters, W. J. et al. 1993. *La Casa di Marcus Lucretius Fronto a Pompei e le sue pitture*, Thesis Publishers, Amsterdam.

Pietri, C. ed. 1987. *L'Urbs: espace urbain et histoire (1er siècle av. J.C. – IIIe siècle ap J.C.)*, École française de Rome, Rome.

Pinsent, J. 1975. *Military Tribunes and Plebeian Consuls: The Fasti from 444–342*, Steiner, Wiesbaden.

Pirson, F. 1997. 'Rented Accommodation at Pompeii: The Insula Arriana Polliana' in eds. Laurence, R. and Wallace-Hadrill, H.: 165–181.

Polfer, M. 2000. 'Reconstructing Funerary Rituals: the Evidence of *ustrina* and Related Archaeological Structures' in eds. Pearce, J., Millett, M. and Struck, M.: 30–37.

Platts, H. 2011. '"Keeping up with the Joneses": Competitive Display within the Roman Villa Landscape' in eds. Fisher, N. and Van Wees, H.: 239–279.

Platts, H. 2016. 'Approaching a lived experience of Ancient Domestic Space' in eds. Griffiths, S. and von Lünen, A.: 43–53.

Platts, H. 2018. 'Housing in the City of Rome' in eds. Claridge, A. and Holleran, C.: 299–316.

Platts, H. 2019 (forthcoming). 'Experiencing Sense, Place and Space in the Roman Villa' in eds. Baird, J. and Pudsey, A.

Plett, H. 2012. *Enargeia in Classical Antiquity and the Early Modern Age. The Aesthetics of Evidence*, Brill, Leiden.

Poehler, E. E. 2006. 'The Circulation of Traffic in Pompeii's *Regio VI*'. *JRA* 19: 53–74.

Poehler, E. E. 2017. *The Traffic Systems of Pompeii*, Oxford University Press, New York.

Poehler, E., Flohr, M., and Cole, K. 2011. *Pompeii: Art, Industry and Infrastructure*, Oxbow, Oxford.

Polansky, R. 2007. *Aristotle's De Anima: A Critical Commentary*, Cambridge University Press, Cambridge.

Porteous, J. D. 2006. 'Smellscape' in ed. Drobnik, J.: 89–106.

Porter, J. I. ed. 1999. *Constructions of the Classical Body*, Ann Arbor, Michigan.

Potter, D. 2015. 'The Scent of Roman Dining' in ed. Bradley, M. 2015: 120–32, Routledge, London and New York.

Potter, D. 2014. 'The Senses in Public and Private Life' in Toner, J.: 23–4.

Potter, D. 1999. 'Scent and Power in the Roman World' in ed. Porter J. I.: 160–89.

Proudfoot, E. 2013. 'Secondary Doors in Entranceways at Pompeii: Reconsidering Access and the "View from the Street"' in eds. Bokern, A., Bolder-Boos, M., Krmnicek, S., Maschek, D., and Page, S.: 93–111.

Puelma, M. 1996. 'Ἐπίγραμμα–epigramma: Aspekte einer Wortgeschichte', *MH* 53: 123–39.

Purcell, N. 1985 'Wine and Wealth in Ancient Italy' in *JRS* 75: 1–19.

Purcell, N. 1987. 'Town in Country and Country in Town' in Macdougall, E.: 185–203.

Purves, A. 2017. *Touch and the Ancient Senses*, Routledge, Abingdon.

Quilici, L. and Quilici Gigli, S. 1978. 'Ville dell'agro Cosano con fronte a torrette', *RivIstArch* 3,1: 11–64.

Quilici, L. 1990. *Le strade: Viabilità fra Roma e il Lazio*, Quasar, Rome.

Quintero, R. ed. 2007, *A Companion to Satire*, Malden, MA.
Raaflaub K. A. 1986. *Social Struggles in Archaic Rome: New Perspectives on the Conflict of the Orders*, Wiley, London.
Radice, B. 1968. 'Pliny and the Panegyricus', *G & R* 15.2: 166–172.
Rainbird, P. 2002. 'Making sense of petroglyphs: the sound of rock art' in eds. David, B. and Wilson, M.: 93–103.
Ramieri, A. M. 1995. 'La villa di Plinio a Castel Fusano', *Archeologia Laziale* 12.2: 407–16.
Randsborg, K. ed. 1989. *The Birth of Europe: archaeology and social development in the first millenium A.D.* L'Erma di Bretschneider, Rome.
Raper, R. A. 1977. 'The Analysis of the Urban Structure of Pompeii: A Socialogical Examination of Land Use (Semi Micro)' in ed. Clarke, D. L.: 189–222.
Rathbone, D. W. 2003. 'The Control and Exploitation of *ager publicus* in Italy during the Roman Republic' in ed. J.-J. Aubert: 135–138.
Rawson, B. 1990. 'The antiquarian tradition: spoils and representations of foreign armour', in ed. Eder, E.: 582–598.
Rawson, B. and P. Weaver eds. 1997. *The Roman Family in Italy: Status, Sentiment and Space*, Clarendon Press, Oxford.
Rawson, B. 2003. *Children and Childhood in Roman Italy*, Oxford University Press, Oxford and New York.
Rawson, B. 2010. *A Companion to Families in the Greek and Roman Worlds*, Wiley-Blackwell, London.
Reimers, P. 1991. 'Roman Sewers and Sewerage Networks – Neglected Areas of Study' *Munuscula Romana*: 111–116.
Reinarz, J. 2014. *Past Scents*, University of Illinois Press, Chicago.
Reinsberg, C. 2006. *Die Sarkophage mit Darstellungen aus dem Menschenleben: Vita Romana* (Die antiken Sarkophagrenreliefs 1.3) Gebr. Mann Verlag, Berlin.
Richardson, Jr. L. 1955. 'The Casa dei Dioscuri and its painters', *MAAR* 23: 1–165.
Richardson Jr., L. 1983. 'A Contribution to the Study of Pompeiian Dining-rooms', *Pompeii Herculaneum Stabiae (1)*, 61–71.
Richardson Jr., L. 1988a. *Pompeii: an Architectural History*, Johns Hopkins University Press, Baltimore.
Richardson Jr., L. 1988b. 'Water *triclinia* and *biclinia* in Pompeii' in R. Curtius, ed.: 305–312.
Richardson Jr., L. 1991. 'Innovations in domestic architecture at Pompeii, A.D. 62–79', *ArchNews* 16: 21–35.
Richardson, Jr. L. 2000. *A Catalog of Identifiable Figure Painters of Ancient Pompeii, Herculaneum, and Stabiae*, Johns Hopkins University Press, Baltimore and London.
Richardson, K. 1976. *Daggers in the Forum*, Cassell, London.
Ricouer, P. 1970. 'The Model of the Text: Meaningful Action Considered as a Text.' *Social Research*, 38: 529–62.
Riggbsy, A. 1997. '"Public" and "Private" in Roman Culture: The Case of the *Cubiculum*', *JRA* 10: 36–56.
Rivet, A. L. F. ed. 1969. *The Roman Villa in Britain*, Routledge and P. Kegan, London.

Roberts, P. 2013. *Life and Death in Pompeii and Herculaneum*, British Museum Press, London.

Robertson, E. C., Seiber, J. D., Fernandez, D. C. and Zender, M. U. 2006. *Space and Spatial Analysis in Archaeology*, University of Calgary Press, Calgary.

Robinson, O. F. 1994. *Ancient Rome: City Planning and Administration*, Routledge, London.

Robinson, D. 2005. 'Re-thinking the Social Organisation of Trade and Industry in First Century AD Pompeii' in eds. MacMahon, A. and Price, J.: 88–105.

Robinson, M. and Rowan, E. 2015. 'Roman Food Remains in Archaeology and the Contents of a Roman Sewer at Herculaneum' in eds. Wilkins, J. and Nadeau, R.: 105–115.

Roby, C. 2016. *Technical Ekphrasis in Greek and Roman Science and Literature*, Cambridge University Press, Cambridge.

Roche, P. 2011. *Pliny's Praise: The Panegyricus in the Roman World*, Cambridge University Press, Cambridge.

Rolandi et al. 2007. 'The 79 AD eruption of Somma: The relationship between the date of the eruption and the southeast tephra dispersion', *Science Direct, Journal of Volcanology and Geothermal Research* 169: 87–98.

Romizzi, L. 2001. *Ville d'otium dell'Italia antica*, Aucnus, Napoli.

Roodenburg, H. ed. 2016. *A Cultural History of the Senses in the Renaissance*, Bloomsbury, London.

Rosenstein, N. 2006. 'Aristocratic values' in *A Companion to the Roman Republic*, edited by Rosenstein, N. and Morstein-Marx, R., pp. 365–82, Blackwell, Oxford.

Rosenstein, N. and Morstein-Marx, R. eds. 2006. *A Companion to the Roman Republic*, Blackwell, Oxford.

Rostovtzeff, M. I. 1904. 'Pompeianische Landschaften und römische Villen', *Jahrbuch des Kaiserlich Deutschen Archäologischen Instituts* XIX: 10–126.

Rostovtzeff, M. I. 1911. 'Die hellenistisch-römische Architekturlandschaft', *RM* 26: 1–185.

Rostovtzeff, M. I. 1926. *The Social and Economic History of the Roman Empire*, Clarendon Press, Oxford.

Rowlandson, I. D. and Howe, T. N. 2001. *Vitruvius: Ten Books on Architecture*, Cambridge University Press, Cambridge.

Rudd, N. trans. 1999. *Juvenal: The Satires*, Oxford University Press, Oxford.

Rudolph, K. 2018. *Taste and the Ancient Senses*, Routledge, Abingdon.

Rüpke, J. 2001. *Die Religion der Römer: Einer Einführung*, C. H. Beck. Munich.

Russell, A. 2016. *The Politics of Public Space in Republican Rome*, Cambridge University Press, Cambridge.

Saliou, C. 1999. 'Les Trottoirs de Pompéi: une première approche', *BABesch* 74: 161–218.

Saller, R. P. and Garnsey, P. D. A. 1987. *The Roman Empire: Economy, Society and Culture*, University of California Press, Los Angeles.

Salza Prina Ricotti, E. 1978/80. 'Cucine e quartieri servili in epoca romana', *RendPontAcc*. 51.2: 237–94.

Salza Prina Ricotti, E. 1984: 'The importance of water in Roman garden triclinia', in ed. MacDougall, E.: 137–184.

Salza Prina Ricotti, E. 1985. 'La Villa Magna a Grotte di Piastra' in *Castelporziano I. Campagna di scavo e restauro*, 1984. Rome: 53–66.

Salza Prina Ricotti, E. 1987. 'Alimentazione, cibi, tavola e cucine nell'età imperiale' in *Ministero per I Beni Culturali e Ambientali, L'alimentazione nel mondo antico-i Romani, età imperial*, Istituto poligrafico e Zecca dello Stato: 71–130.

Sauer, E. ed. 2004. *Archaeology and Ancient History: Breaking Down the Boundaries*, Routledge, London and New York.

Scarborough, J. 1981. 'Roman Medicine and Public Health' in ed. Ogawa, T.: 33–73.

Schmeling, G. 2011. *A Commentary on the Satyrica of Petronius*, Oxford University Press, Oxford.

Schultz, V. 2016. 'Historiography and Panegyric. The Deconstruction on Imperial Representation in Cassius Dio' in eds. Lange, C. H. and Madsen, J. M.: 276–296.

Schwalb, H. 1902 *Römische villa bei Pola*, Wien: A. Hölder.

Scobie, A. 1986. 'Slums, Sanitation, and Mortality in the Roman world' in *Klio* 68: 399–433.

Scott, M. 2013. *Space and Society in the Greek and Roman Worlds*, Cambridge University Press, Cambridge.

Scott, S. 2000. *Art and Society in Fourth-Century Britain: Villa Mosaics in Context*, Oxbow, Oxford.

Scullard, H. H. 1981. *Festivals and Ceremonies of the Roman Republic*, Cornell University Press, Ithaca.

Seiler, F. 1992. 'Casa degli Amorini Dorati', *Häuser in Pompeji* 5, Hirmir, Munich.

Semper, G. 1984. 'Structural Elements of Assyrian-Chaldean Architecture' in *Gottfried Semper: In Search of Architecture*, trans. Herrmann W., MIT Press, Cambridge Mass.

Serres, M. 2008/1985. *The Five Senses: a Philosophy of Mingled Bodies (I)*. trans. Stankey, M. and Cowley, P., Continuum, London.

Serres, M. with Latour, B. 1995/1990. *Conversations on Science, Culture and Time*, trans. Lapidus, R., University of Michigan Press, Michigan.

Sgubini-Moretti, A. M. 1998. *Fastosa Rusticatio: la Villa dei Volusii a Lucus Feroniae*, Rome.

Sherwin-White, A. N. 1966. *The Letters of Pliny. A Historical and Social Commentary*, Clarendon Press, Oxford.

Shumka, L. 1999. 'A Bone Doll from the Infant Cemetary at Poggio Garmignano' in eds. Soren, D. and Soren, N.: 615–618.

Skeates, R. 2008. 'Making Sense of the Maltese Temple Period: an Archaeology of Sensory Experience and Perception', *Time and Mind* I (2): 207–238.

Skeates, R. 2010. *An Archaeology of the Senses: Prehistoric Malta*, Oxford University Press, Oxford.

Slater, W. ed. 1991. *Dining in a Classical Context*, Ann Arbor, MI.
Smith, B. 1999. *The Acoustic World of Early Modern England: Attending to the O-Factor*, University Press of Chicago, Chicago.
Smith, J. T. 1997. *Roman Villas: A Study in Social Structure*, Routledge, London.
Smith, M. M. 2007a. *Sensing the Past: Seeing, Hearing, Smelling, Tasting, and Touching in History*, University of California Press, Berkeley.
Smith, M. M. 2007b. *Sensory History*, Berg, Oxford.
Smith, W., Wayte, W., and Marindin, G. E. 1875. *A Dictionary of Greek and Roman Antiquities*. 2 Vols. John Murray, London.
Sogliano, A. 1886. 'Pompei', *NSc*. R. Accademia dei Lincei, Rome.
Sogliano, A. 1887. 'Pompei', *NSc*. R. Accademia dei Lincei, Rome.
Sogliano, A. 1888. 'Pompei – Degli edifici recentemente scoperti, e degli oggetti raccolti negli scavi dal dicembre 1887 al guigno 1888', *NSc*. R. Accademia dei Lincei, Rome.
Sogliano, A. 1893. 'Pompei – 2. Degli edifici disterrati nell'Isola 2a, Regione VIII', *NSc*. R. Accademia dei Lincei, Rome.
Sogliano, A. 1895. 'Pompei – Giornale degli Scavi redatto dagli assissenti', *NSc*. R. Accademia dei Lincei, Rome.
Sogliano, A. 1896. 'Pompei – Edifici scoperti nell'Isola 2a, Regione V', *NSc*. R. Accademia dei Lincei, Rome.
Sogliano, A. 1897. 'Pompei – Degli edifizi scoperti nell'isola XI, Regione VI', *NSc*. 5.5. R. Accademia dei Lincei, Rome.
Sogliano, A. 1898a. 'La Casa dei Vetti in Pompei', *Monumenti Antichi* 8.
Sogliano, A. 1898b. 'Pompei – Relazione degli scavi fatti durante 1898', *NSc*. R. Accademia dei Lincei, Rome.
Sogliano, A. 1899. 'Pompei – Relazione degli scavi fatti durante 1899', *NSc*. R. Accademia dei Lincei, Rome.
Sogliano, A. 1900. 'Pompei – Relazione degli scavi fatti durante i mese di 1900', *NSc*. 5. 8. R. Accademia dei Lincei, Rome.
Sogliano, A. 1901. 'Pompei – Relazioni degli scavi fatti durante il meso di febbraio 1901', *NSc*. 5. 9. R. Accademia dei Lincei, Rome.
Sogliano, A. 1905. 'Pompei – Relazione degli scavi fatti dal dicembre 1902 a tutto marzo 1905', *NSc*. 5. 2. R. Accademia dei Lincei, Rome.
Sogliano, A. 1906. 'Pompei – Relazione degli scavi fatti dal dicembre 1902 a tutto marzo 1905', *NSc*. 5. 3. R. Accademia dei Lincei, Rome.
Sogliano, A. 1907. 'Pompei – Relazione degli scavi fatti dal dicembre 1902 a tutto marzo 1905', *NSc*. 5. 4. R. Accademia dei Lincei, Rome.
Sogliano, A. 1908. 'Pompei – Relazione degli scavi esegueti dal dicembre 1902 a tutto marzo 1905', *NSc*. 5. 5. R. Accademia dei Lincei, Rome.
Soprano, P. 1950. *I triclini all'aperto di Pompei, Pompeiana. Raccolta di studi per il secondo centenario degli Scavi di Pompei*, Naples: Bibliotheca della Parola del passato. 4: 288–310.

Soren, D. and Soren, N. eds. *A Roman Villa and a Late-Roman Infant Cemetary: Excavations at Poggio Gramignano, Lugnano in Teverina*, L'Erma di Bretschneider.
Spano, G. 1910. 'Relazione degli scavi eseguiti nell'anno 1907', *NSc.* 5. 7. R. Accademia dei Lincei, Rome.
Spano, G. 1911. 'Pompei – Scavi eseguiti durante il mese di ottobre 1911', *NSc.* 5. 8. R. Accademia dei Lincei, Rome.
Spano, G. 1915. 'Pompei – Scavi sulla via dell'Abbondanza durante il mese di giugno', *NSc.* 5. 12. R. Accademia dei Lincei, Rome: 336–341.
Spano, G. 1916. 'Pompei – Continuazione dello scavo della via dell'Abbondanza', *NSc.* 5. 13. R. Accademia dei Lincei, Rome: 231–235.
Speksnijder, S. 2015. 'Beyond "public" and "private": accessibility and visibility during *salutationes*', in eds. Tuori, K. and Nissen, L.: 87–100.
Spinazzola, V. 1916. 'Pompei rinvenimento di quattro sepolti dal lapillo nel peristilio della casa di Trebio Valente', *NSc.* 5. 13: 87–90.
Spinazzola, V. 1917. 'Continuazione degli scavi in via dell'Abbondanza', *NSc.* 5. 14.
Spinazzola, V. 1953. *Pompei alla luce degli Scavi Nuovi di Via dell'Abbondanza (anni 1910–1923) I–II*. La Libreria dello Stato, Roma.
Spivey, N. 1998. 'Review of J. T. Smith's "Roman Villas: a Study in Social Structure"', *G & R* XVL (2): 252–255.
Squire, M. 2015. *Sight and the Ancient Senses*, Routledge, Abingdon.
Staub Gierow, M. 1994. 'Casa del Granduca un Casa dei Capitelli Figurati', *Häuser in Pompeji* 7, Hirmir, Munich.
Steinby, E. M. 1993–2000. *LTUR* 1–6. Edizioni Quasar, Rome.
Stemmer, K. 1992. 'Casa dell'Ara Massima', *Häuser in Pompeji* 6, Hirmir, Munich.
Stephenson, J. W. 2014. 'Veiling the Late Roman House', *Textile History* 45. 1: 3–31.
Stewart, S. 2007. *Cosmetics and Perfumes in the Roman World*, Tempus, Stroud.
Stockton, D. 1979 *The Gracchi*, Oxford University Press, Oxford.
Stöger, H. 2011. 'The Spatial Organization of the Movement Economy: The Analysis of Ostia's *Scholae*' in eds. Laurence, R. and Newsome, D.: 215–242.
Storey, G. R. 1999. 'Archaeological and Roman Society: Integrating Textual and Archaeological Data', *JAR* 7. 3: 203–248.
Storey, G. R. 2002. 'Regionaries-Type Insulae 2: Architectural/Residential Units at Rome', *AJA* 106. 3: 411–434.
Storey, G. R. 2004. 'The Meaning of "Insula" in Roman Residential Terminology', *MAAR*. 49: 47–84.
Storey G. R. 2018. 'All Rome is at my Bedside: Nightlife in the Roman Empire' in eds. Gonlin, N. and Nowell, A.: 307–332.
Stroka, V. M. 1984. 'Casa del Principe di Napoli', *Häuser in Pompeji* 1, Wasmuth, Tübingen.
Strocka, V. M. 1991. 'Casa del Labirinto: (VI, 11, 8–10)', *Häuser in Pompeji* 4, Hirmir, Munich.
Strocka, V. M. 2007. 'Domestic Decoration: Painting and the "Four Styles"' in eds. Dobbins, J. H. and Foss, P.: 302–322.

Stuardo, R. I. 2003. 'Access Patterns in Maya Royal Precincts' in ed. Christie *Maya Palaces and Elite Residences: An Interdisciplinary Approach*, University of Texas Press, Austin: 184–203.

Suter, A. ed. 2008. *Lament: Studies in the Ancient Mediterranean and Beyond*, Oxford University Press, Oxford.

Sutherland, I. 1990. *Colonnaded* cenacula *in Pompeian domestic architecture*, Ph.D. dissertation, Duke University.

Swoboda, K. M. 1919. *Römische und romanische Paläste: Eine architekturgeschichtliche Untersuchung*, A. Schroll and Co, Vienna.

Syme, R. 1939. *The Roman Revolution*, Oxford Paperbacks, Oxford.

Syme, R. 1968. *Ammianus and the Historia Augusta*, Clarendon Press and Toronto: Oxford University Press, Oxford.

Synnott, A. 1991. 'Puzzling over the Senses: From Plato to Marx' in ed. Howes, D. 1991: 61–76.

Talbert, R. 1984. *The Senate of Imperial Rome*, Princeton University Press, Princeton.

Taylor Lauritsen, M. 2011. 'Doors in Domestic Space at Pompeii and Herculaneum: A Preliminary Study' in eds. Mladenović, D. and Russell, B.: 59–75.

Taylor Lauritsen, M. 2013. 'The form and function of boundaries in the Campanian house' in ed. Anguissola, A.: 95–114.

Taylor Lauritsen, M. 2015. '*Ter Limen Tetigi*: Exploring the Roles of Thresholds in the Houses of Pompeii and Beyond' in *Houses and Habitat in the Ancient Mediterranean*, eds. Andrea di Castro, A. and Hope, C. A.: 299–312.

Terrenato, N. and Becker, J. eds. 2012. *Roman Republican Villas: Architecture, Context and Ideology*, University of Michigan Press, Michigan.

Terrenato, N. and Becker, J. 2012. 'Introduction' In *Roman Republican Villas: Architecture, Context and Ideology*. Eds. N. Terrenato and J. A. Becker, pp. 1–7, University of Michigan Press, Michigan.

Terrenato, N. 2001. 'The Origins of the Roman Villa', *JRA* 14: 5–32.

Terrenato, N. 2012. 'The Enigma of 'Catonian' Villas: The *De agri cultura* in the Context of Second-Century BC Italian Architecture' in eds. N. Terrenato and J. A. Becker: 69–93.

Thébert, Y. 1987. 'Private life and domestic architecture in Roman North Africa' in ed. Veyne, P. trans. Goldhammer, A.: 313–409.

Thompson, H. 2017. *Reviewing Blindness in French Fiction, 1789–2013*, Palgrave Macmillan, London.

Tilley, C. 1994. *A Phenomenology of Landscape*, Berg, Oxford.

Tilley, C. (with the assistance of Bennett, W.), 2004. *The Materiality of Stone: Explorations in Landscape Phenomenology*, Berg, Oxford.

Tilley, C. 2010. 'Interpreting Landscape: Geologies, Topographies, Identities', *Explorations in Landscape Phenomenology* 3, Left Coast Press, Walnut Creek, California.

Torelli, M. 2012. 'The Early Villa: Roman Contributions to the Development of a Greek Prototype' in eds. Terrenato, N. and Becker, J. A. : 8–31.

Toynbee, J. M. C. 1971. *Death and Burial in the Roman World*, Thames and Hudson, London.
Treggiari, S. 1998. 'Home and Forum: Cicero between "Public" and "Private"', *TAPA* 128: 1–23.
Trendelenburg, A. Von. 1873. 'Erotenfries aus Pompeji', *AZ* 31: 44–48.
Tsakirgis, B. 2007. 'Fire and Smoke: Hearths, Braziers and Chimneys in the Greek House' in eds. Westgate, R. Fisher, N. and Whitley, J.: 225–231.
Tsujimura, S. 1991. 'Ruts in Pompeii. The Traffic System in the Roman City', *Opuscula Pompeiana* 2:58–86.
Tuori, K. and Nissin, L. eds. 2015. *Public and Private in the Roman House and Society*, JRA Supp. Series 102, Portsmouth, RI.
Tuori, K. 2015. 'Introduction: Investigating Public and private in the Roman House' in eds. Tuori, K. and Nissin, L.: 7–16.
Tybout, R. A. 'Rooms with a View: Residences Built on a Terrace Along the Edge of Pompeii (Regions VI, VII, and VIII)' in eds. Dobbins, J. and Foss, P.: 407–420.
Van der Meer, L. B. 1998. 'L'affresco sotto le Terme di Traiano del Colle Oppio, Roma: real'a e progetto'. *Oudheidkundige Mededelingen uit het Rijksmuseum van Oudheden te Leiden* 78: 63–73.
van Tilberg, C. 2007. *Traffic and Congestion in the Roman Empire*, Routledge, Abingdon.
Vandenbroeck, P. J. J. 1986. 'Homo Novus Again' *Chiron* 16: 239–42.
Varone, A. 1989. 'Pompei Attività dell'Ufficio Scavi: 1987–1988', *RStPomp* 2: 225–238.
Varone, A. and Franchi Dell'Orto, L. 1990. *Rediscovering Pompeii*, L'Erma di Bretschneider, Rome.
Varone, A. 1993. 'Scavi recenti a Pompei lungo via dell'Abbondanza (Regio IX, ins. 12,6–7)' in Franchi Dell'Orto, L.: 617–40.
Varone, A. 1995. 'L'organizzazione del lavoro di una bottega di decoratori: le evidenze dal recente scavo pompeiano lungo via dell'Abbondanza' in Moormann, E.: 124–136.
Veal, R. 2017. 'Fuel in ancient food production' in eds. Heinrich, F. B. J. and Hansen, A. M.: 1–5.
Veitch, J. 2017. 'Soundscape of the Street: Architectural acoustics in Ostia' in ed. Betts, E. *Senses of the Empire*.: 54–70.
Versnel, H. S. 1992. *Inconsistencies in Greek and Roman Religion*, Brill, Leiden.
Veyne, P. ed. 1987. *A History of Private Life; from Pagan Rome to Byzantium*, trans. Goldhammer, A. Harvard University Press, London and Cambridge.
Vigne, L. 2009. 'The Five Senses in Classical Science and Ethics' in *The Sixth Sense Reader*, ed. Howes, D.: 107–118.
Vigneron, P. 1968. *Le Cheval dans l'Antiquité gréco-romain*, Faculté des Lettres et des Sciences humains de l'Université de Nancy, Nancy.
Vila, A. 2016. *A Cultural History of the Senses in the Age of Enlightenment*, Bloomsbury, London.

Villedieu, F. ed. 2001. *Il Giardino dei Cesari. Dai pallazi antichi alla Vigna Barberini sul Monte Palatino. Scavi dell'École française de Rome, 1985-1999*, Ministero per I Beni e le Attitvità Culturali Soprintendenza Archeologica di Roma, Rome.

Vogt J. 1926. *Homo Novus, ein Typus der römischen Republik,* W. Kohlhammer, Stuttgart.

Volpe, R. 2012. 'Republican Villas in the *Suburbium* of Rome' in eds. N. Terrenato and Becker, J. A.: 94–110.

von Blanckenhagen, P. H. and Alexander, C. 1990. *The Augustan Villa at Boscotrecase*, Mainz am Rhein: P. von Zabern.

Vout, C. 1996. '*The Myth of the Toga*: Understanding the History of Roman Dress', *G & R* 43.2: 204–220.

Vout, C. 2007. 'Sizing Up Rome, or Theorizing the Overview' in eds. Larmour, D. H. J. and Spencer, D.: 295–322.

Vuolanto, V. 2017. 'Experience, Agency, and the Children in the Past: The Case of Roman Childhood' in Laes, C. and Vuolanto, V.: 11–24.

Wallace-Hadrill, A. 1988. 'The Social Structure of the Roman House', *PBSR* 56: 58–77.

Wallace-Hadrill, A. 1991. 'Introduction' in eds. Wallace-Hadrill A. and Rich J. W.: ix–xviii.

Wallace-Hadrill, A. 1994. *Housing and Society in Pompeii and Herculaneum*, Princeton University Press, Princeton.

Wallace-Hadrill, A. 1995. 'Public honour and private shame: the urban texture of Pompeii' in eds. Cornell, T. and Lomas, K.: 39–62.

Wallace-Hadrill, A. 2003. '*Domus* and *Insulae* in Rome: Families and Housefuls' in eds. Balch, D. L. and Osiek, C.: 3–18.

Wallace-Hadrill, A. 2008. *Rome's Cultural Revolution*, Cambridge University Press, Cambridge.

Wallace-Hadrill, A. 2011. *Herculaneum: Past and Future*, Frances Lincoln, London.

Wallace-Hadrill A. and Rich, J. W. eds. 1991. *City and Country in the Ancient World*, Routledge, London.

Wallis, B. 1984. *Art After Modernism: Rethinking Representation,* David R. Godine, Boston and New York.

Warde-Fowler, W. 1899. *The Roman Festivals of the Period of the Roman Republic: An Introduction to the Study of the Religion of the Romans*, Macmillan and Co., London.

Watson, L. 2005. 'Epigram' in ed. Harrison S.: 201–212.

Watson, A. and Keating, D. 1999. 'Architecture and Sound: An Acoustic Analysis of Megalithic Monuments in Prehistoric Britain', *Antiquity* 73: 325–336.

Watts, C. M. 1987. *A Pattern Language for Houses at Pompeii, Herculaneum and Ostia*, PhD Diss. University of Texas at Austin.

Watts, G. R., Pheasant, R. J., Horoshenkov, K. V., and Ragonesi, L. 2009. 'Measurement and subjective assessment of water generated sounds,' *Acta Acust united with Acustia* 95: 1032–1039.

Webb, R. 2006. 'The *Imagines* as a Fictional Text: Ekphrasis, apatê and Illusion' *La Licorne* 75: 113–136.

Webb, R. 2009. *Ekphrasis, Imagination and Persuasion in Ancient Rhetorical Theory and Practice*, Farnham, Ashgate.
Weddle, C. 2017. 'Blood, Fire and Feasting: The Role of Touch and Taste in Graeco-Roman Animal Sacrifice' in ed. Betts, E.: 104–119.
Weekes, J. 2005. 'Reconstructing Syntheses in Romano-British Cremation' in eds. Bruhn, J., Croxford, B. and Grigoropoulos, D.: 16–26.
Welsch, K. 2010. *The Roman Wedding*, Cambridge University Press, Cambridge.
Westgate, R., Fisher, N. and Whitley, J. eds. 2007. *Building Communities: House, Settlement and Society in the Aegean World*, British School at Athens, London.
Whitby, M. 1998. 'Introduction' in Whitby, M. ed.: 1–16.
Whitby, M. ed. 1998. *The Propaganda of Power: The Role of Panegyric in Late Antiquity*, Brill, Leiden.
Wilkins, J. and Nadeau, R. 2015. *Food in the Ancient World*, Wiley Blackwell, Chichester.
Williams, C. 2011. *A Martial Reader: Selections from the Epigrams*. Bolchazy-Carducci Publishers, Illinois.
Williams, C. 2011. 'Introduction' in Williams, C.: ix–xxx.
Williams, J. 2013. 'Musical Space and Quiet Space in Medieval Monastic Canterbury' in ed. Day J.: 196–221.
Wilson, L. M. 1924. *The Roman Toga*, Johns Hopkins Press, Baltimore.
Wilson, A. 2000. 'Timgad and Textile Production' in eds. Mattingly, D. J. and Salmon, J.: 271–296.
Wilson, A. and Flohr, M. 2016. *Urban Craftsmen and Traders in the Roman World*, Oxford University Press, Oxford.
Wilson, R. 1983 *Piazza Armerina*, Granada, London.
Wiseman, T. P. 1971 *New Men in the Roman Senate 139 BC – AD 14*, Oxford University Press, Oxford.
Wiseman, T. P. 1987. 'Conspicuipostes tectaque Digna deo: The Public Image of Aristocratic Houses in the Late Republic and Early Empire' in ed. Pietri, C.: 393–413.
Witcher, R. 2005 'The Extended Metropolis: Urbs, Suburbium and Population', *JRA* 18:120–138.
Wittgenstein, L. 1958. *Philosophical Investigations*, 2nd ed. Basil Blackwell, Oxford.
Wojcik, M. R. 1986. *La Villa dei Papiri ad Ercolano: contributo alla ricostruzione dell'ideologia della nobilitas tardo repubblicana*, L'Erma di Bretschneider, Rome.
Wolf, E. R. 1990. 'Facing Power – Old Insights, New Questions' *American Anthropologists*: 586–596.
Wynia, S.L. ed. 1982. *La regione sotterata dal Vesuvio. Studi e prospettive, Atti del convegno internazionale 11–15 novembre 1979*. Università degli Studi di Napoli, Naples.
Wynia, S.L. 1982. 'The excavations in and around the house of M. Lucretius Fronto' in ed. Wynia, S.L.: 329–340.
Zaccaria Ruggiu, A. 1995. *Spazio private e spazio pubblico nella città romana*, École française de Rome, Rome.
Zanker, G. 1981. '*Enargeia* in the Ancient Criticism of Poetry', *RhM NF* 124: 297–311.

Zanker, P. 1987. *Drei Stadtbilder aus dem Augustischen Rom*, in ed. Pietro, C.: 475–489.

Zanker, P. 1998. *Pompeii: Public and Private Life,* Harvard University Press, Cambridge MA.

Zarmakoupi, M., ed. 2010. *The Villa of the Papyri at Herculaneum: Archaeology, Reception, and Digital Reconstruction*. Sozomena: Studies in the Recovery of Ancient Texts 1, Walter de Gruyter, Berlin and New York

Zarmakoupi, M. 2014. *Designing for Luxury on the Bay of Naples: Villas and Landscapes (c.100 BCE–79 CE)*, Oxford University Press, Oxford.

Index

age 11
Allison, P. 107, 109, 134, 138, 146
   dining rooms 163, 164
   house VI.16.26 149
   light/dark 152
   Pompeii survey 199–200, 207
amphitheatres 55
   Pompeii 54–62
ancient experiences 10
animals 49, 50
Apicius 274 n. 54
Apuleius 154
   Metamorphoses 143, 149
archaeology 9–11, 12–13, 136, 138–9, 142–3
architecture (*see also* buildings)
   private/public 17
   theory 2–3
   textual properties 6–7
Aristotle 4
atria 78, 84, 85, 104–5 (see also *atria-tablina*)
   function 105–9, 142–3
   kitchens 204–5, 207–8
   multisensory experiences 106–27, 139–54
   private/public 105–6, 112, 150–4
   relationship with *cubicula* and *peristylia* 135–9
   rituals 113–27
   weaving 105
atria-tablina 78–80, 121
   fauces-atria-tablina 89
   function 104–9
   funerals 122–7
   multisensory experiences 80–9, 106–29
   openness 80–9
   private/public 80–9, 105, 112–13, 128
   rituals 113–27
   salutationes 115–19
   weddings 119–22

Augustus, Emperor of Rome 86
   Res Gestae 86
authepsea 277 n. 92
autism 239n. 42

Balch, David 91–104
Bay of Naples, the 18, 52
benches 34, 37, 118, 262 n. 128
bereavement 88
birds 49–50
blindness 233
Boman, H. 152–3
Bradley, M. 13
braziers 107, 109–10, 149, 164, 172, 251 n. 85 (*see also* food warmers)
buildings, interpreting 7–8
burials 37–8

calendar 272 n. 15
Caligula, Emperor of Rome 55, 170
Catullus, Gaius Valerius 154
cenacula 162, 163
cenationes 162
chamber pots 38, 263 n. 134 (*see also* toilets)
children 107–8
Cicero, Marcus Tullius 199
   Ad Herrenium 167–7
cities. *See* urban life
Classen, Constance 12
clothing 116–17
Colloquia of the Hermeneumata Pseudodositheana 166, 170–1, 172
context 7–8
conversation 50–1, 167, 254 n. 123
convivia 164–77, 189, 190 (*see also* dining)
cooking 59–60, 109–12, 182, 183
cookshops 62–9, 182
corporeal bias 11
corridors 212, 229
couches 164, 172, 185
cremations 38, 71–2

cubicula 18
   function 133–5, 142–3
   multisensory experiences 139–54
   Pliny the Younger 131–3
   private/public 132–3, 150–5
   relationship with *atria* and *peristylia* 135–9
culinae 194 (*see also* kitchens)
curtains 103, 136, 138

Dans Le Noir restaurant 157, 158
D'Arms, J. H. 166–7
Day, J. 4
Descaves, Lucien
   Emmurés, Les 233
Dickman, J. A. 105–6
dining 112–13, 145–9, 157–62
   doors 208–11
   feasts 72, 158–9, 160–1, 167
   furniture 172, 186
   gardens 177–88, 224–5, 226–9
   kitchens 193–4
   multisensory experiences 164–77, 189–91
   rooms 162–4
   separation, corridors, spaces and rooms 212–16, 229
   separation, different storeys 225–6
   separation, walls, obstacles and floors 216–25
   serving food 228–9
   social status 160–1, 169, 189–91, 193
Dio, Cassius 157–8, 159–60, 161
disease 205, 206
domestic space-codes 8
Domitian, Emperor of Rome 157–61, 170
domus 14–15, 19, 91 (*see also* Roman homes)
doors 136, 138–41, 142, 151, 208–11
doorways 39–42, 45–7, 59, 68, 81–9 (see also *salutationes*)
   archaeology 136, 138–9
   entrances 92–104

education 166
elite, the 15, 85–7, 113 (*see also* social status)
   funerals 123
Ellis, S. 153

enargeia 166–7, 168, 171
entrances 92–104
exedrae 162, 163

fabric 172
family, the 26, 113
   funerals 122–3
fauces 34, 65–6, 78–9, 83–4, 92
   house of the Golden Bracelet 183
   villa of Cicero 72–3
   villa of the Four Mosaic Columns 73
fauces-atria-tablina 89
Flohr, M. 63, 65
food 165, 171, 184, 196
food warmers 177
Forma Urbis Romae 33
Foss, P. 162
fountains 28, 178, 179, 184
frescoes 117, 172, 186, 258 n. 50
funerals 114–15, 122–7, 158, 167
furniture 172, 186

games 54–62, 175
gardens 139
   dining 177–88, 224–5, 226–9
   kitchens 224–5, 226–9
gender 11
gladiator contests 55, 58–9
Goldbeck, F. 104
graffiti 45–7, 59, 108
Grahame, Mark 6–7, 8
Greek myths 232

Hales, S. 67
Hamilton, S. 13
Hanson, J. 6, 8, 9
Hartnett, J. 118
hearing 28, 31, 33–4 (*see also* sound)
hearths 110, 195–6
Herculaneum 18, 19
   doors/doorways 39, 41, 83, 209–10
   frescoes 174
   house of the Bicentenary 136–7
   house of the Corinthian *Atrium* 215, 216
   house of the Deer 222–3, 224
   house of the Great Portal 287 n. 66
   house of the Mosaic *Atrium* 179–80, 222, 223, 225

house of the Neptune Mosaic 212, 213
house of the Wooden Partition 136–7, 138
kitchens 200, 203–5, 207–8
map 41
multisensory streetscapes 51
toilets 207
topography 206, 207
waste disposal 206–7
Hillier, B. 6
home, the (*see also* Roman homes)
Pallasmaa, Juhani 2–3
Horace 82
food 165
Satires 81
town and country mouse story, the 1–2
house I.6.8-9 110
house of Caesius Blandus 94–7
house of Gavius Rufus 218
house of Holconius Rufus 99, 102–3
house of M. Lucretius Fronto 146–7
house of Marine Venus 57
house of Menander 146, 147, 152, 164
house of Octavius Quarto 56, 57
house of P. Casca Longus 63, 64, 65
house of Pansa 79, 98–9, 100–1
house of Paquis Proculus 92–4, 95, 215–16, 229
house of Queen Margherita 226, 227
house of Quietus 57
house of Siricus 219–21
house of Stallius Eros 110
house of the Anchor 84
house of the Ara Maxima 99, 101–2, 212
house of the Bicentenary 136–7
house of the Bronze Bull 221–2, 223
house of the Cabinet Maker 175, 176, 226–7, 228
house of the Ceii 63, 64, 65, 68–9, 83, 111, 198, 219
house of the Centennial 214–15
house of the Chaste Lovers 65–6, 172, 172, 174, 186, 189
house of the Corinthian *Atrium* 215, 216
house of the Cryptoporticus 63, 64, 65
house of the Deer 222–3, 224
house of the Floral *Lararium* 57
house of the Garden of Hercules 57, 58, 185, 186–8

house of the Golden Bracelet 181–4, 226
house of the Golden Cupids 214
house of the Great Portal 287 n. 66
house of the *Lararium* of Achilles 63, 64, 65, 66–8
house of the Mosaic *Atrium* 179–80, 222, 223, 225
house of the Neptune Mosaic 212, 213
house of the Priest of Amandus 212–14
house of the Prince of Naples 144, 145
house of the Tragic Poet 92, 93, 196, 216–17, 229
house of the *Triclinium* 172, 173, 176, 186, 189
house of the Vettii 61, 62, 144–5, 146, 175, 204
house of the Wooden Partition 136–7, 138
house of Trebius Valens 144, 185, 228–9
house of Vetutius Placidus 34, 36
house VI.16.26 146, 147, 149
Howes, David 12
human remains 38
Huntley, K. V. 108
hygiene 205

insulae 19, 283 n. 5

justified access-maps 6, 8
Juvenal 39, 42
Satire III 39

kitchens 110–12, 193–4
atria 204–5, 207–8
doors 208–11
gardens 224–5, 226–9
Herculaneum 200, 203, 207
layouts 199
locations 199–208, 226–30
multisensory experiences 195–208
Pompeii 199–202, 204, 207
separation, corridors, spaces and rooms 212–16, 229
separation, different storeys 225–6
separation, walls, obstacles and floors 216–25
serving food 228–9
Koloski-Ostrow, A. 206

language 166, 167

lararia 109
Latin 166, 167
latrina/lavatrina 194 (*see also* toilets)
Laurence, R. 45–6, 85, 86, 87
'leaky' house concept 92–104, 128
Lefebvre, H. 25
light/dark 106–7, 134–5, 151–3
   amphitheatres 55, 58
   cubicula 143, 151–3
   dining 157–8, 159
   kitchens 196, 197
literary evidence 19
   reservations 31, 39, 42, 88
Livy 86–7
Lucan
   Pharsalia 124–5
Lucian 127

manufacturing 62–9
Martial 33–4, 39, 42, 82
   dining 168–9, 170
   Epigram 'Bedroom Lamp' 143
   Epigram to Mamurianus 111
   Epigrams 42, 81, 195
Mayer, E. 15
Merleau-Ponty, M. 5
military success 26, 39
mirabilis/mirari 167
modern experiences 10, 12
Morley, N. 206
mosaics 117, 258 n. 50
mourning 123–5
movement 8, 9, 116
multisensory experiences 3–4, 232 (*see also* multisensory streetscapes *and* senses)
   atria 106–27, 139–54
   atria-tablina 80–9, 106–29
   cubicula 139–54
   dining 164–77, 189–91
   dining in gardens 177–88
   funerals 122–7, 158
   Greek myths 232
   house of the Garden of Hercules 186–7
   house of the Golden Bracelet 181–4
   kitchens 195–208
   Pallasmaa, Juhani 2–3, 26–7
   Pliny the Younger 23–4, 28–9, 233–4
   research 13–14

salutationes 115–19
   transmission between *atria* and *cubicula* 139–50
   weddings 119–22
multisensory streetscapes 51–3
   Herculaneum 51
   Ostia 51
   Pompeii. *See* Pompeii, multisensory streetscapes
   Rome 32–3, 38, 39, 42, 43–4
music 126, 175

noise. *See* sound

oeci 162, 163
officiae lanifricariae 62–3
Oken, Lorenz 4
ostentatio/ostentatione 167–8
Ostia 51
Ovid 123–4
   Consolation to Livia 123

pain 195–6
Pallasmaa, Juhani 26–7
   Eyes of the Skin: Architecture and the Senses, The 2–3
partitions 85, 103, 136–8
paterfamilias 26, 121, 122, 127
   atria-tablina 128–9
perfume 144–5, 154, 175–7, 186
peristylia 135–9
Petronius 151
   Cena Trimalchionis 189
physical sensation 20, 29
plans 9
plants 180, 187, 188, 280 n. 118
Pliny the Younger 23–4, 132, 134–6, 233–4
   corridors 212
   cubicula 131–2, 148–9
   dining 170
   Epistles 162
   Letters 23–4, 26–9, 131–2
Pompeii 18, 19 (*see also* Pompeii, multisensory streetscapes)
   animals 49, 50
   bakery of Popidius Priscus 34
   birds 50
   burials 37–8
   climate 52–3

cremations 38, 71–2
doors/doorways 39–40, 45–7, 59, 68, 83–4, 208–11
fauces 34, 65–6, 83–4, 72–3, 183
feasts 72
fullonica of Stephanus 63–5, 68–9
graffiti 45–7, 59
house I.6.8–9 110
house layouts 199
house of Caesius Blandus 94–7
house of Gavius Rufus 218
house of Holconius Rufus 99, 102–3
house of M. Lucretius Fronto 146–7
house of Marine Venus 57
house of Menander 146, 147, 152, 164
house of Octavius Quarto 56, 57
house of P. Casca Longus 63, 64, 65
house of Pansa 79, 98–9, 100–1
house of Paquis Proculus 92–4, 95, 215–16, 229
house of Queen Margherita 226, 227
house of Quietus 57
house of Siricus 219–21
house of Stallius Eros 110
house of the Anchor 84
house of the Ara Maxima 99, 101–2, 212
house of the Bronze Bull 221–2, 223
house of the Cabinet Maker 175, 176, 226–7, 228
house of the Ceii 63, 64, 65, 68–9, 83, 111, 196, 219
house of the Centennial 214–15
house of the Chaste Lovers 65–6, 172, 173, 174, 186, 189
house of the Corinthian *Atrium* 215, 216
house of the Cryptoporticus 63, 64, 65
house of the Floral *Lararium* 57
house of the Garden of Hercules 57, 58, 185, 186–8
house of the Golden Bracelet 181–4, 226
house of the Golden Cupids 214
house of the *Lararium* of Achilles 63, 64, 65, 66–8
house of the Neptune Mosaic 212, 213
house of the Priest of Amandus 212–14
house of the Prince of Naples 144, 145

house of the Tragic Poet 92, 93, 196, 216–17, 229
house of the *Triclinium* 172, 173, 176, 186, 189
house of the Vettii 61, 62, 144–5, 146, 175, 204
house of Trebius Valens 144, 185, 228–9
house of Vetutius Placidus 34, 36
house VI.16.26 146, 147, 149
human remains 38
kitchens 199–202, 204, 207, 208
levels 182–3 (*see also* topography)
maps 35, 40, 55, 63, 70
pedestrians 39
smell 37–8, 59–61, 65, 71, 118
sound 48, 49, 50–1, 65
sensory buffer zones 68–9
street vendors 59–60
streets 43–8, 59, 71–2
toilets 207
topography 71, 103–4, 206, 207
traffic 39, 43, 44–7
travel in 43, 59
villa of Cicero 69, 71, 72–3
villa of Diomedes 69–71, 73–5, 185, 225
villa of Mysteries 69–71
villa of the Four Mosaic Columns 69, 71, 72, 73
waste disposal 206, 207
windows 67–8
zoning 34–7, 62
Pompeii, multisensory streetscapes 34–8, 39, 40–1, 43–51, 52–4
amphitheatre, the 54–62
extramural dwellings 69–75
fulleries, workshops and cookshops 62–9, 182
postica 92
Potter, D. 176–7, 190
power 24–6, 160–2, 169, 189
private, the 15–18, 77, 82–3, 88, 150, 232
atria 105–6, 112, 150–4
atria-tablina 80–9, 105, 112–13, 128
cubicula 132–3, 150–5
family, the 113
rituals 113
weddings 122

processions 120, 122
Proudfoot, E. 84
public, the 15–18, 77, 78, 89–92, 150, 232
    atria 105–6, 112, 150–4
    atria-tablina 80–9, 105, 112–13, 128
    cubicula 132–3, 150–5
    family, the 113
    Martial 82
    rituals 113
    weddings 122
Publicola, Publius Valerius 39

Quintilian 154
    Institutio Oratoria 134

race 4
research 12–14
Riggsby, A. 15–16, 133–4, 150–1
rituals 104–5, 112
    funerals 114–15, 122–7, 158
    lararia 109
    mourning 88, 123–5, 126
    salutationes 81, 90, 105, 114–19
    weddings 114–15, 119–22
roads 48 (*see also* streets)
Roman calendar 272 n. 15
Roman homes 3–4, 14–15, 77–80, 234–5 (*see also names of individual house and villas*)
    atria. See *atria*
    atria-tablina. See *atria-tablina*
    children 107–8
    closure for mourning 123–5
    cooking 109–11
    cubicula. See *cubicula*
    curtains 103, 136, 138
    dining. See dining
    domus 14–15, 19, 91
    doors 136, 138–41, 142, 151, 208–11 (*see also* doorways)
    doorways. See doorways
    Empire-wide 5–6
    fauces-atria-tablina 89
    fauces. See *fauces*
    floor plan 79
    gardens 139
    hearths 110, 195–6
    insulae 19, 283 n. 5
    kitchens. See kitchens

lararia 109
layouts 199
literary evidence 19
mosaics and frescoes 117, 258 n. 50
multi-functionality of rooms 78
multisensory experiences. See multisensory experiences
partitions 85, 103, 136–8
Pliny the Younger 23–4, 27–8, 212, 233–4
postica 92
power 24–6
private/public 15–18, 77 , 78, 80–1, 89–92, 232
public accessibility 89–92 (*see also* 'leaky' house concept)
relationship with street. See streetscapes
research 14
Roman villas. See Roman villas
salutationes 81, 90
social status. See social status
space syntax analysis 6–7
tablina 78
toilets. See toilets
windows 67–8
Roman time 106–7, 267 n. 22
Roman villas 14–15
    Pliny the Younger 23–4, 27–9 , 131–2, 148–9, 233–4
    villa of Cicero 69, 71, 72–3
    villa of Diomedes 69–71, 73–5, 185, 225
    villa of Mysteries 69–71
    villa of the Four Mosaic Columns 69, 71, 72, 73
Rome 18–19
    human remains 38
    multisensory streetscapes 32–3, 38, 39, 42, 43–4
    noise 31, 32–4, 39
    streets 43
    zoning 33–4
rural life
    Horace 1–2

salutationes 81, 90, 105, 114
Scipio Africanus 231–2
seasons, the 52–3, 106–7

secrecy 241 n. 66
Seneca the Younger 81–2, 111
   Consolation to Marcia 149
   De Ira 149
   Letters 81
   Moral Letters 189, 205–6, 231–2
   On Quiet and Study 31
   salutationes 115–16, 118–19
   social status 90
senses 4–5, 289 n. 3
   hearing 28, 31, 33–4 (*see also* sound)
   hierarchies of 4
   Merleau-Ponty, M. 5
   movement 8, 9, 116
   physical sensation 20, 29
   Serres, M. 5
   sight. *See* vision
   smell. *See* smell
   taste 13, 28, 170, 197 (*see also* food)
   touch 10, 28, 116, 118–9, 195 (*see also* temperature)
sensory archaeology 13
Sensory Formation Series 12
sensory streetscapes. *See* streetscapes
Serres, M. 5
serving hatches 228
sexuality 82, 88, 154
slaves 112, 117, 191, 195, 197–8, 229
sleep 134, 135
smell 10, 37–8, 199, 229–30 (*see also* unpleasant smells)
   atria 109, 111–12, 126, 142, 143–4
   cities 205–6
   cooking 59–60, 110, 111, 182, 183
   cubicula 142, 143–4
   death 125–6
   dining 170, 175–6, 190–1
   doors 142
   gardens 188
   habituation to 206
   house layouts 199
   kitchens 195, 196, 230
   manufacturing workshops 63
   perfume 144–5, 154, 175–7
   Pliny the Younger 28
   Pompeii 37–8, 59–61, 65, 71, 118
   research 13
   rituals 109
   salutationes 118

   Seneca 205–6
   social status 111–12, 117
   sensory buffer zones 68–9
   street vendors 59–61
   togas 116–17
   toilets 205–7, 230
   waste 206
   wind 52
   windows 67–8
Smith, B. 50–1
social class 6, 11, 15, 24 (*see also* social status)
   dining 160–1, 169
   Domitian, Emperor of Rome 160–1
   power 24–6, 160–2, 169
   private/public 16–17
   taverns 182
social identity 8
social status 80, 85–7, 89–91, 232, 234 (*see also* power)
   clothing 116–17
   dining 160–1, 169, 189–91, 193
   elite, the 15, 85–7, 113, 123
   funerals 123
   rituals 114–15
   salutationes 116–17
   smell 111–12, 117, 183
   Vitruvius 77, 78
   weddings 120–1
sound 48–9, 73–4
   amphitheatres 56, 57–9, 61
   animals/birds 49–50
   atria 49, 106, 107, 108, 126, 140–1
   children 108
   conversation 50–1, 167, 254 n. 123
   cooking 110, 182, 183
   cubicula 141–2, 143, 149, 154
   dining 112, 170, 174
   doors 140–1
   fountains 179, 184
   gardens 178, 179–80, 184, 186–7
   Imperial deaths 123–4
   Juvenal 39
   kitchens 197
   Martial 33–4
   mirabilis/mirari 167
   mourning 123–5, 126
   music 175
   ostentatio/ostentatione 167–8

Pliny the Younger 28
Pompeii 48, 49, 50–1, 65
rituals 109
Rome 31, 32–4, 39
salutationes 117
Seneca the Younger 31
sensory buffer zones 68–9
street venders 59
streets 48
temperature 53
villa of Diomedes 73–4
weather 52–3
weaving 106–7
windows 67–8
space syntax analysis 6–8
speciosus 167
spectabilis 167
speech 7
spolia 26
Statius 159
   Silvae 158–61
street vendors 59–60
streets (*see also* streetscapes)
   Pompeii 43–8, 59, 71–2
   processions 120, 122
   Rome 43
streetscapes 31–2
   impact of animals 49–51
   impact of neighbouring buildings and areas 32–8
   impact of pedestrians 45–7, 50–1
   impact of streets 43–8
   impact of traffic 45–8
   multisensory 51–3
   Pompeii. *See* Pompeii, multisensory streetscapes
   Rome 32–3, 38, 39, 42, 43–4
Suetonius 167
summer *triclinia* 178–87, 227–9

tablina 78, 164 (see also *atria-tablina*)
Tacitus, Publius Cornelius 123–4
taste 13, 28, 170, 197 (*see also* food)
taverns 182
Taylor Lauritsen, M. 136
temperature 52
   braziers 107, 109–10, 149, 164, 172, 251 n. 85
   death 125

dining 172, 174
fountains 184
gardens 187
kitchens 195
Pliny the Younger 29
weaving 107
texts 7
   interpreting 7–8
thresholds. *See* doors *and* doorways *and* streetscapes
time 106–7, 267 n. 22
togas 116–17
toilets 16, 194–5, 205–8, 229–30 (*see also* chamber pots *and* waste)
topography 71, 103–4
touch 10, 28, 116, 118–9, 195 (*see also* temperature)
traffic 43–7, 182
Trichuriasis 205, 206
triclinia 162–3, 171–2 (*see also* dining)
   house of the Golden Bracelet 181–4
   summer *triclinia* 178–87, 227–9

unpleasant smells 118, 183, 188, 199, 205–6, 229–30
   death 126
   dining 176–7
   gardens 183
   kitchens 111–12, 194, 195, 205, 230
   manufacturing 63
   Seneca 205
   slaves 195
   social class 111–2, 195
   toilets 194, 199, 205, 206, 230
urban life (*see also* streetscapes)
   Horace 1–2

Varro, Marcus Terentius 133, 206
Vergil
   Georgics 167
villa of Cicero 69, 71, 72–3
villa of Diomedes 69–71, 73–5, 185, 225
villa of Mysteries 69–71
villa of the Four Mosaic Columns 69, 71, 72, 73
vision (*see also* light/dark)
   blindness 233
   Boman, H. 152–3
   clothing 116, 117

   cubicula 151–3
   dining 166–7, 170, 219
   domination of 4–5, 8–9, 13, 151, 232–3
   enargeia 166–7, 168
   fountains 184
   gardens 180, 184
   kitchens 198, 219
   mourning 123–5
   ostentatio 167
   Pliny the Younger 27–8
   Pompeii amphitheatre 61
   research 13
   Riggsby, A. 166
   rituals 109
   weddings 120
Vitruvius 16–18, 89–91
   cubicula 132, 133
   De Architectura 77–8
   oeci 163

Wallace-Hadrill, A. 8, 9, 91–2
   private/public 17–18, 105
waste 118, 205–7 (*see also* toilets)
weather 10, 29, 52–3, 67–8, 107
weaving 106–7
weddings 114–15, 119–22
whipworm 205, 206
Whitehouse, R. 13
wind 52–3
windows 67–8
Wolf, E. R. 25, 26
worship 109

zoning 33–4, 36–7, 62